WHAT THE WOMAN LIVED

POETRY
Body of This Death
(1923)
Dark Summer
(1929)
The Sleeping Fury
(1937)
Poems and New Poems
(1941)
Collected Poems 1923–1953
(1954)
The Blue Estuaries: Poems 1923–1968
(1968)

CRITICISM
Achievement in American Poetry, 1900–1950
(1951)
Selected Criticism: Poetry and Prose
(1955)
A Poet's Alphabet: Reflections on the Literary Art and Vocation
(1970)

TRANSLATIONS *with Elizabeth Mayer*
The Glass Bees by Ernst Juenger
(1961)
Elective Affinities by Goethe
(1963)
The Sorrows of Young Werther *and* Novella by Goethe
(1971)

With Elizabeth Roget
The Journal of Jules Renard
(1964)

ANTHOLOGY *with William Jay Smith*
The Golden Journey: Poems for Young People
(1965)

What the Woman Lived

SELECTED LETTERS OF LOUISE BOGAN 1920-1970

Edited and with an Introduction by
RUTH LIMMER

Harcourt Brace Jovanovich, Inc. New York

Library of Congress Cataloging in Publication Data
Bogan, Louise, 1897–1970.
    What the woman lived; selected letters of Louise Bogan, 1920–1970.

    I. Title.
PS3503.0195Z53 1973   811'.5'2 [B]   73–9737
ISBN 0–15–195878–5

First edition

B C D E

CONTENTS

When Louise Bogan died in February 1970, she left behind, in the files of friends and libraries, more than a thousand letters spanning precisely fifty years of literary and personal history. Even the smallest collection gave evidence of a voice still reverberating with humor and wisdom. It soon became clear that those letters told a story, and that the story was important not merely to those who knew her, but also to all who cared about twentieth-century writers and writing.

To reveal the story required only that the letters be selected to provide the fullest record possible of the complicated woman who gave her energies—in an elegant and remarkably self-effacing way—to the creation, encouragement and appraisal of poetry in particular and of literature in general.

But Louise Bogan stood for public reticence. Her way of life precluded publicity seeking, loud noises and vulgar gestures; she joined no groups, signed no manifestoes. Her name was *not* a household word, and she did not want it to be: for most of her life she lived, wholly apart from literary cliques, on the upper reaches of Manhattan Island, where the slit beside the bell in her apartment house read "Holden."

The fact of her determined privacy opens the question of whether, for the value of the story, it is permissible to publish such a collection. Obviously I have judged it is, as have those who shared her letters with me. The reasons are clear but, in view of Louise Bogan's disdain for lifting veils in public, may need specification.

First, I believe the public should have access to information about the woman who helped to shape poetic tastes for nearly half a century and who added to the body of poetry in English some of its finest lyrics. Second, because the persons she wrote to and about were so often major figures on the literary scene, the reflections we get of them also deserve to be part of the public record. It is a charming corrective to our present view, for example, to see a rubicund and merry Edmund Wilson, and instructive to see, up close, Theodore Roethke's poetic apprenticeship.

This is not to say that the lifework of Wilson or Roethke, or Bogan herself, needs the support of biographical revelation to give it richness or meaning. I do suggest that when—as here—it is experienced consciously and described finely, with the precision instruments of art and insight, then the artist's life has its own significance. That significance may cast no light whatever on the work produced; I do not think, in fact, that these letters will provide many new interpretations of Louise Bogan's poetry. But I am convinced that the letters—of irreducible value in themselves—will bring readers to her poetry, and to the books of a great many other writers who live in these pages. If, because of Miss Bogan's enthusiasms, *The Princess Casamassima* or *Follow Thy Fair Sun* or *The Dog Beneath the Skin* or *Open House* is again taken from the shelves, then no one, least of all Louise Bogan, is going to begrudge the action because of the (perhaps) impure motive.

But reading lists do not animate themselves. Another reason for the invasion of privacy is the joy of her style. And her wit, taste and largeness of spirit hearten and refresh at a time when such qualities are unfashionable. There is the additional fact of Miss Bogan's professionalism. A professional, no matter how little she herself participates in "entrepreneurism" on her own account, knows that she is, ultimately, a public person, whose work and personality will be dissected by scholars and strangers. It is well, then, to provide the future with clarifying documents from her own hand. And because these documents also dramatize the suffering and growth of a personality that struggled to adjust the demands of its own genius to the many-sided realities of private life, they are additionally valuable as a psychological study of exceptional penetration and honesty. It is no small thing to know, as precisely as Louise Bogan did, what it is to be a woman.

For such reasons, then, I believe that she, too, would have accepted this volume as an inevitable next step, perhaps even as a posthumous responsibility. —And in any case she suspected it would come: as she once joked to Rolfe Humphries, toward the end of a typographically snarled missive, "God help the man who has to edit our letters."

At the same time, she would undoubtedly have insisted on limitations and excisions. She deplored as academic tedium all hour-by-hour accounts, for she knew that while details give life, trivia turn into social history only after many decades. Much of the dailiness of these letters has been excised; only enough has been included to give a sense of the pressures she worked under as a journalist, and to remind us that a poet's reality can include both Flaubert and flounder. Further deletions contain repetitions, irrelevancies and material more fully covered in subsequent letters; and a few have been made to provide her friends with a privacy that is their right.

The author, too, deserves privacy, although the distinction between prissy concealment and responsible reticence is probably never as sharp as the editor thinks it is. The solution was forthrightly to include items of an intimate nature whenever I thought them humanly instructive or important either as personal or literary history. Hence, for example, Louise Bogan's various breakdowns and recoveries, being part of the fabric of her life, neither could nor should be concealed. On the other hand, the smaller privacies—those that I believe can make little difference in the assessment of character or in sharpening a view of the American literary scene—were cut whenever I felt it appropriate to do so.

With less confidence, some further cuts have been made to avoid gratuitous pain to people still alive. And yet, to have removed all such discomforting remarks would have been to denature the letters and distort the record. I have followed a rather intuitive line here; often: the more public the person, the more unkindness I thought he or she could survive. But certainly cuts for this purpose (as, indeed, for the purpose of privacy) are infrequent and would not, if restored, change the picture we form of the writer. It is clear from the letters that Miss Bogan was both tough and vulnerable, sharp-tongued and generous, intemperate and serene, wildly prejudiced and wholly fair. Which is to say: she was grandly human. It need merely be noted, in defense of the acerb comments which remain, that they may be wholly revised a hundred pages later, and that no single letter can safely be used to define her response to her contemporaries. In the last years, in fact, and without any diminution of intellectual power, she came to an almost absolute charity and forgiveness. The human sin then was to be boring, or coldhearted.

Her critical opinions, on the other hand, wavered hardly at all, for published judgment never depended upon her feelings toward the author in question (although, inevitably, just as some of her friends wrote works she esteemed, some of the people she didn't like wrote things she deplored). The letters attest to her incorruptibility; she was simply not buyable. In this regard it is instructive to read her collected criticism (*A Poet's Alphabet*, 1970) alongside the letters. A stinging remark dropped in a letter becomes, on the printed page, a no more favorable but now thoroughly tempered comment stemming from the inviolable principle that one judges from within the poem, from within the poet. And when, having done so, she found the poetry weak or unworthy, she increasingly often left it unreviewed. To squash flies against walls, which she could do with unerring skill—and which her friend Edmund Wilson had more than once urged upon her—was a sport she came to relish less and less. "Why bother with the bad," she asked, "when there's so little space for the good?" And, indeed, why enter into so uninviting a talent? This entering-into explains, in part, the difficulty she faced in her last years: the creative energy her kind of criticism demanded was frequently beyond her strength. As she said in 1960, faced with a request to do an extended article on Robert Frost: "The notion of spending all those months in close relations to that wicked old man is rather daunting." But she undertook the job because "he *is* a fine poet, essentially."

Such was the heart of the matter, and what these letters demonstrate: that Art justifies the struggle. For if she earned her living by writing criticism, she earned her life by writing poetry, poetry as pure, as intense, as permanent as any ever published. She was, I believe, too severe; out of all the poems she had written, she chose to preserve only one hundred and three, all but twelve less than a page in length; but in them, as W. H. Auden has said, she wrested "beauty and truth out of dark places." That, surely, is the ultimate triumph. So while it is possible to read this volume without at the same time reading her poetry, to do so is to grasp only partially the meaning, and the force —and the joy—of a singular life.

Among Louise Bogan's papers were probably no more than two dozen carbons of letters she had written; many of them, properly for a person who lived on Manhattan Island, were directed to the landlord; of the rest, mainly business letters of one sort or another, only three have been included here. Except for letters to Ruth Benedict, which at some point in the past had been returned, and for letters to me, the letters from which this selection was compiled were made available with great kindness and generosity by the following persons, to whom I owe personal pleasure and public gratitude:

Sister M. Angela, I.B.V.M., Kay Boyle, LaVerne H. Clark, Malcolm Cowley, Babette Deutsch, Rufina McCarthy Helmer, Howard Hollister, Helen Spencer Humphries, Tenney K. Lehman, Katie Louchheim, Beatrice Roethke Lushington, Margaret Marshall, William Maxwell, Howard Moss, Sylvie Pasche, Robert Phelps, Ann Rogers, May Sarton, Josephine O'Brien Schaefer, Karl Shapiro, William Jay Smith, Allen Tate, Glenway Wescott, John Hall Wheelock, Katharine S. White (for letters to herself and to the staff of *The New Yorker*), Edmund Wilson and Walter Wynn York.

I am also grateful to many of the above, and to those persons listed below, who in a variety of ways aided in the search:

Mrs. Charles Abbott, Léonie Adams, Nina Alonzo, Wystan H. Auden, Peggy Bacon, Johnfried Bergschneider, Constance Carrier, Marshall Clements, Caroline Delteil, Richard Eberhart, Abbie Huston Evans, Caroline Gordon, Zoltan Haraszti, Diana Haskell, Jacqueline Froom Hinden, Jacques Hnizdovsky, Caroline G. Hogue, Arthur C. Holden, Mary E. Knapp, Stanley Kunitz, Margaret Mead, Henry Allen Moe, Ned O'Gorman, Dorothy Olding, William Pratt, J. D. Salinger, Evalyn Shapiro, Robert Sward, Louise Talma, Louis Untermeyer and Janet Lewis Winters.

The following institutions opened their manuscript collections to me, and I gratefully acknowledge:

The American Academy of Arts and Letters and the National Institute of Arts and Letters Library, for letters to Rolfe Humphries.

The University of Chicago, *Poetry* Magazine Papers, 1912–1936, for letters to Harriet Monroe; and *Poetry* Magazine Papers, 1936–1953, for the letter to Hayden Carruth.

The Newberry Library, for letters to Malcolm Cowley, Paul Scott Mowrer and Morton Dauwen Zabel.

The Princeton University Library, Allen Tate Papers and Archives of Charles Scribner's Sons, for letters to Allen Tate and John Hall Wheelock, respectively.

The Poetry Collection of the Lockwood Memorial Library, State University of New York at Buffalo, New York, for the letter to William Carlos Williams.

The University of Washington Libraries, for letters from the Theodore Roethke Papers.

Collection of American Literature, Beinecke Rare Book and Manuscript Library, Yale University, as owner of the original letters to Edmund Wilson.

Others whom I am delighted to acknowledge and thank: Maidie Alexander Scannell, Louise Bogan's daughter, who in reading the letters through made important suggestions; Carin Watling, who transcribed the bulk of the letters; my colleagues Professors Karen Brockmann and Jacqueline Wallace for advice on translations; Williard Keebler, whose generosity facilitated many tasks; Josephine O'Brien Schaefer, who read the manuscript in its fullest form and gave me the benefit of her informed enthusiasm; Margaret A. Barrier, who in happily supportive ways made the project additionally pleasurable.

But surely almost everyone in extending help and courtesy to me had as his or her central concern the volume to be produced; it is to Louise Bogan, then, and her hold on the memory and respect of so many persons, that ultimate acknowledgment must be made.

Arrangement: The poems used as decade breaks were chosen for applicability and do not necessarily follow chronology.

Dates and Addresses: Meticulous about form, LB almost always headed her letters with a date and an address block. Where the date is missing but known, it has been included without added apparatus; where it has been approximated, the date appears in brackets. She changed the style of her dating from the American month-day-year to the English day-month-year, but to avoid confusion the former is followed throughout. From June of 1937 on, the address read 709 West 169th Street, New York City; address blocks thereafter are included, when she gave them, only when this Manhattan address was not the place of origin.

Identification: In an attempt to keep the total MS as readable as the letters themselves, identification of recipients follows the first mention of the name in a letter, even if that precedes the first received. Because most of the other persons mentioned are either sufficiently identified in the text itself or carry names that are known to all readers, additional identification has been included only when LB's remarks might otherwise be significantly obscured. In all cases, persons are identified only once. When in doubt consult the index, where *i* refers to the identification page.

Footnotes: In order to avoid blighting pedantry, I have held footnotes to a minimum. I have, however, dropped in explanatory notes where necessary understanding depends upon them or where the spirit seemed to call for them. Sometimes LB included in a letter a newly written poem; when these are not footnoted, the poem is un-identifiable and an additional footnote to say so seemed extravagant. Likewise, unless described as unpublished, uncollected or culled, all of LB's poems mentioned in the text can be found in her final collection, *The Blue Estuaries* (1968). Where possible and appropriate, I have quoted LB's own words in the footnotes; when no source is given, they have been taken from unpublished writings, from letters to me, or (very rarely) from conversation.

Selection: The reader must not assume that any series of letters to the same correspondent necessarily began with the first, or ended with the last, printed; or that gaps in correspondence necessarily mean no correspondence. Further, LB used postcards with delight and abandon; almost none have been included. In addition it should be noted that LB carried on a much more extensive correspondence than is sampled here. Beyond the omissions and deletions explained in the introduction, one must add the essentially unprincipled omissions demanded by restricted space; the occasional recipient who did not choose to make letters available; and the recognition that some of the smaller collections were unsuitable for inclusion because they added little or nothing to what was already revealed in letters having more narrative cohesion. Finally, some few people did not save her letters or lost them in fires or other literary catastrophes.

Omissions, whether slight or substantial, are indicated by three asterisks, except in the case of postscripts. When postscripts have been omitted, no apparatus shows it, but when any part of the postscript is printed, the rule of asterisks is maintained.

Text: About half of these letters were written by hand, occasionally in pencil, generally in blue or black ink. The loveliness of LB's script has often been commented upon by her friends; inevitably, however, since she wrote very swiftly, the handwriting (which changed from large and angular to small and flowing) is at some points illegible. In such cases, conjectures are designated by [?], full uncertainty by –?–.

Like all *New Yorker* writers, LB expected editing, and to the extent that it was reasonable, she had no quarrel with it; therefore, I have felt no need to call attention in the text to such changes as have been made. In any case, they are infrequent and insignificant: on the order of correcting spelling and typing errors, adjusting punctuation, repairing oversights and reducing a few names to initials or blanks. Verbal additions, however, are indicated by brackets, except for those on p. 379, which are LB's own.

1920-1929

SONNET

Since you would claim the sources of my thought
Recall the meshes whence it sprang unlimed,
The reedy traps which other hands have timed
To close upon it. Conjure up the hot
Blaze that it cleared so cleanly, or the snow
Devised to strike it down. It will be free.
Whatever nets draw in to prison me
At length your eyes must turn to watch it go.

My mouth, perhaps, may learn one thing too well,
My body hear no echo save its own,
Yet will the desperate mind, maddened and proud,
Seek out the storm, escape the bitter spell
That we obey, strain to the wind, be thrown
Straight to its freedom in the thunderous cloud.

/ to William Carlos Williams /

24 West Ninth Street
New York, N.Y.
[July] 1920

My dear Dr. Williams,[1]

Your article was forwarded to me from Farley [Massachusetts]. My family, immediately authority-stamp[ing] John as a maniac, made a concerted effort to back up authority with the result that all communication between John and myself has been cut off. The medical director at Matteawan in numerous letters has assured me that John is decidedly insane and of marked criminal tendencies. —So it was good to know that you feel what I feel for him, and that you have tried as I have tried, to make the word he wishes to say articulate.

Write to John. Tell him, as well as you can in a letter which will be read by various people before it reaches him, that because of the thing he knows endurance can become the long reality. Tell him that there are sources undiscovered and not yet spilled out.

And see him, Dr. Williams. I work, and cannot for some weeks. Write him in any case.

When you hear from him remember that I have not heard.

Very truly yours,
Louise Bogan

1. LB was a month away from her twenty-third birthday when she wrote to the poet and physician William Carlos Williams. Under discussion is John Coffey, a young Irishman who, so he claimed, thought to call attention to the needs of the poor by shoplifting (his specialty was furs) and then, in court, with attendant publicity, testifying to their plight. The plan went awry: having told the police of his long-term, successful thefts, he was sent not to court but to Matteawan, an insane asylum. With typical generosity, Williams wrote a somewhat opaque article for *The Freeman* in support of Coffey, and a poem, "An Early Martyr," not published until 1935.

/ to Harriet Monroe /

155 Lake Avenue
Worcester, Massachusetts
July 23, 1921

My dear Harriet Monroe,[1]

Beginning and End,[2] is, I think, the title for the group you suggest, with the order as it stands. I cannot think of any other general title that would do. Except, perhaps, *Poems* simply.

In "Leave-taking":

> Though you defeat me
> And I be heavy upon you

—reads better.

I can only trust in the early date.

Sincerely yours,
Louise Bogan

1. Harriet Monroe, the founder and, until her death in 1936, the editor of *Poetry: A Magazine of Verse,* probably had as much to do with supporting and encouraging the writing of poetry in English as anyone in America.

2. Under this title in the August 1922 issue of *Poetry* were five poems: "Elders," "Resolve," "Knowledge," "Leave-taking" and "To a Dead Lover." In putting together her first volume of poems, *Body of This Death* (Robert McBride, 1923), LB discarded all but "Knowledge." She was to remain a most severe critic of her own work.

c/o T. Cook and Son
Stefansplatz 2
Wien I
[August] 1922

Dear Harriet Monroe,

The draft on Vienna arrived safely. It represents an unheard of amount, in kronen: a million and a half or so. But in this disintegrating city, where dinner costs twenty or thirty thousand of the newspaper-ish bank-notes, that doesn't mean very much.

I must wait until I return to New York, in October, to see an August *Poetry.* This has been a sort of sabbatical six months, since April, during which I have written nothing. Sometime, when I recover the English language, I want very much to send other things to you. I am coming into the belief that in order to write English, you must, occasionally, hear it spoken!

Sincerely yours,
Louise Bogan

/ to Edmund Wilson /

99 Henry Street
Brooklyn
March 1, 1924

Dear Edmund,[1]

I liked your valentine very much, although it did err a little on the side of discretion. Am I never to see you? This next week I'll be busy finishing up a job at cataloguing,[2] and haven't a lot of time. Do, however, try to see me at some odd moment, soon.

The Dial certainly gave the book [*Body of This Death*] a rotten smack, didn't it? Johnny Weaver in the *Brooklyn Eagle* put me down as *very slight* and wanted to know why all the hosannas had been raised. [John Gould] Fletcher in *The Freeman* said my "lack of thought" was painful.

Well, try some time to pass an idle word with the put-upon.

Louise

1. Edmund Wilson, America's most wide-ranging man of letters, was one of the first friends LB made upon coming to New York. Her third volume of poetry, *The Sleeping Fury,* was dedicated to him.

2. The cataloguing job was for William Fielding Ogburn, professor of sociology at Columbia University. In the introduction to *An Anthropologist at Work: Writings of Ruth Benedict* (1959), Margaret Mead notes that, holding an assistantship under Ogburn, she "filled his office with working poets—Louise Bogan, Léonie Adams, Louise Townsend Nicholl. . . ."

/ to Rolfe Humphries /

Brooklyn
March 19, 1924

Dear Rolfe,[1]

I had a suitcase, ½ doz. apples, a child,[2] and a copy of *The American Mercury,* to hoist onto the train at New Milford: your letter got lost in the melée. To hand is another copy that was to go off to you today. I'm glad "A Girl to Juan" hits you right. Canby [3] turned it down once with the sad note that it showed poetic power but wouldn't quite do. Are you sure it isn't *too* Housman? God knows what I'll do with the first couplet—how long have I? Expect it the day before you put the magazine to bed.[4]

New Milford put so much electricity into the old nervous digestive system that yesterday I went up to see the animals at the Bronx Zoo.

Did you ever see a mandrill? A few gnus and cassowaries and curaçaos were pawing the cages; other than that nobody obliged with any amusement. Do see the mandrill sometime. (Monkey house; third cage on the right.)

* * *

> Yours for the advancement of the Ideal.
>
> Louise

1. Rolfe Humphries, classicist, poet and translator, had served as a lieutenant of infantry during World War I and was currently teaching Latin at the Woodmere Academy on Long Island. Describing him as he was at this time, LB said: "Rolfe presented * * * a seemingly uncomplicated attitude toward life and art. He was continually belying what was patently a gentle and cultivated nature by flights of rather tough and fanciful humor." Among his translations are the *Aeneid,* Ovid's *Metamorphoses* and *The Art of Love,* Juvenal's *Satires* and ("oddly enough") Lorca's only surrealist work, *The Poet in New York.*

2. The child, Maidie Alexander, had been born to LB and her first husband, Curt Alexander, in the Panama Canal Zone, a few years earlier. Alexander, an army officer, died in 1920.

"I never was a member of a 'lost generation,'" she once explained. "I was the highly charged and neurotically inclined product of an extraordinary childhood and an unfortunate early marriage, into which last state I had rushed to escape the first.* * * I had no relations whatever with the world about me; I lived in a dream, populated by figures out of Maeterlinck and Pater and Arthur Symons and Compton Mackenzie (*Sinister Street* and *Sylvia Scarlett* made a great impression on me) and H. G. Wells and Francis Thompson and Alice Meynell and Swinburne and John Masefield and other oddly assorted authors. What I did and what I felt was, I assure you, *sui generis.*" (To Morton D. Zabel, June 11, 1937)

3. Henry Seidel Canby was then editor of *The Saturday Review of Literature.*

4. The lines originally read: "Winter, that is a roofless room, / Tavern to rain, was our love's home." The problem was the tavern image, which LB had used elsewhere. She changed the couplet to read: "Winter, that is a fireless room / In a locked house . . ." and when collected in *Dark Summer* the title became "Girl's Song." But first the poem was published in the May 1924 issue of *The Measure.* Both LB and Humphries were on the nine-man editorial board (which, in its five-year existence, included—among others—Maxwell Anderson, Joseph Auslander, Padraic Colum, Louise Townsend Nicholl, Genevieve Taggard and Elinor Wylie).

May 19, 1924

Dear Rolfe—

Here I am back in the paper-pulp atmosphere of my youth, and a rather bracing atmosphere it is. This is a reticent countryside. The buds are still closed in, and the woodlots look bleak and wintry. In the pasture there are red branches and orange and yellow ones, but as yet little green. —Do you always sleep for a week solid whenever you get into the great open spaces? I sleep until my brain goes poorly; just now; I'll get over that.

Why get mad about Frost and the Pulitzer? He's 48 or so, and just getting crabbed, so it's better he get it now than later. By the time we're 48 we'll get it; and then we can shut up and tell the boys around the cracker-box all about it for the rest of our days.

What's a nice smooth little treatise on atoms? Can you suggest any other rousing country reading? I want to read *Wilhelm Meister* and other Goethe—he was a good guy, I've been told. Did you ever read Landor—and what do you think of him? Give three reasons for your answer.

You could write me a letter, if you'd like. I'll be here for quite a spell,—it's pleasant enough, even though they have a Hupmobile in the barn crowding out the cows. I may be able to stitch up a few pages of literature here.

Yours, imperturbe,
Louise

[P.S.] My legal name (used only on occasions of living in towns where they think it's strange to be a spinster with a child):

> Mrs. Louise Alexander
> % D. J. Bogan
> Otter River, Mass.

242 Lexington
July 22, 1924

Dear Rolfe:

I wrote you a note yesterday—to 12th Street—will you get it?

I've been reading about Keats sitting down every morning and writing 200 lines, fully and easily, and felt *very* minor—perhaps [John Gould] Fletcher was right. Of course, *Endymion* is a lot of junk, mostly, but:

> —like a common weed
> The sea-swell took her hair

isn't so terrible. In fact it's maddeningly lovely. Read Keats' letters on the train. He must have been a fine guy and deserved a better sweetie.

Here, there's the usual amount of young-children-attacked-by-fiend-on-Staten-Island, Davis-gives-speech-accepting-nomination-to-all-the-locusts-in-Locust-Valley, girl-of-fifteen-weds-world-air-flyer-in-London, and other startling events. I've written almost 12 pages of poem—it's pretty awful. The first three pages have a real kick but after that it gets Frostian, with added beats at the ends of lines. I want to do a lyric called "Thunder." [1] Did you ever have that kind of mindless, idealess compulsion—that you must do a lyric called "Thunder" (or any other name)?

The woods were fine—all save the concentrated soup, which tasted the same: potato, oxtail, mushroom, pea—all the same. We took some fine "art study" pictures which the developing place refused to print.

A various world—or is it varied?—is the best, I think. All things stem from that water, stone and vegetable rot—but I can't help thanking my stars that the two bits of protoplasm which meant *me*, met in an age after all the toughest inventing and hewing and moulding had been done. I do love tables, chairs, libraries, silk underwear, clean sheets, food cooked to order, paper and pencil and music.

I finished [Huysmans'] *Là-Bas*: the *messe noir* scene was pretty good. Thank God my thrills come easier.

Write me exactly when you'll be here, so I won't go gallivanting.

> Yours for the life complicated,
> Louise

1. When completed, the thunder poem was called "The Flume" and, after periodical publication in *The Measure* (June 1925), would be collected in *Dark Summer*. It was one of the poems LB culled from later volumes because: "I have never been quite sure about 'The Flume.' It came from the right place, and I worked hard on it, and it has some nice moments—the hot stove and the no-sound of water—which were actually observed and lived with, at one period of my life. Perhaps I have the feeling that one doesn't get out of that kind of obsession so easily—the 'facts' are false, at the end. When I'm dead, someone will gather it up and insert it in the *works*, I suppose. With notes!"(November 23, 1956)

July 24, 1924

Dear Rolfe:

You'll think me slightly crazed when I tell you I'm reading Goethe's biography now—on the advice, supposedly, that lives of g. m. all remind us we can make our l. sublime. I never have read anything about anybody, really, so now, when the passion is on me, I might just as well wade through the *Dict. of Nat. Biog.* from beginning to end. There's such choice bits. Goethe had five love-affairs before he was twenty; at the age of 70 he fell in love again (when he should have been drawing up plans for a pleasant little steam-heated grave) and wrote the *Westöstlicher Diwan* (snappy title, that). O, you great male poets! Think of the life ahead of you, Rolfe! No rest! No hope! I should think you'd shudder at the thought of being 83, with no relief in sight. You'll fall for a girl of 19, at 83 (vide Goethe) whom you'll see one morning chasing the ducks, you will leap out of bed, write an immortal sonnet, clutch the grizzled throat, and breathe your last. Cicero, with all his talk of escaping from the tiger, didn't count on the capacities of octogenarian male poets.

My German is faulty, but the Goethe lyrics ring the bell.

> *Über allen Gipfeln*
> *Ist Ruh,*
> *In allen Wipfeln*
> *Spürest du*
> *Kaum einen Hauch;*
> *Die Vögelein schweigen im Walde.*
> *Warte nur, balde*
> *Ruhest du auch.*[1]

. . . that's from the *Wandrers Nachtlied*—the title is so beautiful, too. The stripped, still lyric moves me more, invariably, than any flummery ode ever written—although, of course, Keats and the Romantics were only partly flummery—but

> *Über allen Gipfeln*
> *Ist Ruh*

gives me such happiness that I want to cry.

Today I hope to finish my lightning passage. I'll send it to you—since you're a brother in fright. Mine is more thunder than lightning, as I told you. The lightning startles me merely, the thunder would wring me with fright were I a mole underground.

What about that horse poem you did? May I see it?

O God, why were women born with ambition! I wish I could sit and tat, instead of wanting to go and write THE poem, or lie and kiss the ground.

If all this is mad blame the weather and an aftermath of Raymond's new Scotch.[2]

> Yours for the stripped and maddening earth,
> Louise

1. "Over all the mountains is peace, in all the treetops you sense hardly a breath; the birds are silent in the forest. Only wait; soon you too will be at peace."
2. Raymond Holden, poet, novelist and, from 1929 to 1932, managing editor of *The New Yorker*, was to become LB's second husband. He died in the summer of 1972.

> 242 Lexington
> July 31, 1924

Dear Rolfe:

I felt awfully dumb—after a visit from the strenuous Wolfs,[1] but I think you rate a couple pages, anyhow, what with malaria and verbs to help, please, serve, resist, and their opposites. —The Wolfs arrived Tuesday noon: Jed looked very fresh and beautiful, and Bob seemed just stomping with vigor. Jed liked my long poem. What there is of it. You'll never believe me when I say that I'll finish the lightning part —sometime, and you can see it. Jed has written one or two very fine things, one about being lost (written after 45 grains of quinine, she says. Do you know the quinine sensation? You're dry from your palate right down through your whole body to the soles of your feet, and a great wheel goes Ummmm–mmmmmmmmmmmmmmmmmmmmmmmmmmmmm through your nose and ear and everything is slow motion—but these are all female experiences, of course).

* * * Bob and Jed and Raymond and me and Scudder Middleton [2] went over, Tuesday night, to see one of Scudder's girl friends who lives in Turtle Bay. We made dinner—corn-on-the-cob, lettuce and cold roast beef, cocktails and claret—and ate it on a balcony over a swell garden full of willow trees. Bob and Scudder had a feverish argument about the effect of alcohol on the carburetor—you know Bob's line. Scudder went for him quite hard. The lady was charming if a little dumb—very much given to showing her very long, very charming legs. She sang after dinner—"What'll I Do" and "Kiss Me Again" and all the desert-Omar stuff that sopranos love and a nice one about three ducks on a pond and why do I remember them with tears. No one got drunk; Jed sang a swell song about a whale with adenoids and

Bob obliged with David and Goliath, and Scudder did a soft shoe dance.

When are you coming down again? We should have a party, I think. Wouldn't you like one? We've drunk all the good liquor, but Scudder always has pure alcohol which, he says, is much better for the tripes than gin. He's awfully amusing, and is sure to try to prove something to you.

If you're not coming this week you won't see me for ages—(wheedle, wheedle, inveigh, inveigh) because I've got to go up and see my great girl, who is catching fish, I hear, and developing in grand style. I'll be gone up to and including my birthday, which occurs around the juncture of Leo and Virgo, in the middle of August. (No pun intended.) I'll be 27, Rolfe. O God, I thought I'd be a great poet by 27 with fat works ranged on shelves. O well.

* * *

> Yours for entasis and entity [?],
> Louise

1. The Wolfs—Robert and Jed—were young poets connected with *The Measure*. Jed, who will more often appear in these letters as Genevieve Taggard, had already published one volume of poetry, *For Eager Lovers*, and was to continue publishing until her death in 1948.

2. Scudder Middleton was a poet and, in the 1930s, managing editor of *The New Yorker*.

> 242 Lexington Avenue
> New York
> August 6, 1924

Dear Rolfe:

It appears you really have had a lot of malaria. I expected to see you Sunday—but there wasn't any note in the box or anything, so I thought you might have gone to see your girl-friend, or something. For goodness sake, lay off the gerunds and gerundives for a while and lie in bed and drink whiskey and quinine alternately and in great gulps. I wish you could come down here, and I could feed you a *lot* of liquor—so that you were really drunk—you bum. You should get good and hilarious oftener than you do. (You resent advice, of course. All unmarried guys over 25 do. Also, who am I to get maternal over a great hulk like you. I'm really scared to death of you, you know.

I'm always scared of great hulks—you especially (confidence No!)) I think you would be like-you-are-at-a-ball-game *all* the time if you went around under weigh [1] a little.

There's a girl on here staying with me (the Otter River expedition having been postponed a little) whom I want you to meet. She's not beautiful, yet very much alive—energetic and vital as the devil. She's a blond with brown eyes and Percy MacKaye is her cousin—which isn't exactly to her credit. * * * She has a cuckoo mother, and I have one, too, so we sit about comparing notes on our blighted lives. Our (hers and mine) lives really were blighted *very* early, you know, by big strong dominating women with crowds of admiring gents in tow. I think you'd like her awfully. * * * Well, all I can say is—if you come down Saturday—let me know ahead of time, so she can be around. You can go into your shell if you want to. —I rather think it would be worth your while to come out of it a while in this case.

Poe's prose is pretty exciting, between you and me. Did you ever read *The Narrative of A. Gordon Pym?* That used to keep me awake in my youth. And "Bon-Bon," the "Red Death," "The Devil in the Belfry," "The Pit and the Pendulum,"—golly, they're pretty harrowing. They stick with me most out of my earliest reading—together with a swell story about a tin mine in Cornwall—one of my brother's books. I read all of my brother's books and *Salammbô* and *Pilgrim's Progress,* when I was at no age to digest them.

Rolfe, do come and see the Scotch girl. She's charming. And admit I scare you too. It would be very satisfying to feel I'm not the only frightened person in this combination. (I shan't use any such admission against you. I'll forget it, if you wish.)

Yours for plaids and pleasures,
Louise

1. The odd form stands uncorrected because it suggests deliberate choice: LB was both an impeccable speller and the granddaughter of a sea captain.

242 Lexington
August 23, 1924

Dear Rolfe:

I wrote you a wild letter once last spring, and you told Jed and Bob you thought I had anxiety hysteria, or something, so I shan't wish another one on you now. I've been feeling like several combined hells for the last two weeks for all the reasons. Yesterday I said farewell to poesy forever, after telling it that it was the last refuge of fools and unsatisfied Uranians. (This was precipitated because I discovered I couldn't write a poem.) I'm mad with Raymond, and work and places to live, and limited incomes and my face and my mind and my will, and with you and with Scotch virgins. I wish you'd met the woman and beaten her to a pulp. I discover she's rather poisonous.

In fact, if you have any free afternoons next week, you can come in and beat me to a pulp (I realize that that's Freudian—but I need a good licking and there isn't anyone around big enough to give it to me). Raymond talks to me when he should kick me down stairs, and say: "If you don't like that come back and I'll break the three other ribs and your medulla oblongata."

The winter opens up as a wide cold period wherein I shall work as a check-girl at the New Roosevelt, or as a file-clerk for the Socony People. To hell with art! It's a waste of time, and besides, it breaks my heart. Go away, little girl, I won't buy your damned violets.

Ring Lardner's *How to Write Short Stories* is great. "Some Like Them Cold" and the story about the cuckoo ball-player are as good as (or better than) the entire *Theatre* of Racine, with Caesar's Gallic Wars thrown in for good measure.

In God's name, write to me, and bawl me out, if not beat me up.

Yours,
Louise

242 Lexington
August 28, 1924

Dear Rolfe:

Just at present, having snuck out of the center of the whirlwind, I'm taking a nice nap, and polishing my fingernails on its edge. No one can stay alive very long in the mood out of which I wrote you that letter. While the storm still yelled around I wrote telling the Taggard-Wolfs good-bye forever—and it's broken them all up, I guess. They are fond of me and I of them. Their fondness this morning took the shape of two letters, in which they called both Raymond and myself habitual drunkards and reminded me that I probably would fill a

dipso's grave because it was in the blood. It may be being cruel to
them, but I've got to be my own kind of damn fool, and not anybody
else's kind. Meantime, my (own) d. foolishness has led me into finding a new place to live, and without breaking up our (yours and
mine) jolly, if inconsequential, habit of letter-writing.

It would be a shame if I should disappoint you by breaking out into
Louise-Nichollishness. I shan't, don't worry. I don't want to do or say
or feel anything that would spoil a lot of silly times we ought to have
next winter, when you can come up five flights of stairs, drape your
legs over the chair, and indulge in a complete excoriation of the New
York School of Poetry. I hereby forgo the Bobbish Schemes in favor
of the rotten jokes we are sure to make if we are left to ourselves.
—Genevieve says I'll never be a great woman until I let myself be
damned. —But there'll be plenty of time for that when my neck begins to go. So we'll forgo the licking, too.

Yesterday I and Raymond (as R[ing] L[ardner] would say) went
to see a double-header between Cleveland and New York. It was
split up and there weren't any three baggers that you could notice.
The guy that pitched the second game for the Yanks—Shawkey, I think
—did everything to the ball except swallow it before he decided to
throw it. The first game was beautifully scientific, with no lost time
by anyone. Babe Ruth got into a fight with the umpire once or twice.
—I like the figures of the Yankee heavy hitters very much (the woman
speaks). One man—Pipp—looks startlingly like you. Your boy-friend,
Waite Hoyt, relieved Shawkey when he began to blow up. You would
have enjoyed that. He looked very nice and plump, but everyone hit
him all over the field.

How about going to see Washington play this / next Saturday? Write
and tell me when you expect to get in. Raymond is having a vacation
this week, so we are open for all sorts of screaming pranks.

Will you listen to the first cantos of my narrative—which probably
will go down the ages in the *Christabel* class? I am going to finish
the lightning part, and call it a day, I think. I've lost all interest in
the woman in it, who used to rush around the house hoping she'd be
betrayed. I'm sure she's been betrayed by this time and has taken to
washing dishes and having babies, like any other milky-breasted female, married to a he-man.

I'm reading *The Education of Henry Adams;* thank God my ancestors were coast-guards and paper-mill supts., not Presidents of the U.S.

Yours for cleanliness and safety
(as opposed to dirt and danger).
Louise

September 6, 1924

Dear Rolfe:

Here comes the September *Measure*, full of moons of grandeur and sunrise trumpets, sponsored by the great Yosef Auslander.[1] A *Reply to Mr. Wolf*, goes the caption of the editorial, by one Ernest Walsh,[2] K. (it is to be supposed) of C.—of Serrahassa-Abetone, Provincia de Modena, Italia. Mr. Wolf's properly dragged over the coals. Miss Millay is called a poet for young girls, and poetry societies of married ladies (as opposed to married harlots), and Carl Sandburg, Ezra Pound and—Robert Frost, the old rail-splitting rascal, are cited as America's great poets.

O, it's worth 25¢ any day of the week.

We met Yosef on the street the other day, looking more like a fruit man than ever. He was perspiring freely, which didn't improve his appearance much. (Rule 1—vary your epithets as much as possible.)

The sonnet's very fine. No joke, it's very fine. You can think up a title any time now and sell it to R. T[orrence].[3]

The lightning's done, as I have before intimated. There's only going to be one more part, making four in all. I have kept the parts to an even four because of the thirteenth cross-reference in the ninth book of the *Upanishads*—after the manner of the Spanish Lully and the Christian mystic, St. Bee. (See footnote ‡ * §.)

How are the murders along 12th Street?

Yours,
Louise

‡ * § A phenomenon I have often observed.[4]

1. The editorship of *The Measure* was a revolving one, and Joseph Auslander held it at this point. He is perhaps best known as the compiler, with Frank Ernest Hill, of *The Winged Horse Anthology*.
2. Ernest Walsh edited the little magazine *This Quarter*.
3. The poet and playwright Ridgely Torrence chose poetry for *The New Republic*.
4. *The Waste Land* had been published in 1922. Clearly LB and Humphries were amused by the scholarly notes Eliot had appended to it.

October 23, 1924

My God, who said poetry was being writ in America? I've read manuscripts for hours: they're no more poetry than I'm the Piltdown Man.[1] Your letter was lovely. —I haven't any liquor in me—ichor—élan vital: what you will—at the moment to make jokes. I've got to go over to Bklyn to see if my mother is alive or dead.

    * * *

Joey Auslander called on me this morning. He looked lustfully at my legs.

M. Van Doren [2] took "Cassandra."

Yours (as the critics would say) for being like Ossian out of Bion and Moschus.

Write me.

Louise

1. LB was elected acting editor of *The Measure* from November 1924 to February 1925. ("I'll accept *The Measure* appointment," she wrote to Humphries earlier in the month; "I'll accept anything to bolster me out of all this lares and penates.") In the first issue under her editorship there appeared reviews by Edith Sitwell and by Countee Cullen, identified as "a New Yorker, colored, a student at New York University."

2. Mark Van Doren was then literary editor of *The Nation*.

The Measure
449 West 22nd St.
New York, N.Y.
[November] 1924

Dear Rolfe:

I can't see you this week: I've got to keep alive, and the backwash is too bitter and too much. You can do a Gunnar Gunnarson on a waiter; all I can do is get ugly and insult people who are good to me. Do you want to come see the stuff I'm collecting for the above w. k. periodical, say Monday afternoon next week? Scudder came across with three good poems; the little [Léonie] Adams girl is going to give me some.[1] The rest will come from the sticks.

Nothing is new, and I haven't a rowdy idea in my whole frame.

It is lunch-time. The cloak-and-suiters clink heavy plates in Woolworth's Improved Lunch, below. These are soft days.

> O help me leave life alone!
>
> Yours,
>
> Louise

1. "The little Adams girl" was at this point just two years out of Barnard College and most reluctant to submit her poems to editors, but by 1925 a remarkable book of poems, *Those Not Elect,* would be published. Miss Adams, who will appear frequently in these letters, shared with LB the Bollingen Prize for 1954.

/ to Ruth Benedict /

> 93 West Cedar Street
> Boston, Mass.
> July 1, 1925

Dear Ruth: [1]

This is a little letter to tell you of my new address, which you will see above—rather a nice horse-hair-and-black-walnut kind of address, don't you think? The place is *way* down on the wrong side of the Hill, almost against the Charles Street jail (over against, as the old printers used to say on title pages). You may address me that way if you wish:

> 93 West Cedar Street
> over against the Charles Street Jail

A very fine neighborhood, on the whole, for as my mother (from whom I inherit my skepticism, I may well believe!) said when I told her of the jail's proximity to my new home, "Well, there's many a good man in jail, and many a smooth rascal out of it." A comforting thought, that. A fine world to go about in, crammed with smooth, unjailed rascals!

Margaret [Mead] and Luther [2] rushed through here last Sunday, on their way to see you. They said that you had told them to look for quite incredible signs and portents by this way: to turn left by the red cow and other fairy-tale directions. Is the way to West Alton [New Hampshire] like that really?

Margaret gave me some beautiful hand-hemmed dishtowels. She would! She said she omitted the aspidistra she intended decorating them with, merely out of lack of time.

Boston is quite beautiful. The people aren't up to much, but occasionally one hears a beautiful voice, which is more than New York ever grants (with one or *two* exceptions). There are real tree-shaped trees as well, and startling sparrows that make a sound like a pebble being dropped into water. There are *marvelous* antiques. Such piles of lovely old things no one ever saw before. Antique dealers sit on my door-step on Saturday mornings, hawking exquisite chairs, and lovely unimaginable tables. *They're* too smooth ever to see jail!

Will you come down before you go to Zuñi or wherever, and talk to me? I'm so dying to talk to someone human. Do, if you can. I think I'm marrying next week. Don't believe it until you hear it, however.

And write me in any case.

Yours—
Louise

[P.S.] I liked the latest poems.

1. Ruth Benedict, the distinguished anthropologist, and author of *Patterns of Culture,* wrote poetry under the name "Anne Singleton." The posthumous *An Anthropologist at Work,* which contains many examples of her poetry, was assembled by Margaret Mead, who also gave time to verse in the twenties. Identifying her as one "leaving shortly for a year's field study in Samoa," *The Measure* published Miss Mead's "For a Proud Lady" (written for LB) in its June 1925 issue.

2. Luther Cressman was Miss Mead's first husband.

/ *to Edmund Wilson* /

93 West Cedar Street
Boston, Massachusetts
July 10, 1925

Dear Edmund:

This is my address throughout July and August. The house is pleasantly old and, after the New York fashion, set in the middle of a slum. West Cedar Street mounts the Hill and comes down on the other side in a welter of brick tenements, jails, and other necessary if unsightly institutions. The up-hill part is beautiful: one stretch meets the eye as absolutely unbroken eighteenth century. You must see that stretch on your journey over the continent.

I have been reading Henry James very swiftly, so that I might, if such a thing were possible, get the color without too much of the sense. I am enchanted by the absolute sureness in method. —Even though he does the thing all wrong sometimes, he is always sure of how he wants to do it. The people that mirror the action never slip up, lose their outline and become merely Tom, Dick or Harriet. But I am not sure that they are invariably the right mirrors. Fleda Vetch is right in the first part of *The Spoils of Poynton:*—she is the last person in the world to reflect the second part—she is much too concerned. James realized this, and just left her out for a time, after the man married the other girl. I think that the scenes after Fleda and the mother find out about the marriage are pitifully inadequate. How can this calm contained creature, that takes a blow in the face without a word, be the same girl that rushed upstairs crying, "I should never give you up!" a little earlier? Some of the mercury gets rubbed off on the back of the mirror. James is impotent and afraid, suddenly. If Fleda made a fine dramatic row—took her shirt-waist off under the Poynton parlor windows, after the manner of George Sand —that would have been vulgar. So we are treated to a great peeled patch in the reflecting glass, with bright rich vision all around it.

That impotence crops up again and again. Even the earliest, gayest things have a touch of it in them. Someone could do an entire doctor's thesis on the Interrogatory Method in the Development of Conversation in the Novels of Henry James. Such people—at once so sharp-nosed and so subtle and so dull witted! [text missing] has the weak-minded habit of repeating the last word uttered by the first voice. Echolalia is the clinical name for that. After this fashion:

Hic: "She was ill and we brought her some beef-broth."

Ille: "Ill?"

Hic: "Well, perhaps not ill, but having about her some sense of the shawl across the knees."

Ille: "Hardly knees."

Hic: "Shoulder would give the arrangement better. She drank the soup."

Ille: "Drank?"

Hic: "Sniffed it, rather."

That is not *echt* James, but there's very little reason why it shouldn't be. Lubbock says that there has only been one Awkward Age—one novel wherein all the action is expressed as action merely, wherein the characters acquit themselves like actors in a stage setting, wherein the setting itself, described as so much malleable stuff upon which these people make dents or cast shadows, suffices for all the "He thoughts" and "She felts" of less artful drama. The implications were terrific, the oblique conversational method immense, the *mise en scène* marvelous, but the book almost drove me mad. God knows what would have happened to the thing if the Duchess hadn't said a few plain words now and again. Someday when I am eighty and have a game leg, I'll make a list of the repetitions and variations of the "You are of a fineness" construction scattered through the book. It's like a little boy who has just learned that literal translations sound amusing, and who goes about doing his best for the ablative absolute. O, too much sharpening down of the fine cedar wood around the lead in the pencil, so that at last the lead itself is powdered away.

I thought that *The Europeans,* for all its nonsensical sense of moral values, really came off. *Washington Square* has about everything. *The Aspern Papers* rings the bell completely, as well, as far as I am concerned. There's another thesis for some young wise person in *The Princess Casamassima:* The Dime Novel Converted into Literature. Did you ever read it, and apart from its magnificent writing, its sheer fearless massing of word and sentence, isn't it a scream?

What was the matter with this man, Edmund? It wasn't exile merely. Part of him had been excised. The pity and terror were somehow misplaced. *The Other House* is such a failure, because the wires get crossed, the puppets go on talking after the play has run down; the voices go on like the horrid sound when the Victrola needle gets stuck in one groove of a record.

I think his sense that all sexual play is essentially evil is an extremely important detail. The array of innocent enough people who are made subtly monstrous because they have slept with someone outside the banns of holy matrimony—it's a child's sense of evil. I used to have it when I almost knew how babies were born, almost but not entirely. That's why *The Turn of the Screw* is so terrific. Miss Jessel died of an abortion, it is intimated, and it is made fearful—as though an abortion weren't a rather heart-breaking thing to die of. What Quint told the children was perhaps how babies were born. I think that James' greatest effects are built up out of that very horror, that outrageous mad fear. Whenever he is about to cave in under his own style, that sense of evil gets him through. Every one of his low sneaks is sexually irregular first. The rest, to him, followed in natural course.

I bore you, perhaps, dear Edmund, by all this. You have had it figured out for yourself years ago, no doubt. No one has really tried to get the clinical details on James, however. Why doesn't someone? The West and the [Van Wyck] Brooks had their biases all against them. Rebecca [West] gets very mad at him because his young girls try to act as though they were suitable creatures for marriage, and had never heard of Mary Wollstonecraft. I get mad at him because he is at once a great artist—such a sense of life, of differentiation, of light and movement!—and an old fool.

I have no one to talk to, you see, so you will let me steam at you occasionally, won't you? I'm reading Jacques Loeb on the physico-chemical aspects of existence, in the midst of the stream of James. He rides his points somewhat. Thank heaven for art, that doesn't need to prove anything.

> Write me more.
> Ever with love,
> Louise

P.S. Raymond's best, too.

/ to Ruth Benedict /

> 93 West Cedar Street
> July 17, 1925

Dear Ruth:
   * * *

Forgive my not answering your letter before this, but everything *has* been upset. We have moved, we have married. Anything, pretty near, is understandable, after matters of that import.

My entire exchequer is being ruined by visits to the dentist. Dear, dear, with autumn coming on and all. I'm reading Marcel Proust, after having given up H. James as an old senile creature. He's not so bad up to 1896—but after that he's awful! But you probably know—

The lovely trees alone heal my inquietude. O, lovely trees: catalpas (Indian bean) just spilling flowers, and lindens—real silver lindens. We ate our wedding supper under a linden tree, just outside of the august town of Putnam. A great flowering branch just swung into the car through the door as we got out. "The bride carried linden flowers"—could anything be lovelier? Raymond had a beautiful button-hole full, and I had a whole armful of branches. Delicate down drop-ping heaven smelling things.

The wedding itself was awfully *jolly*: by a young Congregationalist minister, in a parsonage. A real parsonage—it said so in the window, carefully enwrought with colored glass. The license came out of the village dry goods store, which happened to be owned by the Town

Clerk. We were catechised about our names and color in the back of the place—a corner heavy with dry calico smell, Singer machine oil smell, the smell of old Butterick patterns. Wasn't that jolly?

Write me, from wherever, and do you know Léonie's address? The creature didn't give it me.

Yours,
Louise

66 Fayette Street
Boston
August 25, 1925

Dear Ruth:

This letter has been in my mind for longer than I care to think. There's no reason that it shouldn't have gone off before this, save sheer inertia. Not that I sit about all day, chin on fist, revolving within my head great schemes of poetry and empire. But I do so love to do nothing. If there weren't so much pounding to be done: if I didn't even have to *say* anything again, or if time were *not* time: and there would be space without end, and not this bother of being older every year!

There *has* been a new poem—which *The Nation* took [1] and a story —such a dull story! Prose is so terribly unsatisfactory. Everything in it could be said in any number of ways. While a poem is itself, inevitably, unerringly.

Dr. Sapir [2] came to see me, on a rather unfortunate day, when Raymond's mother had elected to come and give her sanction to our wedded state. She made such a ceremony of it—impressive no end. I was all strung up, being tactful—what a strain that is, even after years of stubborn training—when Dr. Sapir rang the bell. I was a little "away," I'm afraid, with him. He's very swell, and I wish I could have seen him really.

* * *

[He] thought that Margaret looked very worn and tired when he last saw her. Do you think that she'll bear up under that journey's long grind? Perhaps Samoa hasn't the aching, tearing kind of tropical oppression that Central America has. Perhaps it's higher and wilder. I trust Margaret to make something out of nothing in almost any circumstances.

* * * We have taken a little apartment with a big sunny *kitchen*— you see, I did get one after all. It's going to be extremely jolly, and

I must admit that domesticity thrills me to the bone. Yesterday I made peach jam!

Do write me again soon. I'm quite a good correspondent, really.

All very best wishes,
Louise

1. "If We Take All Gold," published in October.

2. Then chief of the division of anthropology at the Canadian National Museum, Edward Sapir was another of the remarkable group of anthropologists who involved themselves in the writing of poetry. A group of his poems appeared in the January 1925 issue of *The Measure,* and shortly thereafter he began publishing poems and reviews for Harriet Monroe in *Poetry.*

/ to Edmund Wilson /

66 Fayette Street
Boston
October 27, 1925

Dear Edmund,

I am returning the Beasly to you, after a frightful lapse, and in rather a sad condition. What appear to be butter marks have sprung into view upon the chaste blue cover. Perhaps they are merely stigmata of my struggle for beauty with Ponds Two Creams, Favored by the QUEEN OF ROMANIA and Mrs. Ordway Q. Spilt of New York, the Lido and points West. Anyhow, the Beasly looks perfectly terrible. Maybe you can never pass it on to anyone else now. O dear, O dear.

We have a new canary. His name is Archad. Also four fish, called I Gaspiri, or, The Upholsterers.

The Beasly, in its galumphing way, is quite interesting. It's not art, but it's good sociological documentation. The definition of terms, especially the kind of terms that little boys chalk up on walls, is especially good data for future students of Early Life in East Texas, I think.

I still read Chekhov. Music has begun here, and every Friday I go to see Koussevitzky get perfectly clottedly crimson in the back of the neck in all *ff*s.

Do write sometime. All best,

Louise

/ to Rolfe Humphries /

66 Fayette Street
Boston, Mass.
December 27, 1925

Dear Rolfe:

In answer to your letter of the 20th, would say that "Xmas" is now over, everyone's worst fears have been realized, and the cleaning woman has swept the artificial snow up from around the "Xmas" tree. The menagerie has gained two charming mice, called Ossip and Wossip, or, The Brothers Karamazov. They are all white with black ears, and have very cunning habits, pink noses and paws, and rather large tails. They eat Pettijohns, drink water, and run in circles.

Gargle, the bird, has pretty habits of letting himself out of his cage. He is out at present, fleeing around the kitchen as I write, and he can stay out, for all of me.

A missive from Léonie informs us that the Great Wilson made some hearty passes at her, inviting her to stay at his house, and all. Are we to allow this sort of thing to happen to our blond Nordic females? Don't say such a thing!

She has the Keats, too, you big bum?

Re poems, Irita Van Doren * * * has had a poem by me for the past month and a half. [1] What do you advise me to do? Is that what she did with your "Man in the Midst of Nature" one? Just grab it off and not write you a line about it? Because I want to send this one, which is called "Winter Swan," out to someone else. What kind of letter shall I write to her? Please advise.

The Taggard-Wylies send us a swell birthday greeting. A new poem is rapidly coming on, to be called "Didactic Piece," but really nothing but the title can be divulged at this moment because I don't know anything else about it myself.

The great Alexander is getting very big and handsome, and is just as certain as ever that the world is her oyster, scallop and clam. No new boy friends have appeared but she drags a couple of mangy girls around occasionally under the pretense of superintending their reading. She got two *excellents* for the month of December, in conduct and lessons. Think of that. What is this younger generation coming to?

My husband snapped to with a swell line of presents, and I presented him with the mice among other things. Their names are Pip and Gyp, and they clean their faces regularly and similarly.

Please go and see Fannie Hurst's *Mannequins* in the movies and see how low one has to fall to win $50,000. It has everything in it except Eliza crossing the ice.

How's for going to Sweden this summer? I see earthquakes are promised in the East this coming year. Also many scandals in high circles.

Well, old friend, will close. Hope you and Jim Tully [2] are still the best of friends. Give my regards to the missus.[3] How are conditions in the Holden-Bogan family?

Hm [?]—dunt esk!

> Yours for movie rights,
> Louise

1. Mrs. Van Doren finally published the poem in the *Herald Tribune Books*, which she edited, in 1926.

2. Jim Tully, according to his own description in *Twentieth Century Authors*, was an "Irish spinner of fairy-tales and a poet whom a hard life twisted into a hobo, a pugilist, and a realistic writer."

3. Humphries had married Helen Spencer, a physician, earlier in the year.

> 66 Fayette Street
> March 19, 1926

Dear Rolfe et Cie:

Welcome home to our side of the Rockies, the Adirondacks and the Orange Mts! Now bawdy repartee should fly through the air much more fluently, New York and Boston being what and where they are.

Our little nest is rapidly becoming the swellest in town. The air of common lewdness has left it. Which is rather a loss, but respectability has not yet crept too securely in. In our backyard we have a lot of nice railroad tracks and the American Rescue Workers. Also several loads of bricks. In our front yard is a public school full of undernourished children who chant:

"One-and-one-are-two"

in the most harrowing monotone. The machine beginning, alas! No chance for *them* to discover anything about a non-Euclidian world.

We have a lot of social lepers on our street. Also some employment bureaus and a few interior decorating establishments. They don't seem to have much to do with one another.

Did you see Léonie's book? It's swell. Also (add literary news) H.

Monroe accepted three sonnets by Raymond Holden. Laugh that off. She states that she isn't crazy about the title, which is quite a shame, I think. Why should H. have a hiatus in her madness?

We wrote some swell *bouts rimés* the other evening. What about a few long-distance ones? The rhyme scheme was:

feather — ooze — booze — weather
together — choose — moos — leather
drench — cloy — yard — stench — joy — card —

from which Raymond evolved a beautiful little thing entitled "A Catch of Old Catarrh," and I a slight song called "Dick Deeps, the –?– Dust Man," or, "The Influence of Climate Upon Environment." [1]

See what you can do. $500,000 to the winner. Look for Lucky Bucks in today's *Herald Tribune*.

The great Alexander will no doubt be put into the pound, or wherever they deposit truant children, because she hasn't gone to school yet, and doesn't know when she is going to go, or where, or anything. She can swim swell. We expect to espouse a new cat very soon. Raymond says it will have to come from Düsseldorf and spout eau-de-cologne.

※ ※ ※

Yours, straining for a reply,
Louise

1. LB never lost her pleasure in *bouts rimés*. In 1958, faced with the following rhymes set by William Jay Smith—reek, speak, turn, tweak / learn, burn, lodge, churn / dodge, hodge-podge, fat, wodge / drat, hat, flat, flat—she turned out "The Confrontation":

O horrible the filthy reek!
I stand still, and can hardly speak.
How terrible to meet this turn!
How frightful to receive this tweak!

What is this horror I must learn?
As once I froze, I now must burn.
And hang around the lonely lodge
My heart become a broken churn.

For it is nothing I can dodge
Caught as I am in a hodge-podge
As I was lean I must be fat
And have Fate use me as a wodge.

Now I must utter "Damn" and "Drat"
Now I must rush and get my hat
And run six miles in nothing flat
And run six miles in nothing flat.

/ to Ruth Benedict /

66 Fayette Street
April 9, 1926

Dear Ruth:

* * * Did I tell you about the invitation from Yaddo, which is a sort of imitation Peterborough in [Saratoga Springs], N.Y.? They give you a studio, bedroom and bath, to say nothing of meals and much landscape architecture, all (if you're a creative lady or gent) for $10 a week! Raymond says that all the most *awful* people will be there, but perhaps that's jealousy. It might be fun for the month of August. Would I work?

* * *

I've discovered a wonderful man—Ernest Hemingway—who really can write simple declarative sentences. He has a book called *In Our Time*, published by Boni and Liveright, that's thrilling. Did you see that awful Joey Auslander blurb about Lady [Leonora] Speyer, and Virginia Moore and Genevieve Taggard in last Sunday's *World*? That sort of thing is one reason why the s. d. sentence should propagate and flourish.

Margaret I have neglected most shamefully. My letters would have been so domestic, and she would have so girned and girded at me. Léonie would really like a job, I think. She said she might come up and help me plant a seed or two of the garden.

Could you come too? * * *

Ever, the domestic and vanishing
Bogan

Yaddo
Saratoga Springs, New York
August 23, 1926

Dear Ruth:
* * *

This place ["Yoohoo"] is an 1890 conception of Haddon Hall. There is a fountain in the enormous hall downstairs, Renaissance theme, bronzes, and whatnot scattered over a room as big as the waiting room in the Grand Central Station. The creative workers have, apiece, an enormous bedroom and a studio that could accommodate the larger part of the N.Y. police, drawn up in squads. The studios, for the most part, succeed in being restful and beautiful, in spite of cream-colored Gothic moulding and bird's-eye maple desks. Mine is indeed magnificent, with pines seen through lattices on three sides, and with a fourth side given over to a great plate glass window looking over a golden oat-field, a baroque marble pool, pines, fields beyond, and mountains on the horizon. The gardens are very lovely; roses and pines and marble pergolas. Such grandeur!

I have done two stories and two poems,[1] since I came. Curiously enough, the place does make you feel like working. And such food! Never have I tasted such food! —The people, pretty terrible at first glance, have all become human on acquaintance. There's a Polish composer and his singing wife; Joseph Anthony, who writes novels; Joseph Warren Beach, a sad example of the academic mind, and some other rather minor examples of artists. Do you think Léonie would care for any of this? I am giving her name for next year. She could get a great deal of inspiration for that wonderful mimetic gift of hers, here.

We are in N.Y. this winter! Really, I could live behind a billboard or on a roof, to be back among people I know. —Let me give you a full account of my paranoiac behavior *viva voce*, when I see you. I'm sure you would appreciate it more, rather than seeing it set down in cold script.

Under separate cover, I send you the two poems I have done here, and one other, that I was too upset to show you at Melrose. I am writing to Margaret. I trust she has not crossed me off her heart. Will you show her the poems, considering them communal copies?

With all best love,
Louise

---

1. Not well known is the fact that, until the mid-thirties, LB wrote short stories, nearly all of which were published in *The New Yorker*. The poems were "Feuernacht" and "Dark Summer"; the "one other" mentioned in the last paragraph is unidentifiable.

432 East Manhattan St.
Santa Fe, N.M.
December 16, 1926

Dear Ruth:

Today I feel my existence more or less justified—I don't many days—because I have made a *lemon* pie, with a meringue baked to the most delicate nuance of an extremely delicate octoroon's skin! Cooking is really more fun than eating one book after another, in a kind of drug-incited fever. * * *

O Ruth, how Santa Fe depressed me at first! [1] The day after we arrived—and we came into town on a pitch black evening—we walked up one of the more awful streets—out beyond the Old Palace —all red brick bungalows. I was for turning and running home immediately. It was Thanksgiving and we [were] in the hotel, in a very depressing pair of rooms, and even our small remaining quota of Scotch failed to cheer us up, the hotel's splendid dinner, which included Long Island duck and frogs'-legs, even less. —The air was lovely, like clear October at home, but I kept saying, I knew it, I knew it—just another American town. Fortunately Raymond heard about a house that afternoon from Dr. M.—and we went out to see it. It was so nice that we took it at once, and moved in that day, deserting the hotel, where our hands struck sparks from the door knobs and the faucets.

The house is snug, and pleasantly furnished—there's an adobe fireplace and a sumptuous bathroom, a bedroom for Maidie, an adequate kitchen, a dining room, and a sleeping porch—all with rough round timbers in the ceiling and plaster walls. The sun streams onto the porch every afternoon, and Raymond and I bask in it, drink cups of tea, and read or write. (We're brewing some raisin wine in a great crock, and will be drinking that merrily by the New Year.) You will have a picture of the little house soon.
* * *

Léonie hasn't sent me *any* of her works yet. I think she's a bad one, not to. * * * I'm so pleased about the Museum job. That World Peace thing has such terrible offices—full of ballots. Now, at least, Léonie can go willingly through the corridors and get hopelessly lost amid the Stiegel glass and the delicate old furniture. She says the guards call her "young lady." Darling lady?

We expect to get a little extra money soon and get out to see the country roundabout. We've been very restricted by our finances up to now. * * *

All greetings of the Good Season,

and best love—

Louise

1. The move to Santa Fe was made for Raymond Holden's health.

/ to Edmund Wilson /

432 East Manhattan St.
Santa Fe, N.M.
January 13, 1927

Dear Edmund:

It was very sweet of you to send me [Dorothy Parker's] *Enough Rope.*
I had been wanting to see it. I didn't think that the poems in the
beginning—the first section—were so hot, rather diluted Edna [Millay],
to my mind, but the to-hell-my-love-with-you stuff is excellent. Perhaps we gals are at our best on that note.

Well, you'd be surprised * * * at the way writers and artists wring
the last drop out of their subjects in these parts! My, my, such
writing and art! What with W[ytter] Bynner and A[rthur] D[avidson]
Ficke there is really no bound that can be set to *Real Achievement*
in the great Southwest.¹ We had quite a lot of liquor at W. Bynner's
the other night and the stories he didn't tell about the old crowd
back in 1902. Rolling under cabs and lying in gullies in silk hats
was nothing to that young crew. Them was the days.

By now you have reviewed the latest work of R. Holden, his really
beautiful sonnet to John Banister Tabb.² Really a rousing talent, that
young man's.

There is nothing much here with what Raymond would call the
cortex. I have read one million novels, the latest world vision of Mr.
Wells, and a book by Mr. Archer on how to write plays. In writing
a play care must be taken to have a beginning, a middle and an end
—you know. —I haven't written a line, and do not care for literature as
such.

I liked your remarks on hell and the demon poems.

We went to an Indian dance and saw all the hunters making con-
ciliatory if not amorous passes at the deer and mountain sheep. The
Indian girls were very snappy. They had little feet trimmed with fur.

Paul Rosenfield took "Keramik" [a short story, for *The American
Caravan*] so that the old man has found a place to die at last. What do
you think of the future of American prose? I think it vastly overrated.

Léonie is up with all the *objets de vertu* at the Metropolitan. She
says that the guards are a little cuckoo from gazing upon the marbles.

Let's have a letter sometimes.

Yours ever affectionately,
Louise

1. Bynner and Ficke were poets who, today, are best remembered as the perpetrators (under the names of Emanuel Morgan and Anne Knish) of the *Spectra* hoax, wherein they all too convincingly parodied imagism.

2. John Banister Tabb, an American poet-priest of the nineteenth century, wrote, among other works, *The Rosary in Rhyme.*

432 East Manhattan Street
Santa Fe, New Mexico
February 1927

Dear Edmund: Don't, I beg you, think
That I have sunk my wits in drink
When you were sweet enough to send me
Your book,[1] as one who would befriend me.
I grabbed that book from out its cover
And cozened it as would a lover.
Out in the open sun I read it,
And did I like it? O you said it!
The long play I liked even better
Set out in paragraph and letter
Than on the Provincetown's rough boards
The dialogues were sharp as swords.
In fact, I think it's not excessive
To say the whole thing's very impressive.
I much admire the way you tucked your
Sly points into your sentence structure.

The reason why I've been so tardy
To write you, is, like Thomas Hardy
I've seen life show its seasoned fangs
These last weeks, in a lot of pangs.
A large tooth in my lower jaw
Has filled me with a kind of awe.
I've had long mystic thoughts on pain
Each time the thing began again.
It would shut up, then it would roar.
I said, "What am I living for?"
I wept and groaned and writhed upon
The floor at interval, till dawn.
The worser thought I tried to scout
Was, that I really should have it out.

In Santa Fe there is a dentist
To whom all others should be apprenticed.
He gave me a local shot of dope
When I was nearly losing hope,
My looks, my humor, and my reason.
That tooth came out in shortest season.
And my, it was a horrid long one—
How nature contrives with roots to wrong one!
Why didn't she make ball-bearing teeth
With never a root at all beneath?

Then Raymond's mother came to see
The great Southwest. We gave her tea,
She gave us dinners and rides around
So that we hardly ever found
Time to sit down and write a word.
That's another reason you haven't heard.

We saw some Indians dance a wild
Greek comedy dance, at which you'd have smiled.
Not a calm rite to grey-eyed Pallas
But a lot of leaping with a phallus.
I told Mrs. Holden succinctly how
These things come out of *The Golden Bough.*
A nice short talk to distract her attention
From a lot of actions I really can't mention.
She took it all in very good part
Although I thought it might break her heart.
Then we went digging for ancient bones
In a pueblo fallen to stones.
Raymond dug skulls and arms and legs
And other pre-historic dregs.
Armed with shovel, axe and pick
And every kind of digging trick
He scaled abysses quite unscalable
Proving that his joints are malleable.
We found a lot of artifacts
And almost broke our fronts and backs.

Edmund, though the air's not sticky
I cannot stomach Arthur Ficke.

W. Bynner gets on my nerves
For all his gentle boyish curves.
I wish that kindly for my sake
They'd both go plunge into the lake.
I'm dying to get back to town
And leave this lot of brawny, brown
New Mexicans to their own devices.
A nice hot New York summer entices
My thought far more than the open spaces.
I think my friends have jolly faces,
I'd like to kiss them all much better
Than wait for the postman to bring a letter.

But won't you write me, anyhow—
It will be May when I kiss your brow.
And meantime there's April and maybe March
To loosen my spirit from its starch.
Raymond would like to know if you got
The Father Tabb sonnet, which he thought quite hot.
And did you get this letter? Tell me
Before the Bynner-Fickes quell me.

And send me some poems, if you please.
Yours highly [?] for Life and Art—

                                        Louise

1. *Discordant Encounters,* a collection of plays and dialogues (1926).

/ *to Allen Tate* /

                              432 East Manhattan Street
                              Santa Fe, New Mexico
                              February 19, 1927

Dear Mr. Tate: [1]
I was very much interested in your letter but I fear that my branch of
the Bogans will not help you a lot in your researches. In fact, my knowledge of my branch does not go beyond my grandfather. His name was
James Bogan; he was born in Ulster—Londonderry, I believe, was the
town—in the 1830's. He shipped out to sea when a young boy, and settled in Maine, where he was a captain of sailing vessels out of Portland

Harbor for many years. The one other branch of the Bogan family that I knew about before receiving your letter was a New England lot that went to California in '49.

You are quite right in saying that there are very few Bogans in this country, so perhaps the parent Irish stem may be the same. I have never been certain that it was a definitely Irish stem. I came across a form of the name in "The Battle of Otterburn," one of the ballads in Percy's *Reliques*. The form given there is Bowghan, and a footnote credits the name to a corruption of the English *Buchan*. I have never really liked to believe that. I think *Bowghan* is a jolly forerunner of *Bogan*, or should be.[2]

Have you, by chance, seen the seventeenth-century work on Athens and the Athenians in the New York Public Library, written by a Zachary Bogan, who was a fellow of Oxford? I came across it by chance one day, in the card catalogue. Perhaps the name was English before it got over to Ireland. It would be fun, if you are not concerning yourself wholly with your genealogy in this country, to find out something about old Zachary, to say nothing of the fourteenth-century Bowghans who seem to have been a lively crew.

Would you write me if this has given you anything? It was nice to hear from you.

Sincerely yours—
Louise Bogan

1. Allen Tate's first volume of poetry, *Mr. Pope and Other Poems,* had not yet been published, but he had already helped found *The Fugitive* and written extensive criticism. Tate met LB for the first time a few months after this letter was written, when she and Raymond Holden, and Léonie Adams, who had been visiting in Santa Fe, returned to New York.

2. On March 4, 1941, LB wrote again to Tate about her ancestry: "I never bothered to look up the Bogans, when in Ireland. I don't know if I ever mentioned it to you, but I never cared for the Bogans. My mother, who was a Murphy and a Dublin O'Neil, adopted by a Shields, always held them in a certain amount of scorn; and all my talent comes from my mother's side. The only Bogan I ever really cared about was my brother, Charles, who was killed, as you know, three weeks before the Armistice in the 1914–1918 War, and is buried in France."

1927

432 East Manhattan Street
Santa Fe
March 13, 1927

Dear Ruth:

Somehow I don't write letters, and then the mail is parsimonious and I'm left lonely. —The winter has turned into spring for one day, at least. We've had lots of snow and wind lately—such wind, that made feints at knocking down three-foot adobe walls. The iris in the garden is up— and there are lots of real-looking bulbs in the San Miguel Garden, but it doesn't seem to mean much. Maidie has the mumps, and perhaps that's a sign of spring. Raymond and I will start having them too, presently I have no doubt, since we both missed them in youth.

Today *is* lovely, pure blue with lots of finches singing their heads off. And one day last week we had a visit from a friend of yours—none other than Inocia. We went to Cochiti about a month ago, fully armed with the clock, but Inocia was dancing. We met Carolina Q., a beautiful rather Americanized Indian who also remembered you, and Mr. Boyd. They both sent you their best wishes. The dance was lovely—with lots of little boys in it, and some fine singing. In fact, I think it was the liveliest dance we have seen. Maidie loved it. She has a wonderful time feeding Indian babies cookies whenever we go to a pueblo, which they usually proceed to bury in the sand—and then wipe off and eat.

Well, Inocia found out about us and came to call on a frightfully snowy, windy day. She had come up on a truck that morning, and I didn't envy her the drive from La Bajada on. —She was quite beautifully dressed, and kept popping presents out from under her shawl. First it was two little dishes for me, and then two rings, one, as she said, for Mr. Benedict, although she did not know him, and one for you. Shall we send them, or bring them? We gave her lunch, and Raymond drove her downtown, where she had left another "lady"—I put it in quotations not invidiously, but merely to show her exact word. —They were to stay the night at St. Catharine's School because the day was so snowy. She is so nice, with such a dignified mien. We're going to Cochiti again soon, and at Easter. She is saving a bowl for me, and Raymond has his heart set on a drum!

* * *

We've had some rather funny times here. What with one thing and person, and another. Bynner gives the funniest parties in the world. Did you meet Dorothy Harvey here? She was Dorothy Dudley, whom Harriet used to publish years ago.[1] We went to dinner at Bynner's, and she was there, and a Mrs. M. who is living with a Mr. B.—and it was very funny indeed. Mrs. M. got very drunk and turned out to be an Italian countess, after all, like the snark, or something, and sat saying "You are all subservient," and poor Mr. B. became violently ill all over the carpet (that sounds nice and discreet, like Lorelei Lee, who said, "And suddenly, the gentleman became short"), and Mrs. Harvey and I, none too sober, made scrambled eggs, which the countess spilled and trod upon, thinking them subservient also, no doubt. Later, we had tea with Mrs. Harvey, and she *is* a scream, completely cuckoo. Then the M.'s or the B.'s, came to call. I like them. I like her very much, she is pretty and smart and a little fat-headed. Fancy trying to live in sin in Santa Fe! As well try to live in sin in New York. There's the same lack of privacy.

Bynner is all right in small doses. He came in the other night at 3:30 in the morning—and invited us to a party of townspeople, who were going to take off their clothes. We refused gently but firmly—we see the Fickes occasionally, but cannot give them much.

Léonie * * * hasn't sounded awfully spry this winter, but I think the job at the Metropolitan amuses her somewhat, and she's a dear resisting [?] thing—nothing really matters and her poems come in any case. Did you see the new lot in *Poetry*?

What's this about Margaret thinking that life is strange? Léonie said she had a dreadful blue fit a while back. And is she really going to Samoa again soon? [2]

I haven't a poem in me or about me—and feel useless and incompetent, but then summer is my time for poems, mostly, or perhaps there aren't any more. I think I'll go to Dr. Frink [3] and get hypnotized or have suggestional therapeutics worked on me when I get back, so I can work.
* * *

I think I need some new clothes. They may help. And some emotional winding up. But Raymond says I can't have a love affair. Maybe it's just as well.

Raymond, for all that the above sounds tyrannical, is as sweet as ever, and much much better, I'm sure, although what a summer in New York will do for him, I don't know. —If you hear of a nice slave job anywhere at $100 a month, do bag it for me. I'll be back about May 1st and free after the 18th.

Perhaps I should have my hair cut off again.

Will you write to me soon, because I'll be back before, unless you do it promptly. Do write, and send poems if there are some.

With every good wish.

Affectionately,
Louise

1. Describing her to Theodore Roethke in 1935, LB said of Mrs. Harvey, "She was my closest batty friend for years. Rich, or rather, ex-rich Chicago saloniste type, who has had breakfast with Bertrand Russell, *and* Brancusi, on separate occasions. Brancusi fed her beef-steak."

2. "I read Margaret's book [*Coming of Age in Samoa*] with much pleasure. The argument goes as cleanly as a piston; the cause falls, the effect rises. But not mechanically—brightly and humanly set going. She sent me her At Home announcement. Margaret is one to be *quite* at home in whatever Mandatory Province!" (To Benedict, December 1, 1928)

3. Further comments on Dr. H. W. Frink appear on p. 334.

Hillsdale, N.Y.
October 11, 1928

Dear Ruth:

Yes, we shall be away all winter, and all forever, if the plans for buying, on a long-term mortgage, a fruit-farm, come through. Forty plum trees, a view of two townships, a little house, pear trees as tall as poplars, and hollyhocks to be the background of hardy borders. Farewell, farewell! We fade into the bucolic!

But we *are* coming to town soon, and should love to take your offer of a night's bed with alacrity. I have wanted to see and talk with you. It's not long on talk, this country life. * * *

The Arthur D. Fickes are staying here until their new house is ready. They are rather nice, but not anything to exclaim over. The ever-blooming Millay came over one day last week with a copy of her new book [*The Buck in the Snow*] for me—that was swell of her, I thought. Have you read the Cameo poem? It made the room turn round, when I read it.

Léonie writes of H. D.'s teas, Bryher, and Robert McAlmon. I wish she'd see someone more robust. She's been ill, and sounds a little sad. London is too work-a-day for people with a Guggenheim. I think she should flee to the continent as soon as possible.

The country is unbelievably beautiful. For the first time in a year, I have heard things in the head while dining under these fabulous trees.

Do write if you can have us come see you.

> Ever affectionately,
> Louise

/ *to Edmund Wilson* /

> Hillsdale
> Columbia County, New York
> Thanksgiving
> November 22, 1928

Darling Edmund:

I thought that you had forgotten me, so at the receipt of your letter, my joy knew no bounds. Californeye-ay must be grand, but upper New York State isn't so bad, even in this bleak season, when a tree's a tree, and not a fat cushion, littered up with a lot of birds and leaves. Our fruit farm defies description. Wait until you see it. It is embowered in lilacs and roses; plum trees circle it round, and vines fill up the interstices. We are indebted to a friend for a fireplace and chimney; even at this moment the mason and his helper are fitting brick to brick with immemorial gestures of the trowel. We'll never have a bath-room, so take several baths to last you over some little period of time, before you come up to see us. Raymond has put in windows, and worked wonders with sheetrock and miter-box. I have scraped wallpaper, and planted an extensive bulb garden. We are to have some Blue Andalusian hens, and a small black goat, in the spring, so that our friends will not lack fauna to observe when they come to visit us.

I'm rather sorry that I shouldn't be able to recognize *Daisy* in her present form.[1] I liked her in her old form. However, onward and upward.

Edna Millay has a lovely new Cadillac car. She is off reading now, at $600 a throw. I have not seen much of her. They are going on a motor trip through France in January.

Scribner's has me on the rack. All sorts of jolly reports roll in—they are on the point of taking the book—in fact, it is in the printer's hands—but no one ever really verifies any of this news. Mr. Scribner, I fear, will ultimately shake his head and sigh. I liked Max Perkins.[2] "We'll write to you," he said. That was seven weeks ago.

There's been a big turnover in verse these last few months. I have written more and worse verse than at any other time in my career. I think it is all wonderful, too, which makes it all the funnier. Does it rain —do I look out the window and see a barn, or a cow, or a tree, or a horse and wagon, or a stray dog—does it snow, or shine, or blow? Out comes the pencil, and down go a few nature notes. How happy I feel! How easy art really is! Almost at once I realize that the thing is just terrible.

I am sending you a poem that I do not hesitate to claim as mine. In fact, I think it one of the most remarkable works ever penned.[3] I make you a present of it, together with the best wishes of the season.

Léonie has concealed from us that she felt rotten. The last time I heard from her, she wrote that Dickensian drunks acclaimed her in pubs as a sweet little thing, and that she and the Tates were about to settle in Oxford, along with Red Warren.[4] I thought that that would turn out to be rather a dull idea. She should go to Spain—to some warm climate, and mingle in a social way with persons other than the Tates. * * * This cozening by academic friends will ruin her. I'll write her recommending a more torrid life.

Now, dear Edmund, I can do no more than ask you to write us, and plan to come to see us, when you get back. Or we can go to see you, if we ever get to town. Don't work too hard, and keep away from Greta Garbo and Dolores Del Rio, who are your neighbors, we hear.

Ever, with truest affection,
Louise
(The Hermit Crab)

1. *I Thought of Daisy*, Wilson's first novel, was revised heavily in MS before Scribner published it in 1929.

2. Maxwell E. Perkins worked for the publishing house of Scribner from 1914 to his death in 1947. His letters, *Editor to Author*, were selected and edited by John Hall Wheelock, who is about to appear as a correspondent.

3. Most probably "I Saw Eternity." LB wrote it, she told Ruth Benedict, in a "mood of katharsis. * * * To think that I should come, at the age of thirty-one, to the stage where I write poems about Eternity!" (December 1, 1928)

4. A future Pulitzer Prize winner in both fiction and poetry, Robert Penn Warren was then twenty-three years old and a member of the Fugitives group.

/ to John Hall Wheelock /

> Hillsdale
> Columbia County, New York
> December 7, 1928

My dear Mr. Wheelock: [1]

Thank you for your letter. Your decision on the manuscript has encouraged me more than I can say. I thoroughly appreciate the time and thought you have been good enough to give to the matter.

I see no objection to the format you suggest. I realize that the poems you now have are really too few for a volume. However, I have a strong feeling that there should never be too many poems in a book of poetry. Thirty-five is, I think, the greatest number I should wish to publish at one time. I have as many poems again as the manuscript contains, that have been kept back, because I do not wholly trust them, and feel that by their inclusion the effect of the others might be blurred. You understand this feeling, I am sure. Perhaps, by the end of next summer, I may have ten new poems to add to the manuscript as it now stands—one of them a fairly long dramatic dialogue that I plan to do. With ten poems from *Body of This Death,* would that be enough?

I should be very glad if I could send you, from time to time, new work as it comes. There are perhaps five more things that you could see immediately. I may not always be right, but it is, you will agree, a true instinct to wish to scant, rather than to fatten.

I am glad that you like "The Flume." I spent my childhood in milltowns, and was happy to be able to do something with that remembered noise of water.

Again thanking you for your thought and courtesy.

> Sincerely yours,
> Louise Bogan

1. The poet John Hall Wheelock was, throughout his professional career, an editor and, after Maxwell Perkins' death, editor-in-chief of Charles Scribner's Sons. On p. 337 LB describes the occasion when, as one of the judges, she helped to select Wheelock for the Bollingen Prize.

/ to Rolfe Humphries /

> Hillsdale
> December 16, 1928

Dear Rolfe:

Before we sink into the spell of literary coadjutation, let me express my own delight, nay, I might almost say, happiness, in receiving the *lovely* record of your voice, recorded by Speak-o-Phone Inc. on a nice metal disc. In fact, I could write a review of that alone, and may, before I finish. It certainly was fine, as Mark Van Doren wrote me, in the highest critical vein, of my new volume of verse. The only drawback is that, due either to inordinate shyness, fear of the microphone, or of the attendant, or of the velvet curtains in the cubicle (it was a cubicle, wasn't it?) you forgot your early training in ventriloquism (speaking from or to the stomach, or voice issuing out from or in accordance with the stomach) and swallowed your vocables with such inconsiderate ease that I could hardly make out, in the first sonnet, at least, what you were saying. Raymond says that your greeting is "Hello R and L, you big wheats," but I insist that you say "Hello, R and L, tweet-tweet." Please clear this up for me. The second sonnet was rendered more clearly, but yet a little too *bas*. However, we cannot say how pleased we were to have you thus canned, on the music shelf in this, our little mountain cot, available at all times. We'll make some for you and you can get one of those $4.98 toy phonographs in Macy's to play them on. Wait until you hear me *throw* my voice! What a pleasure that will be!

Now, for serious literary matters:

You are very sweet (my God, how long am I going to keep this up!) to want to couple my name with yours, on the hind-end of the [Robinson] Jeffers review. You are far too self-effacing, however. The ideas are really yours, you just hadn't thought out a review for so long that they came hard, and a conversation just cleared them up a little, that's all. I know just what a lot of concomitant reading in the library will do for me, on the edge of writing a review. One gets all costive and queer. You had the dope on the man from the first, really.

I think the review is excellent as it stands. The first paragraph is short and snappy, and the writing in the second, third and fourth beautifully ordered. My few suggestions are these (and if you want you can buy a couple of tickets for *Fifty Million Frenchmen* for next Monday night in full payment). * * *

The point should be *emphasized* that the figures in "Loving S[hepherdess]" have been seen *over* and *over* again—in *all* the volumes. That the projection works automatically, like one of these machines that puts records on by itself, by means of a mechanical arm. That if he'd written *Tamar* (that book) alone and then shut up, he'd be extraordinary, but his fluency has given the emotional mechanism away. No great dramatic writer could possibly slip into such a groove—and this leads to:

2. Lyric poets can lack a sense of humor and still be great, but dramatic poets, *never*. And there's not a drop of humor in one single poem. (Such nice humor as "Well, let's go to bed!" or "Get the hell out of here, you cock-eyed bastard!")

3. Our time (whatever it is) just loves poems about the internal organs of the body, the mechanisms of sex, abortion, fecal processes, etc. It's like looking inside the hood of an automobile, or watching the shafts and gears and sprockets in a factory. (Don't you think that's a good point? I really think it explains why people think J. has terrific profundity because he makes remarks about women menstruating.) (I'll take another quarter for that.)

4. (And this is the last.) The split up lines make a *hypnotic* rhythm, so that he can be banal (as God knows he often is) right on top of being awfully good (and he has a grand ear for phrase and eye for detail, indubitably). All's one for that, when the reader gets all hopped up with the trick rhythm.

That's all. And do you need *two* renderings into prose? I'd take one good emotional one, as the best proof of that point. And oh, doesn't that prose rendering slap him down! Swell!

It's grand that you could do it, thanks to Edmund's ideas on California by Californians, and not have to read a lot of guff about his great genius from Babette Deutsch or someone, all dished up in the *N. R.* And speaking of Babette, *who's* a rood-screen? Have you [seen] that review? [1] * * *

Now dearies, we are planning a little *coup*. We are planning to come down the Saturday before Yule or Noel, and go to a show. Then, after Yule, you can drive up to Katonah and meet us, and we'll all come up here for a jolly Wassail together. How's that? We'll talk it over.

And how about four cheap seats for next Monday night at *Fifty Million Frenchmen?* Will you get them? Wouldn't that be fun? And you can take us to the Speak-o-Phone place and yell "Louder and funnier!" from behind the curtains.

Well, yours for intrauterine mechanics and the life of the soul.

Louise

1. Babette Deutsch, best known as a poet and translator, is here viewed as a critic of LB's poetry; a happier view is taken on p. 279.

/ *to Ruth Benedict* /

Hillsdale
December 28, 1928

Dear Ruth:

The Blake filled me with joy as I wildly tore off the wrapper. Thank you for it, dear Ruth. —I did want it with real gluttony, and had no idea where to find it, even if I could have afforded it. * * *

Raymond and I have taken up chess and given up liquor—almost, that is. Chess, I find, is quite terrifying. That closing in on the king is like time and fate sitting in opposite quarters, and chuckling quietly, because their designs are not immediately apparent. It's no game for a person afflicted with claustrophobia. Somewhere at this moment, behind these pleasant hills, there is a great fat Bishop and a round ponderous Rook. . . . O dear, O dear.

* * *

Ever with love—
Louise

[March] 1929

Dear Ruth:
* * *

I delayed writing to Léonie, during my spell of flu, so that heaven alone knows when I shall hear from her again. We received a letter from Allen Tate, yesterday; he said that real virtue is not time's fool, and that Léonie had real virtue; reports of her romance with Mr. D., the demon poker player, were therefore much exaggerated. The Tates and Léonie are now living in [Ford Madox] Ford's apartment, where, Allen remarks, the bathroom is level with the floor, whatever that means. They all have had a touch of flu. Allen sent on two works of his: neither of them have much sinew; they are full of fine phrases, delineating the problem of a frontiersman on the quais.

A great depth of snow has fallen here. A party of ski-ers with Yale voices have taken over the Inn for the holiday. I lie awake at night and shudder at the thought that they will inherit the earth. The sum of $10,000 was actually mentioned during the first evening, also the statement was made that money makes money. I never felt more like joining the Communist party. I have had the pleasure, during the month, of turning down an invitation to join the Poetry Society of America. So you can see that I have been warped from childhood, and will never learn the trick of mingling in a social way.

My reading has been ponderous and varied, these last weeks. I have read lives of Zola and of Baudelaire; Iwan Bloch on the sexual life of our times; Thomas Hardy's early years, by his second wife (this is very illuminating); a grand novel, *The Last September*, by Elizabeth Bowen, full of rich sub-acid wit; five or ten garden books; Jane Austen's letters; and, as I think I told you, all the comedies of Shakespeare. —I'd like you to send the [Archibald] MacLeish book [*The Hamlet of A. Mac-Leish?*]. He has a real talent, without any doubt; he has been too friendly with Conrad Aiken, T. S. Eliot, and others: his ear is too good. You saw Elinor [Wylie]'s sonnets, didn't you? Did you like them? I thought them the best things that she had done.

Sunday and Monday were quite soft; I heard a whole brook going very fast down a hillside, and felt real full-bodied sunlight behind a haystack, on Sunday, and thought that spring was managing at least a hoarse whisper, and then this snow came. What will happen when it begins to thaw is beyond my imagination. The iris are nicely mulched, so that they, at least, cannot be washed from the ground. I think it would be amusing if the bulbs really did come up, don't you? Of course, I don't expect them to.

R. Torrence is still off my works, no doubt rightly. I am sending you a sonnet [1] that I thought quite good, at the time. Please be *perfectly* critical about it. Is all this bone business just funny? The other isn't right yet, and in any event, hasn't much importance, beyond some rather good phrases pointing to regression towards the infantile. Dear me. Pretty elusive, these talents.

* * *

Ever, with love,
Louise

1. Called "Sonnet," the poem begins, "Dark, underground, is furnished with the bone."

/ to John Hall Wheelock /

Hillsdale
March 26, 1929

My dear Mr. Wheelock:
The dedication is *To Raymond Holden.* On all sides the eye is assailed

by *Dark*—Dark Freight, Dark Hester, Dark Star. I really shuddered, reading the new lists. But for me, Dark Summer stands, and I am glad you now think it feasible.

For your praise of the book, I can only give you my deepest gratitude. Whatever the poems are, they are all I know how to do. The lack of indentation I have a taste for. With every good wish, and greetings from us both.

Sincerely yours,
Louise Bogan

/ to Ruth Benedict /

Hillsdale
Columbia County, N.Y.
April 16, 1929

Dear Ruth:

It has indeed been a wearing week: my daily trips to Hudson involved a train and a bus, and a station waiting room superficially like a scene in hell.[1] Then the weather—that was indeed beyond belief. Every morning the window presented a jolly snowy mid-winter scene. It has snowed since last Wednesday, off and on. Three days rain is enough to empty any sky, says the adage, and that's another adage disproved.

However, some of the house got painted, and a man cleaned up the orchard, so that the brush is piled on the vegetable garden to be burned, the grape trellis is mended, the outhouse cleaned out, and one thing and another. —I have painted the kitchen, the walls by choice and the floor by chance. Tomorrow I start in on the living room and that will be indeed a blessed day. Literary works went by the board. I got down some notes on Philmont (that's where the station waiting room is; that waiting room where yesterday everything suddenly became insignificant and I had some sort of great mystic revelation—due purely to fatigue). —A little man in a lunch room who served me delicious coffee and an immaculate sandwich, all set out on a tray spread with a pristine napkin, almost had me in tears, because he put such faith in a new electric sign that someone had sold him. When illuminated this sign goes through all the colors of the rainbow—they fade off—he told me about it with such hope and passion. Then he slyly started the pop-corn machine, poor dear, and I bought a whole bushel with my remaining money. God keep me extroverted so that I can always see such saintly little men.

    * * *

Ever with love,
Louise

1. Raymond Holden was in the Hudson, New York, hospital, having been operated on for acute appendicitis eight days previously.

/ *to John Hall Wheelock* /

Hillsdale
May 1, 1929

My dear Mr. Wheelock:

The sample pages delighted me more than I can say. The leaf ornaments are exquisite; the hips and haws on the title page are equally lovely. I can only thank the single and collective taste of all concerned. The type I like, too, and the squarish, rather than oblong look of the pages. In fact, I have nothing to object to: it all seems like a materialization of a happier kind of dream.

The longer poem is really coming to life. For a time I despaired of it; now it has its shape and sound, a climax or two and an ending that really excites me, all in the mind; one or two good intensive spurts will finish it, I trust. You have been good to believe in it, and clever to goad [?] me. It will be about five typewritten pages, I should think, in the form of a colloquy between *This One* and *The Other*.[1]

The success of the garden book depends upon the success of my garden, which I am now planting. The point of the book would be rich and varied flowers for little money, from the care of one pair of hands. Most garden books presuppose ten men with spading forks, a greenhouse, and an enormous balance at the bank. . . .[2]

    * * *

Again with all gratitude for the lovely job on the book—

Ever sincerely yours,
Louise Bogan

1. "Summer Wish."
2. The book never came to pass.

Hillsdale
July 12, 1929

Dear Mr. Wheelock:

The proofs came; I am working on them little by little, and should get them back to you early in the week. I shall try to work out some order of poems that will have relation and coherence; the chronological order is not a good idea, I find.

I want to ask you how I am to deal with Mr. [Louis] Untermeyer, who has written me concerning poems for his new edition of *Modern American Poetry*. He himself suggested that I send him fair copies of any poems I chose, and I was about to comply with this suggestion when Edmund Wilson told me I must by no means do so, until Mr. Untermeyer had made definite advances for the poems through Scribner's. Edmund seems to think that Mr. Untermeyer has odd ideas about anthology fees; he (Edmund) has talked to Mr. Perkins about Mr. Untermeyer's use of his own poems, and Mr. Perkins told him to have no dealings with Mr. Untermeyer direct. This all sounds very sinister—however, will you advise me what to do? Could I send him the poems in proof?

Thank you for your kindness in encouraging me about the book. I have moments when I could cheerfully consign it in shreds—to the air. With our every good wish,

> Sincerely yours,
> Louise Bogan

Hillsdale
July 29, 1929

Dear Mr. Wheelock:

I have forgotten to write you about anthology fees. Last week I wrote Mr. Untermeyer that Scribner's would be glad to give him permission to reprint a group of poems in the new anthology, were he to write and ask for that permission. While I think it hard on the author to receive no compensation for this privilege, in view of Mr. Untermeyer's command of publicity, perhaps you could waive the full amount per poem, since the group is to be made up of seven poems.[1] Mr. Untermeyer has had my permission for the use of the group.

> In haste,
> Sincerely yours,
> Louise Bogan

/ 47

1. The standard anthology fee was $10 per poem. Given this request, Scribner lowered it to $5. Untermeyer used from this new collection "Simple Autumnal," "Come, Break with Time" and "Cassandra." The other poems, coming from *Body of This Death*, were not paid for, since they had previously appeared in the Untermeyer anthology.

Hillsdale
October 12, 1929

Dear Mr. Wheelock:

Harriet Monroe writes me that she is sending out *Dark Summer* to the Poetry Clan (which numbers, I believe, two hundred members) as its sixth book. I don't know just what that means in prestige, but Raymond says it means two hundred copies sold, at least. Scribner's will like that, from the monetary point of view. Personally, I think that two hundred lonely, isolated clan-members is a picture to weep over.

Yvor Winters' review [of *Dark Summer* in *The New Republic*] was typical of him, wasn't it? He is *such* a serious, learned, conscientious boy, so passionately for style and dignity in writing, and for ethics and humanism in life. Edmund said that the Hardy comparison was something that would occur to Yvor alone. I thought the review so serious and intelligent that perhaps it will make people flee in horror from this modern *soi-disant* combination of Campion, Jonson, and Dryden! Yvor loves argument; he cannot write a review without dragging in special pleading for the restitution of metaphysical birthright to modern American writers. I have seen him, at a very gay dinner party, when all the other guests were making themselves wreaths out of the centerpieces, almost come to fisticuffs with Arthur Ficke over Gerard Manley Hopkins!

Louis Untermeyer wrote me a nice letter. —Edmund's book came; I think that there are eight or ten fine poems in it—poems full of great style and really noble thinking—noble in the passionate sense; like music.[1]

Have you seen Léonie Adams' book, *High Falcon?* It is dedicated to Raymond and me. We are very proud. It is full of extraordinary loveliness—and a sharpness that I, for one, could not put a name to. She has the greatest talent in the really grand manner of anyone writing in America today. I wish it were not so near, and dependent on, the dreadful dream in her own heart.

I shall never get over that Poetry Clan business!
With every good wish.

> Sincerely yours,
> Louise Bogan

1. Scribner had published *Poets, Farewell!* The title poem describes a visit Wilson made to the Bogan-Holden household in Hillsdale and ends with a valedictory to poetry: "Voices, farewell!—the silver and the brass— / I leave that speech to you who have a tongue." The renunciation was temporary; over the years Wilson turned out a number of poems remarkable for their technical virtuosity and multilingual wit.

/ *to Harriet Monroe* /

> Hillsdale
> Columbia County
> October 12, 1929

Dear Harriet Monroe:
   * * *

I should be very glad to do Mrs. [Marjorie] Seiffert's book for you, if I did not think it rather a breach of etiquette for one to do so. I have tried never to review a book of poetry by a woman contemporary. The review of Hildegarde Flanner in a recent *New Republic* was done only after much urging on the part of Edmund Wilson. Again, I have met Mrs. Seiffert, and I have another silly prejudice against saying anything in print concerning even the most casual acquaintance.[1] All these ideas are rather stupid, I know, but I have seen so much nonsense arising from friendship (or even enmity) between author and reviewer. Since Mrs. Seiffert's book and mine are on the same publisher's list in the same season, I must say no, with regret. However, if you would tell me, another time, of a book you considered sympathetic, I should be delighted to do it for you.

Raymond and I have often spoken of the delightful hospitality you tendered us in Chicago. And I have often thought of the extraordinarily exciting influence on my own early work, of *Poetry*: it was a great thing to have it in the same country, to be able to read its bound volume in the library, for a young person at once eager for, and abashed by, its achievements. You must be very proud, Miss Monroe, of the influence you made spread and blossom in a singularly arid time, and now watch still in proud life, in a time grown a little more kind to originality and ideas in poetry.

* * *

Believe me to be, with every fortunate wish,

Cordially yours,
Louise Bogan

1. Marjorie Allen Seiffert's book, *The King with Three Faces,* was ultimately reviewed for *Poetry* by Miss Monroe herself.

/ *to John Hall Wheelock* /

Hillsdale
November 13, 1929

Dear Mr. Wheelock:

New York, and not its literary figures, can tire me with hysteria, and I hope that you did not think me too hysterical over the phone. I never see any literary figures—if I can possibly help it, and believe me, my protective mechanisms work beautifully at this period [?]. But if anyone has one word to say, or has any ideas, or drive, or talent, in New York, he (or she) ultimately turns out to be a maniac, or to have been a maniac, or about to be a maniac. And that is so tiresome, isn't it? By the time one is able to call up, or see, one's stable friends, everything has become too horrible to contemplate. . . . But you will think me on the verge, if I go on in this vein. . . . In any case, I am sorry that the lunch was made impossible. Next time, I'll write you hour and day beforehand.

I am enclosing a very affecting letter, from the state library of my native state. Will it be possible for Scribner's to gather up a copy of *Body of This Death,* and send it and *Dark Summer* to the librarian? Also, would Scribner's send a glossy print of the picture that you have? I'll send them a picture of my birthplace, which will strike them dumb, I am sure. The house has *such* a cupola and eaves made of gingerbread, and in the picture's foreground my mother is holding me, an infant of six months, of extremely simple appearance, in her arms. * * *

With every good wish from us both, and with my sincere regret over our non-lunching.—

Believe me to be—

Sincerely yours—
Louise Bogan

1929

Hillsdale
December 15, 1929

Dear Ruth:

It's a lovely quiet Sunday—Maidie has been sent on a little vacation week-end to her grandmother's—and I should be doing a review of Rebecca West—in fact, I must do it this very afternoon (at the moment I am taking time out to write to you, but the drag [?] is at the back of the mind). From three o'clock on, of course, on all Sundays, I listen to the Philharmonic over the radio. Unfortunately, Raymond does not give over his carpentry even on Sundays, so that at this very minute Brahms' First is going on with much sublimity at the same time that Raymond is shingling the little new porch. What *would* happen were a neighbor at the Philharmonic suddenly taken with a fit of shingling, I do not know. I can't murder Raymond, because I love him too much, but really, something should be done. . . .

❋ ❋ ❋

Reviews really mean nothing. After reading Mr. Tate on I. A. Richards—that the greatest minds can hardly encompass the simplest lyric—there's nothing left but to write prose. Write the winter through.

I have discovered Colette and become a great *philosophe,* in these last months. You would laugh at me. Do let's tie down the visit in January, so that I shall *really* see you. Make a real hour and minute for the encounter!

Raymond sends love. Write me what time in January.

Ever with love—
Louise

EXHORTATION

Give over seeking bastard joy
Nor cast for fortune's side-long look.
Indifference can be your toy;
The bitter heart can be your book.
(Its lesson torment never shook.)

In the cold heart, as on a page,
Spell out the gentle syllable
That puts short limit to your rage
And curdles the straight fire of hell,
Compassing all, so all is well.

Read how, though passion sets in storm
And grief's a comfort, and the young
Touch at the flint when it is warm,
It is the dead we live among,
The dead given motion, and a tongue.

The dead, long trained to cruel sport
And the crude gossip of the grave;
The dead, who pass in motley sort,
Whom sun nor sufferance can save.
Face them. They sneer. Do not be brave.

Know once for all: their snare is set
Even now; be sure their trap is laid;
And you will see your lifetime yet
Come to their terms, your plans unmade,–
And be belied, and be betrayed.

5 Prospect Place
New York City
January 6, 1930

Dear Miss Monroe:

The day after Christmas, while we were away on a visit, our house in the country took fire through the carelessness of the man who was tending the furnace, and burned completely. All our things went, too— books, pictures, and almost all our manuscripts. —We are insured, both for the house and its contents, but insurance does not give back the things gathered over years, nor the books, never to be exactly replaced, and our work put into walls and rooms. We have recovered somewhat from the shock: after all, it is more important to be alive without possessions than dead either with or without them. We have come to New York to get work and start again. —[Lola Ridge's] *Firehead* came today, forwarded from Hillsdale, and I shall get it done this week. We have an apartment now, and as soon as we can get a few pieces of furniture together, literary production can go on. I am sorry for the delay in getting the review to you, but it can be put down to an act of God, and most delays have worse reasons.

We are really quite well. Do not think us tragic figures. Our best greetings to you, as always, for this year, and all others.

Ever sincerely,
Louise Bogan

5 Prospect Place
January 17, 1930

Dear Miss Monroe:

I have read *Firehead* and begun a review, but I am puzzled by what may very well be my biased ideas concerning it. And since I know that Miss Ridge is ill, and no doubt puts much store by good reviews—especially a good review in *Poetry*—I do not feel that you should allow me to go on with my article, since my attitude must be a purely critical one. I can only say what I myself feel, and perhaps there is some lack in my nature that does not permit me to believe that Miss Ridge has been successful in this poem.

I have found from bitter experience that one woman poet is at a disadvantage in reviewing another, if the review be not laudatory. I do not feel capable, at the present moment, of taking upon myself Miss Ridge's hurt feelings, so would you allow me to send *Firehead* to you and to another reviewer? Were my own mind and heart more settled, I could more easily banish the idea of my inadequacy in this matter. Perhaps I put all this badly. You understand, I am sure. It is difficult for you to have to put up with this backing and filling on my part, but I must say what I feel and think. And in this case, it is my (perhaps mistaken) idea that Miss Ridge would take my remarks too much to heart.

With every good wish from us both—

Cordially yours,
Louise Bogan

October 24, 1930

Dear Miss Monroe:

I am enclosing the letter that lay on my desk ready to be mailed to you, when the news of *Poetry*'s 1930 prize awards reached me.[1] I cannot think of any recognition that has ever touched me so deeply. At the risk of seeming to air difficulties that are important to myself alone, I want you to know how successfully for the past year I have suppressed any impulse toward creative work. A set of unfortunate incidents brought this condition about. I can truthfully say that childish pique and even more childish pride had nothing to do with this creative despair. I should prefer to think that it was complete weariness with the continued reappearance of a personal legend that colored, in the minds of many people who might be expected to be without bias, opinion of my work. For some years I had been out of touch with writers and cities and had forgotten the deadly persistence of rumor in a specialized group. At the second or third meeting with a kind of subtle and refined cruelty, I abjured poetry. I no longer wished to say myself.

I tell you these reasons because your award has not only made them clear in my mind, but to a great extent has nullified them. I am refreshed, and hope to get out of this fog a sane and balanced person. —That the prize was given to my work in general delights me, because I have never been able to compete, in contests, or to write to order or on terms.

Please do not think my frankness to you a breach of decorum. I hope you can feel that I do not say these things easily. But it is better to say them, and thereby work through to some kind of power over circumstance. I want you to know that your thought for me has had a broader influence than you could have planned.

Again take my gratitude, and the promise that when anything gets done, it will go to you.

Believe me to be,

Sincerely yours,
Louise Bogan

1. The award referred to was the John Reed Memorial Prize, given for LB's first two volumes and for poems published in *Poetry*. In this same year the two other major prize winners were Hart Crane, for "The Bridge," and Abbie Huston Evans, a poet whom LB very much admired. Many years later (see p. 337) LB urged her claims on fellow members of the Bollingen Prize jury.

/ to John Hall Wheelock /

The Neurological Institute
Fort Washington Avenue and
West 168 Street, New York
April 11, 1931

Dear Jack:

I missed the Psychiatric Institute, or whatever it is, by a hair, so don't be too perturbed by the heading. I refused to fall apart, so I have been taken apart, like a watch. I can truthfully say that the fires of hell can hold no terrors for me now.

Whatever happens after this, I shall no longer sneer and fleer. One of my component parts, strangely enough, turned out to be the capacity to love. I still can love. Isn't that wonderful? I still can go into love humbly and take it, no matter to what end, and feel humble and ashamed [?]: "Love comes in at the eyes"—A pretty pass for one of my stiff-necked pride, don't you think? It comes in at the eyes and subdues the body. An army with banners. My God, every poet in the world knew about it, except me.

Regularly, every day, I read *Uncle Vanya*. Do read it again. It is the lexicon of wisdom and pity.

Say a prayer for me, won't you? Thank you always for your friendship and kindness.

Yours—as ever
Louise

/to Edmund Wilson /

The Lafayette
Portland, Maine
May 2, 1931

Dear Edmund:

Thank you for the left and right wing books. And of course you realize that I'm not at the Hotel Lafayette, in Portland, Maine. I just put that in to make it harder.[1] So much literature has flowed from my fertile brain, these last few days, that the stationery has not been able to stand the gaff. Like sun in April, to use a tried and true simile, it has disappeared.

* * *

My life here is one grand sweet song. I have aroused pain in at least three hearts. Two of the hearts are nonagenarian, but what cares saucy Bogan?[2] One aged lady passed the remark to me that I looked precisely like a rose. I may say, in reference to this, that such a remark has never been passed to, or on, me before. One aged gentleman gazes at me to such an extent that he totally forgets to eat his soup. And as for the third heart: it belongs to none other than the gymnasium instructress. She actually up and kissed me this very afternoon. She has restrained her passion up to this time. But southern blood will out. She's Italian. An odd place, Italy.

I'm glad you liked the Swift poem. The *Journal to Stella* wrung my heart. The passion is so real, so imperfectly dissembled, and the wit is such a strange mixture of roughness and elegance. I'm eager to have the poems. Thank you, my dear, for getting them.

In addition to some love, I must add that I have stirred up a little enmity. An old mussel called Miss Agnew sits outside my door and says, crustily, "There seems to be a great deal of smoking around here!" Poor old thing! How I love her. How I love everyone, even the worms in the worm-casts, the snails in snail shells, the maggots in the cheese.

Well, my dear fellow, my charming old syringa, I must now close. Warn men, women and children of my reappearance. Tell them to buy smoked glasses. For, verily, yea, let it be said, that nothing or no one will be safe from me from now on.

Yours with much love—

Rosily—
Louise

[P.S.] You didn't sound sententious. What an idea. *Anna Livia Plura-belle* got me, too. Did you note that he uses *Bogan* as a verb?

1. She was recuperating in a sanitarium in Connecticut, where the therapeutic regime included weaving, needle-spray showers, sunbaths and "most simple-minded tasks." Describing it to Wilson in a poem appended to this letter, LB ended:

> My God, what was the crime. Did I deserve
> Therapy, out of possible punishments?
> What the betrayal, that the faded nerve
> Must bloom again by means not making sense?
> O, I shall mend! Even now I grow quite well,
> Knitting round wash-cloths on the paths of hell.

2. "What care I; what cares saucy Presto?" from the poem "Hypocrite Swift," referred to in the next paragraph, and in the following letters.

/ to Harriet Monroe /

5 Prospect Place
June 23, 1931

Dear Miss Monroe:
  * * *

The Swift poem was the kind of thing I do not care to do very often: extreme allusiveness has little place in poetry. I was surprised and pleased to find, after starting it as a literary exercise, that it turned out really to be a poem.

I am much better, although by no means completely well. Several mechanisms have broken down and a strange new period has set in, in my heart and mind. I feel at once renewed and disinherited. Different people say different things. My doctor insists that I love; Robert Frost, whom we saw recently, recommends fear and hatred. But I have lost faith in universal panaceas—work is the one thing in which I really believe.

Ever, my dear Miss Monroe, in friendship,
Louise Bogan

/ *to Allen Tate* /

306 Lexington Avenue
New York City
October 8, 1931

Dear Allen:

It was nice of you to write me about the poem. I do not think that its *genre* is as different from the *D. S.* lyrics as you suppose. In fact, I thought it pretty read into and subjective after it was finished. It began as a literary exercise when I was in the country getting over what is popularly known as a nervous breakdown, this spring. When I struck the stanza with the nice long *a* sounds (beginning "On walls at court") I suddenly realized that it *was* a poem, after all, and I lay my rapid recovery, from then on, to precisely that discovery.

Poor correspondents rarely have honest nervous breakdowns to bolster their defection. Mine began almost immediately after the Tennessee trip. It lasted well into the early summer. It was punctuated by stays in Neurological Institutes, nursing homes, and by long passionate visits to neurologists—all delightful fellows with Southern accents that wrung the heart. In fact, my heart was wrung so long and so hard by the chief neurologist (and the chief Southerner) that I had to forbear and decide that my nerves could take care of themselves. Better defective nerves than defective ethics, has always (almost always) been my battle cry.

The Swift poem was all that came out of this, in the form of art. Tough, isn't it?

Caroline's book came,[1] and she can just put me down as a dog [?] for not acknowledging it. I read it all day long, in bed, during a relapse, and thought it a fine workmanlike and in parts inspired job.

There isn't any news. We saw Edmund several times before he went to California and Santa Fe, but not since. He said he was giving up the *N. R.* job because he wanted to travel light. * * * I am now a journalist and do character sketches for the papers. Have you read the extraordinary *Exile's Return*? I may be prejudiced (Mr. Cowley having made up for lost time as a literary arbiter in the last year and a half)[2] but I must quote you a sentence (or two sentences) from a letter I received this morning—from a mutual friend, I may make so bold to say. —"as goofy an attempt at self-justification as print has lately been obliged to carry. One had thought that the notion of acquiring literary characteristics by living in rope-soled shoes in Normandy went out with Dowson and the Boxer Rebellion. . . ."

(I like the Boxer Rebellion.) "—and as for those letters to Kenneth, Joseph, et al., and the lovely twilight reminiscences over the lost youthhood of 1923, and the belt-hitching pride in nose-punchings [?]! It is all too good to be true!"

Raymond will write. Do write again. I thought the article on taste grand. How are you all? With regard, Allen and Caroline,

Louise

1. Caroline Gordon was then married to Allen Tate. Her novel was titled *Penhally*.

2. Malcolm Cowley, a literary critic then working for *The New Republic*, will come under increasing attack for what LB felt were his "opportunistic" political-literary activities. In later years, both members of the National Institute of Arts and Letters, they became reconciled.

/ *to Morton D. Zabel* /

January 23, 1932

Dear Morton: 1

Let me explain my new defection. The [Viola] Meynell article should have gone to you in the 2:45 air mail this afternoon. (Do not despair: it *shall* go this week, as hereinafter explained.) The truth of the matter is: for the first time in my experience I have come straight up against a job of writing and *cannot do it*. My old trick has played me false. This trick pushed the matter off and back, knew it and forgot it, summoned it at the last moment, ground into it, as you say, fitted it into form, squared it out. What has failed? The mind that feels, the emotions that think, the silent, in the background, stayer, gatherer, watcher? I should prefer ignorance or fear as reasons. —I can manage all differently. Knowledge can be pulled out in threads, sentence by sentence, and reintegrated. No lovely frenzy then, but no matter.

—I fight in all sorts of ways. I fight by tearing into pieces my whole pride and character, and by smashing everything slick in sight. You cannot think what life with a shell resolves into. All this leaves very little margin for creative effort. (And that sentence is the mope and mow of the jolly grinner in the soul who can keep even misery and malevolence sane.)

Not a *femme fatale*, Morton. Only people with a good wide streak of *chi-chi* and attitudinizing can manage that. Believe, believe that I am proof against my own obsessions. There's mature irony in these bones, my good sir. When the time comes—in the twenty supposititious poems, perhaps—it will serve. *For certain moments at the least,*

*that crafty demon and that loud beast that plague me day and night
Ran out of my sight; . . . I saw my freedom won and all laugh in the
sun.*

[Ford Madox] Ford is, I fear, an old fool. *The waves were bar-
barous and abrupt* after all this time and repetition sticks in my crop.
Certainly, in the last thirty years, other and as good phrases have risen
into his vision. We heard some enlightening things concerning Ford
from Wyndham Lewis, who was in town for a short time this fall.
Quite an odd one. The Messianic delusion, I should say. But *what*
a scathing lot of scurrilous stories! His account of Robert Graves,
Laura Riding, and the Irish Adonis: ("She-devil! She-devil!" remarked the Irish Adonis' grandfather from behind *The Times* in the
chimney corner) was a masterpiece. * * *

Have you read Violet Hunt on Ford? Do get it. The funniest book
in years. Léonie and I were beside ourselves over it, in those dear
dead days before the rue Vaugirard. (Léonie was a sub-leaser in that,
too, and what did *she* get out of it?)

I distrust Béhaine,[2] saving your grace, because of Ford. But I shall
start reading him immediately—because of you. Your determination to
get more out of me sets all manner of notions stampeding through my
thoughts. Those three definite and intelligent *précis* slapped me like
a tonic air, this morning, as I drank my hot coffee and cold orange
juice. (Not in a sunny chair: this unfortunate bedroom faces west and
only lacks "a great opal" to make it peculiarly sinister.) * * *

"C'était l'hiver: un dimanche soir. Il pleurait." Isn't that beautiful?
It is the beginning of a novel which haunts my dreams. Indoors
someone is sitting beside a lamp with a green shade. Outside the
steel cars make a noise like water running into a bottle. Come, come.
Tell me it will happen.

This letter has made me feel much better. I'll write another soon
again. The review will go to you this week, *parole d'honneur.*

Yours etc.
Louise

1. Morton Dauwen Zabel was then the associate editor of *Poetry* and continued
in that position until, for one year, he took over the editorship on Miss Monroe's
death. The author of numerous books of criticism, Zabel was a professor of English
at the University of Chicago when he died in 1964.

2. René Béhaine, born in 1880, was considered by Ford Madox Ford to be the
greatest of living French novelists; he continued to think so as late as his *March of
Literature,* published in 1938. On the other hand, LB says that Ford considered
Georges Simenon the greatest French novelist (see p. 307).

1932

306 Lexington
New York City
April 1, 1932

Dear Allen:

I had feared that my review would distress you. I am sorry that you thought it full of personal bias, and even venom. I can only say that I was not estimating you as a person or as a friend. I was reviewing a book of poetry which aroused in me respect and irritation in about equal measure. If you objected to the tone of my review, I objected, straight down to a core beyond detachment, to the tone of some of the poems. I hesitated to accept the book [*Poems: 1928–1931*] for review because I suspected that a flavor of irritation would get through to the critical page.

When I did accept it, I tried in every way both to clarify and minimize the irritation. The review copies contained some misprints; I called up Scribner's and had them read me the passages as they should appear. Our copy of *Mr. Pope* had been burned; I got another from Balch in order not to pass upon it from memory. And I went to the Library and read a file of *The Fugitive* in order to get that background straight in my mind. You may not consider these efforts gestures toward detachment; I intended them to be. And I read every printed version of the "Ode to the Confederate Dead."

The first thing that annoyed me was the slightly pontifical air of the foreword. But perhaps this is stupid of me; I thought: Allen is merely serious, and that is commendable. When I sat down to the book, "Last Days of Alice," "The Paradigm" (in spite of its extraordinary insight), the eagle poem, "Ignis Fatuus," and some passages in "Causerie" disturbed me to such an extent that I simply did not know what to do. "Here," I said to myself, "is cold legerdemain, metaphysical arrogance (perhaps a phrase as meaningless as 'philosophic ambition,' but let it go—), deliberately conceived, put down without a qualm, managed to the last degree. These poems are sterile: Allen should not do this thing, and having done it, he should be brought to book therefor." As you know, Allen, in a poem, not only can the feeling be in excess to the matter, but devices, crotchets, and all skilled traps for the unwary, can exceed. In short, these poems struck me as elaborate ruses, as poetic sophistry (in the non-Protagorean sense of the term). They would have struck me as such in the work of my son, my father, my enemy, or the friend of my bosom.

I should have tried to define them just as definitely in these hypothetical cases, as in yours. More especially if the writer had a talent such as yours concealed beneath them.

As for the points you bring up in your letter, shall we go into them? I stand accused as one who stabs a friend in the back—presumptuous and ignorant. —The reference to the boldness or non-boldness of the Fugitives' program was not intended to be invidious; I did not intend to imply that they *should* have been bold. You interpret the quotation from *The Fugitive* (but the word *astute* still sticks in my crop. The picture of an *astute* poet is as queer as the vulgar idea of a deranged one). You define the term sophist, talking down a little to unlearned ears. You ask me how a poem can have authority. I cannot answer, except to say that some poems do. And finally you turn away with an ill-dissembled "Faugh!" from what you consider my presumptuous infringement on a specialized nomenclature.

You were being a schoolmaster a little, weren't you? [1]

Yours—

Louise

1. Reviewing this letter in 1972, Allen Tate said that there *was* personal animosity, but that the review would probably have been much the same had there not been. ("My poems were never Louise's dish of tea.") Certainly their friendship was not broken by the disagreement here. As they parted for the last time, the year before her death, LB said to Tate: "Never a cross word these forty years." She had forgotten the review, and, as Tate recalled, "Well, so had I!"

/ to Morton D. Zabel /

April 29, 1932

HART SUICIDE BOAT DOCKS TONIGHT DETAILS LATER—

LOUISE

306 Lexington Avenue
New York City
May 5, 1932

Dear Morton:

By now perhaps you have all the bulletins concerning Hart [Crane] from other sources. —Peggy Cowley [1] had lunch with me yesterday. She said that Hart had begun to go to pieces in Havana. He ramped about the boat all Tuesday night and Wednesday morning. Wednesday noon he rushed into her cabin in pajamas, for a dramatic fare-well to her and to life. (Peggy did not take this seriously: she had heard Hart's farewells before.) Then he made for the saloon, rushed through crowds of passengers to the afterdeck, and took a fifty-foot dive into the sea. The ship stopped; boats were lowered but nothing could be done. *The New Republic* is publishing a poem or poems found among his effects. Is this the poem which should have gone to you? Peggy mentioned Hart's intention to send you something; she was rather vague on this point, however. —It is a great loss, but Hart could not have gone on, dashing [?] himself against people, places, against night, morning and midday. He could accept nothing simply; he had no defenses. Had he done much work on the Montezuma-Toltec theme, do you know? —The story went dead the day the boat arrived because all the ship's newsmen had been drawn off to meet Mrs. Hargreaves (Lewis Carroll's "Alice"). Hart would have appre-ciated that detail, don't you think?

* * *

A strange tea with Willa Cather, early in April.[2] She is already an old woman, querulous and set in her ways. She bullies the waiter. She bewails the good old days when gentlefolk had the Metropolitan and Carnegie Hall all to themselves. (Women collapse so thoroughly, so soon.) But she has a taste for high comedy; *Dead Souls* seems the greatest novel in the world to her still hearty appreciation.

I have read *Conquistador* though hurriedly and with some inatten-tion. He [MacLeish] is a fine craftsman and a man of feeling. Hating life and action as he does, the poem manages a point of view and a flavor. You do not think the feeling in the poem suspect, do you? Bour-geois poignancy or no, I am all for some rigidity [?] of emotion in writing, and appreciate it wherever it is modernly found, and cherish it, from Valéry's passionate apostrophe to Zeus, on.

Do let me hear from you soon. I have some things to say about [Dorothy] Richardson, another time.

Yours ever—

Louise

1. Malcolm Cowley's first wife, Marguerite.

2. Presumably this meeting was in connection with a profile LB was doing of Miss Cather for *The New Yorker*. Her article, called "American-classic," was reprinted in the volume *Willa Cather and Her Critics*, edited by James Schroeter for the Cornell University Press (1967).

Dear Morton:

This is to inform you that a cold little note this day has gone forth, from me to The John Simon Guggenheim Foundation, meekly asking for an application blank. It was like pulling teeth, but I did it, and you are the only begetter of that deed. Now I am in a terrible funk as to backers. I frankly do not know where to turn; I think up people and immediately reject them. Perhaps my state of mind on this point will improve when I get used to the idea. Never having played politics, I am pretty well stumped. Then too, I remember your counsel; that if I kept my mouth shut, no one need know anything about it in any case. But surely, if I ask for recommendation from even *one* of any gang, the *coterie sprache* will begin like mad, and then where will my fine plans for secrecy land? O dear!

Malcolm Cowley, no; and will not Yvor turn and rend me, and why call on them at all? Then, tentatively:

You

Katharine White of *The New Yorker* [1] and Edna Millay (because they are on the Vie Femina Heureuse Committee and may sound impressive). (You see how all sorts of nasty little grabbing ideas get into the thing immediately; I knew it!)

Horace Gregory   Torrence
Edmund Wilson   Mark Van Doren

and there I end. Not Untermeyer; not Allen [Tate]; not Léonie; not anyone else you could mention. Should I write to little Mr. [Robert] Hillyer, medium-sized Mr. [S. Foster] Damon, and nebulous Mr. Winfield Scott, just because they sent me a word of praise recently? (I don't know any of them, and I respect only Mr. Damon.) No; that would be straw-clutching in the extreme. No straw-clutching. I'll name a few kind and discreet people, send in a sheaf of reviews—Scribner's will lend me those—remark in passing that my unworthy name appears on the roster of Who's Who, 1932, and let it go at that. —Forgive all this groaning. —Something, perhaps your presence among the masterpieces at the Metropolitan, and your well-taken but hard-to-bear remarks on my mode of life, has made me feel horribly like a worm. Dissatisfaction with my mode of life runs riot through my veins, and I *would* choose just such a time to apply for rest and refreshment in Europe from an adamantine Foundation.

Forget that I ever brought any of this up.

I have a grand, nasty piece of gossip for you, but I shall not sully this paper or my noble mood of the moment with it. Ask me about it sometime. As the modern and female de Goncourt I am going to put it down in my note-book, wherein it will be found one day, in the cellar with the croquet balls.[2] *Never* have I heard a more distressing and peculiar piece of news. —It's a shame that I can't tell it to you. But no.

Just to prove that I have some spirit left, and hold courageous convictions, I am forwarding *Ces plaisirs . . .* to you. (I shall never forget the venom with which you pronounced Madame Colette's name over that third glass of wine.) Do write me and tell me how you enjoyed your trip back to Chicago.

> Yours ever, for intense personal loyalties,
> Louise

1. Katharine S. White, wife of E. B. White, was until her retirement in 1961 the fiction and poetry editor of *The New Yorker*.

2. The notebooks LB left were closer to commonplace books than to Goncourt journals. There was no gossip whatever. And, indeed, the passage sounds as if she were teasing Zabel in kind. He really did enjoy retailing gossip.

October 14, 1932

Dear Morton:

* * * Do bear down on native quality of mind, will you? That awful blank [on the Guggenheim application] after academic honors frightens me. Tate and Adams and Taggard all had degrees; Tate and Adams were ΦBK; Taggard made it up in ambition. Crane and K[atherine] A[nne] P[orter] hadn't academic backgrounds, but Crane has probably put the Aydelottes and the Bowmans on their guard forevermore.

Bear, bear on the mind, on the capacity of the brain, on the long scholar's head, on the know-without-having-learned intuition, on the bred-in-the-bone aptitude, on the up-from-Livermore-Falls-Maine coming-through, on the seeking-out-as-her-own nicety of choice, on the made-a-life-for-herself-through-choice-in-spite-of-evil-chance stamina. O Morton, I hate this like poison, but since I have committed myself (and through your urging), be he who burns with intense loyalties, and *bear*.

Yours, without the benefit of Academe, but with the firm intention of seeing light over Corfu in the near future—

Louise

[P.S.] Isn't this a NICE letter?

306 Lexington Avenue
New York City
November 29, 1932

Dear Morton:

Yours of last month sometime has lain unanswered; all sorts of minor evils and near catastrophes have kept my nimble pen from letter paper, these four weeks back. The lady downstairs committed suicide by gas, for one thing, and, since the lethal chamber was situated directly under Maidie's bedroom, Maidie got a good gassing, too, and was laid up for three days. This occurred the night of Harriet Monroe's visit to us. H. M. did not seem as well as formerly; we gave her one and a half glasses of Bacardi cum ginger ale: she said she liked it better than tea. I meant to get some flowers to her hotel before she left town but the suicide put a stop to my activities for that week. I'll write her soon. —The minor evils do not bear recounting—they're nothing much and leave hardly any mark on a spirit finally resigned, though quite unembittered, a mind open to joy, if any happens to be around, and refreshed, under the descending cloud of winter, more than I dared hope. —One evil, hardly minor, was the death of Margaret Wilson,[1] of whom, as you know, I was very fond. She died suddenly in California, just a day or two before she planned to come back to the east. Edmund bore the matter better than any of us thought he could. He flew out to the coast for the funeral, and returned, saddened but by no means in psychic pieces. —He's now gone off observing cities and won't be back until the new year. —I do miss Margaret.

The great *nice letter* campaign panned out admirably. All prospects came through with pleasant replies; I hope that their O-so-secret remarks to the Guggenheims followed their protestations to me rather closely. Robert Frost surprised me by the vigor of his reply. I had written him that I wouldn't bear any grudge if he could not honestly commend me; he reminded me that I shouldn't know anything about what he said, in any case, so that grudges were out of place. "But I shan't decide against you," said he. Poetic politics being what they are,

God knows if Frost's word means anything. But I can't bother about that. —For the others: R. Hillyer, very pleased; S. Foster Damon, very pleased— ("It was kind of you to call upon me." This seems an odd reaction somehow—); M. Van Doren, very friendly, very pleased; R. Torrence, very pleased but quite dubious; John Hall Wheelock, excessively gracious; [2] E. Millay, nice as can be (she takes the Guggenheim recommendations quite seriously, H. M. says); you, not specifically pleased, but very gracious, none the less; H. M., rather puzzled as to whether or not I had sent her a blank, but I did.

So there you are. I've put the whole matter to one side now, and am planning an annual flower garden in Maine. In Maine, flowers grow to great size and extraordinary coloring. Sown in June, they make a brave show the first week in August. . . .

News in brief: A fine, frightfully angry, terrifically compressed poem written and sold to *Scribner's* (I owed them one this last two and one half years—) called "Exhortation" or perhaps, "All Souls' Eve." [3] You may receive a copy on application. One or two guinea hens absorbed at one or two dinners. An invitation to meet Bernard Faÿ, whoever he is,[4] turned down. An invitation to the P.E.N. club dinner, to meet Pearl Buck, Léonie Adams, Genevieve Taggard and Henry Pringle, among others, also turned down. No literary wowsing for me this winter, and besides, I have met the Misses Adams and Taggard and can probably live a little longer without meeting Mrs. Buck and Mr. Pringle.[5] (L. Adams is now a Communist. She once said to me, "Whenever I meet a new man, something in my mind says '*gentleman?*' —or '*not* gentleman?' It's very hard for me to be interested if he is *not* a gentleman!" I wonder how this attitude works among the members of the Party.) —Saw *The Playboy* and *The New Gossoon, The Playboy* in the company of that fine prig, William Troy,[6] who is proud and pleased that his mother's people came from the same town which produced George Moore. *The Playboy* is *not* an Irish play, say what you will. The main idea is an intellectual and rather decadent one, the first, perhaps, of café-sitting in Paris in the '90's. It's the play of a decadent *Anglo*-Irishman [Synge] and I don't blame the true Irish, the Gaels, for not swallowing it. It sounds very nice, however. The company is so-so; all the excellent people are rather decrepit, which detracts from some moments; the younger people have pretty ankles and pleasant smiles. [George Shiels'] *The New Gossoon* is delightful: new generation Irish: motor-bikes mixed up with mountainy goats. Not a patch on [Denis Johnston's] *The Moon in the Yellow*

River, of course. (You can read that now; it's been published recently. I recommend it to you.) —Read Lawrence's letters; C[atherine] Carswell on Lawrence and re-read J[ohn] M[iddleton] Murry on same. The letters are beautiful and terrible; Lawrence's lapse from being an artist into trying to be a prophet very well defined. "The conscience of our time," someone said to me the other day. Sure, and the poor, sad raggedy conscience, the self-tortured conscience it turned out to be. (I want to read T. E. Shaw's *Odyssey*. *His* life I somewhat admire, undercover agent or no. A ditty box, a motor-bike, books and the works of Mozart, a hard, pressed-upon existence with one or two necessities of the spirit squeezed out therefrom—far more admirable than D. H.'s globe-girdlings tied to a wife's apron strings.) Read D. H. L.'s *Etruscan Places*. He *could* throw off effects, almost by chance, that seize the imagination. Perhaps that is enough. But O, the blather surrounding the few excellences! And do you know, Murry isn't so far off in his estimate as you might imagine. Certainly he gets Lawrence down more thoroughly than A. Huxley in the introduction to the *Letters*. The C. Carswell book is entirely negligible.

* * *

For Christmas I expect a warm dressing gown and a set of Thoreau's *Journals*. All I expect, and all I'll get. Enough. —Did you hear Stokowski's concert last Sunday, by radio? So beautiful: Handel, my lovely Gluck, the Leonora 3rd and Brahms' double concerto. Toscanini's programs have been dull: Sibelius, the *Eroica* (which I detest), Enesco, lots of Wagner (whom I dislike more and more as time drifts by under the eye of eternity). For five weeks now, I have done real work in piano technique with a severe friend, a girl who has carried over some of Leschetizky's method into her teaching, but not all. We do not *read* things together, we shred them out, note by note. Too much piano reading dulls the mind, destroys the fingers and deadens the nerves. We're doing the C major Mozart sonata (No. 3): and I mean *doing*!

* * *

Yours for the contemplative life,
Louise

1. Edmund Wilson's second wife, whom he had married in 1930.

2. In asking Wheelock for a recommendation, she said: "The case for me is not as poor as you might think. It's not as good as it should be, either. But I say to myself: 'They gave it to Genevieve Taggard.' (But they didn't give it to Elinor Wylie. . . .)" (October 21, 1932)

3. "I think it good, because, on a second reading, it sounded like something I had never seen before, and I always take that as a sign that the vulgar upper consciousness had nothing to do with it." (To Wheelock, October 31, 1932)

4. Faÿ, a French historian with American passions, wrote biographies of Franklin, Washington and Theodore Roosevelt.

5. Mrs. Buck and Pringle were that year's Pulitzer Prize winners in the novel and biography.

6. William Troy, critic and teacher, was to marry Léonie Adams in June 1933.

/ to Katharine S. White /

November 30, 1932

Dear Katharine:

Your note and the [*New Yorker*] check came this morning, and saved me from experiencing one of the most humiliating moments possible: that moment when one's last mossy vestment falls in rags at one's feet. Directly I sign my name to this note, I am going out and buy $145.00 worth of clothes, regardless, as my mother used to say, of cost or expense.

I feel guilty about the two missing pieces. —I can plead Thanksgiving (grisly festival!) and a fit of the sulks over the merits of work in progress. —Tomorrow, wearing four dresses, five pairs of shoes and two hats, I'll begin a new one and get it to you by *noon on Tuesday*.

Yours in great haste!
Louise

/ to Morton D. Zabel /

306 Lexington Avenue
New York City
February 14, 1933

Dear Morton:

I began a letter to you on the 24th of January. How time has flown, that is, by what means, I can't correctly say. My review of [John] Masefield was hardly off the typewriter before I had to begin my winter's verse review for *The New Yorker*. That review (ten books polished off in 1100 words) always disaffects me thoroughly, so that I have to take long ferry rides to Hoboken, long walks all over town, and long drinks of beer at four in the afternoon (alone, in Lüchow's, with the reflection of my self going up into infinity in the long funereal mirrors). The review had to be cut; the meticulous queries of the

NYer's proof-readers had to be answered, and then I was called upon to write an editorial for *The New Republic* on the subject of Sara Teasdale's death. * * * E. Wilson chided me for the flip tone taken in the *New Yorker* review. What else can one take? I take it for the good round sum of $75; I do not seek to justify this action, and if this piece of journalism cheapens me in the eyes of men and angels, I have no retort to make, save that I was paid $75 for the effort, and that I spoke my mind honestly, if glibly.

All this served to make time pass. Miss Monroe came to dinner. She seemed very happy and full of insouciance; I trust that this bodes well for the Guggenheim affair. She had come from a meeting of the jury that afternoon. Judging by intuition, I should say that she had had her will of them. Maybe not. We sent her a large bunch of bright short-stemmed tulips, to the boat, and I heard from her from Havana: a delightful journey so far. No word from the G.'s. E. Wilson keeps assuring me that he is confident in my success. We have seen a great deal of Mr. Wilson since Christmas. He comes in after supper and we play at the game whose name I have forgotten: you write a line of poetry and pass it on, and soon an entire poem is revealed, written by several hands. And very funny some of these efforts turn out to be. Edmund is a master at topical songs, too, written at high speed and sung to a tune that borrows Kern's rhythms and Gershwin's melodic line. * * *

There have been some very amusing parties in town of late. One was at Berenice Abbott's (the photographer), last Friday. I went at six, expecting to get home in time for supper. I went with some qualms, having been bored to death at a party in her studio last summer, where large androgynous females took up a lot of room and contributed little or nothing to the gaiety of life or the dignity of art. This party was quite different. The first person my eyes lit upon, as I entered the room, was Escudero in the flesh.[1] One of his little gypsy girl friends was with him—also his manager and interpreter. Also present were about a dozen charming Negroes from Harlem, all talented in the extreme, and a scattering of the less objectionable type of Lesbian. There was a bar; the drinks were excellent; the food was good; a blind pianist played for dancing; I looked well and danced continuously until far into the night, and Raymond engaged M. Escudero in conversation until early in the morning. It was the best party I have been to in years, and only goes to show that too many intellectuals in the same room have a negative and depressing effect, while a great many natural, happy and unaffected Negroes liven things up masterfully. Escudero told R. that he could not read and write. "What is all that to me?" he exclaimed. I conveyed to E. that I thought him a great artist; we raised glasses to each other frequently. He would not dance or even make noises with his finger-nails. I wish I could give such a good party. No M. Josephsons and K. Burkes and e. e. cummingses and M. Cowleys. Just a happy crew of gentle voluptuaries. * * *

> Yours, with admiration and esteem,
> Louise

1. Escudero is said to have been the greatest flamenco dancer of his time.

/ to Harriet Monroe /

> 306 Lexington Avenue
> March 15, 1933

Dear Miss Monroe:

Mr. Moe wrote me on Saturday last that the trustees of the Foundation had awarded me a fellowship "for creative writing abroad"— for one year, beginning with April 1st. —I can't tell you the happiness and enthusiasm that this news has given my heart and mind. And for your good offices in the matter, I cannot express my gratitude. I am a little abnormal, because I fear so much and expect so little; help from outside has come so infrequently to me that I have taught myself never to expect it, and never, if possible, to ask for it. So that this fellowship gives me great confidence in myself and in the possibilities of future work that I may do. Nothing like it has ever happened to me before, I can assure you. I hope that some work will come through, and that it will be worth your faith in my abilities.

I plan to sail early in April for Genoa, and go down to Sicily before I visit Florence, the hill towns and Venice. I'll write to you again before I sail.

Again, with all gratitude, affection and esteem—

> Louise

1930-1939

/ *to Wolcott Gibbs* /

March 28, 1933

Dear Wolcott: [1]

Here are the corrections. Thank you for saving me from "the opposite direction as herself"—(as one would say, from worse than death). —If Mr. Ross wants the house in "Conversation Piece" placed on the north side of 37th Street, and described in detail as a "large old-fashioned brownstone mansion, with a stoop," I'm afraid someone will have to write that in for me, because I certainly don't see any sense in writing it in, as myself. I've placed the house in New York (as opposed to Jersey City) and even the most bewildered person in the world, in the sense of the person most prone to bewilderment, ought to be able to read the rest in.

    * * *

> Yours—
>
> Louise

1. The writer Wolcott Gibbs was substituting for Mrs. White on this occasion when Harold Ross, the founder and editor of *The New Yorker*, struck another blow for absolute clarity in the short story. For a more positive example of LB's regard for Ross' editorial skills, see p. 199.

/ *to Harriet Monroe* /

> Villefranche
> Alpes-Maritimes
> June 12, 1933

Dear Miss Monroe:

After two months in Italy, I have come to France, to visit Dorothy Dudley Harvey, who has lived here for a little over a year. Villefranche is built on the side of a rocky hill; it is full of cats and of people who look like cats. The inhabitants fish and raise carnations. Dorothy's house is truly remarkable, even more remarkable than any Dudley house seen up to this time. Formerly it was an hotel. Now the restaurant windows are papered over, and the former restaurant is a studio, which looks out, through perhaps eight windows, over the bay. The rooms are papered with kindergarten colors. Books, paintings, lithographs, Chinese hangings and bowls of carnations and geraniums and bougainvillea and cherries and squashes and oranges hang on the wall, crowd the tables, the desks and very often the chairs. Outside the bay is aquamarine, when seen from a height, and Prussian blue, when seen in the distance.

My daughter will arrive late this month. I plan to take her up to Austria, perhaps stopping at Lake Garda and Venice on the way. The rapid shrinkage of the dollar makes any broad plan impossible. I think we shall manage somehow. And now I shall begin to work.

Why does one hardly ever hear of the Carpaccios in Venice? I loved them. One afternoon I went to Padua and saw the Giottos and Mantegnas there. The Mantegnas are magnificent. He was a great intellectual master. The Giottos are so pure that they break the heart. His stern gentle Virgin goes off [to] Egypt; Christ raises Lazarus; Christ is taken down from the Cross—unbelievably sincere, felt, beautiful.

Venice was more beautiful than I had hoped it could be. Palermo, Rome, Siena, Venice met my hopes. Florence was a great disappointment. The dry, hard, dead look of the streets, feel of the air, look of the people, destroyed my delight in its treasures almost at once. But Venice!

Will you write me sometime? I'll send you poems when they are written.

Ever with affection,
Louise

/ *to Morton D. Zabel* /

Les Muriers
Cap Brun
Toulon-Var
June 29, 1933

Dear Morton:

* * * Last Friday I left the cliff-dwellings of Villefranche to have lunch with [Ford Madox] Ford and I have been here ever since. In fact, my one social *succès fou* has come off in Cap Brun, Toulon (Var). Painters want to paint me; young Communists (brother to Madame Ford) want to convert me. Ford wishes that I stay here all summer *and* all winter. I have been fed, housed, given to drink, cosseted and posseted all round. Ford lives in a villa overlooking the Mediterranean, surrounded by a garden, and waited upon by his new wife, also a Communist. She [Janice Biala] is really a kind, sweet, gentle girl; she paints rather poorly and lives rather meagerly. Ford produces

large complicated dishes for every meal. Red wine flows like water and dinner comes to an end with a great burst of *marc*, the most fiery liqueur that ever went down anyone's throat. Many tales concerning the Tates are told, around the *marc*, in the evening, when the big stars of the Midi show in the heavens, none of which I shall repeat here. Nothing scabrous, you understand. Just kind idle gossip.

* * *

[unsigned]

August 27, 1933

Dear Morton:

* * *

No more shall I lament my lot, for having been vouchsafed a few close glimpses into the lots of other people, I do not think mine so dreadful after all. Perhaps God's own chosen happy people at this moment are sitting in cafés in Paris or in beer-stuberls in Copenhagen, but I doubt it. Everyone is more or less miserable everywhere, and the one thing to remember is that intellectual curiosity and the life of the mind are man's hope, and let it go at that. Since the gift of faith has been denied me, I cannot be heartened by the magic in dogma or ritual. But I have an ear for music, some talent for writing, a wonderful sense of humor, a fine constitution, and (the unexpected blessing given to my declining years!) an appreciable amount of good horse sense. So I shall settle down and let my intellectual curiosity work, with the aid of these above mentioned God-given gifts. And if those aren't the words of a sensible woman, what would the words of a s. w. be?

* * *

Ever,
Louise

/ *to Katharine S. White* /

White Plains
[January] 1934

Dear Katharine:

Thank you so very much for your sweet letter. It is not, my dear, that I am nervously puzzled; rather, let us say, I am nervously prostrated, having lost the power to take "an objective view," to make "clear-cut decisions."

As soon as I can manage even to peer around the corner of the pretty little emotional cul-de-sac I've managed to sew myself into, burning words will again begin to flow from my pen and I'll send samples on to you.

Maidie is at home, behaving very well as the poor child always does in crises. She's really a fine girl and objective as hell, thank God.

I have every confidence in this place and plan to stay here until I'm good and cured. I do hope that you and Andy [E. B. White] are now better of grippe germs.

Again with gratitude for your lovely card and with much love.

Louise

/ to John Hall Wheelock /

White Plains
March 23, 1934

Dear Jack:

Your kind letter came months ago, it seems. I appreciated it with all my heart, but I hesitated to answer it until I really had begun to work again. My general inability to produce anything wore me down to such an extent that I determined never to write anyone again until I had produced at least a page or two of writing, and could therefore omit the moans and groans that come into sterile inactivity.

But now, for an hour a day, at least, I am able to put down chance words on paper. These words will soon make the first two chapters of the book—a volume tentatively entitled *Laura Dailey's Story*.[1] Shall I bring this little sheaf in to your office one day next month? I am spending every other week-end in town now, so you can see that I am nearly well once more.

The doctor does not think that I should return to New York for good until I have creative work under weigh, and perhaps, in addition, a part-time job to keep me under routine. Would Mr. A[lfred] Dashiell want a capable woman to lick stamps and place them on envelopes, do you suppose? Do you think it would do any good to ask him? —O, you have a lot of trouble with me, do you not? If it's not one thing, it's another, and very little reward do you get in return! Whereas your other authors produce grand manuscripts such as *Ten-*

der Is the Night. That really is swell. I congratulate the magazine upon
it.

Another little bit about the book: Its title page would bear the remark of La Rochefoucauld:

> *L'accent et le caractère du pays où
> l'on est né demeure dans l'esprit
> et dans le coeur comme dans le langage.*[2]

And I told you how the thing should be a "play of sensibility" over
the mill-towns of my childhood. Very little sensibility has played over
New England since Thoreau. —Did you see [my] piece in *The New
Yorker* last November, called "Dove and Serpent"? The book will be
a little like that.

I shan't go near your office footlessly again. I'd love to see you, but
the sheaf must be ready to go along too.

You have been so kind, Jack. Thank you a thousand times, and
write me if you'd like.

Ever with affection,
Louise

1. LB worked at this prose piece occasionally all through her life. The only sur-
viving fragment—handwritten on yellow foolscap sheets—was dated June 1959.
2. "The accent and the character of the region where one is born live as much
in the language as they do in the mind and the heart."

/ *to Morton D. Zabel* /

The Bryant House
Provincetown, Mass.
July 27, 1934

Dear Morton:

* * * Then E. Wilson invited me down here. In New York the one
bright spot in my horrid early summer had been our German evening. We got together two nights a week and read Heine, aided by
two dictionaries. E. W. plans to thread the morass of 19th century
German thought and literature; Heine is his first step in the process
of mastering the entire German language. We paid absolutely no
attention to verb-forms or case-endings; we merely read the poems
with the aid of TWO dictionaries. So that now we have Heine's early
vocabulary (a pretty ghoulish one, as you no doubt realize) at our
fingers' ends. We have fought through the early youth—native Jew-

ish—early 19th cent.—moanings and broodings, the pure little lyrical intermezzi before us. —Edmund hopes to step into Goethe's *Faust* very soon. And from thence to Hegel, and from thence to Marx and Engels, I presume. —He is writing a long piece on the development of the science of history, beginning with Vico, continuing with Michelet, ending with Lenin. He has read every word Michelet ever wrote, including his letters: the 86 volumes (or so) are neatly piled along his study. —In case you thought that scholarship was dead, along these salty shores. . . .[1]

Morton, I produced two poems, and sold them both for bread and shoes.[2] I shall produce two or three more, if only to keep my promises to *Poetry* and to you. But thereafter the fountain will be sealed for good, I'm thinking. With Eliot, I pronounce poetry a mug's game (I called it a gull's game for years). I can no longer put on the "lofty dissolute air" necessary for poetry's production; I cannot and I will not suffer for it any longer. With detachment and sanity I shall, in the future, observe; if to fall to the ground with my material makes me a madwoman, I abjure the trade. Having definitely given up alcohol and romantic dreams, having excised my own neurosis with my own hand, having felt the knife of the perfectionist attitude in art and life at my throat. . . . But you can't stand this, I know.

* * *

Forgive me for not being a female Dante: write to me soon: lots of news.

Ever, dear Morton—
Louise

1. The activity described culminated in *To the Finland Station: A Study in the Writing and Acting of History,* not published until 1940.
2. Presumably "Short Summary" and "Man Alone," published in *The New Yorker.*

/ *to Edmund Wilson* /

100 W. 55th Street
New York City
August 12, 1934

Dear Edmund:

I open this note with a request that will raise every hackle on your spine with fury and distaste, and that request is: Could you have someone in your ménage, say, Hortense, readdress and send off to me the brown paper parcel left with you and, I believe, stored in the bottom part of the living room cupboard? Do have the address clear, like a true friend: otherwise, my entire fall wardrobe may go astray.

I have thought about you with solicitude and tenderness, my dear, and I trust that by now your plagues have somewhat subsided. —I came back to town expecting a hell of a month, but I have had a surprisingly good time with that remnant of the population still infesting the walls and sewers of this Modern Babylon. I have done a lot of subliminal mewings, roarings, and retchings, on odd scraps of paper; this week I shall lick some of these into shape and perhaps favor you with a look at the results. —I missed you and Heine to such an extent that I gave up beer, turning to solitary drinking of small portions of hard liquor instead. This sipping is excellent for releasing the subconscious at the time; it is rather bad for the next morning's clarity of mind.

At the moment it looks like divorce in the Holden family; you never can tell with these pure individualists, however.[1] —By the way, I met M. Gold [2] the other night in Bohemian surroundings. He looked very neat, and was surrounded by a bevy of dressy Jewish girls with false eyebrows.

Do write me a line, my dear, saying that you are better.

Ever with love,
Louise

[P.S.] Love to Rosalind.[3]

---

1. Marital difficulties grew serious upon LB's return from Europe. Although they stopped living together shortly after that, Raymond Holden and LB were not divorced until 1937.

2. Mike Gold, a leading Communist, wrote *Jews without Money.*

3. Wilson's first and, at that time, only child.

100 W. 55th Street
August 22, 1934

Dear Uncle Ed:

Your letter, with its enclosed currency, appeared this morning: I had given you up as liquidated or estranged, so that I was very happy to see your old cuneiform handwriting on the envelope. —Glad to hear that you are well, kid (note change of style: this one is known as the LACONIC, or BOLDFACED). And I cannot bear the idea of your lonely communings with Heine. How did you ever bear it; without you at my elbow, prodding me on to look up all the verbs beginning with Q, the sight of a page of Heine would bring on nostalgia verging on the hysterical.

I wish that we were absolutely compatible, and then I could go to Russia with you, on my alimony. But you would continually growl at me, I know.

PLEASE TELL ME IMMEDIATELY WHAT "To THE FINLAND STATION" MEANS. It's a grand title, and why did you keep it from me all this time?

I write and write—more than I've done in years—and I read and read, and I study nature as well as books (Agassiz), and I miss you. Do come back sometime, and how about another letter, one of these autumn evenings? —I'd send you the new poem I wrote and just sold to *Scribner's*—it's called "Poem in Prose"—but it really is *so* woodwind and cello that perhaps you couldn't bear it. I'll send it later.

Ever with love,
Louise

[P.S.] O hell, here's the poem anyhow. It will get a letter out of that crusty old heart, at least!

I blurbed [1] [Eliot's] *The Rock* for *The New Yorker:* I said, "This work must be prized more for its value as an act of piety than for its virtue as a piece of literature." Pretty snappy, what?

---

1. "Blurb" is a word LB used for paragraph reviews in *The New Yorker,* for flap copy and advertising squibs on book jackets and for those about-the-contributor passages found in many magazines and newspapers.

82 Washington Place
New York City
October 16, 1934

Dear Edmund:
* * *

I liked these last poems so much that there's no use of my making quibbling remarks about the technical effects which I might or might not be right about in any case. The pictures of Provincetown in September and of your grandfather's house touched me particularly. There's an abyss in each one—is it a sociological abyss in each?

Genevieve's book [*Not Mine to Finish*] came to hand the other day: in one poem she takes me to task for being a mocker and a fritterer; I sat down and composed the enclosed work after reading her opus. She's really very talented, but she is *so* transparent. The new gag is being and becoming a second Emily Dickinson: the Taggards came from Amherst after all, it would appear! O God save us all from harm and danger!

I miss you. Come to town soon.

Love—
Louise

Lines Written After Detecting in Myself a Yearning Toward the Large, Wise, Calm, Richly Resigned, Benignant Act Put on by a Great Many People After Having Passed the Age of Thirty-Five.

For every great soul who died in his house and his wisdom
Several did otherwise.
God, keep me from the fat heart that looks vaingloriously
      toward peace and maturity;
Protect me not from lies.
In Thy infinite certitude, tenderness and mercy
Allow me to be sick and well,
So that I may never tread with swollen foot the calm and
      obscene intentions
That pave hell.
Shakespeare, Milton, Matthew Arnold died in their beds,
Dante above the stranger's stair.
They were not absolved from either the courage or
      the cowardice
With which they bore what they had to bear.
Swift died blind, deaf and mad;
Socrates died in his cell;
Baudelaire died in his drool;
Proving no rule.[1]

---

1. These lines were later reduced to four and published under the title "To an Artist, to Take Heart."

> Slipping in blood, by his own hand, through pride,
> Hamlet, Othello, Coriolanus fall.
> Upon his bed, however, Shakespeare died,
> Having endured them all.

/ *to Morton D. Zabel* /

82 Washington Place
New York City
January 17, 1935

Dear Morton:

* * * The problem of evil and the concept of man's imperfectibility have recently struck me all of a heap. I have even pondered over the possibility: does the doctrine of original sin throw any light on the matter? Edmund is quite at a loss, to discover his formerly highly intuitive friend bent upon problems that need a richly stocked arsenal of philosophical weapons, in order that they be pried apart!

I've read all the mental-collapse-period in Shakespeare: *Timon* and *Troilus* and straight through the big dramas to the heath in *Lear*, full of real and simulated madmen. Rather rewarding! (Do you remember Eliot's phrase: "The less rewarding Waller"? E. W. and I have a joke about it. Everything, to our minds, is now more or less "rewarding.")
* * *

Some morning, when the blood runs high, I'll sit down and write you an account of what goes on. Everyone is about to go to a party for Señor Dali, dressed in anatomical charts. Poor old F. M. F. is here, in a dreadful dingy flat, among onion skins, his wife's paintings and old newspapers. Great God! * * *

Thank you again, dear Morton.

Ever your sincere though unrewarding friend,
Louise

February 5, 1935

Dear Morton:

* * * I met Virgil Thomson [1] last week, at dinner in an amusing house. He played Methodist hymn tunes. I recommended Swift's *Polite Conversation* as a possible libretto. Pope would sound well, rendered by the human voice, too. Thomson is fat, mean and effeminate; he is also witty and informed. Lanvin designs his clothes and they are fierce.

I had a run-in with Rolfe, after having absorbed a fair quantity of his liquor, recently. He is experiencing a violent Marxist conversion, and that troubles and annoys me, and I am not so charitable as I should be. The reconciliation of the warring elements in my own nature was effected in such an unconscious and unknowable Jungian manner that I have become rather impatient with surrogates for religion, and life-

lines and rocks of ages and snug harbors and other dogmatic frame-
works. Rolfe sounds too much like an impotent artist, for my liking, and
I told him so. I am very fond of him, and I respect his crucial state. Why
does he eat from the hand of the *New Masses* group? To ally oneself
with those great critical intelligences, Stanley Burnshaw and Granville
Hicks!

⁕ ⁕ ⁕ Do write to me, Morton. I miss you. The next letter will swing
more and creak less.

Ever, with affection and respect,
Louise

1. The composer of, among other music, *Four Saints in Three Acts,* set to a libretto
by Gertrude Stein.

/ to Edmund Wilson /

82 Washington Place
Manhattan
June 22, 1935

Edmund dear:
Your collection of Persian miniatures arrived this morning, and I was
so happy to hear the tone of your humor again: you and your ladies
swigging out of not one, but two decanters, and your dames with their
stomachs only faintly veiled, tweaking dulcimers! How nice to know
that you are still somewhere, and that the girls and the vodka haven't
gotten you yet. What the Russian cuties don't do, the Hellenic ones
probably will: I expect to see you coming down the gang plank a mere
ghost of your former rubicund self: hollow, *maigre,* worn, shorn, and
staggering. Ah well, a little Guinness will put you on your feet again;
that and the delightfully ripening influence of my mind.

I, myself, have been made to bloom like a Persian rose-bush, by the
enormous love-making of a cross between a Brandenburger and a Pomeranian, one Theodore Roethke by name.[1] He is very, very large (6 ft.
2 and weighing 218 lbs) and he writes very very small lyrics. 26 years
old and a frightful tank. We have poured rivers of liquor down our
throats, these last three days, and, in between, have indulged in such
bearish and St. Bernardish antics as I have never before experienced.
⁕ ⁕ ⁕ Well! Such goings on! A woman of my age! He is amusing, when
not too far gone in liquor; he once won a ΦBK and he has just been
kicked out of Lafayette, from his position of instructor in English. He

is just a ripple on time's stream, really, because he is soon going to Michigan to write a text-book on electrical fields. (How is the Dnieperstroi, by the way? I expect pictures of the Dnieperstroi, and get depraved Persians instead! What would Marx and Engels say?) —I hope that one or two immortal lyrics will come out of all this tumbling about.

* * *

So they still give Tchaikovsky, do they? Fancy that. I'll *bet* everything is gayer than you expected. How is the pink subway (why not a *red* subway)? Maidie has a whole act, depicting you in the pink subway: sort of a short operetta, with incidental songs. You must hear it sometime.

Well, my dear, we both love you very deeply, and Maidie is writing a separate note. God knows what's going to become of me. I feel so terribly happy, with or without Brandenburger: a form of incipient idiocy, no doubt. I wake each morning feeling younger and younger and I dance through each day with the abandon of at least an emu. I am also becoming quite pretty, so that, for the first time in years, gents try to make me on the streets. —Well, we'll all collapse like the one-horse shay, no doubt, during the next decade.

Send us more pretty pictures, my dove, my coney, and write, too. I DO miss you a lot.

Ever with love,
Louise

1. Roethke first met LB in late 1934, on an occasion not wholly comfortable for the twenty-six-year-old apprentice poet. "Damn her anyway," wrote Roethke to Rolfe Humphries. "She and her Irish digs." (*Selected Letters of Theodore Roethke*, November 2, 1934)

/ to John Hall Wheelock /

82 Washington Place
Manhattan
July 1, 1935

Dear Jack:
You mustn't take the request about to appear in the next paragraph amiss. I ask the favor of you without, I trust, the least flavor of rancor in my heart. I am faced by a problem, and I wonder if you can help me solve it. —There is, or will be, once I get it written out on this fair sheet, in a postscript, some rancor in my last paragraph. Don't look at that yet. It might prejudice you.

The point is: Malcolm Cowley, a month or so ago, asked me to edit an anthology of female verse, to be used in the pages of the N. R. They have, as you know, already published groups of Middle-Western verse, and whatnot. They are now about to divide mankind horizontally rather than vertically, sexually rather than geographically. —As you might have expected, I turned this pretty job down; the thought of corresponding with a lot of female songbirds made me acutely ill. It is hard enough to bear with my own lyric side. The idea and the task have gone on, however, to Hildegarde Flanner, and she has written me asking for an immediate contribution.

Now, I haven't anything, at the moment, to send her. The Lucretius stuff I am at work on has been promised to *Poetry*, along with any lyrics that may occur during the summer. The one thing that came to mind, the one poem I should like them to have, in order to raise the tone of the whole thing from the level of Marie de L. Welch and Frances Frost, is "Italian Morning," which has been on the bank of your magazine since last May. Could you persuade Dashiell, or someone, to release this poem, before it finally settles down to the bottom as irremediable residue? It is the best poem I have done in years, and I would like to see it in the N. R., as a kind of proud gesture against the Malcolm Cowleys, the Kenneth Burkes and the Bruce Blivens of this world.

I know that this request is both bad literary manners, and all sorts of other things that I haven't the time to enumerate. But it isn't real mean-spiritedness. Wait for my last paragraph for a taste of that!

I have a poem on hand, which I'm not quite sure of, yet, called "Baroque Comment," which I'll send you as a substitute after it is writ out fair. It has some really beautiful lines in it, but it isn't a lyric, and I want the N. R. to have a swell lyric from me. Do you see? [1]

You do see, don't you, Jack?

—I had the peculiar experience of falling mildly in love, about a week ago, with an enormous young man from Ann Arbor, Mich. He brought out all my Catherine the Great side, let me tell you, he being six feet two and weighing [fifteen] stone if he weighs a pebble. We had a magnificent week (he is aged twenty-six, by the way), and I found myself writing the most extraordinary Ella Wheeler Wilcoxism, as a consequence. This last will never be seen by human eye, I trust. Never shall I give the feminine sonneteers any competition. O, I'm a strange one, amen't I?

And I've just discovered Rilke. Why did you never tell me about Rilke? My God, the man's wonderful. Perhaps, sometime this summer, you will come down, in the late afternoon, and I'll provide some rye, and you can help me with some of the harder verses in the *Neue Gedichte*. My German is still so poor.

* * *

So let me hear from you, Jack.

Louise

P.S. (And this is the nasty part.)

In your current magazine, you blurb Raymond Holden as the author of a second book of poetry, *Landscape with Figures*,[2] published in 1930. Now, I don't know whether you know it or not, but there was no such book. (I particularly loved the date, to give the whole thing some authority.) I don't think you had anything to do with this strange notice, * * * but such an out and out fabrication really shocked and alarmed me. That sort of thing lets the human race down, I always say. But if Scribner's wants non-existent books listed for their authors (*with* dates), don't forget, when *Sleeping Fury* comes out, to list the following non-existent volumes of mine:

> *Five Fingers* (1902)
> *The Werewolf of Amalfi* (1905)
> *The Goat in the Manger* (1912)
> *The Midnight Blue Cineraria* (1916)
> *The Splendor Falls* (1918)
> *Moles and Marmots: Their Life and Art* (1921)
> *Up the Workers* (1925)
> *My Life in a Mustache Cup* (1926)
> *Can We Forgive Her?* (1927)
> *Guide to the Bowery Savings Bank* (1930)
> *Gentle Gimcracks* (1931)
> *Father of Flamingoes* (1932)
> *Five Bedpillows and a Breeze* (1933)
> *A Short Talk on the Messina Earthquake* (1934) AND
> *My Ornaments Are Arms* (1935)

! ! ! !
L.

---

1. *Scribner's Magazine* got around to publishing "Italian Morning" the following month. Lyric or not, *The New Republic* got "Baroque Comment," for $7.50.

2. Lionel Wiggam, who would later publish a volume of poetry under this title, but who is not under attack here, is dealt with on p. 132.

/ to Rolfe Humphries /

82 Washington Place
Manhattan
July 2, 1935

Dear Rolfe:

It was nice of you, damned nice, to write me such a swell letter. You really are a great guy in many ways. I have moments when I'd like to kill you; on the other hand, there are moments when I'd like you to live forever. —At the present writing I feel that I shall live forever, and moreover, I feel that I want to live forever. Hangover. Why I should embark, in my present state, on a letter to you, I can't think. I really have been drinking far too much these last weeks, but I comfort myself with the thought that it's merely beer, as opposed to Jamaica rum and *fine champagne,* mixed. All that beer does to me is swell me up to hideous proportions; I'm rapidly getting a large corporation, and soon won't be able to see my feet. But to hell with it. I am so deliriously happy, most of the time, over nothing, over the fact of being able to breathe the daylight, of getting up in the morning, of eating, of sleeping. I hope that I haven't finally turned into a real manic depressive, and that this isn't the high state. I don't think so. Just a psychopathic personality with paranoid touches, as they say of people who cut other people up and mince them into the bath-tub.

　＊　＊　＊

Now, look, here's another poem, but first let me tell you what brought it about. It's really a terribly funny story. I was so mad last night, over the whole thing, that I was on the point of withdrawing my immortal lyrics from Scribner's in a huff. I wrote Wheelock such a funny letter that I cracked my side laughing over it, and haven't been able to think of it without roars ever since. I'm afraid I can't be as funny about it right this minute as I was yesterday. ＊ ＊ ＊

Such swine as there are in the world!

You and I aren't swine, although we may have our swinish moments. I hate a lie, O Christ, how I hate a lie. However. . . .

Looking for a moment at this new poem. Forgive me for doing so much looking at my own works, my dove, my coney, but, my God, I haven't written any poetry in so long that you must forgive me. I am becoming practically Jewish in my bounding egotism in this new phase, you see. And I'm coming to your works in a moment. So be patient.

The Lie

First met when I was young:
Within the sliding eye,
Upon the sidling tongue
I knew the lie.

Innocent, saw the look,
Dupe, heard the dreadful beat
When beautiful eye and mouth
Gave forth deceit.

Was truth bred in the bone,
Fast in the flesh, of that child,
And is it I alone
Whom shifts drive wild?

What curse, then, living truth,
Long upon me has lain,
That I should seek the whole
Sound word, in vain?

My whole life, with the lie
Has lived. At night it moved,
In daylight, with a cry,
It loved.

Inchworm, O you, O crude,
Horrible mouth, abate;
Move from me, long withstood,
Lest I must touch your state.[1]

The first stanza is admittedly lousy. There's something terribly wrong
with it; I don't know what. I thought it would be fun to say—Within
the sliding eye. Upon the sidling tongue,—but that's too much like
anagrams, I admit. It is rather a good trick though, now isn't it?

The second stanza is good, except I wish to God I could get away
from the word *beat*. The book will be sown with *beats*, one to a page,
and sometimes two. The third stanza begins to get too noble for anything, and that's bad, I suppose. As a matter of fact, I was a nervous,
frightened kind of brat, with no particular claim to truthful bones, but
I did hate to have my mother lie to me, but all kids do. Whom shifts
drive wild is nice; I like that. I looked in the thesaurus for a one sylla-

ble word meaning lie, and when I found *shift* I fell upon it like a mad thing. It's a superb word.

In the fourth stanza *whole* is right, but I wish I could think of something else. I'm terribly fond of *whole*, as well as of *beat*.

I mean to repeat *whole*, in the 5th. An effect. What do you think?

Now, about inchworm. There's nothing particularly loathsome about an inchworm, is there; it's the dry rather attractive type of worm, as I remember. *Lugworm* is the word at the back of my mind, of course; you remember the Yeats poem. What is the kind of worm that raises itself up and looks around, as distinguished from writhing forward all over? If that's an inchworm, then it's all right; that is a horrid kind of worm. The rest of the stanza I like: how it came out so well, I can't think.

I was shaking with rage when I wrote it.

Now for your *Graffiti*, and what a lovely word, to be sure. Where did you learn it? Is it a technical term, like *gloss*?

"Melody for the Virginals" is beyond words beautiful. Be pretty any more, after the long open a's, is an effect fit to wring the heart. O God, it *is* so fine, Rolfe. What in hell have you been doing, for the last ten years? They should lock you up in a room and make you write poetry, as they did to Alfieri, whoever the hell he was.[2] Edmund is always telling me about him. If I could write a poem like that I'd crown myself with bays. ("You go pretty far in that direction, anyhow," says you.) I shall crown you with bays the next time I see you. I'll meet you in the Library, and I'll filch some marble bays off Cato, or Spinoza, or whoever that is in the corridor, and crown you with them.

"Meditation for Sext" (and where in God's name did you get those beautiful musical terms. You always gave out, formerly, that you couldn't hear music. Maybe you can't; that's no crime; Yeats can't either). Me, with all my proud boasts of musical breadth and culture, I don't know what *sext* is.[3] Is it six voices, or an instrument with six strings; or is it a religious term, perhaps like *compline*. There's another lovely word. Can't you do something with *compline*? It's a time of day in a breviary, I believe. A mediaeval time of day, no doubt.

One word in the "Meditation" I am doubtful of, is *areas*. Auden, Spender, Lewis. Areas lie around railheads, under the shadow of kestrels. It's fitting and fine where it is, in the line, however.

I don't like *garish*. It's the right sound, but it always sounds like red paper roses to me.

And does rain have a brown stain? Where? It is more a slatey stain, when you see it, isn't it? You usually see it on stone. It changes the color of the stone to a deeper color.

I don't like quintessential certitude. Not at all. And then two adjectives in the next line. Be a love, and do something about this, to please old mummy Bogan.

O, but, Give us our daily darkness. O but. O but. Jesus lover of my soul.

Listen, where have you sent these? For God's sake, send them to Andy White, or Harriet. I know you would rather see them in *The Yale Review* or somewhere. Send them to *The Yale Review*. But don't snoot at *The New Yorker*. Those poems of Edmund's they printed were pretty good. And they might give you a spread, with decoration: They are fools if they don't. Look, tell me that I can send them to Andy, who is now in Maine. I'll write an accompanying letter that will take the hair right off his head. Let me. Do.

What a letter, to be sure. I'll send you the two poems for keepsy-weepsy in another one. This letter will be too fat as it is.

I don't know what to do about "Roman Fountain." It's so sort of footless, as it is. *Clear* would be better before *gouts*; I'll change it. I wanted to get *thick* in, because the point about the fountains of Rome is, that there's so much water in them. None of your piddling little streams. Big gushes as thick as your arm, simply leaping up and scattering around; making a lovely big strong noise; rushing up like whole rivers. Great big bronze gents with great big bronze cornucopias or shells, or something, on their shoulders, and from that, great, enormous thick jumping water. To hell with that poem. It's minor, all save the first stanza. It doesn't do it. It should be all fountain, and no Louise looking at it.

And I'll change it to considered sacrifice.[4] Of course. Just sluttish writing on my part. The whole thing is rather meek and soft sounding, I think. There should be an *axe* or a *xylophone* in it somewhere, to edge the sound.

God help the man who has to edit our letters.

Write me again, and come to town soon.

Yours,
Louise

[P.S.] Morton wrote me from Naples. The moon, the green and white goddess? The moon? He is *such* an ass, and yet so pathetic. I don't

admire him exactly, but there's something there that touches me.
Naples, I may add, moon or no moon, is a hovel.

L.

1. "The Lie" was never published.

2. "I read about the poet Alfieri in an Italian reader. You know: 'The story is told of the poet Alfieri (and then a lot of gerunds and gerundives and indirect discourse contrary to fact and verbs taking the dative) that, in order to have him produce at all, they had to lock him in. His brothers and sisters took the key away and hid it in the (some perfectly terrible noun beginning with *s* impure). This bothered Alfieri, so he wrote tanti belli sonnetti in order to get out again. . . .'" (To Roethke, November 6, 1935)

3. "Concerning my 'musical terms,' I grew up in a family of singers: my mother and my brother were constantly 'bursting into song.' And I began to study the piano at seven. —You will remember, I'm sure, in dealing with my work, that you are dealing with emotion under high pressure—so that *symbols* are its only release." (To Sister M. Angela, July 5, 1969)

4. In "Baroque Comment."

July 6, 1935

Dear Rolfe:

This will be shorter and less manic, because it is horribly hot, and because I must harbor my strength to write a long and polished screed to Morton, tomorrow. I have a hard time thinking up things to say to him, because I never want to tell him all, and because what I do tell him is often held over me like a sword when he sees signs of my spiritual discipline, God save the mark, slipping.

E. Wilson has sent back nothing, evidently, on post cards from the Soviet U., but veiled enthusiasm over the fact that the boys are reading Pushkin and going to see Chekhov's plays. * * * Well, that's fine. I have always thought that the pure artist had his place, and should stick right in it, being as productive as possible and as pure as hell, whatever was going on outside. And that place doesn't have to be an ivory tower. But it shouldn't be right in the middle of a boiler-works or a Red Square, or a propagandist's office, either, no matter what Eda Lou Walton [1] has to say about dead boughs. Of course pre-revolutionary art is the hardest to keep pure and free. But a great effort should be made in that direction. In spite of all you had to say last winter on the subject of the elegiac quality of lyric poetry, it should be written all the time, right now. For after the revolution there will be a reversal, back to more sensitive and delicate values, and when some poet-revolutionary fellow, who has poetic energy, suddenly gets into a creative fit after discovering that he loves his mother or wants to kill his wife or somebody's husband, or even himself, or even after looking at the post-revolutionary evening air, it would be hell if the only person's works left whose style he could imitate would be Granville Hicks or Horace Gregory or Mike Gold or Eda Lou Walton. I believe the great human change into a new world should be expressed, but I also believe that when the Soviet arbiters say that Hamlet is foolish, they are talking nonsense, and destructive nonsense at that. And I hope the human race will never be purged of those types, who, like Shakespeare, are victims all their mature life of the most dreadful form of morbid jealousy, or of unconscious homosexuals like Hopkins and Housman, or of perfectly batty people, who drive themselves into extreme fits over the fact that the landlady looked at them sideways, like Beethoven. God keep me from a world, even without poverty and human degradation, in which there were no delicate sensibilities that could produce a remark like *Margaret, are you grieving*; or *An expense of spirit in a waste of shame*; that could not feel horror over mutability and an excess of joy over the facts of perfectly physical passion, or pity for the maladjusted or horror over the senseless cruel. A world in which everyone rides in pink subways and does physical jerks and marches round and round in formation and flies in gyroscopes from one senseless and blatant kind of mass-gymkhana to another. No. The channels must be kept open. The post- must feed from the pre-. By the way, do you realize that Auden got two of his best phrases from Katherine Mansfield's letters: *a change of heart* and *the old gang*. There you are. If we do nothing else, we may give a phrase to the post-. That's enough.

You may get out of this last par. a criticism of your par. which begins: "If we agree that 'a poet's value is the function of two independent variables' . . ." I don't think, to go on into the matter a little farther, that your question "Is not the agony of the human spirit adequate matter for genius to function on?" has enough effect, seeing as how you don't answer it, but slide off into *reductio ad absurdum* of the Princess and the pea, and then hop to the S.U.'s idea of Hamlet. There were poets who went out into battle and didn't always fall. And the value that we must attach to them now, and in the future, is, and must be, pretty much the value that the human race has always given to them. As Edmund has found out: Chekhov's plays sound just as swell to post-rev. audiences as they did to pre-rev. audiences. Also Pushkin. And the Persian color looks just as beautiful on the panel, even if it depicts nothing more useful than a houri surrounded by decanters, and seated on cushions, giving herself a quick drink. And if you do hear music, you can't say that Mozart will ever go out, or that Beethoven's last quartets will ever need other values pinned onto them but their very own. No, and let the guys with equal poetic power or whatnot and more usefulness in changing the world be damned glad that they can excel in the last job, since in the first they can never exceed what has already been done in all lines. I don't think that many things can ever be done any better. Italian poetry and piano variations, for example (Dante and Mozart). And my God, what about Bach?

* * * I am going to Boston early in August, and to Maine thereafter, to see the Whites. * * * So do let's have the bay-crowning before that. Come on, Rolfe, I shan't eat you. And we used to look so nice together in the street, if you remember. I have a very pretty great big hat.

To take one last look at Hopkins' early Communism: all sorts of gentle and sensitive people held the same views, after they had gotten a good look at the industrially bred Victorian slums. Ruskin, for example. Did you ever read Ruskin's late tracts on the subject? All sorts of endowed Victorians felt terrible about everything, and in America we have hard words from Emerson and Thoreau. The reason I get so mad at the comrades is that they always sound as though they had discovered everything yesterday; just after the slump. The iniquity had been going on for a long time before their fathers were born. When I was a child, in Ballardvale [Massachusetts], and heard about the Lawrence strike, even I knew that the system was iniquitous. The only point I can make is that there seemed to be nothing I could do about it, and, since the days of barricades have gone out, there still seems to be nothing. So, although you tell Edmund that my ideas of social justice are depraved, I tell you that I want a little peace, a little troubled peace, in which to finish out the time allotted to me in life as a human being. So you'd have me an Eda Lou Walton, huh? Or a Comradess Leane Zugsmith! Faugh! (Always a good word, Faugh, I always think.)
* * *

Do let me see you soon.

Louise

1. Eda Lou Walton, a teacher, critic and political activist, was one of the poets in Ruth Benedict's circle of friends. Humphries had first met her in San Francisco,

where, with Genevieve Taggard, they had attended poetry workshops in the early twenties.

"[According to Edmund Wilson] art and poesy seem to be flourishing in the United Soviet Socialist Republic; theaters are jammed to the doors, and they are celebrating the 74th anniversary of Chekhov's birth with some fervor. All that makes me feel much better, after having been called a dead leaf on a dead branch by Eda Lou Walton." (To Humphries, June 28, 1935)

/ *to Morton D. Zabel* /

82 Washington Place
August 2, 1935

Dear Morton:

I feel the reproaches. Directly after your sailing, a month and a half of mixed pleasant and disagreeable events began. Many of the events I cannot now recount to you; it would be hard to put them down, unless I suddenly managed to become equipped with some of H. James' subtlety and wind. People fell out of the sky; and such people! Very large people, some of them endowed with strength, erratic natures, wit, humor, a pronounced taste for liquor and late hours, as well as with real talents of one sort or another. Young, strong people. Young strong admiring people, who, when I, in my strong-minded way, tried to stem their tide, would turn to me with some disarming remark as "Louise, you're a great minor poet and I'm a bastard, but kiss me." One of these strange creatures got a flat A under I. A. Richards at Harvard.

Don't be shocked, Morton. I have it all under control. I know all about the disrupting influence of such things, and I hope you, as my biographer, will pass over this period in silence. Although there's no real reason why you should. I wrote poetry during it. If it weren't so frightfully hot today, I'd send you two of same: "Roman Fountain" and "Baroque Comment." These are the best of the lot; there were perhaps five others. —Now I am extremely tired. The weather has been frightful, and the wear and tear of the city's noises practically unbearable. Then just lately I have had to fend off the, I must say tempting, offers of material help from another sudden admirer: cottages in the country, motor-trips to Jones Beach, the use of a really good piano and, of course, the delights implicit in his own person. One would think that I was too old for all this. A second blooming, and the bough can hardly bear it.

* * *

Ever,
Louise

/ to Theodore Roethke /

82 Washington Place
August 23, 1935

Dear Ted:

* * *

I sold *Scribner's* a poem, one you haven't seen and won't see for a while, and they gave me $10 for it,[1] which I immediately took out in books from their bookstore, although, I must say, $10 doesn't buy many books. I got the [R. P.] Blackmur compilation of the James prefaces, thinking that I might while away my time among the blackberry bushes with them. Did you ever hear Wells' remark that a James novel was like a cathedral, all soft lights and subtle splendor, and traceries and old music, on the altar of which, once you got to it, was displayed a piece of string, an eggshell, or a dead kitten. . . . Well, I bought the James and Jean Cocteau's reminiscences and the new Paul Morand and a volume of Rilke's letters, and then I thought of you, my feathered friend, and I bought you [Rilke's] *Letters to a Young Poet,* and if you read it, you should get something from it. And in this letter I am enclosing two Rilke poems, to illustrate a point I shall shortly make.

The difficulty with you now, as I see it, is that you are afraid to suffer, or to feel in any way, and that is what you'll have to get over, lamb pie, before you can toss off the masterpieces. And you will have to *look* at things until you don't know whether you are they or they are you. The lack of fundamental brain-work, so apparent in most lyrics, is not apparent in yours; you have a hell of a good mind, and real intelligence; real, natural, rich, full (in the best sense) intelligence. Your mind isn't a piece of ticker tape, going from left to right, like many minds, and it isn't full of gulfs and blank spots and arid areas. But it *is,* half the time, hiding from itself and its agonies, and until you let it do more than peek out, from time to time, you aren't going to get much done. "To My Sister" is a swell poem, because, as I said, you are right in it, mad as hell, and agonized as hell, and proud as hell. . . .

Now in these Rilke poems (said she, ascending the podium) you get two things. You get a terrific patience and power of *looking,* in "The Blue Hortensia" one, and in the other [2] you get a magnificent single poetic concept carried through with perfect ease, because it is thoroughly informed by passion, in the first place. In the latter poem Rilke is terribly upset about his inability to get away from it all—you know that without my telling you, but let me maunder on. So he starts to write a poem, and he turns the lack of freedom into a perfectly frightful metaphor: he is unable to see any distance, any horizon (lovely word!), and he is so unable to see any that he feels himself *inside* a mountain, like a vein of ore. Everything is nearness, and all the nearness stone. Magnificent. And then what happens? Well, he can't stand it, so he turns to someone for help, and he drags the person into the metaphor. *I* am not adept at pain, he says, but if *you* are, make yourself heavy (isn't that *schwer* wonderful?) and break in, so that your whole hand may fall upon me and I on you with my whole cry. . . . Now, a poem like that cannot be written by technique alone. It is carved out of agony, just as a statue is carved out of marble. And you must let yourself suffer, once in a while, lovey, in order that you may do same. Stay sober for a week. Anyone capable of writing "The veil long violated by Caresses of the hand and eye," plus the "To My Sister" lyric, *might* come to the point of tearing off a lyric cry that would be, as someone I once knew used to say, heart-rendering. . . .[3]

"The Blue Hortensia" plumbs blue hortensia to their depths. Here all sorts of comparisons are brought in, to aid the plumbing process. The color of the flowers is the color of old writing paper, faded into yellow and violet and gray, and it is like a child's many-times-washed apron— and by the time the reader gets to that, he is in a state of collapse, for Rilke has re-created the color in such a moving way that it's as though something new had been created in the universe. You see all that, I'm sure. Now, my duck, go and look at some of the flora, or even fauna of the electrical area, and do likewise.

    * * *

I'd like to go off with you either to 1) Venice or 2) Salzburg, or 3) a fold in the hills, for one week. After that period one or the other of us would come back on his or her shield, I have no doubt.

    * * *

Now start in sobering and suffering, my fine boy-o.

Louise

1. LB's *Scribner's* poem was "Evening-Star," published in October.

2. Untitled, this poem stands first in Rilke's *Das Buch von der Armut und vom Tode* (1903). The German *Hortensie* might be more usefully translated as "hydrangeas."

3. Like most of the Roethke poems mentioned in these letters up to 1941, "To My Sister" was, after periodical publication, reprinted in *Open House*. "It is good," LB wrote to him in an undated letter, "because it is *felt* first, outside of literature. Some of your things have been put into literature at once, so that the reverberation is lacking. —Beware of poems leaning on the repeated imperative for their main effect, however. There's been far too much of the O-do-(don't)-such-and-such note in the lyric, of late years."

"The veil long violated . . ." comes from "Epidermal Macabre."

82 Washington Place
September 4, 1935

Dear Ted:

A fine pair we turned out to be. —I nearly died last week from a touch of ptomaine; that is, I had a slow temp. of 101 or so for two days, and then I got up and started to run around town and caved in again. And then Raymond sent me a copy of his remarkable novel [*Chance Has a Whip*], in which a sort of deBoganized Bogan goes through some paces I once went through, in the full flush of my youth and pride, and that made me very mad, and I sent the book back, and Raymond got mad, and sent it back, and then we began a row through the mails.[1] My letters were masterpieces of invective, I will admit, and I hope they find a place in my collected works. (Two volumes of poems and eighteen volumes of invective.) —And then, worn out by these happenings, and a mere shadow of myself, I went out to Léonie Adams and Bill Troy's expecting some sunshine, peace and a little Irish whiskey, and what I got was 2 martinis and a liqueur after one meal. —I have stopped drinking hard liquor, as a matter of fact, because an extremely difficult time, full of decisions, is ahead of me. I always stop drinking when I have to fight or take trains in foreign countries. If I'm to be left at the junction, in either case, I want to have some speech and hauteur left, in order to pull it off, and I have neither, in a long hangover.

Now, darling, you left me a great opening for a great inspirational letter, and I am not going to take it, in the way you expect, perhaps. But let me say one or two things. In the first place, the loss of face is the worst thing that can happen to anyone, man or woman. I know, because I have lost mine, not once, but many times. And believe me, the only way to get it back is to put your back against the wall and fight for it. You can't brood or sulk or smash around in a drunken frenzy. Smashing around gives the world's insects and worms the upper hand, and if you smash yourself dead, they won't give a damn; it won't impress them in the least; they'll get up every morning and gargle with Listerine, just as though you never had been. —I, too, have been imprisoned by a family, who held out the bait of a nice hot cup of tea and a nice clean bed, and no questions asked, until the mould starts in effacing the last noble lineaments of the soul. (That's wonderful, isn't it?) And let me tell you right now, the only way to get away is to get away: pack up and go. Anywhere. I had a child, from the age of 20, remember that, to hold me back, but I got up and went just the same, and I was, God help us, a woman. I took the first job that came along. And there was a depression on, as there is now, not quite so bad, but still pretty poor, and I lived on 18 bucks a week and spent a winter in a thin suit and a muffler. But I was free. And when, this last time, I couldn't free myself by my own will, because my will was suffering from a disease peculiar to it, I went to the mad-house for six months, under my own steam, mind you, for no one sent me there, and I got free. —When one isn't free, one is a *thing*, the *thing* of others, and the only point, in this rotten world, is to be your own, to hold the scepter and mitre over yourself, in the immortal words of Dante.

I don't know what to say about the drinking. If you didn't have such a good, happy and sensitive mind, I'd say, go on and drink, if you want to. Lots of excellent people have drunk and drunk and produced. But drinking seems to have you down, at the moment, and to hell with anything that gets a person of your potentialities down. If, as someone once said, Kenneth Burke is one of those providential characters put into the world to show how the human mind should not be used, you may well be a person put into t. w. to show how it should. I've already written to Malcolm, telling him he's a damned fool if he doesn't give you some poetry to review. And what would you do if you got it? Throw it against the wall, most likely, and go back to your pie, rye and sauerbraten mit nudeln, washed down with a little beer and ice-cream. I don't know, Ted. I don't indeed. You're 26 and should know your own mind. But believe me, I saw my brother, from the age of 26 to 33, when death providentially took him, and he stayed at home and didn't put up a fight, except toward the last, when he used to knock down doors and smash windows with chairs, and be brought home, beaten to a pulp, and I tell you, anything in God's world is better than that. . . .

* * * You are thoughtless and unhappy and spoiled, and I wish I had $10,000. Perhaps I could shake you out of it, on that sum. You could shake yourself out of it, for much less. And, take the word of one who has lain on the icy floor of the ninth circle of hell, without speech and will and hope, it's the self that must do it. You, Ted Roethke, for Ted Roethke. I, Louise Bogan, for Louise Bogan.

Forgive me if I sound melodramatic, my pickled pear. I am fond of you, and I think there are so few of our kind that you should stay in the ranks.

Ever,
Louise

1. Holden's novel, which provides a worshipful portrait of LB, tells of Hendrick Fillmore, a childish but outwardly forceful businessman, who leaves his wife and

children for the boss's daughter, the "beautiful and mysterious" Leda Putnam. Despite—or because of—her prior history of promiscuity, she is warm, supportive and emotionally generous. Through her love, and the healthy introspection it generates in him, the hero—who bears strong biographical resemblances to Holden himself—comes to understand the nature of the forces in American society that entrap man's spirit.

The charge of deBoganization is a real one. Having virtually no ear for dialogue, Holden created a nearly inarticulate character who, when she does speak, is given to murmuring, "Oh darling, oh Rick!" Additionally, he turned the poet into a woman whose only desire was to fulfill the hero's needs (". . . at once hull, anchor, sail, ocean and wind to the vessel of his being"). But except that she was dead on the page—not, after all, the author's intention—and for the fictionalizing of some actual events, it is hard for the outsider to see what in this continuously adoring portrait could have brought LB to invective. For despite the novel's inadequacies, it is about a man who, freed by love to discover himself, pays homage to the source and mainstay of that freedom.

/ *to Rolfe Humphries* /

September 5, 1935

Dear Rolfe:

I think it undialectical and childish of you to be affected by the rain. Undialectical, because if we have one sort of weather, it stands to reason that we have to have another kind, and a good thing, too. Childish, because the mature soul rather enjoys the rain: clouded skies let you alone, and you don't have all that play and inter-play of nerve-wracking light and shadow to cope with. I admit that everything is rather damp in my house at the moment, particularly as I seized upon yesterday or the day before to do a little laundry, and now I am surrounded by the lank form of towels that will not dry. Just a foretaste of my life in a cold-water flat, and I must recognize it and use it (I don't know what those *its* refer to, exactly) as such. Old philosophic Bogan, the weather sage.

But really, one thing I decided, after my sojourn in the mad-house, was that I should never let the weather get me down. I used to be at the mercy of clouds no bigger than a man's hand, and in that hour of twilight, when animals howl, I used to feel that all hell was rising up to oppress me, and frequently, I would weep. No more. I am serene from dawn to dark, and even the horrid watches of the night afford me no qualms. Grown-up. Mature.

Because mankind has coped pretty well with the weather. Whatever its faults, you must give it that credit. It *has* coped with the weather. Look at caves and hurricane cellars and oil-burners and air-conditioning. . . .

After this meteorological treatise, there seems little more to say. I am gathering together my little fugitive poemsie-woemsies of the last five or six years, and I want your help in arranging them, sooner or later. I may have to get the batch off to Scribner's before you are back, because I want to borrow 100 dollars from them, in order to get Maidie into an institution of the higher learning. Get an advance, I should say. I really think it's a sin to take money for a suppositious book of mine: but there *are* twenty poems, and I only need ten more, and I have a year to write them in, and I will have to *write* them, as opposed to waiting until they waft down to me from heaven on the wings of the Enclitic, or what do they call the Holy Ghost?

* * * I am reading the George Sand-Flaubert letters, and they are very rewarding. I am copying out the choice bits and will relay them to you. Flaubert was so sour and she was so full of love-love-love, that they make a fine pair. I admire her tremendously; she was not an artist, but she was a big woman, and there have been few enough of those in the world. She went through a life that would have killed ten men, and at the end, at seventy, she was wonderful: full of gumption and wisdom and good sense, and she loved children and the oppressed and fruit and flowers and wine and marionette plays and she worked like a tiger. I am going to put myself in training, these next ten years, to have such an old age, if I have an old age at all.

Flaubert said that most novels are written by disguised bourgeois, as distinguished from artists, and I think this very good. After the Commune, he said that what he feared was that the proletariat would rise into the stuffiness and the stupidity of the bourgeoisie, and there's something in that, too. I don't know just what, but I feel, as an artist, that there's something in it.

* * *

Louise

/ *to Theodore Roethke* /

September 9, 1935

Dear Ted:

Well, that's something like it! It's as good a piece as you have done to date, and it sounds like you, and it sounds like a poem, the two ultimate tests. And it sounds felt, not written. Great, lovey. Splendid. Now I'll go for the last few lines, and you must realize that Rolfe and I do this sort of thing all the time with each other's works, and mutual criticism often results in mutual improvement, so don't think I'm treating you like a novice, for I'm not. To illustrate R.'s methods with me, I will quote you an eight line and about fourteen syllable lyric, torn off by me last month. In its first form, it had a lamp that had to be lit in it, and the 2nd line was different, *undsw*. Well, Rolfe attacked it, one evening when he was here, and for a week we wrote and re-wrote it, knowing all the time that it was only an eight line, fourteen syllable poem, not much damn good in any case. Variant readings ran through the mail like wild, and after all this fuss, I put it in a drawer and forgot about it. But you see that such things can happen, and not be tampering. . . .

> *Lines Written on Coming To*
> *Late in the Afternoon*
>
> My God, Louise
> Here it is night!
> Snap on the light
> And write out plain
>
> Again with labor,
> Written as heard,—
> Set the fit word
> To its fit neighbor.[1]

Now, to tackle your last lines:

> In language fit and pure
> I stop the lying mouth

is perfect, really fine. But I don't like *lyric cry*: it's a cliché, as old Malcolm would say. And it seems to me what you need in the last line is a synonym for *open* or *apparent,* as opposed to the tongueless idea. A fine sounding word meaning *apparent* would, to my mind, bring the intensity of the last stanza to a practically unbearable point of crisis, and that, my dear, is as you know, the great triumph of the short lyric: that it can be brought up, at the end, into a sound that tears the heart in twain. Of course, you could have it, as you suggested: This is my (something) cry, and then, My rage, my agony. That is what you were working toward, I think. Or you could delete the colon after mouth, and say I stop the lying mouth, *With* something or other, something or other. I like the colon after that swell line, however. I leave the job of writing the penultimate line to you—nice of me, isn't it—and I go back to a word meaning *apparent* that could be clapped in front of *agony,* to make the last line. And here are all the words the thesaurus gives: conspicuous, manifest, definite, explicit, apparent, notable, notorious, starkstaring, literal, plainspoken, producible, and above board. (I don't *really* think that above board would do, but some of the others might!) Now go ahead, my dove. It's your poem, after all.[2]

I expect to be evicted tomorrow, and tonight little Morton Zabel is coming to see me. He's back from Europe: Naples, Rimini, Ferrara, Venice, Vienna, Paris, Cambridge and Greatham, near Pulborough, Sussex. He has been sending me Alinari prints and manuscript books bound in Florentine paper and inscribed copies of books by people I admire, so I think I must not chaff him too lightly on the subject of St. Thomas Aquinas and the Jesuit order in general. He is a pathetic fellow in many ways, the real don type, but he has a heart of gold, and I have certainly treated him like a dog, all these years. He has a horrible habit of creeping up my arm, that unnerves me. Well, I'll have some dinner and hear about the great and the shades of the great. If he has any money left for dinner, after that pilgrimage with the dollar at 57 cents.

* * *

I'd like to see your beautiful teeth again. And a very good cure for a cold is to go to bed with a bottle of rum. This thought has crossed your mind, I'm sure.

It *is* a good poem, my dear. Immaculate.

> With a buss and a wave of the hand,
> Louise

Sept. 10—Coincidentally with breakfast

Your two Sunday letters came this morning, and you seem rather low, but you're not as low as you think. You're bored, that's what's your trouble. You should be somewhere where there's a really good library, wherein you could roil and read. The N.Y.P.L. is the only thing that keeps me in this fearsome town. I go there and wall myself in with everything I can think of; and when I think of something else that's pertinent to the matter in hand, I look it up, and there it is, by God, in three languages!

Not that I recommend a winter in New York for you. You'd soon be sucking up mixed drinks at some salon, and the fairies would be after you. You don't have to fear women in N.Y. It's the men who get you down. . . .

Darling, you're in a spot, and I can't see what you can do but grin and bear it. Marry your girl, and that will do you a lot of good for a time. —If I had some money I would pick up today and go to the middle of the Pennsylvania grain country—there used to be a town called Rowlett with a frame hotel and piles of fried cakes and fried chicken and grain in sheaves all over the rolling countryside—and meet you there, and we would laugh, fit to kill, for a week. But I have no money. And after a week we'd hate each other, so it's just as well that this idea can't work out.—

* * *

O sweet, the picture of you in bed, with the V.O., worrying about Ellen Glasgow! Ellen Glasgow is a lending-library set-up. The G. Am. public likes pompous spinsters to tell them what life is really like. —And you're right: what good *are* novelists? No good unless they're half poets, like Joyce, or half-nuts, like Dostoevski or sharp as hell like Jane Austen—(a spinster, I grant, poor dear, but a good spinster).

1. Unpublished.

2. The Roethke lines quoted are from the last stanza of the title poem of *Open House*. His published solution reads, ". . . In language strict and pure. / I stop the lying mouth: / Rage warps my clearest cry / To witless agony."

> Hotel Albert
> University Place, Tenth Street
> New York
> September 23, 1935

Dear Ted:

* * * Maidie and I are now inhabiting a little nest which, as far as the light filtering into it is concerned, closely resembles a coal-mine. —The eviction went off very nicely considering the inexperience of the evictees. I tried to fight with the sheriff, but decided it wasn't such a good idea, after all. It was exactly like Death or Inexorable Fate, or something of that kind, knocking at the door and saying "Allo!" You can't kick sheriffs or the Sable Herald in the shins and get away with it. . . .

I know just how you feel about Auden cum Shakespeare. I've felt that way myself. But if one is minor, one is minor: being good AND minor is something.

I think I have a new apt. but my fingers are crossed. You could never do your great bounding-from-wall-to-wall act on the stairs. They're too narrow: You'd catapult down into the basement and be found a husk of your former self (wrecking the entire house in transit, no doubt).

> In haste, but with affection,
> Louise

1935

October 1, 1935

Dear Rolfe:

I was much surprised and pleased to see my fugitive verses, long hidden in your bureau drawer. I think it's a shame I didn't do more rhymed reviews, but [Raymond] sort of had a sinecure on that, in those days, and he was so fluent and clever at it that I thought I was just a runner up and so stood back and watched. First chop or nothing, that's my unfortunate tendency.

The vaudeville one is just a curiosity now, since there isn't any vaudeville any more, not the shabby kind that we knew as children, which is the kind described in the poem. No child ever sits with its heart wrung because the Jap balancing on the picket fence is so obviously old and tired, or because the soubrette has asthma and varicose veins and fallen chops, or because the monologist is so obviously dead drunk. Radio and the talking pictures have winnowed out the totterers, and now everything is slick and smooth and shouting and full of revolving floors and glass trees and superb tap dancers and slick sopranos. No. I don't see where that poem could go, now.

I'm feeling wonderfully peaceful and rested, now that the roof has finally caved in, and if this typewriter behaves for a week or so, I intend to turn out work. *The Dog Beneath the Skin; or, Where is Francis?* is a wow. Of course all that knocking down of the straw men of the British gentility will get tiresome, if Auden sticks to it for the next fifty years, but he does write superbly, there's not the slightest doubt of that. Some of the choruses in this are unbeatable, and put against Eliot's present-day liturgy, they shine and resound. The comedy is very good, really Gilbertian, in spots, and he has learned a lot from Gilbert and from *Sweeney Agonistes* and even from Swift, or maybe he doesn't realize how much his line of stupid middle-class talk sounds like *Advice to Servants* and *Polite Conversation*. I must read those again. The long poetry review is due Oct. 28, and *The Dog*, for the *N. R.*, this week. I've sold most of the books to be included in the review; they went last summer, this summer, when I felt the need to eat. I had to sell the Yeats *Collected Plays*, even, and that made me sore, because the two Greek translations are included and one of them is unobtainable elsewhere. Ah well, there's nothing like eating, after all. . . .

I'm not mad at Roethke; one of his letters took a long time to arrive, and he may never have received my answer, sent to Ann Arbor. Thank God he's working, and I hope the reviews come out well. The *N. R.*

called me up for his address. Malcolm seems very open to suggestion, these days. I can't imagine how he allowed himself to send me the Auden. In the old days it would have gone to Allen Tate, or Horace Gregory, and Horace would have begun his review, "I think that this is a very interesting play . . ." and Allen would have said, "In fusing the basis of the intellect out of the microscopic dualisms concurrent in the derivative dichotomies so uselessly prevalent, and notwithstanding the disuse fallen upon the gentility, destroyed by General Bragg. . . ."
* * *

I'm reading like wild, and have just finished *Some Makers of the Modern Spirit*, edited by J. Macmurray, and containing pieces on all the main thinkers and doers (in the best sense) since Aquinas, so now I know all about Bentham and Newton and Rousseau and Goethe and Nietzsche and Marx. Everything. * * * And I've had a sort of mild illumination about how important money is, since I saw the sheriff standing on my floor, and saw the furniture whisked out the door onto the side-walk. I wanted to do nothing and see what would happen, but after they got about ten pieces out I ran for a moving van. * * * Yes; I understand now that all the spirited uppishness in the world wouldn't have stopped the Greenwood Cemetery (that was my landlord, I discovered, and a grisly one, too) from throwing me into the gutter, and I could have sat and quoted middle-class gush about the necessity for gracious living to them, and that would have been a laugh. I'm sorry I didn't kick the sheriff in the shins: I did stand up to him and tell him to get the hell out, and that was a good one. I really should have seen if he'd have drawn on me. . . .

I think the women's magazines ought to be liquidated first. And all this business about Alice Adams having nice things if she could have gotten ahold of Macy's. On What?

Well, my friend, I could ramble on for hours! Try and get to be an editor of the *New Masses* and I'll send you some work. Not that I think you're any more a man of action than the rest of them. But you have got some humor and some sense. I really don't think you're quite as much a Presbyterian in disguise as the rest.

I'll be in the Lib. on Sat. A.M., and call me when you can. I'll send the manuscript poems back to you. You never have anything happen to you, in the way of fires in the hold or moth and rust. . . .

Louise

1935

/ *to Theodore Roethke* /

Hotel Albert
October 3, 1935

Dear Ted:

* * * This will be brief. I want you to look up my poem in the October *Scribner's*; it is incomplete as it stands in print, since someone, perhaps because of the exigencies of space, left out an entire line. The second stanza, as it came from my pen, read:

> Light, pure and round, without heat or shadow,
> Big in the cirrus sky at evening,
> Accompany what we do.[1]

The *cirrus* is important, because it echoes the *us*-es, or how do you make a plural of *us,* my sweet Master of Arts? I was very much touched when I saw this in print. Wheelock, as I wrote you, ravished it away from me, that night when we two plumbed the depths of German food and drink. I thought it a little album piece, and was keeping it in my bottom bureau drawer, for my literary executors to find, after my death. But I must say that it looks extraordinarily pure and defined as compared to the overstuffed effusions of Bernice Lesbia Kenyon (she's deleted the Lesbia, of late years: you should see her: she closely resembles a Swedish cook and she wears false furs (meow, meow) in profusion), and even of old False Face Jeffers. What an ass that man is! Him and his Pacific Ocean!

* * * I got $7.50 for my great "Baroque Comment" poem, and I spent it on soap (I love soap) and a new fountain-pen and a bottle of very poor whiskey, and then I had $2.50 left over and I thought I might buy some highly expensive comestibles with that, but my deeper nature arose, and I called up Terence Holliday, who imports all the new English editions, and I asked him how much the Auden-Garrett anthology, *The Poet's Tongue,* was, and it was $2.40, so I rushed up to the highly refined Holliday Bookshop (he can't come it over me, for we worked in Brentano's together, just about the time you were getting that lovely set of second teeth), and I bought the damned thing, and it's marvelous: alphabetically arranged [by first lines] so that "Casey Jones" comes right before "Song for St. Cecilia's Day" practically, and it has nursery rhymes, and the wonderful nightmare song from *Iolanthe,* and God knows what else. I shall send it to you, if you send me a written certificate, in your fine Brandenburger hand, that you'll send it back, and not will it to your bastards. I'll send you *The Dog,* too, under the same conditions. I can't trust anything with a man after whom husbands (and a new lot of husbands, God help us) go gunning. . . .[2]

It's a damned shame, since the number of my autumns are now numbered, that I can't laugh through this one with you, for you are the best laugher I know . . . the teeth and the mind combined have something to do with this. I have such an insane delight in beautiful teeth; the major disasters of my life have been based on them. Me and Poe. . . .

Rolfe dug up two poems I wrote years ago, from my letters, sent to him, and I am trying to sell them to *The New Yorker*.[3] One of them is really very good. I don't know when I wrote it: it's amazing, coming upon such a poem.

The weather is beyond words beautiful: the weather of heaven will be bright autumn, I always think. I hope to see you there, dear Theodore. I expect never to see you again on this horrid globe,[4] since I am rapidly falling into all the sins of the middle-aged, which include acedia and a cold and trumpery disaffection for feeling.

Pick the wives whose husbands' hands would tremble on the trigger, my fine one!

> Yours etc.,
> Louise

1. The lines from "Evening-Star" were, when collected in *The Sleeping Fury*, adjusted slightly: instead of "big" the line began "held."
2. When Roethke called her on this, she replied: "No particular husbands. And you were the one who told me about the legend. *I* never thought you a sexual athlete. No indeed. Just a boy who was eight years old at the date of my first marriage. . . ." (October 9, 1935)
3. The poems found in her letters to Humphries were "To My Brother" and "Hidden," both of which the magazine bought. "Hidden" was never collected.
4. LB was at this moment aged thirty-eight, and in perfect health.

/ *to Morton D. Zabel* /

> Hotel Albert
> New York City
> October 7, 1935

Dear Morton:

I have been very much at peace, since the roof fell in; in fact, I haven't felt so peaceful in my life as now. Being evicted isn't really a tragedy, you know, if you are still youngish, and can scrape some money together, and have your work and a few friends. It's only tragic to the old, who have no money at all, and have to go to the work-house. Yes; the entire lack of money makes it tragic. The entire lack of money makes anything tragic, don't you think? It's damned difficult to go on graciously living, or living graciously, faced with an entire lack of money.

I don't know why you think I am going to sit down and hope I shall be happy when I am seventy. I am happy now—happy for the first time in my life. At peace for the first time. I thought you gathered that when you were here. I'm just going to try to keep that way, that is all. I know it takes work. I worked and fought for thirty-seven years, to gain serenity at thirty-eight. Now I have it. And it's not dependent upon the whim of any fallible human creature, or upon economic security or upon the weather. I don't know where it comes from. Jung states that such serenity is always a miracle, and I think the saints said that, too. Though there are certain ways, and a certain road that may bring it about, when it comes, it is always a miracle. I am so glad that the therapists of my maturity and the saints of my childhood agree on one score.

* * *

The greatly whooped up *Europa,* by Robert Briffault, gives me a pain, I must say. The man is a humorless and tiresomely egoistic prig; and his stories about the libidinous and concupiscent pre-War aristocracy smell just as badly when he writes them down as when some tired old creature tells them over the last round of highballs in some painfully modern Victorian parlors, uptown. They smell badly because they are told without an ounce of sensibility or pity, and therefore, of course, without an ounce of understanding. I took the bad taste out of my mouth, this morning, by re-reading the Blunden preface to Wilfred Owen's *Poems,* and the poems themselves. There was a real sensibility for you, and such a person is the only real realist, because he *feels* the horror, instead of merely recording it in a knowing and anthropological way. I suddenly knew, this morning, that such sensibility is so ennobling that, were it to come into contact with the group, it would ennoble even the Communist Party of America, and I knew, too, that until such a person, or such persons, became Communists, that the Revolution, if any, would be worthless and bleak slaughter, only. Perhaps Lenin was such a man. Everyone says he was; the Christ-mantle has descended on him so swiftly that we will never know. But certainly Wilfred Owen was a great poet, in all senses, and he might have been a great leader as well. I very nearly wept over him, and I shall read no more Briffault. Those harsh, certain, beak-faced egoists unnerve me. If they become the Revolution, God help us all!

* * *

Ever with affection,
Louise

/ *to Theodore Roethke* /

October 16, 1935

Dear Ted:

The *N. R.* piece is finished and sent in, but somehow it's all wrong, and it fell into Otis Ferguson's hands, because Malcolm has appendicitis, and I lay awake half of last night trying to figure out what was wrong with it, and I know I must get hold of it and tear it apart again, so I called up this morning and asked for it back and it will come back and I will tear it apart and do it over.

(That's what happens to one's lit. style when one reads Mabel Dodge Luhan.) I've just finished her *European Experiences.* My God, the money she had, and how she threw it around, and the people who let themselves know [?] her because she had money! A marvelous villa and all the ease and freedom in the world, and a rather vulgar, dumb woman at the center, dealing it out. Importing Swamis and whooping up a ghost in the bed rooms and sleeping with her son's tutors (although nothing *happened,* according to her) and really hating the only real people who came near her. It's a grand book, in a way, because she HAS got guts and power and a feeling for life. But what *I* could have done with the same chances! Or what I could do now. I was pretty much in stupor over a long period of years.

But I really wouldn't want to do that *salon* thing, even given money. I hate people too much, I can't stand them near me, any more; they give off an actual stench, if there's more than one or two of them in a close room. I run out into the air. The human scent is rather like old meat, I find. I never used to notice it before. . . .

Old morbid Bogan!

Poor pet, I do feel for you in your isolated state. What you need is a nice strong energetic wife, with some money, and a few brats that you could teach to repeat bawdy Elizabethan snatches for you. That's really the truth! You should marry, right away, a good *strong* managing girl. Like Helen Spencer, in strength! Now what about the girl in Ellston?

Then you'd never have to run out at night for beer: she'd feed it to you: a spigot beside your bed, and platters of *kalter aufschnitt* and bread and butter and whole cheeses. Now think about this.

My pal Edmund W. returned from Russia last night and ran around town frantically trying to find me. He traced me here this afternoon: came in and had a long talk, or rather, delivered a long soliloquy—Russian letters seem to be very much like American letters, only not so good. That is, there are cliques who refuse to be propagandistic and who sneer at the Soviet "melodramas" as the propaganda plays are called. The *cognoscenti* function just as ours do: they try to stand clear. He says the theatre is superb and the Russian girls splendid. He came down with scarlatina in Odessa: in hospital 40 days. —He's much thinner, poor dear, and looks rather hunted. But he's in fine spirits and we're having dinner together tomorrow. He's staying at the Lafayette, having been evicted or sold up or something while away. (You see what a strong wife can do? *Rolfe* never gets evicted!)

The Russians are wild over Hemingway, whom they've just discovered and they're translating *Ulysses*!

I wish I could do something for you with Eda Lou. No hope, however. She and I are antipathetic and always have been. I wish your father had taught you the florist business as a side-line, and then you could come on and open a green-house in Queens.

* * *

Love,

L.

[P.S.] I'll never get mad at you, darling. I might just forget about you if I ever should start suffering on your account, but not mad. —I'm so closed up!

October 20, 1935

Dear Ted:

* * *

Rolfe showed up last night. * * * We went over to the Lafayette and had 2 T. Collinses apiece, and then Edmund showed up and we went up to his bedroom and had 2 more again. Edmund is *wonderful* on Russia. His story of how Poland looked (all pompous conductors in gold braid who, as he said, "got my overcoat mixed up with their whiskers") after the jolly camaraderie of the Soviet Union (where passengers read poetry to the locomotive engineers and everyone shakes

hands with everyone after having completed a successful railway journey, at 20 miles an hour)—is priceless. E. came back to the hotel with
me and we had some beer, and sat here on my bed, going through the
S.U. yet again. E. has picked up a S.U. form of embrace, rough yet
chaste: he sits upright, talking diligently, and grasps your neck with
his whole right arm, in a sort of bear-hug. He told me of how he was
cupped in the hospital in Odessa, with 20 brass cups, twice a day. He
says it was like being buried under a pile of horse-shoes. Then the
doctor, to cheer him up, gave him *Little Women* in German to read,
and E. suddenly remembered that Beth, in that book, dies of scarlatina
(the disease he was suffering from) and that wasn't so good. Also, the
doctor read him a great many poems by one Sir Alfred Lyle, a sort of
denatured Kipling, and E.'s account of these poems was so immense
that I slipped out of the bear-hug and rocked on the counterpane with
mirth. O, it's so good to have him back! "And there I was in Odessa,
reading Sir Alfred Lyle!"

I wish you could come to Boston with me. We'd have much fun. But
all you middle-Westerners are so afraid of shell-fish. They give you
rashes, don't they?

The lovely weather holds.

Be a fine upstanding M.A. and send those *N. R.* things in *right away*.

Love,
L.

[October] 1935

Dear Ted:

Well, I certainly locked myself up and made myself work, yesterday. I
labored from dawn until dark, stayed only by a pork chop and a piece
of pumpkin pie and some coffee. These vittles I ate at my desk, pen in
hand, peppering my copy with commas, crossing out, putting in, and
shifting back to front. For long periods, nothing would happen at all,
and then when I got my second wind I was ready to give up, but I
know from long experience that that is the moment to keep on. So I
kept on, until the bitter end, and it is my impression that I reviewed 23
books of verse in 1200 words. I may be wrong. By the time Maidie
came home, at 11 P.M., I was speechless and staggering, but I HAD
written some nice periodic sentences and made some good quips.
—This morning I tore it all apart again, compressed Auden and Isher-

wood into 15 lines, as opposed to 30, and got the copy to the *NYer* by 11. Not bad.

You did the same, I trust. It's getting time for those *N. R.* pieces, my sweet.

The people who review by telling the story have it easy, I must say. But how dull that is to write! I can't write anything in prose unless it amuses me and makes ME laugh.

Of course I didn't tell Jack W. to take your poem. I have better things to do with my time than running around wet-nursing brats like you. What do you think I am: a literary agent? You got taken on merit, as usual, I suppose.

The New Yorker Book of Verse will be out this week, and very good, too. I have six poems, as opposed to 12 by F. Frost and about 80 by O. Nash and P. McGinley. —This last week I haven't seen much life: although I wasn't actively working all the time, I was feeling guilty about not so doing, so I turned off the telephone and pretended I was dead. Edmund showed up once or twice and we had fun, talking and drinking beer. He's coming into some money this week and is going to buy me a lobster and a quart of champagne. —I turned Rolfe away from the door, one evening. He has become so gloomy and biddable (to the *New Masses*) lately that he bores me, a little. I hate the delight he takes in being under authority. I hate authority. I hate being told what to do and feeling noble and religious about a cause. That's what growing up in the R. C. Church does for you. I wouldn't take orders from the P. of Rome or Moscow or Thibet.
　＊　＊　＊

All right: getting a Ph.D. ruins the brain. I wouldn't know. I have known Ph.D.'s and Ph.D.'s. ＊ ＊ ＊ M. D. Zabel is a Ph.D. and a Jesuit and Tom C. is a Ph.D. and a rabbit and I once knew a Harvard Ph.D. who used to yearn at me over the tea-cups. Edmund is the best all-round brain I know: he graduated from Princeton and got a job as a leg man for the old [*Sun*]. O, how funny he is! I wish you could hear how they tried to stock the Moscow zoo.

Poor lamb: no wives!

Love and kisses,

L.

/ to John Hall Wheelock /

65 University Place
New York City
October 29, 1935

Dear Jack:

I am sending you, this week, Viola Meynell's new novel, published in England by Cape, *Follow Thy Fair Sun.* Morton brought it back to me from England. He stayed at Wilfrid Meynell's, and met Viola. I have been, for a great many years, an intense admirer of her work, and, because she told Morton that she was looking for a new American publisher, he told her that I would speak to you. Putnam brought out several of her things, rather badly. You people, of course, published her memoir of her mother.

The present book is, I do not hesitate to tell you, in my judgment, the most remarkable study of the agony of love that I have ever read, whether by male or female pen. The course of frustration, disillusion and despair is traced, as is usually not the case, with the author's bare nerves and sensibilities. It is not wrapped up in literature; it occurs on the page before us, as in the best drama and poetry. Colette is the only other woman I know who has looked so closely and felt so *accurately* that her words have the value of some major discovery about life. I am not, as you know, a great admirer of the novel; I even go so far as to deny that Henry James plumbed it or used it to any great purpose, and perhaps the reason is that it cannot be so used. But in this book, once the major theme starts developing, you get the real sound and the almost unbelievable—outside of poetry—evocation.

Do tell me what you think. * * *

Believe me to be, dear Jack

Sincerely yours,
Louise

[P.S.] Roethke says you took his poem. He has it, don't you think? Slight, but unmistakable.

/ to Morton D. Zabel /

November 5, 1935

Dear Morton:
* * *

Edmund, by the way, said that you are more like a well-informed Russian intellectual than anyone he knows. He was astonished when

Mirsky [1] reeled off the stations between New York City and Red Bank, New Jersey, on hearing that E. came from Red Bank. "How do you know them?" asked E. "Oh, I go in a little for the geography," answered M. And he astonished and thrilled E. by being able to recite "poems in a million languages." He sits in a cubicle in Moscow and reads a million poets in a million languages, it would seem, during periods between trips to outlying posts of the Red Army, which he harangues, from time to time, thus earning his bread and butter.

I have been reading perhaps a thousand things: Otto Rank on the artist (this has some fine stuff in it, although you probably pooh-pooh all that clinical and subconscious-delving approach). Rank is by no means a fool; I have gone through the process of a sudden and mysterious cure, and I am willing to listen to men who have plotted out the curve of the subterranean, to some extent. I have read Ridley's book on Keats' craftsmanship—extremely witty and sane, sensitive, too —and Gilbert and Gay (to bolster up some remarks made by me in a review of Auden's *Dog*), and *Bouvard and Pécuchet* (was Flaubert's *sottisier* ever published, or was it all used up in this work?), and Cocteau's *Orphée* (also because of *The Dog*) and Mabel Luhan's latest and *Butterfield 8* and God knows what else. I am now committed to a closed career of reading and writing. * * *

The poem to my brother, in the *NYer*, contained a terrible misprint, by the way. In the fourth stanza, if you can by any chance call it to mind, the fourth line should be "All things remain," as opposed to "All things indeed." The printer put a slug in the wrong place, and their proof-room didn't catch it, and I received profound apologies from everyone, which is as it should be, since the poem, as it appeared, might have been written by an Armenian with a slight command of the English tongue.[2] * * *

I hope to hear Roland Hayes [3] on Friday. He is the greatest concert artist, male or female, I have ever heard. I haven't seen any theatres or gone to any concerts. No piano and no radio. Nothing but this rehabilitated machine, on which I manage to type as badly as ever, it seems.

Now come across with your news, my dear friend.

Ever with respect and admiration,
Louise

1. Prince D. S. Mirsky, whom Wilson had met during his trip to the Soviet Union, although best known for his two-volume history of Russian literature, also wrote on

Walt Whitman and T. S. Eliot. It is assumed that he died in a Soviet concentration camp in 1937.

2. Never one to sit quietly for a typo, LB wrote to *The New Yorker* about another misprint the following September: "You might tell the proof-room from me that, when they get another of my poetic efforts to operate on, they might try printing the lines upside down. That's always a good effect, too."

3. The Negro tenor Roland Hayes remains without peer as an American interpreter of art songs. On this occasion his program included, in addition to the Schumann-Heine *Dichterliebe,* two songs by his accompanist, Percival Parham, set to texts by Langston Hughes.

/ to Theodore Roethke /

November 6, 1935

Now look, my pet, it was fine for you to get into such a lather and to worry so much about sounding like other people, and you should, and that's all to the good, your rage and desperate attempt to find out why it all happened, etc. But if I were you I'd forget about it this time, and let the *Scribner's* poem go through. It isn't a direct echo, in any case, like the one I have recently found in myself and will tell you about in a moment. * * * Write [Stanley Kunitz] and say, "Yes; now that I come to think of it, that does sound somewhat the same; I'm sorry. I have read and admired you so long. I promise not to read you for some time, as an act of contrition."

The thing I did was really far worse. "Evening-Star" echoes a chorus in *The Rock* in a perfectly open way. The chorus about light. The word *praise* and the invocation, repeated invocation to light, are identical. If I put it in the book I'm going to have a note acknowledging the source.[1] As long as you know what you're doing you can do anything. Look what Eliot does to everyone from the Elizabethans down. Cabbages lines. Anything that is conscious and acknowledged is all right. It's the horrible unconscious lifting, and then sticking to, as in [Frances] Frost, that [is] truly reprehensible.[2]

I take back a lot I said about James. I'm reading the letters, which I was unable to read, for years, and they are very fine, once you get used to his eccentricities. And now I can read the later manner like a shot, just as one can get going very fast and smooth with French, after a week of concentration and continued application to the text. It's really a beautiful manner, for anyone who likes periodic sentences. He says that the real test of a real feeling for writing is a passion for adverbs. . . . "I'm glad you like adverbs—I adore them; they are the only qualifications I really much respect, and I agree with the fine author of your quotations in saying—or thinking—that the sense for them is *the* literary sense." That shows the difference between a prose-writer, even a great prose-writer, and a lyric poet. You can't be a lyric poet and love adverbs. Strange, isn't it. For James was a great prose-writer, there's no doubt about that. I am reading *The Bostonians*, which no one ever reads, and which Edmund has been trying to get me to read for years. It's magnificent. The first account in American of a Lesbian attraction. And so closely written, so accurately observed. Do read it. * * *

Think of being a novelist: always in your work, walking around in it, year after year, with never a break. Book after book, year after year. As I lay awake in bed last night I had a magnificent idea for a novel after James' own heart: perfect in form and shape: rather like an hourglass, as is *The Ambassadors*, but not quite. I must say, I get terribly sick of novels that go along, riding a hidden or ostensible *I*, in a straight line, with some bumps, from start to finish. Even Proust is tiresome in that respect. . . .
* * *

Louise Sappho Bogan

[P.S.] Now relax and stop being badgered and stop worrying, for a while. You can't hear anything going on inside yourself, if you can't stay serene once in a while, my coney.

Not that I think for a moment that fiction really is an art. Someone like James takes it and sweats over it for forty years and what thanks does he get, and who in hell cares what he's really doing, and after his death everything falls right back to where it was before. Jane Austen is the only English novelist that a poet can respect. She's clean and onto it all and witty and not just a megarathium * of everything, thrown in a heap. I believe in the short story and the long short story: the novel, never. To hell with the novel. But I have *such* a wonderful idea for one. But my talent is for the cry or the *cahier*. . . .
* * *

* What does this mean? Is there such a word?

1. The acknowledgment was never carried through into print, and for good reason, since LB is speaking more to comfort than to repent. Eliot's "O Light Invisible, we

praise Thee! . . . we worship Thee! . . . we glorify Thee!" was neither the verbal nor the emotional equivalent of her own lines: "Light from the planet Venus, soon to set, / Be with us. . . . Light, lacking words that might praise you; / Wanting and breeding sighs only."

2. Frances Frost's borrowings from LB in *Woman of This Earth* (1934) were caught out and demonstrated by Rolfe Humphries when he reviewed the book for *Poetry*.

/ *to John Hall Wheelock* /

65 University Place
New York
November 8, 1935

Dear Jack:

You can see what I mean, concerning the tone of the Washington letter. You know me well enough to realize that with my chin-in-the-air attitude to the outside world, I would no more think of sitting down and expanding on my early life and development than I would think of flying around in the air on wings. And yet I know that I am being a recalcitrant author, and am passing up O so many sales, among the Washington University ladies, by not so doing. I can see the portfolio of information that G. Taggard will send them, for example. —I suppose I should expand on one or two things, just to let the comfortable creatures know that it is out of poverty, fear and disaster that poetry grows, and the worse the soil, the better the poetry is liable to be, given a good tense temperament in the poet, to begin with. . . .

I should like to know how far I should get, when I am doing a critical piece, if I depended on a personal contact with the author, for my material. I do think I should write a note, a short one, saying that all that is relevant to her talk can be found in certain books of reference, and if she can't find the influence in my work, then she will have to do without them. . . . O no! You see, I need your advice on this. Do set the tone for me, if it will not take up too much of your time.

* * *

Thank you, dear Jack, for your time and trouble.

Ever your erratic and high-spirited friend,
Louise

/ *to Theodore Roethke* /

December 1, 1935

Dear Ted:

I still don't know just what started your trouble: why on earth should you start running around the countryside? It's a mystery to me, but I'm terribly sorry that you were incommoded by nurses et al. * * *

I do hope that the attack of whatever-it-was is temporary merely, and that you'll soon be back on the cinder track once more. I thought you might have gone away like a cat, to do some serious drinking or thinking or whatnot. My own life has been one of suspicious calm. I was in bed for a week myself, but that was just a cold, and I had fun, rather, because Edmund came and fed me caviar and Budweiser and brandied calf's foot jelly.

* * *

Ever with love and kisses,
Louise

/ *to Morton D. Zabel* /

65 University Place
New York City
December 3, 1935

Dear Morton:

It is afternoon, and a cold one, with an assortment of high clouds, cut off from my view by the factory building opposite my window. In the factory building young people fold cardboard and pack children's sewing sets, in spite of the present state of the world. That's one floor; on another people cheerfully make shoes. The man directly opposite has made shoes cheerfully, under my sight, for weeks now. The week before last I watched him microscopically, since I was confined to a bed of pain with a horrible cold. (That's what stopped the Auden Anth. review the first time.) He starts work at eight thirty every morning, and knocks off around six every night, and he rubs and cuts and pastes in the interval between. He is small and Jewish and he wears spectacles and is a "simple organism," no doubt: his briskness and cheer are appalling. He has a gesture of brisk hand-rubbing that punctuates long stretches of his efforts; he makes a wide and tense and cheerful arm-sweep, with a shake of the fingers, high in the air, from time to time, so I suppose that he is talking, from dawn to dark, just as briskly as he works. —Negroes pack mops into mop-wrappers, on the lowest floor of the building, and they are less brisk. But what I can't really understand is the tremendous market for children's sewing sets. I can't, indeed.

* * *

Let me make a swift comment on the Poetry Ball and G. Taggard's Anglo-Saxon Revolutionary soirée. I wasn't even invited to the first (J. Auslander had something to do with that black-balling, I am sure), and E. W. was invited to the second, but declined. * * * He says that he would have liked to have stood up and said, "My friends and comrades, the U.S.S.R. is now passé; Bulgaria has a form of world revolution under weigh that is absolutely the latest thing, and you are all terribly behind the times in showing any sympathy with the Russians." G. T. would then have had to read up on Old Bulgarian, and rush around bringing herself up to date, because she wouldn't suspect a hoax, not she. —Eda Lou Walton gave her ticket to the P. B. to Henry Roth,[1] and bought him a full dress suit to go to it in (actually: she may have rented the suit, but it was tails, I believe, and an opera hat, and everything). She wanted him to see what the upper classes are really like. That's the honest truth, although hardly anyone in their senses would believe it. Well, Henry went, and came back, having observed that the upper classes didn't know anything about Dante (Henry can read him in the original, I have been told), and that they get drunk, and that the upper class women looked cruel and heartless and frightened him. So I suppose Eda Lou's money really wasn't wasted, after all. Dear God.

* * *

I went to the French exhibition at the Metropolitan, the day after I got back on my feet. I really went up to see the winter sunlight on the floor of the long room downstairs in the American Wing. I often do this, during the winter; the room is so gracious and beautiful, and the sunlight pours in, broken up into squares, onto the floor, and the whole thing gives *me* bunches inside, I can tell you. I stand on the stairway and look down, in a trance, for as long as I dare; I fear the Irish muggism of the attendants, to some extent, so I don't dare stand there too long. There's something about the fact that the room is *on ground level* that gets me; H. James could do a story about that, something about genteel atavism, and wanting to live in the 18th cent. Yes; there's something in my blood that wants to look *down* into a long ground floor room with the sunlight in it. You can figure that out, if you can.

* * *

Ever, with appreciation,
Louise

1. Henry Roth is the author of *Call It Sleep.*

December 12, 1935

Dear Morton:

* * * I will tell you a funny story, as a New Year's present. —It seems that Wallace Stevens invaded the little private literary colony inhabited by Hemingway and Dos Passos, and wives, in Key West. He was very drunk (I am telling this to you from Dos Passos' version of it, told to Edmund), and he barged in on Hemingway and began to lay him out. "You're a cad," he said to H., "and all your heroes are cads and you are all your heroes, so you must be a cad!" H. took this very meekly, they say, replying, "Come now, Stevens, I'm really not so bad as all that, am I?" "Yes," said Stevens, and stormed out.[1] He then turned his steps toward the home of Dos Passos, and he found the Dos Passos ménage listening to the phonograph and having a cocktail before dinner. "So you're Dos Passos," said S., "and here I find you, playing cheap things on the phonograph and surrounded by women in pajamas. I thought you were a cripple and a man of culture! Women in pajamas!" and he stormed out of there. Now, Dos Passos' comment on all this is, that Stevens is a disappointed man, who doesn't dare to live the life of an artist, preferring the existence of an insurance broker, so that he tends to idealize men of letters, etc. Dos Passos also remarked that Stevens' poems were all written, very probably, under the influence of liquor. —But as I see it, Stevens was quite right: the sight of the Dos Passos ménage, being O so liberated and free and emancipated and pajamaish was enough to give anyone a turn. * * * Poor sensitive Stevens, I say; and good for him!

With affection, as always—
L.

1. In his biography of Hemingway, Carlos Baker tells of a fight between the two men: "Stevens emerged with a black eye and a badly bruised face." The reasons for the conflict, according to Baker, "remain obscure."

1930-1939

[December] 1935

Dear Ted:

I am so sorry that you are still under the weather, but I am glad that you're having good, sensible professional care. There's nothing like it, when one gets really down, and isn't able to make the motions by oneself. —Believe me, my dear, I've been through it all; not once, but many times (twice, to be exact). And after the first feelings of revolt and rage wear off, there's nothing like the peace that descends upon one with routine, lovely routine. At the Neurological Center, here in town, at one time I went through three weeks of high-class neurology myself. I had a room all done up in noncorrosive greens, and a day and a night nurse, and a private bath, and such food as you never ate, and hydrotherapy, including steam-cabinets, and a beautiful big blond doctor by the name of McKinney. I had a great triumph with McKinney: I made him shed a single tear and when you can make a neurologist shed a tear, you're doing well, as you probably know by now. You wouldn't be able to bring off that feat, because you've had a comparatively happy life, and because you haven't got the Irish gift for histrionics—not that I don't feel assured that you do pretty well in your Pomeranian way. . . .

Well, there I was, and I got worse and worse, rather than better and better, because I hadn't come into myself as a person, and was still a puling child, hanging on to people, and trying to make them tell me the truth. * * * You won't be THAT foolish. The good old normal world is really a lot of fun, once you give in to it, and stop fighting against it. Fight with your work, but let the world go on, bearing you and being borne by you: that's the trick. As old Rilke said:

> *Und wenn dich das Irdische vergass,*
> *zu der stillen Erde sag: Ich rinne.*
> *Zu dem raschen Wasser sprich: Ich bin.*[1]

* * *

Ever with love,

L.

1. The passage from Rilke comes from sonnet 29 of *The Sonnets to Orpheus,* part 2: "And if the worldly forget you, say to the silent earth: I flow. To the swift water say: I am."

1936

Dear Ted:

I am again sorry that I haven't written sooner. I hope you are feeling splendidly, in or out of the bath. I am feeling very well today, now that the fearsome holidays are over, which always tend to make everything and everybody tense and ugly, in this city: the contrast between carols being rung on church-bells—around Twelfth Night, these become increasingly hard to bear—and Christmas trees and whooped-up wassail of all sorts—between these things and the New York streets in general, where, as usual, people flounder and rush, and run in and out of offices to earn things, and in and out of stores to buy things. Christmas and New Year's in Michigan are no doubt far less artificial and wearing.

Today has been dreary and full of slush, but I had a very good time, nevertheless, trying to plan a new set of rooms for Maidie and myself, in which we can have some sunlight and a piano. * * * The rest can wait. For, after a winter spent in this manner, I can look forward to a summer in the country. I may have to take a regular job, but I am resigned to that, as well. For I have had a great deal more freedom than is usually assigned to indigent members of my or any other sex. I have had lots of life and travel and change and fun and love, and now I can get along with little enough, as so many others have had to get along while I was more or less sitting pretty, and being fanned by Senegambian slaves. No, I don't want to lie down now and kick and scream. Or sit weeping into beer-glasses, or emit wild maniacal yells. . . . A hair's breadth of room is all I ask, to take a figure from one of our distinguished women poets. . . .

I have been reading Rilke's *Journal of My Other Self*, and I recommend it to you, when you are all better: it has its depressing side, not to be sampled by invalids. I can heartily recommend to you James' *Notes on Novelists*. You have probably read this; I never tire of re-reading parts of it. The three articles on George Sand are superb. No one should ever take J. to task for lack of human sympathy, or for lack of understanding the erraticism of gifted women, or for narrow moral prejudices, after reading these. He loved G. Sand, and respected her throughout; his understanding of the mixed up de Musset-Italian doctor affair is complete, and he can even laugh at it: not a trace of old-maidish shock. In fact, I have had moments of cynicism over this business, even I, but not Henry. And the article on her worries with Chopin, and her tragic relationship with the daughter who betrayed her, is touching in the extreme. Do read these if they are in the library.

* * * The only human contact that I look forward to with any expectation is the visit of Janet Flanner (she does the Paris Letter in the *NYer*); she wrote that she is looking forward to meeting me this month, and she is quite a person, from all accounts, and writes, as you know, damned good prose.

As to Morton, my dear, he hasn't much—hardly any—intuition, you are right there, and his jesuitical kind of mind flattens out his convictions: his critical remarks are always rather on the fence, as though he must oblige all sides. He is, on the other hand, a true and real and generous friend; he has put up with my howls for years, and during the period when my howls were frequent and boring. And he is the true learned type; he is always fundamentally on the right side; he really knows, because his taste and intelligence are first-rate, even though his nerves are panicky (he is terribly afraid of some things, and runs to cover, poor boy) and his convictions, as I have said, tend to beat around the bush. I admire him more than almost anyone I know, and I should certainly go to him in any real crisis, and be sure of help. So don't write to him nastily. Nicely, rather. R. M. Lovett,[1] by the way, will probably turn his classes over to M. when he leaves Chicago. He as much as said so the night I met him.

* * *

Do write soon, my dear.

> Ever with love—
> Louise

1. Robert Morss Lovett was both a professor of English and an associate editor of *The New Republic*.

/ to Rolfe Humphries /

January 24, 1936

Dear Rolfe:

I can't write any thumping prose on your two questions. I fought out my fight last summer, and, since I stopped being one kind of a neurotic, I don't keep on fighting the same fight over and over. I fight whatever it is out, and then leave it, and go on to something else. Sort of a personal new party line. . . . That's the best way for it to be. I fought one fight—a crusade designed to make the man I loved tell the truth—for about five years, over and over again. Now I take about three months to get a thing laid out, so that I can see it all, and then I either accept it or get over it. That's health.

So you'll have to go back to my letters, if you want thumping prose, on that subject.

I can write you a quiet line or two, in answer. To the first question: I suppose any political regime that includes dictatorship is something for a writer anywhere to worry about. I don't think he should give as much worriment to the possible political set-up as he does to his writing. The less capacity for scattered worrying that a writer possesses, the better. Great artists in any field haven't been great worriers. Minor artists ought to worry about their work, for worry is only valuable when it goes toward making something hard, condensed and durable. Minor art needs to be hard, condensed and durable.

2) An organization of writers for the defense of culture seems to me to be a rather tendentious scheme. If culture is going to be overthrown, it will be, in any case. No puny organization of writers is going to stop it. Perhaps it is best for culture to get knocked on the ear from time to time. It always has been knocked on the ear, before now, and the disguised rubble built into the wall has gone down, and remained, rubble, and the beautiful incised stones and the headless statues and the partial stanzas and the bronze garlands and the pure speech and the rational thought have come through, in any case. Why worry? Why ask for the world without ruins? Why ask for a world in which art never changes or fails or is partially erased? The Fascists burn the books, and the Communists bar the heterodox, and what difference is there between the two? I must say I would just as soon die on the barricades for Mozart's music as not: if someone walked in this minute and said, Louise, if you don't go out and get shot, they'll take Mozart's music and throw it down the drain, I'd put my hat right on and go out and take it. But the thought of spending years moping along with a lot of other writers, defying anti-cultural forces: No. For culture isn't saved that way. Nothing is saved that way. And a lot of precious life is wasted that way. I'm an individualist, as you can easily see.

* * *

> Write again soon.
> Louise

/ to Katharine S. White /

65 University Place
New York City
February 5, 1936

Dear Katharine:

E. Wilson has fallen heir to some Victorian anthologies, or garlands, of female poetry, and he thought it would be a good idea if I did a piece on same, linking them up with modern female verse, the point being that when the girls had a restricted life, they were far more ardent, lauding the virtues of husbands and connubial bliss in general in far from uncertain terms; while modern female verse tends to vilify and belittle the masculine charms, much of it being written just after or just before some disillusion handed to the woman by the man. Do you think that this idea would mean anything to the magazine?[1] The Victorian quotations are howls, I can assure you.

With every good wish,
Louise

1. The resultant essay, called "Poetesses in the Parlor," was published by *The New Yorker* in December.

/ to Theodore Roethke /

February 19, 1936

Dear Ted:

Forgive this long silence: I have been engaged in preliminary divorce proceedings, having finally managed to get a good lawyer who isn't out for my last cent, and who speaks our kind of language. Such men are rare in this town, and it's only by the grace of God that this one turned up. So by April or May I shall again be a free woman, and if I marry again, I should be put away permanently in the manic-depressive ward, it seems to me.

I have thought of you often, and hoped that Saginaw wasn't getting you down too much. There's nothing to do, in some of life's interims, but sit down and live it through. I don't think that you are in the ninth hell, by any means: you are free and well and not being mangled by the thorns of old, cruel love, or of new, cruel jealousy, or of hatred or melancholy. Something has stopped, and something new hasn't started yet, that is all, and when the new thing does start, you'll be better than you ever were, I'm certain. * * *

I saw Léonie and her husband recently, and I was more than ever convinced that a spinster's life is to be the future life for me. Wife-hood is too damned full of hero-husband-worship, for one of my age and disabusedness.

Ever,
Louise

/ to Rolfe Humphries /

Dear Rolfe:

I suppose you are right, but today, after taking bus-rides to various points in this city, and after observing my kind from top of same, I began to feel that what we need is a new race. The Russians have it easier, in producing a new generation. But I think there is no doubt that this generation should be swabbed off the board. For they are sick in their souls, to a woman and to a man. In miles of streets I did not see one clear, feasible face. Dead souls, one and all, and I re-membered the wonderful passage in *The Waste Land*, where Eliot describes the crowd going over the bridge in the twilight.

And I thought: "There will be a race that will go up this street singing, and, perhaps, leading beautiful animals, garlanded with roses, and each one wise and noble in his heart," but I knew it wouldn't be produced by our age, or even by the means thrown up by our age. And a lot of blood will have to flow before it comes, and lots of air will need to be let into the generations before it.

Speaking of blood, why did [Stanley] Kunitz think that by thinking and banding together, that anyone, even an intellectual group, can stop the coming "blur of blood." If revolution is the one means of change, I wish people would stop being sentimental about it, and writ-ing about it as though it might appear by the waving of a wand. How is there to be a synthesis arrived at, in the minds of the young, if they are told that war is hell, and not told that revolution is also hell? I think that this should be made clear to them, and that they should be trained to be bloody-minded and hard, and that they should know that hatred becomes them, but that love lies beyond even that.

I think it would be a good thing if everyone were compelled to shut up for about five years: work in silence, publish nothing. There really is a terrible lot of ego-airing going on, under the guise of thought, now isn't there? I can't read any of it any more.

    * * *

Louise

March 31, 1936

Dear Rolfe:

My name is Mrs. Holden, and I live at 70 Morningside Drive, Apt. 34, and my telephone number is 5100–Univ. 4. And did I tell you that I blew up Louis Untermeyer, in no uncertain way, and that he wrote back, denying all, and intimating that I was having delusions or something? Delusions nothing! He re-wrote an entire review of mine, grabbed off some stray sentences here and there on all sorts of people, including Spender, Millay, and Auden, and then carefully left my biographical note just as it stood in 1930. The louse! I wrote him a second and last time, and told him off again—rather well, but not quite so well as the first time, because I wasn't mad, and I'm never so good as when roused. But I did mention that I was pleased to see that, in 1932, he thought S. Spender derived from Anna Wickham, of all people, and Gerard Hopkins. . . .

My new room is wonderful. I remember, years ago, taking a walk with you to Morningside Drive, and we looked off over the city and you said that that was the way you thought a foreign city would look, and you're quite right, of course. The view is a perfectly print-like one, and I waken in the morning to a great big sweep of sky, and the sun all over the room. This, to one who has spent the winter facing a northern shoe-factory, and who has passed the last two weeks at the bottom of a well, is delightful. Now if I don't make myself work, I ought to be prohibited.

Ted writes me that the birds are bothering him, but that nothing else has happened, or seems likely to happen. Poor boy! He could have such fun in a little job here, now that he seems to bound around with a liquor bottle glued to his lips, a little less.

I feel that I can't have any male visitors, in this place—so very studious and virginal and all, but that's nonsense, of course. Edmund almost had me thrown out of the Albert the other night. —Bell-boys and managers began to telephone informing him that it was 3 in the morning, and about time for him to lower his voice. —He was reading Baudelaire aloud. He thinks that Edna, in the preface, has gone senile.

Well, come to see me, or meet me at the Library, before you are / do.

Louise

April 10, 1936

Dear Rolfe:
* * *

Bunny [1] showed up last night, and the door downstairs was closed at 11:00 P.M. so he stood beside his taxicab and howled, in a rather *refeened* way, "O Louise!" and I had to go down to him, in the rain. We went to a Greek place over on Broadway (the shocking lack of cafés and good restaurants in this center of learning makes me feel that the learning can't be any good), and ate a hot chicken sandwich apiece, and B. drew up a list of American women writers he thinks I should do a series of pieces on—but I am rather cold to the prospect. * * * I came back here, into this virginal nest, at 2:30 A.M. and I fear I am giving a disreputable impression. Do come up some evening after Easter,[2] or some afternoon, and I'll try to repair that impression with you—because you do not have a high voice, or insist on lecturing about moral philosophers far into the night. I do want you to see my view over Harlem. "Jesus Christ Almighty," Bunny cried, last night. "Why do you live in such a place, surrounded by old maids, where you can't entertain anyone!" I told him it was the peace and the view, but he seemed to think that both would be deleterious in their effects.
* * *

Louise

1. Although LB rarely used it, Edmund Wilson's nickname was Bunny.
2. "As a child I solemnly believed that the sun *danced,* on this day; a thought held over from the Druids, I am sure!" (To May Sarton, April 19, 1954)

/ *to Morton D. Zabel* /

April 15, 1936

Dear Morton:
* * * From de Banville, let us skid swiftly to Baudelaire. I know all about Baudelaire now; I have known a lot about him for years, but now I know more. The Millay-Dillon translations gave me quite a turn, I can tell you. I began by thinking that George was doing pretty well: "Lethe" isn't so bad, and that's the first one in this book. But then I began to look up the ones that give me supreme "bunches," and O dear! *"L'invitation au Voyage"* came next, and I whirred my eye over the first stanza, and got down to the refrain, thinking: She'll

really lift this out of the Symons shadow, and what did I find? "Luxury and voluptuousness," that's what I found. I frothed at the mouth, very nearly. Because, as you know, the terrible part of that line, in the French, is the word *calme*—both as to sound and as to meaning. That *l* and that *a* and that *me*, and the thought of peace—the thought of poor Baudelaire looking for peace, between the *luxe* and the *volupté*. (And *luxe* isn't luxury, really, save in the phrase de luxe, is it?) And why "restraint and order"—she could have said "order and beauty," just as easily. And *bless*! —Well, I went on to "*L'Horloge*," and thought: She'll do something really wonderful with "*avec sa voix d'insecte*" . . . and what she had done was to personify that image, which, in B., is right in, embedded in, the idea of the clock's sound, and time's sound, and she put a "wingèd insect," of all things, upon the vein, and she got her mosquito line, all right, but where was the *voix d'insecte*? O, they shouldn't have tried to do a whole volume; she should have let him alone and minded her own business, and allowed his small sheaf of translations to make their small impression. Here the thing has become so portentous and so pompous that you feel that Baudelaire is being dragged into the eminently successful careers of E. M. and G. D. It's all wrong. It was a hard job, no doubt, but it's wrong, just the same. Their insistence on the beats in the line has blinded them to the fact that B. was a master of assonance, that all his effects are embedded and not detachable in any way, that he was a master of the end-stopped line (Millay's run-overs give me the creeps) in much the same way that Racine was, and, as Eliot has pointed out, that "in Baudelaire, *every word counts*." —They might have given the poems in some sort of real order, and kept the "*Hypo-crite lecteur*" one at the beginning where it belongs. And they could have done the magnificent "*Chant d'Automne*," while they were at it; it would translate more easily than some of the others. And what about "*Femmes Damnées*"? * * * Well, I think Valéry is right, with his blurb on the cover: "*Cette traduction est telle qu'il faudrait qu'un autre B. existât pour en donner l'idée au lecteur français*" [1]—it really is a pretty mean cutting-both-ways remark, isn't it? Canny old Valéry!
* * *

Ever, with affection,
Louise

1. "Only another Baudelaire could interpret this translation for the French reader."

1936

70 Morningside Drive
New York City
May 1, 1936

Dear Rolfe:

I wouldn't have missed Bennington for anything, but it is a bad, fancy, three-times-removed-from-reality kind of place, and I pity the girls and fear for their futures. The faculty is almost without exception a bunch of neurotics and would-be's (two members of it have experienced Church of England conversions within the year; I knew one member of it at one time very well, and know her intellectual hollowness and pretension: she now goes for Obey and Auden as she once went for fur-trimmed suits from Altman's. She's a very nice woman, generous and maternal, but she has no business to be on the faculty of a college). —Yes; it's terrible; rather like a large and not-very-well-run tea-room. They sell cocktail mittens with bells on them and little pieces of china and the latest books and God knows what else, in the Commons building, and they listen to Horace Gregory and Josephine Herbst [1] hand out the old rantings, but do they go down and look at the mill in the town; do they ever see a proletarian—no. I saw a few proletarians, nice beery ones, in the station, when I was waiting for my ticket, and I just wanted to go back to the college with same, and push them into the Commons room, and shout, "Go ahead and make a speech! They need you!" —Coming home, I looked out of the window of the train when we were passing through Troy, and I saw a sad, cheerful little parlor, that someone had fixed up, about ten feet from the trains. There were cushions embroidered with daisies and poppies, on the velveteen divan, and a china-closet with white doilies under the dishes, and two plants, with crepe-paper skirts on their pots, in the window, and my heart went out to that room, as it never could go out to anything in Bennington College. I bet it was a railroad tart's room, at that. I hope it was: so cheerful, so warm, so neat. So itself. . . . * * * Did you march today?

Louise

1. Josephine Herbst, a well-known and socially conscious novelist, was the next year to report on the Spanish Civil War from Madrid.

1930-1939

/ *to John Hall Wheelock* /

> The Willey House Hotel
> Swampscott, Massachusetts
> [June] 1936

Dear Jack:

* * *

I recognized my flavor, and my phrase, in L. Wiggam's [*Landscape with Figures*], but what can I do in such a situation? I *do* think that something should be done; I was just out of a hospital for "nervous ailments" when the [Frances] Frost plagiarism occurred, and I then thought that any fuss I should make would be put down to persecution delusions or some such thing. The Wiggam should be shown up in some way, I think. Can't something be done about it by my publishers? The point is that I am the one poet in America, with a definite note, who is almost unknown. *Dark Summer* fell into a dark deep well; it is never stocked in bookstores, and is known to a small group only, so of course it is fair game for the lifters. —I should whoop myself up, in some way, I suppose, by running with some pack, but this I can not and will not do. —So if Scribner's can't do something, nothing can be done. If I, for example, ran with the F. P. A. pack, he'd have parallel passages all over his column, etc., etc.[1]

What does it really matter? (But I *do* have my moments of resenting it.) Let the Viking Press have their fun and sell their 2000 copies. There is a world elsewhere. . . .

I am working on a center, or nucleus for the book. This should consist of:

1.) A poem called "Goodbye at Sea," already on the stocks, which will sum up the Holden suffering, endured so long, but now, at last, completely over.[2]

2.) A longish poem called "The Sleeping Fury." (The book will be called *The Sleeping Fury*, I now think, because, as Morton Zabel rightly observed, *Sleeping Fury* sounds a little like Audrey Wurdemann.)

3.) Some *renderings*, of Lucretius and, perhaps, Rilke.

4.) One or two short sharp epigrammatic things.

And that, unless the demon starts really flowing, will be all. —I was so comforted, this winter, when I came upon Mallarmé's *Poésies*, in one volume, containing about fifty poems. If that was his lifetime work, I haven't done so badly, at 38. And I *cannot,* as you know, write imitation poetry. It isn't any fun!

 * * *

Ever,

Louise

1. The reference is to Franklin P. Adams' column of topical humor, "The Conning Tower," which had originally run in the old New York *World,* and was now a feature of the *Herald Tribune.*

2. The poem will finally be called "Putting to Sea." "I know what it's about, with my upper reason, just a little; it came from pretty far down, thank God." (To Wheelock, July 29, 1936)

/ to Rolfe Humphries /

Willey House
Swampscott
July 1, 1936

Dear Rolfe:

* * * I am sitting down *every morning,* just like those old non-occasional verse writers, Dante and Milton, and writing poetry to order. Can you imagine that? I set myself a theme, and off I go. I'm engaged with a nautical, or maritime, effort, at the moment. If I get the manuscript in by September, Wheelock says, I can achieve book-publication sometime in January. Isn't that swell! And you can review me in the *New Masses.* "Miss Bogan seems to have written some more punk, operatic, prima-donnaish poetry, in which she shows off to a remarkable degree, airing her outmoded, and, we fear by now, rather antiquated charms and sex-agonies in the most futile way imaginable. Nothing can be gained by reading this work, as nothing was gained by writing it. Far better if Miss B. had confined herself to writing articles on hay, grain and mash for *The Breeder's Gazette.* She has a poem on Italy that makes no mention of either Mussolini or Fascism, and the International Clothing Workers of America have not touched her heart. As we said at the beginning, and here re-state, punk is no word for her...."

 An old lady in a street-car in Boston, yesterday, turned to me and said, "It's trying to rain." * * *

Louise

/ *to Robert Hague* /

The Willey House
Swampscott, Massachusetts
July 30, 1936

Dear Mr. Hague: [1]

The Arthur Davison Ficke blurb herewith, at the bottom of this page.
—The blurb sounds like nonsense to me; it is difficult to write anything
about the gentle and tepid sort of thing that Mr. Ficke produces. But
I am trying to live up to Mr. Ross' demands: that everything should
have something said of it. And Mr. Ficke is a pleasant gentle fellow,
concerning whom it would be silly to be sharp. So there you are. Of
course, if you think it sounds too nonsensical, I could struggle to brace
it up, although I can't think how....

＊ ＊ ＊

Sincerely yours,
Louise Bogan

The Secret, and Other Poems, by Arthur Davison Ficke. Poems, in
free-verse narrative and traditional lyric forms, making no great claims,
but written with a heart and an ear. (115 pages, $1.75)

1. Robert Hague was handling the critical pieces at *The New Yorker.*

/ *to Morton D. Zabel* /

Swampscott
August 10, 1936

Dear Morton:

Your very fine letter came this morning and I read it out of doors, at
the ice-cream parlor under the trees, where they serve breakfast
within sound of the sea. How pristine and clear the atmosphere of
such a place is, compared to others we inveterate travelers know, and
I tried to figure out the difference, as I sat there. The quality of the
light has a great deal to do with it, of course, and then, the trees
aren't thick enough and there are no charming and pathetic tablecloths on the tables. (Those out-of-door *tablecloths* have a great deal
to do with European plein-air charm. There's something so assured
about them, so civilized. Man to nature: "Well, I have brought part
of my *house*, my shelter, out into the open. You see, I'm not a bit
afraid, storm, winds and terrors of the sky, [of] what you can do to
me!" —That kind of thought is a civilized one, isn't it? —But Americans
just set tin tables about, and let it go at that. Conceding to nature

a little, you see. Not yet sure enough to go the whole hog, *with* the tablecloths.) —Another difference is: that no beer has ever been spilled on the gravel, and no songs ever sung, under the meagre boughs.

I spent yesterday finishing up a piece on Sandburg [and] Tate * * *. I wonder if it is just the impeccable rightness of our several tastes— yours and mine—or whether we are dreaming each other's dreams, and absorbing, at long distance, each other's critical points: I, too, made the statement, in my remarks on Allen, that the Villon line should be interred for good, or for about twenty years; that it was, by now, to put it mildly, a poetical chestnut.[1] And in your review of S. V. Benét, I noted, the other day in the Library, that you had come out against hortatory remarks. I came out against them, last winter, in letters to Rolfe, making the same point: that they were merely machinery to gain a factitious appearance of strength, and that was relayed to you by spiritual wireless, I have no doubt. —So you see what delicate instruments we both are. Hold, therefore, none but lovely and honest thoughts, so I may have the benefit of your virtue.

I was a little captious with Allen, as you will see, dragging out into the open, from the thicket of classical references, Eliot-Valéry style, oblique images, the essential romantic bitterness of the man. The real weakness of his style and thought comes through when he is off his guard (which isn't, I'll admit, often; but I don't think it a virtue always to be on your guard, in any art. Reticence, yes, but not guardedness; there's a difference). That short passage on Poe, for example, might have been thought up, and written, by an ignorant schoolboy. One doesn't sneer at Poe's bats, these days * (his belfry bats, I mean). —I have had some correspondence with Rolfe about Allen's passion for the *Aeneid.* I wasn't sure about the plate-eating business, having read the *Aeneid,* albeit in the original, for the last (latest?) time, way back in 1915. And Rolfe wrote back that it wasn't the *plates* they ate, but the *tables,* and his interpretation of the picnic at the mouth of the Tiber differs radically from Allen's, I must say. Rolfe is rather good on this whole thing: ". . . the average layman thinks Aeneas is a terrible prig; Allen Tate is a terrible prig; therefore, Allen Tate thinks Aeneas is wonderful . . ." I rather liked the Sandburg book [*The People, Yes*] and drew a parallel between Flaubert's *sottisier* and hatred of the French bourgeoisie, and Sandburg's notebooks of common speech, and *love* for the American crowd. That is rather a good parallel, but *The*

* or at any time, for that matter!

New Yorker may excise it: too high brow for "their readers." (Who are their readers, anyhow? Mostly, I look at the pictures!) * * *

Brief answer to your points on the Freudian discoveries, their use, value and applications:

> 1.) Of course artists and thinkers have known the real secret all along. And primitive people knew it too. (Myths: principally the high-point Greek ones.) No practitioner of the art of mental healing (yes, I know how invidious that sounds) ever omits, at some point in the cure, two great remarks made by two great men: "Know thyself," and "The Kingdom of God is within you." One or two doctors have said to me, as well, again quoting: "He who loseth his life shall find it. . . ."
>
> 2.) No one wants to put all the burden on the Ego, i.e., the conscious will. No one but A. Tate and the Comrades. The thing to do, for happiness and sanity, is to lift the nagging burden of the Super-Ego, and to listen, as much as possible, to the stirrings of the Id, when stirrings are vouchsafed. —Responsibility is, as you say, the rock-bottom indispensable of sanity, but the courage to take responsibility must be trained into most of us—into people of our type. For responsibility is the mark of adulthood, and adulthood is based on "the conquest of fear," God save the mark.
>
> 3.) Therapy does not console; it cures, where it can. There is no cure for some people; just as a man cannot add a cubit to his stature, by taking thought; if you're born with certain things left out, you can't be cured; you can't be "born again."

—I had already noted the [Thomas] Mann essay, and copied out one of the same paragraphs that struck you: the one concerning the heightening which comes to the artist when he acquires the habit of regarding life as mythical and typical. That's only another way of saying that when one lets go, and *recognizes* the stream on which we move as the same stream which moves us within—that it is time and the earth floating our blood and flesh, floating its own child—and stops fighting against the kinship, the light flows in; peace arrives. * * *

The class is dismissed for the day. Please pass the books to the front!

   * * *

Ever with love,
Louise

[P.S.] Do you remember how someone says, in *The Tragic Muse*: "Don't they know *how* to love?" I think that should stand on the title page of some really beautiful modern novel (still unwritten!), don't you?

I thought [Bernard] De Voto (in *Sat. Rev. of Lit.*) pretty good on Dos Passos. If Dos Passos is a *novelist,* I'm a gazelle!

1. ". . . *en l'an trentiesme de mon age.*"

/ to Theodore Roethke /

70 Morningside Drive
August 29, [1936]

Dear Ted:

So you were mad, were you? Well, H. M[onroe] turns us all down, from time to time, and I had a little poem rejected by the *Sat. Rev. of Lit.,* not so long ago. If one insists on being a lyric poet, those things happen. H. M. should have taken the poem, of course. Money should grow on trees, too. It's life, my poor young friend. . . .

When you end up at Red Gap Normal College, I'll go and take your course, in my bonnet and shawl. With little velvet strings tied under my chin, and one of those jet plumes in front.

I'd love to see you helping with the wash. I'll bet you wet everything in sight and play with the soapsuds!
  * * *
Write some and pray for me.

L.

/ to Edmund Wilson /

October 7, 1936

Dear Edmund:

Thank you for the beautiful blurb; I had to condense it a little—and that's a thrill, condensing that old literary master, Wilson—but it was just what was needed, and no doubt we shall both end our careers, in the New World, as a couple of old Trotskyite blurb-writers. On Dry Tortugas, or somewhere. . . .

The sight of your beaming face strengthened me no end. Let me know when you're around here again, in time, and I'll cook you one of those unsurpassed beef-and-kidney pies. The room now has its curtain hung, and looks so pure and unspotted that you'd be astonished. I'm going to introduce the corrupt note by raising one of those plants that eats raw meat: a Venus' flycatcher, or some such thing.

You may have the Fenollosa [*The Chinese Written Character as a Medium to Poetry*], although I must say I'd like to have it myself. Bring it in, anyhow, as I'd like to read it. The blurb will bring in $3.00, and you can have that, too, if you'd like. Generous to a fault, those Bogans.

Still reading Turgenev. Don't forget to look into *Virgin Soil*.

Ever with love,
Louise

/ *to John Hall Wheelock* /

October 28, 1936

Dear Jack:

I have just come back from the country, and I hasten to answer your letter. —Can't someone else write the blurbs? I have to write so many on other people that I can't really bear to write one about myself. Whoever does it might try to make the point, mildly, that I care, really truly care, about the actual *writing* in a poem. That I have given some thought to the effects of tension, sonority, etc., that *language* can produce. That I consider, with Gautier: (here read his *L'Art* through), etc., etc. I also think that our unconscious (Uncs., in Freud's charming phraseology) knows more about us than we know about it.

I supply no biographical note. I have a job reviewing books of poetry for *The New Yorker*, and have had it since 1931. I won a Guggenheim in 1933. I am wild about music, and I read everything but books on Grover Cleveland and novels called *O Genteel Lady!* I don't think I will write very much more, but I should like to go to Ireland. . . . There: they ought to be able to make something really zippy out of that!

* * *

Dear Jack, how I do annoy you! Did you see Benét defending you against my flippancy, in the *Sat. Rev. of Lit.*? —But I wasn't being flippant.[1]

Come up sometime again, and I'll play the songs of the High Auvergne to you. You should hear Madeleine Grey sing them. It's like Paradise. Really!

Ever,
Louise

[P.S.] M. D. Z. writes from Chicago that people are "vastly stricken" and "greatly admiring" when he reads "S. F." to them. The blurb writers might use "vastly stricken," don't you think? "The reader will be *vastly stricken* with this book." That would be enough to keep everyone off it. It sounds, somehow, like coming down with the small-pox, doesn't it?

1. William Rose Benét complained that although she had spoken to the moments of clear and moving expression in Wheelock's *Poems 1911–1936,* she was wrong about everything else. LB had suggested that the poems were not in the modern temper, that the word "belovèd," for example, was no longer usable, since popular songs and the radio had cheapened it. More to the point, she felt, was the sentiment expressed in a line by Auden, which she often quoted: "I had an aunt who loved a plant, but you're my cup of tea."

Her review demonstrates what is patently clear: her incorruptibility. Not even her own publisher, a friend who stood in position to do her favors, could escape what she saw as the truth.

/ *to Theodore Roethke* /

302 West 77
October 28, 1936

Dear Ted:

I am just back from the country, where I spent four days in a rented house of E. Wilson's,[1] listening to the squirrels, as distinguished from the rats, and reading *A Vision,* by W. B. Yeats (full of Frustrators, full of Frustrators!), *Pushkin,* by Prince Mirsky (written before he went back to lick the boots of Gorky, and very good: he is excellent on the "tensions" of Pushkin's emotions, and the "nudeness" of his style), and other works of literature. I did nothing but sit and read, in one spot, on a couch in the living room, and all the leaves in the world, or at least all those in Stamford, Connecticut, were falling outside the French windows (note the effect the word "French" has there; if I said "German" or "Swiss" windows, it would be quite different, wouldn't it?). They fell and fell, and a brook murmured, and I sat on, thinking, from time to time, "What a hell of a lot of leaves!" but feeling exactly nothing. From time to time, I would rise and have a meal, but finally the cook left (the leaves got her!) and then I had to cook, and Bunny kept turning the ice-box off, every night, in some mistaken hope that it would stay cold by itself, and in the morning the food smelled like a charnel house, and there was never enough gin, because he ordered, out of a desire for work and sobriety, only one bottle at a time, and then he and I would polish that off, and it would only be ten o'clock in the evening, and we'd be in the middle of an argument, with no gin to help us carry it on, and Edmund would sit there and say: "I'll get a case of it; that's the thing to do: get a case of it!" —Then I would get up and sadly go to bed, in a room draped with red bunting, or turkey-red, or whatever, to accent the revolutionary note, because the house belongs to rich revolutionaries.

Well, I had quite a time. So Bunny's real pensioner and cook, who does everything for him, was to show up, with her four (colored) grandchildren; but one of the grandchildren (called Dolores, and remarkable for the phobia she has about white people: she shrinks from them in horror) got the croup, and there Bunny and I were, alone with the leaves, but he decided I should go anyhow, even though I am a good cook. (I think he really wanted a whole bottle of gin to himself, for once, don't you?) So I got off, through the really beautiful, if rather undistinguished countryside. (I like things big, in the countrysides I really love: big trees and hills and enormous vistas, embracing counties.)

Darling, the couplets you sent are really good; excise the navel and the toes, if you need money, and send them to Gibbs or Katharine W. The navel and toes are very good, when you aren't thinking of a market. . . .

* * *

Love,
Louise

1. "['Trees'] is a stone house, rather gloomy, and full of bad liberal-anarchist attempts at decoration, and its situation, among saplings, with no real lookout, depresses me, but it is completely equipped with all modern conveniences (the liberal-anarchists, when possessed of a little money, always fit themselves out as comfortably as possible): oil-burner with thermostatic control, bath, telephone, electric stove and God knows what else. Edmund will be happy working here throughout the winter. He is engaged with a long essay on Pushkin which should place that forgotten figure definitely. . . ." (To Zabel, October 26, 1936)

1936

/ to Morton D. Zabel /

November 2, 1936

Dear Morton:

* * *

I discovered, at "Trees," where the whole modern-political-bigotry stems from. It stems from a man called Belinsky, who shut off Russian poetry short, right after Pushkin and Lermontov, by making up rules for *his* side, and imposing them on all the other sides. He thought up that bright one, it appears, about imagination being a low function: "thinking in images." I had "thinking in images" thrown at me by the comrades, all one winter. Why don't you get someone to do an article called "Back to Belinsky"? Someone who can read Russian and who could get some good solid quotations from B., and put them down, as parallels to what the comrades * * * say today? I'll see if there's anything about him, or by him, in English, the next time I go to the Library. * * *

The League for Protecting Culture (?) sent the League of American Writers a sheaf of poems by Spanish poets, now lost in the shuffle, in one way or another, in Spain. The poems are really beautiful; they range from exhortation (Communist) through Parnassian descriptions of the Generalife. Rolfe wants to translate them, and send them out as a group.[1] They are now in French, but could easily be lifted over into English. I want to do one of them—one that doesn't need much effort, I may add. Even the calls to arms throb with emotion, and are really written and observed, not just fried up, in theoretical fat. I was impressed.

The radio is now fixed, at great cost, and last night I heard, for the first time in over a year, a great performance of music that tumbled and poured all over the carpet in my humble room. Bauer playing a movement from the Saint-Saëns concerto, with incredible speed, and a Scarlatti sonata, with speed even more incredible. Also the shawms and innocent voices of Honegger's *King David*. A lovely transparent female chorus in this last. You heard all this too, no doubt. —As I look back on it, I don't see how I lived through last winter, without music of any kind. Now, nothing can really dull my heart; I have only to look back on that room in the Hotel Albert, whenever depression sets in. * * *

The Yeats *Oxford Book of Modern Verse* came through, in sheets, yesterday. It's not full of the horrors Grigson expected. The preface gets crotchety, half-way through, but is full of good sense, nevertheless. * * * There's a lot I would change, but a great deal I think is remarkably chosen. His selections from himself, for example. But where on earth is Wilfred Owen? So much Herbert Read, and no W. O. The Gogarty comes out well, too. I admire him; Edmund thinks he is just a rhymer. No; better than that.

* * *

Am going through Turgenev. I told you, I think, to read *Virgin Soil*. *A Sportsman's Sketches* is also very good: pure lyric poetry, most of it. —Tolstoi hated him, you know, as he well might. Tolstoi didn't have the sensibilities, the real working heart. The working eye and ear, but not the working heart. Turgenev knew. I'm engaged with *Rudin,* now. Be sure to get the Garnett translation; Isabel Hapgood is frightful: ". . . His hands were endued with gloves."

* * *

The book should come out early in February. * * * The title page will bear the legend:

> *Wie ist das klein, womit wir ringen;*
> *was mit uns ringt, wie ist das gross . . .*[2]

Read *"Der Schauende"* (*Buch der Bilder*).

Write soon.
Love,
Louise

1. He did, under the title . . . *And Spain Sings.*
2. This legend from Rilke—"How small it is, that with which we struggle; what struggles with us, how great . . ."—would be repeated in every collection of her poetry from this time on.

/ to Edmund Wilson /

November 14, 1936

Dear Edmund:

Haunted by your woods, I came home and produced a love poem to end love poems—perhaps the only real love poem I ever wrote [1]—and I plan to have it stand against winter and silence and hatred and party politics (if need be, in italics) at the end of my book. (The Sleeping Furry, a Tale of the Russian Steppes, by L. B., dedicated to E. W., in hatitude.)

* * *

Love,
Louise

1. "All my black side tried to stop it from coming, but it would come, and it came just the way it is: all of a piece." (To Wheelock, November 1936) The poem is titled "Song for a Lyre," and its first line—"The landscape where I lie"—LB later carved on one of Wilson's famous windowpanes in Talcottville, New York. In *Upstate,* the journals Wilson published in 1971, he told how this pane, and others, were destroyed by vandals.

/ *to Rolfe Humphries* /

December 2, 1936

Dear Rolfe:

Before the end of the week I'll do my revolutionary duty.[1] IF— I have any time or energy left over from recommending you to the Guggenheims, that is. My, my, don't you wish you knew what I'm going to say! Hmm, hmm, how confidential it will be! Hmm, hmm.

Spent all day putting together two or three old book-reviews, for an article Morton wants, and it irked me terribly. What a horrible prose style I was once prone to write! All sort of awed and oozy. Never will I undertake a thing of this sort again. Unlike Edmund, I have no taste for re-hashing and re-shaping and re-considering. . . .

I enclose a little poem, written late last night. Not too good, I'm afraid. Just as I was about to drop asleep a whole beautiful witty satire rose before my eyes, all about someone showing someone else over a museum, in the New World, wherein all the bourgeois (and human) foibles were embalmed. The last two lines of it were:

> And do not fail to note, as we pass by
> The Stuffed Adultery, Old-fashioned Lie . . .

but I was too cosy in bed to get up and write it all down, and maybe it's just as well, in any case. And then, this morning, I was taken with the following:

> Not being young, nor a whilom haunter of parks,
> I feel I must love you, love, without literary remarks.
> As one who listens, at least once a week, to five hours
>   of discs,
> It is not me, any longer, who exposes the bony structure
>   to risks. . . .

Now I must confess that this doggerel was brought on by Auden's new book, *Look, Stranger!* * * * Not that Auden is doggerel. He is much tighter than formerly and still amusing, and at times wonderfully condensed—Shakespeareanly condensed, in epithet. I really think he's the works, or will be, when he gets a few bones to gnaw, and reaches forty-five or fifty. * * *

You know perfectly well that * * * I wouldn't marry Edmund if he were the last man on earth. Why should I? It's fine the way it is, except for the fact that he should have a Lithuanian to take up the slack in his love-life. The Irish are no good at that.

Boy, am I going to tell the Guggenheims to cut your umbilical cord for you! You and your Forty-second Street Library! Didn't you ever hear of the Bodleian, or the classical libraries in Rome, Italy? But I'll bet you just lurk around, that year, as usual. And never see Ravenna, Palermo, Rome, Venice, Salzburg, Oxford. Just immure yourself in the 42nd Street Library, that's what you'll do! Dope!

Yours, etc.,
Louise

1. To translate one of the Spanish poems that Humphries had received and was now involved in editing. But the translation did not eventuate: ". . . it wasn't good enough. I refuse to do punk translations." (To Humphries, December 23, 1936)

/ to Morton D. Zabel /

December 4, 1936

Dear Morton:

Well, last night I sort of knocked myself out with claret, and you can imagine how much claret it took to knock *me* out: me who should go down in history as the heartiest female drinker among the female poets (closely edged up on, it is true, by E. Millay, L. Adams—who used to astonish Ford by downing pony after pony of brandy, and staying cold sober—and E. Wylie, God rest her soul). —Be that as it may, I attempt these few words to you, just after having undergone a course of treatment, starting with tomato- plus lemon-juice, with Worcestershire sauce (Tabasco would have been better, but I didn't have any), a flagon of hot chocolate, a hot bath, lasting an hour—truly Roman, I can tell you— some food, and two quarts of water. . . .

What was I going to say: O, yes, * * * I do want to state that I have in no way changed, *as a critic*, since I started to write criticism, which was in the fall of 1923, God save the mark. I *have* changed as a writer; my journalistic training has done me the world of good. I now know a periodic sentence from a hand-saw, and manage one quite well, thank you. I now know that you've got to snap into it in the first sentence, pack the first paragraph, and come back, like a Bach fugue, to the point, or an echo of the point, at the end (or a development of the point). —You probably knew these things all along, because you were educated and I was not, although I *did* get A plus with Genung, or whatever his name was, in my one year in college. —But as a *critic* I have undergone no conversions, changes of *standpunkt*, color, creed, skin, faith or place. I write my criticism, what there is of it, out of my innate feeling for form, sincerity, music, truth, beauty, etc., etc., and my innate distaste for nincompoopery, dopishness, chaos, murk and balderdash. So there! Once against nincompoopery, always against nincompoopery, that's my motto. . . .

    ✿ ✿ ✿

Louise

December 8, 1936

Dear Morton:
    ✿ ✿ ✿

The S. F. is now in sections: four of them. It rises and falls, from despair, to exaltation, and back again: Bogan in cothurnus and Bogan in flat heels. "S. for a Lyre" (which, by the way, you can have, since the new *Scrib. Mag.* turned it down and I refuse to peddle it to the *Sat. Rev. of Lit.*, for example) is the last poem in the book, and I want it set in italics, to give M. Rukeyser, K. Patchen, S. Burnshaw, H. Gregory, and M. Zaturenska something *really* to worry about. "Miss Bogan ends on a typical note of feminine love, as might be expected. In her next we no doubt will get the let-down from her latest emotional spree. If we are alive when her next appears . . ." (They won't be, I hope.)

Seriously, the poems shape up pretty well. The 1930–1933 period—despair, neurosis and alcoholism—is set off by itself, ending with "Hypocrite Swift." Then there is the period of further despair, edged in upon by the period of Beautiful Males (ending with "Man Alone"). Then the spiritual side begins, with a few rumbles from the sensual bassoons and the mystic fiddles. All ends on a note of calm: me and the landscape clasped in each other's arms.

    ✿ ✿ ✿

The photographer was wonderful.[1] Maidie, who wanted a hair-wave and a lace-collar and cameo pin, will be furious, and maybe some will have to be taken over again, to please her. Because the hair was straight, and I had on my little silk piqué neckpiece, and I had just consumed 2 very good rye highballs (along with shrimps and scallops creole and Camembert cheese). The man was a nice little 4 ft. Jew called Ossip. He admitted that the whole thing might be a flop because I was going faster than he was, and that showed intelligence on his part. I think he was striving for Irish eye-twinkles rather than Olympian calm. Perhaps a few Irish e.-t. will be all to the good, after that furiously furry and heady and pensive one, taken in Wien, in 1922. How furry that was, to be sure! * * *

I play the *Winterreise* (Tauber) until I am stupefied, sometimes. —Walton's *Façade* is very jolly, isn't it. I heard it last week. The polka one is perfect; and the tarantella. (I grew up on tarantellas, for some reason. Raff, and tarantellas.)

O Morton, so much difficulty has been written and composed! How good life is! How complicated! When I sat behind the stove, in Ballardvale, so complicated and hungry, surrounded by simple, peasant, repetitive hungers and rages, little did I know that all this had been done! What have we to complain of? Nothing! If we love and suffer 8,888 times in our lifetimes, there's always a hero or heroine who has done it 9,999 times!

And on this note of hope, not to say exaltation, I close!

Love—

Louise

1. Scribner had offered to have publicity pictures taken, and LB agreed. "So I'll go to the man in your building willingly," she wrote to Wheelock in November. "And have one taken in a snood, and another in a yashmak, and a third with a rose between my teeth. (You haven't had an author do that in some years, have you?)"

/ *to Rolfe Humphries* /

December 23, 1936

Dear Rolfe:

My mother has pneumonia, and is, I think, dying. After a long struggle with her pride, I managed, this morning, to get her into St. Luke's. —How I feel, with my pride, I don't think you can imagine.
* * *

What we suffer, what we endure, what we muff, what we kill, what we miss, what we are guilty of, is done by us, as individuals, in private. —I wanted to kill a few interns this morning, and I shall want to kill some nurses tonight, and I know that it is a lousy system that keeps the poor, indigent old from dying as they should. But I still hate your way of doing things. To hell with the crowd. To hell with the meetings, and the public speeches. Life and death occur, as they must, but they are all bound up with love and hatred, in the individual bosom, and it is a sin and a shame to try to organize or dictate them.

Thank you for the poem. I shan't ever see you again, I suppose.

Louise

/ *to Morton D. Zabel* /

December 23, 1936

Dear Morton:

The [picture of the] Fury came intact, and it is so beautiful that I cried. —I would have written you before this, but my mother took sick the night before last, and today I managed to persuade her to go to the hospital, and it is pneumonia.

If you could have seen the fight she put up, right to the last. But now she is a poor dying woman. I wish I could stop remembering her in her pride and beauty—in her arrogance, that I had to fight so—and now I feel it would have been better if I hadn't fought at all. Because under it all was so much love, and I had to fight that too.

I'll write soon, after this is over—after I stop feeling that Lucifer should have won. *The damned, niggardly, carroty, begrudging world!*

Louise

December 27, 1936

Dear Morton:

My mother died yesterday afternoon. —In death she looks terribly scornful and proud, but I think she loved up to the end.

All I could do, last night, was read Yeats' later poems, on what old age is, and what it does.

> Somewhere beyond the curtain
> Of distorting days
> Lives that lonely thing
> That shone before these eyes
> Targeted, trod like Spring.[1]

Say a prayer for her. Her name is Mary.

Louise

1. The quotation comes from the last stanza of Yeats' "Quarrel in Old Age."

1930-1939

January 5, 1937

Dear Rolfe:

I enclose a letter which came in the same mail as yours. —Now the question is: is this poor woman's attitude a product of the class war? * * * (Maidie, who was [at my reading,] said that an old lady in a tippet, in the front row, nearly fell out of her seat, so I imagine the letter is from her, or from someone very much like her.) Is she not an end-product of something quite different (or a beginning product, or a middle product)? Are not things, impulses, reasons for bigotry and hatred, mixed? She would willingly put me up against a wall and shoot me, because she hates me, she hates what I am, what I stand for, but would she not be making a mistake? Would I not be making a mistake if I shot her? Or even her saner sister? If I started shooting all the Irish on 77th Street (perhaps three parties) what would happen to me? I'd be sent to the psychopathic ward in Bellevue. —My only point is: that people, when they start a war, should be sent to the psychopathic clinics of their various countries, and be compelled to find themselves, to find the fight in their own hearts. Then, all nicely cured, they could throw snowballs at each other, until one side or the other won.
        * * *

I certainly think factions are fighting in Spain, among other things. It's having the revolution it should have had in the 18th cent., or just after the war. If there's not religious fury involved, why have they picked on churches, nuns, etc. (I know all about the churches' feudal oppression, an economic thing, but you can't tell me there isn't some good old religious frenzy working as well.) And if history has to take its course, why worry: why not let it take its course? Let the best man win (the strongest in battle, since that seems to be the criterion), and then let Europe blow up in general, and let Russia beat all the Fascist countries, in a nice long war lasting for years. Thirty Years, or a Hundred Years. Then Marxism will have won, and what then? * * *

—I had a foul glimpse into the literary world the other night, when M. Zaturenska and H. Gregory walked into Léonie's. She (M. Z.) rehashed all the stale literary gossip that I used to hear, ten years ago, with a few new trimmings: foul orts and gobbets picked up on a trip to England two years ago. I mentioned your name, inadvertently, and a great cold abyss suddenly opened between H. Gregory and me, and hideous silent fumes rose up out of it, and I suddenly remembered that you had said he put pants on Catullus. Then M. Zaturenska tried to get out of me what kind of a book you were writing, and I said I didn't quite know, and then she said: "Has he a publisher for it?"—very quick and sly, and I said I didn't know, and then she opined that she didn't think you'd get the Guggenheim, and I still said nothing. And then H. Gregory gave a short resume of the life of Churton Collins, with whom he seems to identify himself,[1] and then he corrected my pronunciation of Göttingen, and then Bill corrected it too, so I rose and said in a pleasant tone, "To burst into another foreign tongue, '*Moi, je pars*'" and left. My God! * * *

I told the Guggs. that, as a critic, you were lucid, balanced and informed. I don't think you're always balanced, but then. I also said you had an impeccable lyric talent, that you knew how to work, and referred them to the last par. of your project. "That," said I, "is how a poet should sound."

       * * *

I *did* laugh at the Local you belong to.[2] Allow me to sign myself:
       Louise
       Prime Moveress: The Ass. for More
       and Better Psychiatric Clinics; also
       Charwoman: the Ass. for the Removal
       of Visiting Englishmen Whooping up
       Wars.

1. (John) Churton Collins (1848–1908), editor of the works of Cyril Tourneur, was considered a fearsome critic of the literature of his time, and was known to have turned upon his old friend Charles Swinburne by savagely attacking his prose. After a life crowded with literary controversy, amateur criminology, spiritualism and university teaching, he seems to have drowned himself in a ditch, "embittered by overwork and disappointment."

2. The Friends of Rolfe Humphries Society, Local No. 1.

January 18, 1937

Dear Rolfe:

I am sorry that I didn't hear you read your translations: I was out at Bunny's hermitage, that week end, and the cook alone had a radio. And I didn't want to intrude on her Sunday privacy. Just a bourgeois appreciation of other people's feelings. . . . But she had four grandchildren in the servants' quarters, one of them a babe, and I thought some of them might be asleep. So I didn't hear you.

       * * * —It doesn't seem to click, this passing to each other of literary

enthusiasms, but if you ever have a free and disinterested moment, do read C. Isherwood's "The Novaks," in the first number of *New Writing,* to be obtained in the Per[iodical] Room. I thought it a fine piece of work: simple, unpretentious, full of bravery—real spiritual bravery —and detachment and humor. It helped me to bear my mother's death, thus functioning as some people believe art should. I don't think I could have borne all the terrible details, if I hadn't read "The Novaks" the week previous to those events. —And to shoot the guys who are destroying the Cathedral is childish. What good does that do? It is human *nature* which must be changed, and making live ones into dead ones doesn't change it. It hasn't at least, since the days of Lacedaemon, and perhaps not even then. There's nothing so tiresome and old hat as an old war, unless it's old politics. —I think Edmund's point is well taken: if you feel there should be a war, then go and fight in it. Stop breeding childish hatred on the side-lines. Stop trying to shift what we must do with ourselves—the hatreds we must overcome or bear, the egocentricity we must grow out of, into adult life—onto Spanish factions, or Russian factions, or whatnot. Grown-up people do not want to shoot other people. It's axe-murderers and congenital inferiors in general who go in for that, as a way of proving their manhood. . . .

Yours, etc.,
Louise

/ to Edmund Wilson /

February 10, 1937

Dear Ed:

I don't know why I fall for your epistolary gifts, and am willing to make up with you. —You do give me such a pain, sometimes, that I'd like to cut your throat. But I suppose I have given, and still give, you pains, too, so, if we can't really break each other down, let's build each other up, as you say. * * *

The account in this morning's paper of a whole lot of lost but enthusiastic and Trotskyite souls, sitting around in the Hippodrome, waiting for the voice of God to come in on the telephone from Mexico, and then not hearing it after all, because someone had cut the wires, was terribly touching, and funny, as well. —I think Moses managed those things much better. When he promised a voice from God, by heck, there was a voice from God, along with a lot of manna, and Ten Commandments, neatly written out on stone slabs.

The book is being manufactured, and I think the Guggs. will come through. So I'll be off for Cobh in April.

Come and see me when you can.

Ever—

Louise

/ to Theodore Roethke /

February 10, 1937

No, pet, I have no unpublished poems, and I would hesitate to have them fed, even by you, to yearners, if I had. Because I collect on my works, my young one, and nothing of mine can be read in public without emoluments coming to me. —Old Stand Out for Professionalism Bogan.

I'll send you a copy of the book, don't fret. Although many far more deserving creatures should get one-seventh of my free copies.

Loup-Garou
Louise

[February] 1937

Dear Ted:

* * *

—I am sorry to hear about your colleague. It all goes to show how terribly inadequate the higher education really is. Anyone who thinks himself worthy of the town dump, in death, must have suffered from a terrible sense of guilt for some years previous. I always hate to hear of the suicides of self-loathers. Although when rich old retired men treat themselves to the deaths of felons, by hanging themselves in the attic, I never shed many tears. The rich almost always hang themselves, a true felon's end. . . .

That poor boy could have been straightened out, and given some means of love, if there had been any machinery around that would have helped him to divulge. —Believe me, if I ever decide to get rid of the body, because of reasons economic or physical, I'll spend my last cent on a great big bunch of the most assorted flowers I can find, and I'll go right into somebody's softest flower bed, and bed me down nicely, and when they find me they'll find a card tied to the bouquet, reading: TO ONE SWELL DAME. . . .

* * *

Ever,
Louise

/ to Morton D. Zabel /

February 20, 1937

Dear Morton:

＊ ＊ ＊

Items in experience: I had the Fords here to dinner, and cooked them a curry, and played them sea shanties, and then I had to go to one of their blasted teas the next day, and I had a nice talk with charming, intelligent Bruce Rogers,[1] and was insulted by [a woman], and can't I shoot women who insult me, after this? Yes, I think I shall. One little *coup de revolver* (a pearl-handled one, hidden in the handbag, of course) and the world will be well rid of one more punk female novelist. Or I might take a small machine gun, and decimate punk female writers in rows. . . .

＊ ＊ ＊ —[Maidie and I] saw Rosa Ponselle in *Carmen*: I had never seen *Carmen*, before this. Rosa was very thin and tall and mezzo, and she certainly gave José a run for his knife, in the last act. She wore a get-up such as I've never seen: black velvet with gold frogs, very long, with a train, and a matador hat, with pompons on the far east and west edges, and she executed a fall from her full height in this, after leaping about like a gazelle. . . .

＊ ＊ ＊

Louise

1. The distinguished American designer of books.

/ to Edmund Wilson /

March 16, 1937

The Vision of Willie Yeats

Suddenly into my chamber, I certainly would be at a loss to
    say from where,
A large roomy animal with mad abstract eyes, and considerable
    concrete hair
Advanced toward me with astronomical slowness, as I sat glued
    to my Byzantine chair.
While the sizzle of either Mrs. Yeats frying sausages, or
    sausages frying Mrs. Yeats, slouched up the winding stair.

Thoore Ballylee and Coole (about 70 degrees F.)
St. Patrick's Eve, 1937

Dear Mr. Wilson:

What do you think of my latest? —Me and Lou'll be up to see you on Sat'day. Until then, takideasy.

W. B. Yeats

/ *to Morton D. Zabel* /

March 19, 1937

Dear Morton:

What sweet Guggenheims they are, and how glad I am that they exploited nitrate, or whatever it was! Because some mean old fiends might have done it, and produced a lot of Count-marriers, or something; whereas the Guggenheims felt guilty, and took it out on the Arts, and re-granted me my stipend, relinquished when my heart broke, and my psychical structure broke down, in 1933. And they have re-granted me $500, although I think they only owed me $375. . . . Darlings! May their crown shine in Heaven!

. . . You see how Irish I'm getting, already. —I spent today renewing my passport, and *this* picture makes me look like an aging tart. The other one looked like Annie, the Second Girl, merely. —O Morton, now that the Macgillycuddy's Reeks and Grafton Street and the Giant's Causeway loom up before me, I want beyond anything to go to Rome and Vienna. What a woman! And I *will* go to Rome and Vienna, if it kills me! The fare back and forth will cost about $215.00; and from my own earnings [1] and settlements, and whatnot, I should be able to steam across Europe, hard, and end up in Genoa, or some place, shouldn't I? I've never seen the Cluny, or appreciated the Louvre, or seen the National Gallery. But I have no desire to go muffle myself in the Bodleian, oddly enough. *Don't* you think I should make a dash back to Wien, after the beauties of Erin . . . ?

❋ ❋ ❋

Write soon, with a great deal of well-chosen advice. And remember: I didn't get that Mothersill's from you, the last time I sailed. So you might send something nice, this time. Like a cabin-full of roses and freesias, mixed. . . .

Love,
Louise

1. "I'm now on salary—$15 a week—at *The New Yorker.* $780 a year. Isn't that wonderful?" (To Wilson, March 11, 1937)

1930-1939

April 16, 1937

Dear Edmund:

Ireland is lovelier than I thought it could be, and Dublin is beautiful, too: Merrion and Fitzwilliam Squares are magnificent: pure 18th century, and the whole city, with the exception of, perhaps, O'Connell Street, is surprisingly unspoiled. The parks are very wild and pretty, with many rough-looking trees of a lovely purplish color, and the mist, even on a bright day, lies in them, so that you get an eerie effect, something very strange to see in a city. —The people are very dignified and close-mouthed. They talk in a quiet and conspiratorial way. The types in the street are extraordinary, and Joycean Citizens gather in little groups at corners. Burke and Goldsmith and Grattan stand around in bronze, and this morning I went to St. Patrick's, and saw the Dean's and Stella's graves. I had forgotten that they are buried side by side. Also a tablet to the memory of one Magee, Swift's servant, erected by the Dean in gratitude for the man's "diligence and discretion." "Ah yes, his *discretion,*" said the old verger, or whatever he was, who showed me the slab. "His *discretion!*" —Discretion seems to be a highly prized Dublin virtue.

⁂

Love,
Louise

The Northern Counties Hotel
Londonderry
April 21, 1937

Dear Edmund:

Your letter came today, along with a few others, that had been accumulating for me in Dublin, while I swung north. ("Swung" isn't exactly the verb, Irish trains being what they are. There's no, believe me, *swing* in an Irish train.) —I was terribly glad to hear from you, I must admit. You can be very trying, my old one, but you can be very sweet, as well. I will say that this letter was written out of your more rewarding side.

Good God, what a country this is! It's not a country, it's a neurosis. Never come here, when you are apt, or liable, to ideas of reference, or other paranoid symptoms. Dublin is positively terrifying; I was in a state of terror all the time (5 days) I spent there, and I shudder at the thought of going back. It's beautiful: perfectly beautiful. But it's cruel and shut-up and full of conspirators, believe me. James Stephens, in a review he wrote recently for the London *Times*, of Gogarty's book, admits this. Dublin, he said, is not a city; it is a conspiracy. —I had come to the same conclusion, several days before I read the review.

You don't know what's up. The most moveless faces in the world confront you on all sides. I saw one woman, at a matinee, at the Gate Theatre, who looked as though she had never moved her face, from birth. How she managed to eat or speak, I can't imagine. Now I know where Yeats got his idea, his obsession, of the mask. He had to take good looks, from time to time, at Dubliners. And, after I had managed to get away, to Belfast (it seemed, for a while, that I would be in Dublin for the rest of my life. I became so petrified, physically and spiritually), I suddenly remembered the lines:

> What fanatics invent
> In this blind bitter town,
> Fantasy or incident . . .[1]

Well, maybe a town has to be like that, in order that great literature be bred in it. Florence, I'll bet, was much the same in Dante's time. Full of hidden dissension. Hatred. *Sub rosa* activities. Divided allegiance. —I hope the food was better.

Bloated with tea, scones, cold meat, and little pink cakes, as I am, it's a wonder I can put pen to paper at all. If my good sense hadn't scented the reliability of "an egg and a rasher," I might not be alive to write these words. —Whiskey is terribly expensive: 6/6 for a *half* pint. A double whiskey and soda costs anywhere fom 1/10 to 2/6. Yesterday I bought a half pint of Bushmills, since I was in the vicinity of that distillery. Very good, too. But here in Londonderry the whiskey drinker, or buyer, is put down as a fallen person. You should see the liquor stores: they have black hell written all over them.

Londonderry is pretty awful, except for about three streets, and a lovely park, full, just now, of birds and daisies and primroses, and decorated with fine examples of topiary work. From it you can see the whole town, for it is on the top of the hill, and all Co. Donegal, practically, and Co. Derry, lie below, with their lovely little hills cut up into fields. The light is so lovely. Yesterday I spent in Portrush, watching the Atlantic drive in from Iceland, between the dark cliffs. The clouded light makes the water look magical, and the whole country lives under that clouded light. It's incredibly beautiful, as a country, but terribly frightening. America set up, in the blood, some clarity and definiteness that is antipathetic to all this. —I never felt such a coward before. But here in the North, it is warmer hearted than in Dublin. I didn't expect that.

Tomorrow I move on into the Countess Markievicz country (Ben Bulbin, as you'll remember, from one of your favorite poems). Sligo, Yeats' country, too. Then to the West, and down to Cork, and back up to Dublin, through Wexford and Waterford, and Cashel of the Kings. Then, I really think, I'll go home. England in Coronation time is too ridiculous. And my money won't last very long: things are so expensive here. No nice little *pensions*. If you stay anywhere, it has to be a dismal lodging, or a fairly cheerful and expensive hotel.

Did I mention the 1916 collection in the National Museum in Dublin? That's something. All the grisly mementoes of those heroic but gruesome days: farewell letters, written the day before their executions, of Pearse and Connolly; death masks of Terence MacSwiney and Michael Collins; uniforms; photographs of O'Connell Street in ruins; guns; autographed prison biscuits. And the guard, who showed me the Waterford glass, wanted to get right back to the 1916 collection, with me in tow. I made some excuse. I couldn't see it a second time, not with that blood-thirsty guide. There's a photograph of the Countess, in uniform, looking very beautiful with a drawn pistol in her hand, that slew me. —I tell you, it gets you. For it's still going on, and will never end.

How I wish you were here, to be petrified in turn. My God, what a peaceful life I hope to lead! How I envy you your woods and your fritillaries and your orioles, and Hatty, and your vocal crows, and even your disturbed dreams. If I come out of this alive it will be a wonder.

I had notes taken on your poems, but have lost them. Will discuss same on my return. Your dream poem I thought pretty profound. There's a poem by Auden I saw somewhere which resembles it to some extent; one of the lines went:

"The (human?) heart is as crooked as a corkscrew . . ." "Full of leaks" is fine, too.

Ever, my old scuppernong,
Your feeble friend
Louise

1. From Yeats' "Quarrel in Old Age."

/ *to Theodore Roethke* /

709 W. 169th St.
July 12, 1937

Dear Ted:

It's been hellishly hot here, too—so hot that the higher processes of thought were impossible even to *my* elaborately convoluted brain. The clothes stick to the skin, too. But this afternoon it rained like anything, and perhaps things will cool off a little. —New Yorkers are really wonderful, in a heat wave. They *take* it, and just drop in their tracks; you never see anyone really cross or mean about it, and people do not run around in circles, with their tongues hanging out, as you might expect them to do. . . .

Your poem is *very fine*; I mean it. It really is much better to write about objects and people and things, unless a great convulsion takes place within, and tears you apart willy-nilly. These convulsions do not occur very often, as time goes on, I find, and when they do occur, they soon pass off. —I was wildly in love last week, for example, and I can't even remember what it was like, now. —This change would have taken at least six months, twenty years ago.

    ❋ ❋ ❋

I am so glad you are at last getting Rilke. You didn't go for him very strongly two years ago, did you? —I have read a couple of new French books on him, and understand him rather well, now. He was a strange one. On one side he was a snob and an adventurer; on the other he was one of earth's purest mortals. He *was* wise. And he could go off and shut himself into a tower all winter and see no one, and lash himself into a fury of writing. (On the other hand, he could run around Europe like mad, and not write anything for ten years.)

The new Edna Millay book, *Conversation at Midnight,* is enough to make the angels weep.[1] I must polish it off, critically, next week. I feel terrible about having to do it, for I must say what I think, and she was once a very close and generous friend to me. —Why she had to write this doggerel, I can't think. A. Woollcott is quietly mad about it, however, and it will probably get the Pulitzer Prize. . . .[2]

    ❋ ❋ ❋

Am embarking on my long prose, at long last. I wish I could see you too. I think I have broken with my electrician. He was wonderful while he lasted. He said "Nuttun'" and "Know what I mean?" —And that poem wasn't about music, idiot.[3]

Write soon. Will send on horse poem when I finish it.[4]

Love,

Louise

1. "It's certainly regression: back to the smartiness of high school debates, wherein each side tried to *sound* more profound than the other. And better-read. And more blasé. And more snobby. (She is particularly bad, just now, on really great art. She makes Bach sound like blood-brother to the grouse-shooters.)" (To Wilson, July 27, 1937)

2. It didn't; the prize that year went to Robert Frost, for *A Further Range*.

3. The poem *not* about music is, presumably, "Musician," which was written in June.

4. The "horse" poem is one of LB's best known: "The Dream." On February 10, 1937, she wrote to Edmund Wilson, when it was "just hot from the Muse," saying, "I really did have this dream."

/ *to John Hall Wheelock* /

July 22, 1937

Mr. Whellock: (a *new* variation!)

A variation on a wise sentence you dropped, while I was getting more and more alcoholically dramatic and hazy.

Love,

Miss Bogan

> The male bird does not go about puling and mewing
> To the hen-bird (who is also a realist): "O mamma, love *me!*"
> He flies around and finds food,
> He makes love, and sits, and is tender and doing.
>
> Adult as can be
> Is marriage in a tree.

/ *to Rufina McCarthy Helmer* /

August 5, 1937

Dear Rufina: [1]

Well, here I am in my ducky little apartment, as happy as a clam at high water (although just how happy that is, I have always had my doubts!). I have a table, a bed, a few chairs, and a few bibelots and books. Also some dishes and knives and forks and spoons. T. E. Lawrence never allowed more than four cups in his house, and I can understand, now, just how he felt. I have one cup, but a lot of old, superfluous, cupless saucers, and I'll give them to the Morgan Memorial soon. I potter around and clean and dust, and water the plant (yes, I have a plant, with which I soon will be in love: you remember "I had an aunt that loved a plant, but you're my cup of tea"). I also have a phonograph and a lot of records. This is the only way to live, I can tell you. I dread the fall, when, for shame's sake, I'll have to put up some curtains and down some rugs. —The fine view of the back piazza of the Psychiatric Institute, with its male and female patients, keeps me on an even keel, and in good humor. I always remember the three weeks I spent in its sister institution, the Neurological. I remember looking out, from the windows of hydrotherapy, over what must have been the very roof under which I now live, and seeing a woman hanging out clothes, and wishing that I, too, could be a normal resident of Washington Heights, and hang out clothes in a happy, normal way. Well, I've got my wish, and the mere mechanics of going to the grocer's now makes me happier than the present of pecks of diamonds. (All this is morbid euphoria, no doubt!)

* * *

Saturday is my birthday, and I'll be forty, and I never thought I'd live to see the day. —I am so glad you enjoyed *The Princess Casamassima*.[2] It is superb. It settles the problem of the artist in modern society, for one thing. I think the final scene, when the hard-bitten revolutionary and the aristocrat (or at least the member of an upperest class) stand over Hyacinth's (the artist's) death-bed, and don't know what to say, either of them, is one of the finest in modern literature. In ancient literature, too, for that matter. Do read *The Bostonians*, if you haven't already. That is another masterpiece, and no one ever reads it. Everyone starts in, on James, at the wrong end: *The Golden Bowl*, etc. These works often bore and puzzle the beginner, and they drop James, and miss all the wonderful early works. *The Tragic Muse* is fine, too.

I knew *something* was going to be blown up, as I told you. I have a new theory about the Irish: that they're really forest dwellers, with all the forest-dweller's instincts, and that since, or when, the Irish forests disappeared, they all developed a terrible neurosis, from being forced to be out in the open so much. I really think this is true. Just a lot of Druids at heart.

* * *

Louise

1. Rufina McCarthy—later Mrs. William F. Helmer—was, until her retirement, a teacher of English in the Boston-area high schools.

2. LB's enthusiasm for this novel produced, for *The Nation* a year later, "James on a Revolutionary Theme," one of the essays that initiated the James revival.

/ to Morton D. Zabel /

August 11, 1937

Dear Morton:

✿ ✿ ✿

This morning I arose, bathed, made a superb cup of coffee and two pieces of superior toast, ate these, after eating a fine summer pear. Then I took down Yeats, saying to myself: "You'd better begin your forty-first year with a little poetry, my girl" (although I shan't be forty until tonight at half-past eight); so I crossed myself, and said a prayer of thanks for dangers past and surmounted, and opened the Yeats, and this is what met my eye:

> Undying love to buy
> I wrote upon
> The corners of this eye
> All wrongs done.
> What payment were enough
> For undying love?
>
> I broke my heart in two
> So hard I struck.
> What matter? for I know
> That out of rock,
> Out of a desolate source,
> Love leaps upon its course.[1]

So, after this fine omen, I am ready to go into my fifth decade, with a mild kind of confidence, and a subdued kind of joy.

The Swift researches occupy me. I am sure he was neither syphilitic nor impotent. He was just a highly charged neurotic. And, it seems to me, he was certainly Vanessa's lover. Her letters to him are not the letters of the deserted mistress of an impotent man. And did you ever read her will? The repetition in it, of the words "to buy a ring," seems to me to point to the fact that she knew of an actual marriage between S. and Stella. She was afraid of him, but she went as far as she dared.

Aren't editors dopes? So afraid to say what's really so plain, and covering up everything in footnotes! Well, I can make no flat statements, but I certainly will say what I believe. Without footnotes.

> I am content to follow to its source
> Every event in action or in thought;
> Measure the lot; forgive myself the lot!
> When such as I cast out remorse
> So great a sweetness flows into the breast
> We must laugh and we must sing,
> We are blest by everything,
> Everything we look upon is blest.

A thought for this year!
  Happy birthday—

Louise

1. Yeats' "His Confidence." The second quotation, also by Yeats, is the last stanza of "A Dialogue of Self and Soul."

August 22, 1937

Dear Morton:
It has been a little like equatorial Africa, here. Last night it began to rain, and has kept up ever since, and now there's that lovely cool-cold in the air, and everything smells a little like metal and farewell, and this is the smell I most love in the world: the first breath of autumn, smelled in late August. I have tried to figure out just why I love these days, and this light (best just after the rain just after heat) and I once decided that it was because I was born in August, and, maybe, first began to see and smell, and focus on days like this. That's a very good explanation, I think. . . .
❋ ❋ ❋

I saw *The Spanish Earth* this afternoon, along with two audiences: the Communist one, which came in before 1:00, and the regular, or bourgeois audience, which came in later and paid 20 cents more. The first audience cheered the Communist salute (described, by Hemingway, a little misleadingly, I thought, as the "salute of Republican Spain"). —Hemingway was just *too* noble and humanitarian, and clipped-speech, throughout. You'd have thought that he'd never whooped up such a humanitarian spectacle as a bull-fight, in his life, or never been passed bottles of beer by minions, while on safari. All full of the milk of human kindness, and the virtues of the dear *peasants* and the brave civilians. I don't see him doing any labor and union helping at home, however. I suppose an automobile strike isn't colorful enough for him.

It was truly shocking to see innocent people bombed by Fascist planes, I will admit. Of course, not a word was said about Soviet Russia's part in the struggle. And one touching moment in the picture froze my blood, even though I know all about how terrible the Spanish Catholic Church has been, down the ages. A man's body lay on a sidewalk, after an air-raid, and men and women came out to look at it. One woman, in the presence of death, put her hand to her forehead, in the first gesture of the sign of the cross. She was immediately pushed aside, out of the camera range, by another woman. A good many [people] raising clenched fists, in the salute of Republican Spain, followed this.

Well, men make up these gestures. When they're sick of one kind, they make up its opposite. . . .

There was certainly something awfully sentimental and fixed, about that picture. The whole tone of it bothered me, although, God knows, I'd like the Spanish Loyalists to get their country. But Hemingway was having such a hell of a good time, looking at a *War*, and being disgustingly noble about it. —No one will notice things like this, soon, fortunately. When people aren't having wars of their own, they'll be looking at movies of wars, with lots of well-spaced machine-gun fire, and music arranged by the versatile Virgil Thomson, and Marc Blitzstein. . . .

* * *

The point about *Stella Dallas* was this: it showed the genuine, dyed-in-the-wool yearning of the American proletariat, toward the stuffed shirt class. It was really a howl. The saintly goings on of Stella (B. Stanwyck), and her transfigured face, when she had really managed to get her daughter married off to a William Stuyvesant III, was enough to make the brain reel. And all the time there was a character in the film who was, to me, a perfect darling. This was the rowdy and drunken bookmaker, who frequently made John Boles' face freeze, even more than usual. The episode of the Christmas turkey convulsed me, and when the man got down and began looking for some signs of real liquor, among the sarsaparilla bottles, under the sink, I nearly fell off my chair. What the Communist party needs is more jolly proletarian members, partly in liquor, most of the time, if possible. This God damned nobility of all and sundry is making me terribly ill. If the new

world is going to consist of a lot of Communist stuffed shirts, you can count me out of it. I'll take to the roads, or the trees, or the crannies in the rocks. . . .
   * * *

Love,
Louise

/ *to Theodore Roethke* /

[September] 1937

Dear Ted:

The only homily I can send you is this: Stop forcing things. Stop trying to get a certain number of things taken, this year, just because you had a certain number taken, last year. Forget your score, and let yourself dam up a little, inside. Perhaps you're all sluiced out, for a while. Let whatever-it-is fill you up again, and don't write anything, or send out anything, for a couple of months. —That's the only way to get your weight back. A couple of years is better, of course, but I can't see you doing that, just now. But, for God's sake, forget the editors. Pretend you're in Siberia, and couldn't get anything printed if you tried. —I've had those "easy" periods happen to me; the one thing that saved me, after my first real lot of acceptances, was the fact that I went to Austria for six months, and couldn't get quick action from editors. Then I stopped writing like magazines, and went back to hard, painfully produced poems that sounded like myself.
   * * *

And, as far as I'm concerned, you can have anyone who writes "odic poems." I'm going right back to pure music: the Christina Rossetti of our day, only not so good. My aim is to sound so pure and so liquid that travelers will take me across the desert with them, or to the North Pole, or wherever they are going. Up to Mt. Everest, for example. —This ambition has been brought on by my discovering the fact that Lawrence took the *O. Book of E. Verse* with him through Arabia. What more could poets ask than that? You never heard of anyone taking Karl Marx, Sidney Hook, or even Trotsky or Pareto, through Arabia with them. * * *

Love,
Louise

/ to Morton D. Zabel /

October 9, 1937

Morton dear:

I know, I know. It was like a marriage, and a third thing that wasn't you or the magazine, and those third things are terribly hard to root out. —Pitiful! My God, is suffering over an inherently noble renunciation ever pitiful? No.[1] —Haven't you read the Goncourt Journals? Do you remember, in them, the description of a Gavarni lithograph: a bum leaning against a lamp-post and taking the jeers of a well-dressed couple, and saying: "I may be a tramp, but at least I'm not a grocer." * * * —You have a piano, haven't you? Well, take the hatred out on that, and the nobility out on your work, and don't suffer too long (but suffer long *enough,* so that you'll never have to go back to that particular agony, in 1947). Suffer three weeks. * * *

Now, Dr. Zabel, as I shall be forced to call you in the future, allow me to describe the plunge *I* took today. * * * Maidie and I, as bold as brass, walked into Wanamaker's, this noon, and asked if they would be good enough to show us their pianos. A very old guy, with eyelids like a turtle's, took us in hand (he was shadowed, throughout the proceeding, by another, even older guy, who probably wanted to trip up any sale, and get it for himself). We tried the "spinets," and they seemed O.K., until we tried the half-uprights, which weren't nearly so pretty, but had "normal hammers," or some such thing. We tried and tried, and the turtle kept playing beautiful arpeggios, not to mention "The Old Folks at Home" with variations, as against the only things Maidie and I can play, ad lib.: namely, on Maidie's part, a little Grieg number, and a few bars of a Mozart sonata (both of which keep to about an octave, and don't bring out the resonance of the bass or the brilliance of the treble), and on my part, the chords which presage, in P[*élleas] and M[élisande*], the downfall of M.'s hair. The turtle, I may say, was thoroughly unimpressed by both of these performances. —We tried and tried, and he led us to a horrid little instrument, which had been placed so near some steam-pipes that Maidie and I both caught on that it was made of matchwood and glue. The arpeggios kept ringing out. And then Maidie put her foot down for stiffness of action, and that led us to a darling black little "Federal" (American Empire, to you), half-upright, with "normal stringing/hammers," and gilt decorations here and there, and we took it, to the tune of $310. $25 down, and the rest in two years. But I *am* going to earn the two hundred in two months, and meanwhile we are to have a nice, commodious little piano.

How beautiful life is! —I have been waking up, these last few nights, and thinking how I used to waken at night, and toss and turn, worrying about what was going to happen, and rave (whenever there was an audience). But now I waken and stay awake for hours, and think that, after all, the worst has happened, and there's no more fear. * * *

> Ever with love,
> Louise

1. Zabel, who had become editor of *Poetry* upon the sudden death of Harriet Monroe the year before, resigned as of the October 1937 issue. George Dillon followed him in the job.

/ to John Hall Wheelock /

> October 14, 1937

Dear Jack:
* * *

About the circulars: everyone I really currently care for has the book (how account for the 399 copies sold, otherwise?). —So there are two kinds of people left: my enemies, and a lot of pompous people with names, who are better left to themselves in any case. However, I'll turn over my enemies' names in my mind, and the names of a few neutrals, if I can remember any. —The trouble is, when I'm not actively engaged in hating people, or fearing them, I forget all about them, and it is their names which go first. So today I really haven't any enemies, for practical purposes, that is. And tell the Bookstore they might circularize the G's and M's in *Who's Who.* That is as good a scheme as another.

(I really will try to think, in a day or two!)

I have given the eastern situation, the Far Eastern situation up. When two ancient civilizations start fighting, what good does it do to complain?

> Your wise and detached friend and, may I add, admirer,
> Louise

/ *to Morton D. Zabel* /

November 8, 1937

Dear Morton:

* * *

—I have just been reading, God help me, Yeats' complete works, and it stands out very clearly there that he was all shot to pieces when he first met Lady Gregory. He was 34 years old, and had had a hard, emotional youth, with lots of work and frustration in it. And, in spite of himself, in spite of all he could do, he fell to pieces. Maud Gonne had married someone else, and he had worn himself out on her, and on Irish politics and factions, etc. For a little while he could do nothing, but go around with Lady G. to the cottages and listen to the old peasants talk. He hated his work. He had come to a blank wall all round.

And then what happened? In a few years he is back on his feet again, starting an Irish theatre. He was acting in a new and even stronger way. He began learning how to write, all over again. He began to face reality even more. What do you suppose those later poems came out of? A break, a tragic break, which he lived through and got over, and mended from. *And he never repeated the thing again.* And how strong he became; what a fighter! As he says himself, if he had not gone through all that, in the late '90's, where would he have been when some real trouble started, and he had to fight for the plays of Synge, as well as for his own work? In 1905. Where indeed. —There's probably something coming that you'll have to fight, that will be worse than this, and you had better learn your lesson now, once for all. . . .

* * *

Everyone has to shift into maturity at your age, Morton. And most people of our calibre are just infants until they do. . . . Think of Edmund out in the woods. Think of me, up in Wash. Heights. Think of Dante climbing the stranger's stair, and everyone else who were tested *to their full strength,* and came through.

And how about playing the piano, or doing some water-colors or wood-carving?

Write soon.

Love—
Louise

November 27, 1937

Dear Ted:

Well, if a literary career is like this, I don't wonder that people grew beards and took to drink and other forms of dissipation. —For a month, I worked on that Yeats article, and now that *The Atlantic* has it, they don't tell me whether or not they like it, and I roam around fuming.[1] And then all sorts of other jobs appear, none of which I want, because if there's an unambitious woman, it's me, but they all have small sums of money attached to them, and I owe the money, so I have to go on, reading in the Library all day, between men who rustle the leaves of *The Hotel Man's Vade Mecum*, or beside a youth who reads the *New Masses*, sucks sticks of candy, and bites his nails. (This last creature fascinated me, at the last. He would bite and bite, and then stop himself for a short while, by tugging his hair, and wiping what was left of his hands all over his vest. He didn't stop reading the *New Masses* for a minute, however. Of such are the founders of the new world, no doubt.)

* * *

I spent last week-end in Stamford with Edmund, and we had a nice time, even though I was subjected to some of his friends, one afternoon. My, how the women married to literary men hate me! They positively fry in their own juices, while I am in the room, and wig-wag frantic signals to the poor males, who are only trying to be nice, and don't know anything about my more deadly qualities. But the women do. And John Dos Passos does, too. He hates me so it is painful to watch. Thank God he does. For if ever there was a fake human being and a punk writer, J. Dos P. is that one. He is such a Harvard fake. Bunny loves him.

We played Irish songs and Edmund read me Dante, and we drank Dewar's, Black and White and Johnny Walker, and we went for a walk, and Edmund says that I sleep so loudly that it may bring on serious political trouble. He described what happened when Louis XV's waterworks, that ran the fountains at Versailles, kept the residents of Marly awake all night for years with their buzzing and gargling and gurgling. He says Michelet has a whole chapter about it. One of the prime causes of the French Revolution. —Well, no one around here has complained any, up to now. But maybe they will. . . .

* * * Edmund says, by the way, that Hemingway's latest [*To Have and Have Not*] is nothing but Popeye the Sailor Man, and I think he's

right. The Stalinists now have Hemingway, and he'll be having a lovely time stabbing Trotskyites in the back, for the rest of his life.

I seem to be slipping off the keys. Fatigue. Write soon. My hair will be gray, with this literature, if I don't stop in time. . . .

Love,
Louise

1. The article was published by *The Atlantic* in May 1938.

/ to Edmund Wilson /

November 29, 1937

Dear Edmund:

Thank you for the entertainment, and I hope the nice little review of Swift's poems turned out well. —I have to do a nice little review of *Letters from Iceland,* tomorrow, and point out just why they aren't rubbish, as you seem to think. They're a damned sight better than anything Auden has produced since. That "Spain" poem is a new low for him, mainly because he's beginning to mouth the same old tripe everyone else is mouthing: "the necessary guilt for the necessary murder," etc.

Today I read Henry Miller's remarks, in the current *Criterion,* about the Anaïs Nin diaries. Fifty volumes of them, from the time she was thirteen on, and they're going to be the great thing of the forties, I suppose. A woman's saga, told as I have always held it should be told: without malice, but in full. Miller is to bring them out, in Paris. His article I thought quite fine; but you may not like it, because it is full of symbolic mirrors inside of whales. The main point is, that the woman came into life, by writing as she did write, and by experiencing what she did experience, and she came into life whole and free, from all I can make out.[1]

* * *

Your soon-graying-under-the-weight-of-literature-friend
Waterworks Louise

1. "J. Wheelock said Scribner's couldn't possibly [publish them], even after the kindergarten dirt of Hemingway. For one thing, she has slept with some of Scribner's authors, very respectable ones (not John Galsworthy, but someone just as stuffed, evidently), and she put down just what she thought of the experience—in a word, poor." (To Roethke, November 27, 1937)

Twenty-nine years later, LB wrote: "I actually *bought* Anaïs Nin's *Diary!!* I know, I know. But on Monday I sold a bunch of books for a largish sum—so this wasn't a true extravagance. And a peek through the pages had given me one or two unforgettable vignettes of the preoccupations of this totally humorless dame—especially of her 'friendship' with the redoubtable H. Miller. *And* a photograph, taken in 1934, in which her kohl-rimmed eyes and her lamp-black eyebrows stamp themselves upon the retina. What she looks like now, knows God!"

/ *to Theodore Roethke* /

December 14, 1937

* * *

Did I tell you that H[arold] Stearns wants me to do the poetry article for his new *Civilization in the U.S.* volume? I don't want to do it, but I suppose I must, because Maidie wants me to appear in the select company of Deems Taylor, John Chamberlain and Bruce Bliven. And I can at least tell the truth, without biases. I'm not caught up into any gangs, and I'm not a Yale man, so that I'll have to give a great big plug to Archie MacLeish. —But it's a month's hard work for $50. And a share of the profits, which may be something, since Simon and Schuster are publishing the thing.

The latest new poem was what Edmund always calls "very well-written," but it *was* too full of abstractions, and the form is too full of Yeats. And that long form, with short lines, needs some actual objects in it, to come off. You know how full of objects the poem about the man going up to cast flies in the stream, where the stones are dark under froth, is. That's what your poem needs, and I'm terribly tired of these exhortations to be vertical, too. Perhaps what the world needs is more kindly people in comas. Certainly some of the vertical people are cumberers of the ground, even if they *do* have the right political set. * * * My, how happy I am that I stood out for the humanities, even under pressure! But how could I do otherwise? I know, and knew, that politics are nothing but sand and gravel: it is art and life that feed us until we die. Everything else is ambition, hysteria or hatred.

* * *

Your literary friend,
Louise

/ *to Morton D. Zabel* /

May 19, 1938

Spent the week-end in the connubial atmosphere of Trees. Mrs. Wilson is really a darling,[1] and I hope everything lasts. There will be an heir. She's 25; graduated from Vassar in (!) 1933. E. W. is fine; and the dialectic is coming in for some licks, since he has expiated, it seems, his sense of guilt toward the lower classes.

* * *

How about you and me taking the tonsure and the veil, respectively. And raising *waldmeister*. And drinking mead on feast-days. Think this over.

L. (St. Clare) B.

1. This Mrs. Wilson was the redoubtable Mary McCarthy.

/ *to Rolfe Humphries* /

May 21, 1938

Well—you're you and I'm me, and there's no use fighting about it, I guess, but don't ever come over me with this guiding-hand stuff again, or I'll draw off and give you an unorganized hay-maker. —That may be your field and task, but count me out. You and I are evidently working out our respective Karmas in opposite directions. I began with *The Sacred Heart Messenger* and was often told that if I went into a Protestant Church I should suffer the spiritual equivalent of having my ears drop off. You are ending under authority; and *next* time we live, maybe we can have some sense and some fun.[1]

L.

1. After an earlier fight, LB had written to Humphries: "At least you leave the most important part of me alone. We never quarrel about poetry, which, after all, as someone has said, is a region of the mind; it just happens that it is the region wherein, at our best, we both live." (August 4, 1935)

June 13, 1938

Dear Saint Chrysostom:

* * *

Frankly, I don't much care for the lullaby. I have tried to turn things out before sleep, too, and they're always on the noble-sweet side. As Yeats believes that war emotions cannot and should not be made subjects for poetry, so I believe that the lyric poet should never utter when he or she feels sorry for himself or herself.

Have done nothing but make a translation of *Der Tod, das ist die kühle Nacht,* by Heine. You will think this rather feeble, if you haven't the original at hand. The original is superb. Brahms has written an "art-song" to the words, and I'll play it for you, sometime. . . .

The academics I saw looked so terribly innocent, poor things. That kind of innocence always results, in age, in horror, of course. The once-born shouldn't be learned. It takes the twice-born to be that. Or thrice-born. I'd like to see Baudelaire and Emily Brontë and Catullus, in those hoods and things. I suppose all that *is* bourgeois degeneracy. . . .

* * *

Till Wednesday.

Louise

June 21, 1938

Dear Rolfe:

Am spending a quiet afternoon stewing a chicken. All of a sudden I get a wild yen for some stewed chicken. Extraordinary. My childhood was made miserable by my mother's belief that no Sunday was complete without its stewed chicken, and sometimes she'd produce quite a masterpiece, but more often she'd get mad just about the time the dumplings should go in, and sabotage the dish in some way. So I haven't been able to go for stewed chicken very much, in my mature years. But then, late at night I think how nice it would be if there were a nice stewed c. leg in the ice-box. So there will be one there tomorrow night, and if I like the idea, I can just go on boiling fowl all through July and August, and my alimentation will be reduced to great simplicity. —Toscanini says that he had so many things to learn when he was young that he just ate soup and bread, and that he didn't mind going right on eating s. and b. for the rest of his life. —The fewest and the simplest gestures will do me, too, for the remainder of my time on earth. I just want to be quiet and harmless. Perhaps an unmitigated diet of fat old hen will bring about the desired effect. . . .

Am reading a book by Georges Bernanos, a devout Catholic, which tears the pants off the Spanish clergy. He was in Majorca at the outbreak of the war, and does not hesitate to call the archbishop a murderer. The vol.'s called *Les Grands Cimetières sous la lune,* and you should read it.

When I see you on that boat, from Mexico to Marseilles, I'll believe it. —Pretty big of Moe to give you $250 more. And where did you get the idea that $2500 was coming to you? —If I had been given $2500, I might have had some decent places to stay, in Rome and elsewhere, instead of brooding around in damp and greasy pensions. I remember seeing a real desk in one hotel room, and saying: "O wouldn't it be wonderful to have a desk!" But it cost too much.

* * * [Morton] says that M. Zaturenska is preening herself over her prize no end.[1] She says that she has discovered the truth in the saying that only good people can write good books.

Everything seems to cost a great deal.

There are so many ways one can't let oneself feel, in poetry. But that's all to the good. Maidie wants me to write some happy poems.

Write or buzz,

L.

1. The Pulitzer, for *Cold Morning Sky.*

July 8, 1938

Dear Rolfe:

A very nice letter, and I hope you keep on with your observations. —The Lorca poem is beautiful.

It was nice coming back on the train. The funny little towns, and the horrors of the New Jersey cities equally interested me. (Why did A. MacLeish have to go South and West to pick up photographs of disinherited people and places, when the rotting houses in Newark are so near at hand?) —I particularly liked coming into New York by the ferry at 23rd Street. All that waterfront section is the dirty and clumsy and awkward and touching kind of thing I grew up with, and felt and loved. Mankind being kind of stupid. Not too smart. Bungling everything a little. —When the ferry-houses are full of chromium, and the funny corner restaurants are through, I'll be dead, I hope. Yes, I know it's sentiment. But I don't like the human race to get too smart and slick and clean and efficient. I don't know much, but I do know that's death, and it attracts bombs, too. . . .

Have just finished reading A. MacLeish's great speech, all about poets being challengers. It's the most awful tripe I ever read in my life, but I'll bet the League of American Writers feels set up by it. —From now on, I'm not going to pull my punches about that bird. Of all the tub-thumping performances I ever read, it is the worst. It "was delivered with ringing feeling," or some such phrase; and I can well believe it. It's exactly the kind of sophomoric oration that brings the house down at college reunions. (The audience rose to its feet, at the end, and I can see why.)

Well, the poetasters have got us, and we might as well be resigned. Boy, is Archie mean to the people who live alone "in rooms upstairs with a view of the river." (Is that me: and if so, how did he get it?) Boy, does he tell off the "pure" poets, and the leaners toward posterity. Boy, does he sweep away all standards. ("Where are your little rules as applied to the works of Shakespeare? Where are your little rules as applied to the works of Dante? How small your little rules look," etc.) O.K.

I STILL THINK THAT POETRY HAS SOMETHING TO DO WITH THE IMAGINATION; I STILL THINK IT OUGHT TO BE WELL-WRITTEN. I STILL THINK IT IS PRIVATE FEELING, NOT PUBLIC SPEECH.

* * *

You can easily see that I'm terribly mad, at the moment, about the C.P., and all its works. The girls at the subway entrance saying, in soft tones, "Stop the mad dogs of Fascism; help our boys dodging Franco's bombs," frankly make me sick. If the C.P. doesn't stop all this "mad-dogs" "depraved" stuff it will lose—well, I was going to say the respect of all intelligent people. But I take that back. There aren't, as far as I can see, any intelligent people left.

But by gosh, I'm one, and I mean to put up a lot more fight, to stand up for the abstract idea of warm-hearted and humorous detachment, than I have ever put up before. I have nothing to lose.

> Your Fascist friend,
> Louise

/ *to John Hall Wheelock* /

July 17, 1938

Dear Jack:

Thank you for your letter. I hope the peace stayed—"had some abiding."

You know I never could stand a colony. I tried one once, and that was enough. Everything must be done in solitude, if at all. The thrusting egos of others prance around far too much, in such places (and one's own ego too, I suppose). —I heard from a young man, just this week, that sharing other people's difficulties, at that particular colony, was a little like sleeping six in a bed. —And you know how used I have become to pallets (although you sneer at mine!).[1]

* * *

It is so hard for me to spend time in a strange place, even with people I trust, and who trust me. I get into such terrible panics. —But I'll keep your sweet invitation in mind, and thank you for it, in any case.

Perhaps we can share some Macy champagne on my birthday.

Ever with appreciation and affection, dear Jack,
Louise

1. Wheelock had suggested a stay at the MacDowell Colony, which, many years later, LB came to enjoy and respect. Writing to Katharine S. White in 1957, she said: "I shall be sixty in August, and it is time for me to investigate colonies. Up to now, I have been too *young* to think of them!"

/ *to Edmund Wilson* /

September 23, 1938

Dear Edmund:

No: it doesn't sound very much like the worst of MacLeish [1] (and it's the worst it should sound like), but I put this down to the fact that you write well, and it's hard to write punkly when one has a talent for literature, as well as years of training. * * *

The glosses are wonderful, and all the poem now needs is a little more dreadful liquidity, and a few shouts of HA! BUT THE SUN UPON US! MacL. had grabbed so many phrases from Pound—especially about water shining timidly or brassily in the sun—that maybe some of those images should go in, too.

—I have had a few thoughts about the "Kinds of Criticism" parodies. One is: The Sliding Along with the Author Type. You know: telling the story and summing the book up, in a final sentence, as perfectly fine; agreeing with all the points made, with the style, the method of presentation, the general tone, etc. Then there's The Publisher's Pimp Type. And the Reviewer Getting into Bed with the Book Type (Horace Gregory: "And I thought, as I turned the pages, of the Wisconsin fields under the setting sun in that November of 1925 . . ."). And The

Abstruse or Collegiate Philosophical, Propounded in a Kind of Academic Swahili Type (so many of Morton's contributors to *Lit. Opinion in America* are like this, especially R. P. Blackmur).² What one could call Kenneth Burke I leave up to you.

* * *

Love to you and Mary,
Louise

1. Wilson's parody was called "The Omelet of A. MacLeish," after the 1928 book *The Hamlet of A. MacLeish*.
2. LB herself was one of the contributors, with an article on Viola Meynell.

/ to Rolfe Humphries /

September 26, 1938

Dear Rolfe:

I answer at once, although I haven't much news. —I must say that your account of the boat made me happy that this woman will never set foot on a boat again—certainly not a boat going to the tropics. —The flying fish I observed with the sharp and emotional eyes of a pregnant nineteen, and then I got hives, and ate saltines and sucked lemons all the rest of the voyage. O, the terrible heat in the little cabins of that transport! —Your fellow-passengers sound about up to average. Travel and meet nice people! You should have succumbed and taken a bottle along. It's the only solution, on shipboard, modern and ancient. Rum against the bleakness of immensity.

There has been a hurricane in New England, and it looks as though Hitler were going to go right ahead and start a war. My two Tory friends sit glued to the radio, I don't know why. I just look at the headlines on the newspapers. The fatalist in me. What *can* stop a mass-neurosis like the one in Germany? * * *

Am trying to polish off Edith Wharton. She's really pretty bad, in spite of all her seeming good points. A maker of stiff masks and put-up jobs of plots, and a Europe-yearner of the first water. R. M. Lovett did a pretty good little book on her, saying that her trouble was that she never really saw any Americans west of N.Y., and had no idea of the indigenous culture which was rising all around her, in spite of *Ethan Frome*. *E. F.* is a picture of a dying kind of American life; and, of course, she thought the rising living kind merely vulgar. She is always *pitying* workers: poor things, how they do have to work! Or sentimentalizing them. —Morton had just read *The House of Mirth* when he was here, and he thought it wonderful. She saw the frivolity and decay, but thought that *her* finer, older merchant standards were better. Good manners, living a long time in the same genteel surroundings, etc. The sort of thing which has culminated in Groton and Farmington and the Brearley School.

Morton was still pretty shaky when he came back, but we had a few pleasant times together. We saw [Thornton Wilder's] *Our Town*, and it is really very touching, but almost all the hard parts are left out of that, too. The tough town kids with baseball bats and obscene shouts come in just once. The small town bigotry is played way down. There's a romanticized town drunk, and some terribly noble housewives. No small town prostitute, of course. Its power comes from its pull on nostalgia. —He's really not very big potatoes. But then, who is?

* * *

Read a good new book [by Enid Starkie] on Rimbaud, which you must read when Scribner brings it out. I had forgotten what a beautiful young creature he was. He did the only thing that a poet *should* do: he shocked hell out of everyone by a series of semi-criminal acts, and then he *got out*, for good and all. Never wrote another line. Hated everything he had ever done. Whereas poor old Verlaine went back into the mess and started his whole pattern over again. Went back to Mamma; got drunk; lived in filth. In the later years, Verlaine discovered a fine mother substitute. Whenever he got so sick he couldn't stand, he'd borrow the price of a cab and go to the hospital, and be tucked up and taken care of. Then he'd come out and do it all over again. And at the end he was living with *two* prostitutes. —Edith Wharton should have had a good look at Rimbaud and Verlaine. She admired Paul Bourget, however.

* * *

Write soon.

Love,
Louise

[P.S.] No: I won't do a blurb for the book. I've vowed never to pimp for publishers *in any way*. You don't really want me to!

1938

October 16, 1938

Dear Rolfe:

You have been on my mind, and I have received your card and your letters with much pleasure. —I think you are not so isolated in a foreign country as I have always been. There seem to be gatherings to cheer you, and one thing and another. —Your rooms sound wonderful; you will have them as ghosts in your dreams forever. The big room with the endless parquet floor, the enlarged portrait of the Empress Elizabeth, the photograph of two men going up hill in a snowstorm, the big handles on the doors, the wardrobe, the wash-stand and the ashtray on the desk, with which I lived in Vienna, will never leave me. —You must bathe in it all, for it will mean something very nourishing to the subconscious, in a few years. Not now.

And don't be too scornful of the baroque and churrigueresque, or whatever it is. Mexican baroque is the most beautiful in the world, in many ways. Not the simplest and purest, but the most fanciful: a real high point in the form. And if it annoys you in Mexico City, what are you to do in Rome which is almost entirely a baroque city, as it now stands. So study it and analyze it and appreciate it if you can. There must be some books you can get on the subject.

Here there is little new. I had a terrible time moving. The piano leg split from an old scar, and I never will get a chair to sit in, or be able to remove the bookcases from their bleak and soldier-like arrangement, side by side, around the room. The entrance room is rather nice: very empty, with a chest and a couch and a bookcase and two little chairs, and a lot of autumn leaves and some flowers. The front room, which has a really lovely view of the river, is the one which is stuck in semi-disorder. Chairs cost so damn much, and I have a phobia about buying furniture, since my unfortunate experiences with the hand of God, in the form of catastrophes, and the hand of landlords, in the form of evictions. Why make another effort, when all will be swept away by some terrible circumstance or other. My stars are against a settled abode, or always have been up to now, and, in my intuitive, superstitious and primitive way, I feel that it is flying in the face of fate for me to stay in the same house for two years.[1] —But enough of this.

The omen poem is very good. I hope Maxwell[2] takes it. Mrs. White is still the final arbiter, though. She sits up in [North] Brooklin, Maine, and decides finally on everything, as I discovered when they turned down my Heine translation. (No dead classics.) * * *

Well, my dear, don't divert yourself too much. Take some time to be lonely, and to let the horror of the tropics seep in. I don't suppose the horror is so evident, so far above sea-level, but it must be there a little. * * *

Next time I may be funnier. Write soon.

Louise

1. The move involved going from one floor to another in the same house. LB lived in this second apartment until her death thirty-two years later.

2. A *New Yorker* editor, and a novelist, William Maxwell had first come to LB's attention in 1937 when she read a story by him in that magazine. "It made me believe, for a while, again, in the tenderness and strength of the human heart," she wrote to Katharine S. White. The true beginning of their friendship, which lasted all her life, is described in a letter to Morton D. Zabel on June 2, 1941.

October 28, 1938

Dear Rolfe:

Just a short letter, to tell you that the Friends of Rolfe Humphries Society, Local No. 1, is bearing up, and hasn't lost its membership card yet. * * * Last night I listened to a new poetic drama by one A. MacLeish, called *Air Raid,* a radio drama for women. Boy, was it thrilling! I will say that he has, after repeated batterings, decided to write simple declarative sentences once in a while, and there's mention of simple things like aprons and the process of sprinkling clothes. But he can't keep his verbs out of the optative (?) and subjunctive: it's all "they might be, perhaps," and "I should be able to tell you," etc. And, boy, do the studio noises help! Those bombs at the last saved him. —Working it all out psychologically, I *should say* that he is now ready to murder some women, subconsciously. So he does, in a radio drama. —There is no point to the thing but more fear-mongering, really. So people bomb towns. True. So Archie wants to scare hell out of even more people than are scared to hell already. —No catharsis. . . . Of course I may be wrong. Maidie, in her harsh realistic way said: "O, if it were W. B. Yeats you'd think it was wonderful. . . ."
* * *

Well, I told you I thought Mexico was a bad idea to begin with. Think of all the fun you might be having in the British Museum or along the Bois de Boulongue, or however the hell you spell it. * * * —And do try to see something more than exploitation in those churches.

The exploitation is certainly there, but the Catholic religion, in the stage when it threw them up, was an outgrowth of a human need. Simple people need superstition and prayer (so do complicated ones, for that matter), and no religion has ever been *imposed* on a people. The Indians don't dance just to get rain, or because their chiefs tell them to. The golden bough grew out of man's imagination. The Elysian Fields are underground and the Christian heaven is over-head for two deep psychological reasons. So I wish you'd look at the dust-catching architecture as a human being and a poet and child of the universe, once in a while. You might get some refresh-ment from it, then. And unless you get refreshment from your travels (along with loneliness and misery and a little heart-break), how do you expect to get any poetry out of them?

You'll have to wait until it's over, in any case. I do know that. Only affected would-be's can write poems to the scenery right away. "Dawn: Taxco," or "Septuagesima Sunday in Girgenti," etc.

"Must close." More later.

Louise

November 1938

Dear Rolfe:
  * * *

Two large collected poems have come in: W. C. Williams and R. Jeffers. Una Jeffers has done a good job on Robbie, she has eliminated the more ridiculous ones, like "The Women at Point Sur," and that one about the woman who kills her children in the back seat of an automobile, and "Such Counsels." The shorter poems show up better, but O, there's much too much of them! Jeffers is supposed to explain his work, in the preface, and he says nothing at all, of course—nothing to the point. One thing that struck me was: that all his fiends in human shape and even his rough Point Lobos men and women are eminently respectable, really. They might at any moment turn around and say, "Did you pass a comfortable night?" or "Thank you verra moch!" —The W. C. Williams makes a very good show. Collected, the things stand out better, and I have always liked his descriptions of the spring coming to scraggly New Jersey roadsides, and the tenement houses. He has absolutely no sense of drama, and I might do a piece, putting him against Jeffers, who has too much. . . .

Outside, men are raking leaves and women are shaking rugs. There's

a good archaic down-beat to rug-shaking. The leaf-raking also has a
good old rhythm.

* * *

Salud! (Got that from Malraux, God save the mark.)
Louise
(Infantile Deviationists Local No. 8.)

November 27, 1938

Dear Rolfe:

* * * I think, in bed in the mornings, of the terrible things my insistence upon form in life has done to me and to others, and I swear
never to take an active step in life again. —Even expressing opinions
makes me terribly tired. —What men and women now need, I truly
believe, is a long sleep in the sun. The horizontal position. —But the
fools and the children (and I count myself among them) must fight
it out in the open, and that's when the trouble starts. Action usually
comes from meanness and frustration, but inaction is self-love, and
we are all self-lovers to an almost complete degree. So—act only
enough to get yourself a little something to eat, and a bed to sleep
on, and a drink, and a bunch of flowers. Act only enough to get
yourself a little bit of love. This requires a lot of action, you will say.
Less than you think. Or it would be less, if so many people weren't
overacting. (All this is known as Bogan's Law, and it certainly is as
sensible as the thought of Immanuel Kant, for example. Or of Nietzsche.)

* * *

Nothing new here. I have just given Bennett Cerf a slap in the face
(he wrote asking for an opinion of the poems of Laura Riding to use
in publicity), and that is some comfort. —But I am getting more and
more pathologically irascible, and sensitive. I have cut myself away a
little too much, I know—but I used to have no fear about this, because life always landed me a good swift blow, at intervals, which
threw me back, after I had receded. I have been counting on fate or
time or the coils of destiny to pry me out of my more obsessive fears.
But nothing seems to happen. —Well, decay of one sort or another is
part of the scheme, so I'll lay low and take it. I'll not raise a finger to
bring anything on, however. Never again. Let what will be, be, as
our friend Frost puts it. . . .

* * *

Remember—Rome in the spring. The thick rich sod. The fountained gardens.

Write,
Louise

/ *to John Hall Wheelock* /

November 28, 1938

Dear Mr. Wheeler (it *is* Wheeler, isn't it?):
Thank you a thousand times for sending me your *intensely* interesting poem, whose opacity is equalled only by its limpidity. —I am indeed honored to be its first (and I hope not last!) reader. —As the aeons roll, and the turbidities of our temporal assonances dissolve into less atrabilious acquiescences, the exquisite sophistries of this, your later manner, will, to those of us who do not underrate, as you so beautifully put it, "the ideal realm as panorama," exceed in prevision the hierarchal thaumaturge of that, unwillingly alluded to, by some, as the "Voluntary canicular *phlogisis*" (as distinguished from, and opposed to, *phlebitis*).

Do not, I beg, relegate this letter to the Unbalanced File of my previous correspondence. On the contrary.

Ever your frostbitten friend,
Louise ("Maladroit") Bogan

/ *to Morton D. Zabel* /

January 19, 1939

Dear Morton:
 ✻ ✻ ✻

[William] Maxwell came up one evening, and is a perfect darling. He is pretty wise, too. We were talking about a Wisconsin (or Illinois) Miss Havisham that he knew about, and I said: "Then Dickens was right: people do such things," and he said, "People do everything," and that is true. All those odd things that they do, like falling in love with shoes and sewing buttons on themselves, and hearing voices, and thinking themselves Napoleon, are *natural*: have a place. Madness and aberration are not only parts of the whole tremendous set-up, but also, I have come to believe, *important* parts. Life trying new ways out and around and through. The only bad kind of pain and aberration is the kind caused by power wanting to come through, and being pushed back. Then you get suffering, and if it isn't used to grow, it thumps one right back into the bassinet, and the period of playing with one's toes. —But all the rest of the horrors must Mean Something. Do you agree with me or don't you? Can't I give a course on this Great Truth, somewhere?

   * * *

    Best love, and write soon. Don't get all wore out, running round.

Louise

/ to John Hall Wheelock /

January 29, 1939

Dear Jack:

   * * *

    I enclose the signed contract.[1] I can't understand why Scribner's is doing this, and I'm against the book, on principle. Mark Van Doren's *Collected Poems* has just come in, and again I say: "What earthly good does it do?" —I shall endeavor, however, to write a nice series of *Dingedichte* for you. Can you suggest any subjects? The Zoo has been rather overdone, perhaps. I might write an Ode to the Passing of the Sixth Avenue Elevated, on whose platforms I have shed many a tear. —Or I might try my hand at that $1000 World's Fair prize. Mixing praise for Grover Whalen into some extolling of the helicline, or whatever it's called. Getting the American Tel and Tel Building and the Finnish Exhibit into it:

> And then we come to the Finnish Pavilion
> On which the Finns have spent a million;
> As fresh and fine as Grover's teeth,
> With a patent helicline running beneath.

Remember: I want engraved invitations, sort of, issued for the book:

Charles Scribner and Sons has the honor to present
A New Volume by the eminent American Poet Louise Bogan.[2]

Something on that order!

Ever,
L.

1. In September of 1938, LB had written to Roethke saying: "Poor Scribner's is making another feeble attempt to impress me upon an unwilling public. A new

'collected' book will appear in the fall of 1939, just in time for the World's Fair. I thought of calling it *Light Sheaf*. Do you know what the technical term for not very many stalks of wheat or oats or other grain is?"

This book, called finally *Poems and New Poems*, was not published until 1941, just in time for World War II.

2. These lines were penned in a large, flourishing and absolutely nontypical hand: irony made visible.

/ to Morton D. Zabel /

February 2, 1939

Dear Morton:

   ✿ ✿ ✿

Poor Yeats now knows it all, as my mother used to say. I hope it's as beautiful as he expected, and that he will find Donne and Landor waiting for him (both in a good mood). The very last poems, in this month's L[ondon] *Mercury*, are still terribly moving. All those last poems can stand with his greatest, and are remarkable in showing the senile side of an old poet—his reactions to young girls and old bawds, for example—that no one else ever had the nerve to show, in advanced age. Or did Goethe? Let me know about this, as I may have to write a little piece about it. I think it would be nice if poets lasted beyond life. I often wonder what happens to old ladies who belong to Garden Clubs, in Heaven. But old poets, if they persist, must have a lot of fun, twanging on the harp and one thing and another. Don't you agree? Think of the fun we'd have, discussing problems of technique with all the masters, and having heart to heart talks with Truly Great Souls. (Perhaps they give little seminars, the Great Souls. Shakespeare, Sappho and Socrates, 8:00 to 9:00; First Cumulus Cloud to the Left. . . .)

   ✿ ✿ ✿

Love,
Louise

/ to Rufina McCarthy Helmer /

February 23, 1939

Dear Rufina:

   ✿ ✿ ✿

I've given the world up, at least its political side. I am still a violent pacifist, and refuse to be railroaded into any side-taking that might lead to the air being let into people by means of bullet-holes.

The Communists are still whooping it up here, under various disguises, and so are the Fascists, of course, more openly. "Nice people" really hate Jews with a strong and bigoted hatred; I have one friend who is a darling, but has a streak of Jew-baiting right through her: she got this at Wellesley at an early age. I don't think that this period is any worse than all the former ones; whenever was there real peace and gentle-heartedness parading around, in history? Those three years between Christ's first public appearance and his crucifixion showed up the same motives of greed and cowardice, disguised as high thinking, that are now current. Mankind is nuts; always has been, and always will be, maybe. So I try to lead a perfectly harmless life, not even getting mad at the man downstairs who plays the piano even worse than I do, or at the old male and female tarts in the literary world. I pay my bills, and keep out of the way of trouble. Throwing one's weight around is bad, after the age of forty.

   * * *

Louise

/ *to Rolfe Humphries* /

St. Patrick's Day
March 17, 1939

Dear Rolfe:

* * * Hatred, suspicion, malice and madness seem to be reaching new highs everywhere. I heard, recently, of an attempted suicide, by a woman who has had everything, from youth on, to make her secure. She thought that the servants were poisoning her food. So what rule is there? Perhaps madness, like cancer, is a way of life trying to transcend itself. Last week, on a train at night—and how dreadful that experience still is, with one's face glooming at you out of the glass!—I thought that whoever uprooted life, and set it walking around, equipped with brains and a heart, must have been a fiend rather than a god. We do not even know if it is better to have the heart partially erased—to be "normal" and at peace—or whether the mad and damned who "howl away their hearts" are not, after all, the highest manifestation of the life-force. . . . I am sorry to be thinking so cosmically. I have been very tired. I went to Portland—a symbolic return to the womb, I suppose—and now I am a little better.

   * * *

There's a new song which enchants me. It goes:

"Jeepers, creepers! Where'd you get those peepers?"

Best luck. Love,
Louise

/ to Edmund Wilson /

March 22, 1939

Dear Edmund:
Just a note to ask you *not* to bring Auden and Isherwood to see me. I
have no interest in seeing them, in their present phase, and I certainly
don't want to be displayed to them as a curiosity: a female criminal-
poet. Being a poet, I am of course automatically a criminal; but I can't
say that I want to spend an evening being examined by two visiting
Englishmen, as a queer specimen. So let's forget it.[1]

I was very much interested in reading an article on T. Mann by Erika
Mann, in a recent *Vogue.* Thomas certainly has fallen on his feet, and
the whole picture of him neatly wrapped up in an upper-middle class
milieu, in Princeton, with a "couple" to wait on him, his Victrola, his
grand piano, his writing desk with its "old coins" displayed on the top,
and "the beautiful Empire bookcases from our ancestral home in
Lübeck," gives me a pain. —I always said his eyes were too near
together.

I made a visit to my own ancestral home, and am beginning to understand more and more what Yeats meant by "Paudeen," and why my
mother was an admirable person, even if she nearly wrecked every
ordinary life within sight. —She was against the penny-pinchers and the
logic-choppers; she loved beauty and threw everything away, and,
what is most important, she was filled with the strongest vitality I have
ever seen. —And how the "Paudeens" (from which the other side of
my nature unfortunately stems!) hated and feared her!

I'd like to see you, anytime. Best to Mary and the baby.
Louise

1. "I very nearly met Auden last week. This mixed pleasure is, however, still before me." (To Wilson, January 5, 1941) When this remarkable prejudice was
finally broken down, Auden became one of the friends she most admired, as these
letters will show. In May 1970 he gave her eulogy at the American Academy of
Arts and Letters.

/ to Morton D. Zabel /

April 18, 1939

Dear Morton:
* * *

You are dying to hear about Louis [MacNeice], I know. —He came up on a Friday afternoon, and I had had a hard week seeing people and was very talkative indeed. He was obviously abashed by my dwelling and my neighborhood. He is tall and slender, and wears very colorful clothes: a plaid shirt and a striped chocolate suit, and a yellow handkerchief and suede shoes. His eyes are long and a beautiful hazel; he moves beautifully, and talks well. We skimmed everything: Auden and I [sherwood] (I went for them right away, and said the play [On the Frontier] was terrible, and he said they now knew it, and I said that wasn't any excuse, and that the American C.P. was a bunch of gangsters, and they shouldn't allow themselves to be pushed around by it, etc., etc.). I told him Ireland frightened me, and I described Wellesley College, where he was going to speak, and we talked about his poetry * * * and about Yeats and Housman and the integrity of the artist (!). He said that Auden now talks about the i. of the a., and I just raised my eyebrows sneeringly at that. We had three drinks of rye, all of which L. finished right down to the last drop. I told him that it was an act of moral courage to go around seeing literary people in America, and he assured me that he had non-literary friends, as well. —We *did not* indulge in any personal gossip, and I never once mentioned my own work. He looked at me in a rather hetty way—rather appraising and hostile—a couple of times, and I don't blame him, really. But on the whole he was very nice and slid out of the door with a pleasant wave, after about two hours. The next day I received an invitation from the Oxford Press to meet him at tea, and didn't go, of course, so that's the last of Louis. —He also said it was a curse to be Irish, and I said, not at all, that [it's] an advantage you have, and I told him that H. James was Irish, which he didn't know. I also outlined my idea that the Irish went mad when the forest disappeared, and he said, "I hadn't thought of that." So we now must wait until he whips up a nice little book about America. —He is fundamentally a sensitive and talented being, I should say, but spoiled and rather unhappy about the Auden defection to I., maybe. I felt that, a little. * * *

So if you think that any romantic color tinged the afternoon, you

are wrong. I was at my most flushed and blowsiest. And, as I say, I talked his ear off.
* * *

Finnegans Wake came in, and I am going through it in spurts. It's the farthest North in man's struggle with language, but it is ultimately self-indulgent and the product of impulsions, I fear. Edmund, years ago, used to say that it would come to something and prove something, as it went along. This it does not do. It continually breaks down thought and language, and can this be a good thing? (On the other hand, it explores language right up to the Arctic, and down to the Antarctic, regions. No one, as Thibaudet said of the effects of Mallarmé upon French writers, will ever again be forced to compromise, in expression.) —It is remarkably well-written, throughout; the prosodic texture is wonderfully varied and firm. No Cummingsish adverb-avalanches. —I still don't know what in hell I'm going to say about it. Something of the above. —But is it a true picture of what goes on in sleep? —I have very clear conversations, and even receive answers, from my companions in the dream. —Joyce has slighted the problem. The parodies of learned glosses, footnotes, etc., and the parodies of all known forms of style are the most remarkable things in the book. The punning gets tiresome. The prose-poems assigned to the Liffey are lovely. The book ends, in the middle of a sentence, with one.[1]
* * *

> Ever with love,
> Fleda Vetch

1. By April of the next year, LB had turned sharply against the "repulsive" book. "If it breaks the way toward New Art, of The Music of the Spheres, I'm glad I shall be under the sod when the full symphony starts. The *tone*, even through the jargon, is so *little*, so meachin', so infantile, so smarty pants, so SMALL. * * * The cunning got him, boy, the cunning got him. . . ." (To Zabel, April 14, 1940)

/ to —— /

May 1, 1939

Dear Mr. ——: [1]
* * *

My dislike of telling future research students anything about myself is intense and profound. If they know everything to begin with, how in hell can they go on eating up their tidy little fellowships researching? And I believe the less authentic records are, the more "interesting" they automatically become. Then, too, of course, I have many dark deeds in my past which I shall have to cover up, for posterity's sake. I remember very well, at the age of seven or so, making away with a couple of little gold baby-pins, fastened with a chain, a contraption which fascinated me, from the top of a bureau belonging to a girl with long curls, who was older than I was, called Ethel Gardner, in Ballardvale, Massachusetts. I also have liked throwing things away and hiding them, ever since I can remember. I poked a small ring, decorated with a red stone resembling a ruby, down a crack in a staircase, in Bodwell's Hotel, in Milton, New Hampshire, around 1901, and I always used to bury my rag doll, Mag, and dig her up again. In the convent I fell in love with an altar boy, and wrote him a passionate letter, which was later found by a nun, and almost resulted in my getting expelled, then and there. Nothing came of this however, and I won a book, that year, for Catechism, and the Gold Cross for General Excellence, the next. (This cross was later pawned by my unfortunate brother, so I can't send it to you to prove my story.)

So you see, it is just as well if I don't delve into my past. I used to lie in confession regularly, I must warn you, from the time I first confessed, at the ripe moral age of about nine, through a harp draped with a dust-cover, in the convent parlor. (They must have been varnishing the confessionals.)

My great gifts of imagination always took the form of lies, in fact, up to my entrance into puberty, when I became a radical and a Fabian, and discovered Bernard Shaw, Aubrey Beardsley, Arthur Symons, Nietzsche, Wagner, Max Stirner and Walter Pater. My first literary exercises were strongly influenced by William Morris and D. G. Rossetti and I wrote a long poem, or a sonnet sequence, every day, for about four years, after coming home from school. The effect of these labors, after about two years, was that I got conditioned, one June, in Greek, Latin, French, algebra—in everything, in fact, but English Composition. I was always rather good in physics and geometry, although my struggles, in the laboratory, with Bunsen burners and Gilley boilers would have made the hair rise on the head of any competent physicist. —I used to weep, when under the influence of other people's poetry, and have a rush of blood to the head, resulting in violent nose-running and sneezes, when the muse descended on *me*. (This symptom passed, after about eighteen, and I don't suppose

I have ever been authentically visited by Apollo, since.) I used to get very sick to my stomach in public, too, around this time.

My passage from puberty into early maturity was swift, and I prefer to draw the veil over my experiences, sexual and otherwise, from the age of nineteen, when I married for the first time, to the present. I think the researchers of the future should have a little spice to help them on their way, and if they succeed in discovering any of my adventures, in detail, during this period (as I doubt that they can, since, except for ten years passed among the so-called bourgeoisie, my life at this time was lived among the lower-middle class, and they have short memories, owing to defective intellects and short memory spans). That I have no criminal records is entirely due to the kindness of several members of the legal and psychiatric professions, who, I am sure, put me down as nuts, and just let me go on, thinking that a stay in the booby-hatch, now and again, would not run into as much money as a stay in jail.

Well, where were we? O yes. —In regard to your detailed questions, may I reply as follows, taking them up seriatim, as the saying goes.

Birthplace: Livermore Falls, Maine, a town on the Androscoggin River, run by a paper mill. My father has often told me about the excellent hard cider made by Billy Bean, the proprietor of the town's combination brothel and saloon. B. Bean used to add all sorts of things to the original apple juice, including ground up sirloin steak, and the results of drinking this nectar, when it was ripe, were terrific. I often like to think that I bear traces of this fire-water in the ichor which runs in my own veins. . . .

Dates (what do you mean "Dates"?): August 11, 1897. Ten years before Auden, Isherwood, and L. MacNeice, and about two thousand after Sappho. This was quite a while to wait, wasn't it. It is my firm belief that I was Messalina, the Woman of Andros, a couple of nameless Alexandrians, Boadicea, Mary Queen of Scots, Lucrezia Borgia, the feminine side of Leonardo, Shakespeare's Sonnets, Madame Roland, Charlotte Corday, Saint Theresa (of Avila), and Felicia Hemans, before this. Born under Leo, you can readily see what the results would be (and have, I may add, been).

Parentage: Need we go into this?

Education: See parts of above. I got A in everything, one year. (Boston University gave me $5.00 in gold, too, as the finest writer of verse in the place, and you can imagine the effect of *that* upon me.)

Beginnings of career: Peculiar, to say the least.

Influences: I think alcohol comes in here. I began to drink steadily after meeting one Raymond Holden, although I had been known to crook my arm, on two continents, before that. I like Mai-bowle with wild-strawberries in it, champagne, rye, and anything which happens to stay in a bottle, best.

Development: Slow and unsteady.

Literary and social preferences: In a world which makes Louis Bromfield a Chevalier of the Legion of Honor, A. MacL. an unofficial Laureate, and A. Wurdemann a Pulitzer Prize winner, I should give you my preferences! I should live so long! —My social preferences range from truck and taxi drivers who make me laugh, locomotive engineers, when they are good-looking and flirtatious, delivery boys, and touching old people and children, through Chinamen, Japanese, and inarticulate people who just sit and take it. If you had asked for my *non*-preferences, boy, we might get somewhere.

Political convictions: NONE.

Likes and dislikes: My God: what do you think this is: an encyclopedia? —I love food, music, beautiful and *beau / belle–laid(e)* people of both sexes, babes in arms, flowers, clean rooms, aired sheets, oil-lamps, and books about bad taste. I also like love-making, when it is really well-informed, and some varieties of landscape. I dislike swimming, bathing in lakes or the sea, horse-back riding, and dirty fingernails. Also: well-bred accents, loud talk, the professional literati of all ages, other women poets (jealousy!), other men poets, English accents, Yale graduates and bad writing and bad writers.

Favorite Authors: O, you thought you'd get me there! —I like George Herbert, Shakespeare, Dante, Catullus, Lucretius, and anonymous ballad writers (why don't you go and research something about *them*, by the way?). Also, Swift, Stendhal and Lewis Carroll. Also Joyce, Eliot and some of Pound. Also . . . Thomas à Kempis, Jesus Christ and Rimbaud. Also Mallarmé and Yeats and whoever wrote "Johnny I hardly knew yeh". . . .

Favorite Public Figures: Napoleon, Wellington, Herbert Hoover, Alfred Smith, Carrie Chapman Catt, Leonora Speyer, and the old lady in the ladies' washroom at Mouquins (since torn down).

Marriage: Now, now!

Residence: Back of the Bug House, NYC

Work in Progress: NONE.

Bibliography: NONE.

Hoping this covers the ground, and that this finds you as it leaves me.

> Sincerely yours,
> Louise Marie Beatrice Bogan
> ("Butch" to her friends)

1. LB had second thoughts about this letter; and although she shared it with Zabel, who preserved it in his "Bogan Box," she never sent it to the man whose questionnaire called it forth. Given her change of mind, perhaps the nonrecipient has a right to anonymity.

/ *to Morton D. Zabel* /

May 29, 1939

Dear Morton:

* * * [C. S.] Lewis, like Bunny, knows everything about poetry but *the essential thing.* —I have often taken Bunny up on his meanness to people like Thibaudet, who, as you know, does the exact thing which Bunny cannot do. —And I chaffed him for writing that Taggard review, just recently. "But I still think she *writes well*," said he. That a woman should write at all, etc. But I have heard Bunny read poetry aloud by the hour, and he has even written some moving stanzas. —Don't ask me to explain what he lacks, or why (although I know, as you know). Thank God, he never reviewed me, that's all I can say.
* * *

The contestants in the Hopwood Memorial Prize Award, for judging of whom I should receive $75.00 any day now (and do I need it!),[1] were uniformly Yeats-or-Auden soaked, with the exception of the women, who were just plain punk. One poet called upon his guides, "Muriel, Horace, and Wystan . . ." (No; he didn't get first place, but I assure you my motives were pure.) I told the Director that I had read so much imitation Auden, in the last seven years, that my tendency was to hop on same: that, in other words, my judgment was not crystal-clear on that point. —Some poems about listening to trains and feeding the pigs, in Iowa or somewhere, weren't bad. One contestant called himself Robartes, and apologized for not having been able, just yet, to have assumed his Mask. Now, tell me, is that what Education does to people? —Why can't just those people be educated, for whom the process is salutary and invigorating.

Have been reading all of Roger Fry I can lay my hands on: he is so honest, so sensitive, and so amusing. But he didn't write very much, unfortunately. My immersion in literature-as-such, this winter, left me rather limp; I find that cookbooks and books about painting are about all I can take, just now. * * *

Let me see, now, have I covered all the subjects? O (padun!) there's the Universe: I almost forgot the Universe. Badly planned as it may be, does it not bear upon it the Great Signature, not only in the nobler promptings of the Human Heart, but also in the Song of Birds, the Design of a Shell, and the Pattern of a Leaf? And are we not, all of us, Saints and Sinners alike, Part of It, so that we cannot Judge it Truly, any more than we can judge the shape of our own ear, or the workings of the valves of our Heart? Whatever It Is, We Are It, and we might as well take it and Like It. Don't be too hard on yourself, as Dr. Wall said to me. You are what you are, and you can't do anything about it now. Just take it easy.

Write soon, and send back enclosures, *please*. . . .

Love and kisses—

L.

1. "You will be pleased to know that I am now as distinguished as J. Auslander, R. P. T. Coffin, Frances Frost and John Erskine. —The University of Michigan has asked me to judge their Hopwood Awards—to jointly judge the poetry. Boy, am I flattered! —Frances Frost was a judge about five years ago, so you can easily see where I stand in the critical hierarchy of America." (To Humphries, October 26, 1938)

Lemnos

July 29, 1939

Dear Diomedes-Heathcliff:
   * * *

I feel badly about your attributing strange results to Aloneness, and quoting that old gregarious philosopher, Johnson, at me. I know he was a wonderful man, and a fine critic, and all that, but he was no one to listen to on the subject of Solitude, since he never allowed himself to be alone for five minutes, his whole life long, and would have gone screaming mad if he had had to support his own solitude for a week. And he managed to stay *quite* mad, while surrounded by hordes of people, and an adoring Boswell (a thing, this last, which would drive me into a frenzy in one afternoon, as you well know). So please think up a better counselor, next time. —Aloneness is peculiar-making, to some extent, but not any more so (when one isn't in jail or the mad-house or buried in the Antarctic snows with a leaking stove and a temp. of 160 degrees below zero) than lots of Togetherness I've seen. How many bottles of gin do I drink a year? None. How many did I drink when I was With People? Hundreds. Has my tendency toward alcohol increased or decreased, during the last five years? It has decreased, definitely. I now feel rather boozy if I sit at night drinking some white Chianti, *gespritz.* —Do I fear and hate my fellow creatures as I once did, wrapped up in marital bonds, as the Belle of apartment 12B, in Tudor City? [1] No. (O those wonderful summer evenings when the cream of New York literary life played craps on my floor, and I was hard put to choose between the charms of Scudder Middleton, Ogden Nash, and Wolcott Gibbs! (Not the physical charms, although O. Nash did kiss me once, but THE MENTAL AND SOCIAL CHARMS!)

Now, do you actually think that Aloneness has improved me or not? If you say NO, I'll go to Chicago, disguised, in the dead of night, and chisel my way into your home, and escape with my LETTERS. (You must realize that I really can't come, if I can pass up the delight of pawing through the Bogan Box, with a bottle of Canadian Club beside me, or even a bumper of Vat 69, of blessed memory.)

Having canvassed briefly, as I'm sure you say on the lecture platform, the worth of Solitude versus Multitude, I will cease. I have work to do, babe, pretty soon now. * * *

> Ever with love,
> Louise

1. In these letters LB always gives the address as 5 Prospect Place.

/ to Edmund Wilson /

November 2, 1939

Dear Edmund:

Thank you for the post-card. —I thought I had been saying a few things, now and again, for some years—I certainly have been blowing down stuffed owls like A. MacLeish, for example. But perhaps I am beginning to take more in, and, as you say, give it out better. I hope so. —After glancing through the prognostications and the dated whoops of the *N. R.* Anniversary Number, I certainly am glad that *you* weren't among that gathering of old hacks. What I mean: they vitiate life with every stroke of their pens. If that is what AMERICA is going to be, they can have it. Me, I am fond of civilization, past, present and future, wherever it exists, Archie's whippoorwills by the whoopsy wave notwithstanding.

If you have another p. c. handy, do let me know what you think of the Paul Éluard piece in the *P[artisan] Review.* Also, my *coeur mis à nu,* in the same number. Under Q. 5, on p. 107, I do not credit the white collar class with a tendency to *"ripe,"* but with a tendency to *"rise."* (I suppose people will think that what I really meant was a tendency to "rape.") —I certainly would not have opened up like this a few years ago; you're right. And I really think it is a little *vulgar,* to do it now. But what the hell. . . .[1]

* * *

Yours for the promise of the human spirit!
Louise

1. In the magazine's symposium, "The Situation in American Writing," LB spoke to such questions as: "Are you conscious in your own writing of the existence of a 'usable past'?" "Do you place much value on the criticism your work has received?" "Do you find, in retrospect, that your writing reveals any allegiance to any group, class . . . ?" "Have you considered the question of your attitude toward the possible entry of the United States into the next world war?"

Her replies were precisely those the reader of these letters would expect. What Wilson remarks upon, however, is her willingness to speak about herself: her education, her exposure to Roman Catholic ("real") liturgy, her Irish inheritance and so on. As has been shown, her previous attitude toward biographical revelation was one of total avoidance.

/ *to Morton D. Zabel* /

December 11, 1939

Dear Morton:

* * * —I went into the Picasso show with Rolfe, of all people; we had had lunch, and I thought he should see Picasso, since he knew so much about that other Spaniard, Lorca. * * *

The Picasso show is remarkable, of course, but in a way which I don't think will really be defined until this generation has passed away. I certainly do not agree with the bull-necked docent who was leading a flock of well-bred *types* around, that our era will go down in history as the era of Picasso. If it does, it won't be for the reasons he gave: P.'s great originality, force, depth, insight, profundity, etc. As a matter of fact, the show gave me the feeling that Picasso is *not* very original; and I should state without any shadow of doubt, that he is not in the least profound. The point about the pictures—the main point —is that they are *Spanish, Spanish* and not French at all. Then, they are highly derivative; more so than I realized. When he is breaking through on his own he is dull and muddy, or rather sweet and sentimental (the line, in the classic things, is wonderful, of course, always, but the feeling is always banal). His enthusiasm for masks is a Spanish trait; always something African about Spain. The first Afro-Cubist nude things are just blown up versions of Cézanne's early fumbling attempt at the same thing. Picasso, being a Spaniard, is fundamentally a character. He is not at all profound; when he wants to be profound he *elaborates*. See what I mean? Or resorts to design to pass off his essentially (after the very first *saltimbanque* paintings, in which he is still young, and has a kind of tenderness) Spanish inhuman nature. —The *Guernica* is truly remarkable, as an expression of psychological confusion. And as a piece of painting it is effective to an extraordinary degree. It spreads all across one wall; and it was astonishing how people kept their distance from it: as though it might explode. —I don't think a French painter could scare people like that. Spain is perhaps the only country left where the true hell-let-loose-macabre is in the veins of the populace. The *Guernica* is certainly 20th century macabre, in its purest form. Hell and the demons coming through. Last century in America and France; this century in Spain. Next century in Russia, after it casts off the yoke. *See what I mean?* * * *

Another interesting thing is the appearance of P.'s periods in which he is going through a fit of sulks; like a child who says, "I won't paint!" All the true uglies of one of these periods are in one gallery, and it's something, to sit and look at them. * * *

Picasso as a decorator is superb, and, as I have said, the line drawings are exquisite. But I think Braque taught him a great deal about covering a wall. Certainly the one small painting which is truly beautiful—a table before a window, done in off-browns and nigger-taupes and grays—is Braque.
* * *

Best love and write soon,
Louise

Dear Morton:

* * *

Did you read [Isak Dinesen's] *Out of Africa*, last year? I have just re-read it and it is perfectly magnificent: the finest prose narrative of those bad old thirties, I should say. Now get this and *read it*. You can't play that phonograph *all* the time. —I bought *The Cosmological Eye* yesterday, cheap. [Henry] Miller is terribly funny when he just tears loose. Very German and Till Eulenspiegel. He just tears along and writes and writes, and [James] Laughlin [of New Directions] publishes and publishes. Never a blue-pencilling anywhere. Miller's account of *his* idea of what happens in *Hamlet* is superb. On the other hand, his piece on the Nin woman is astonishingly profound, complex, and well-written. And the story, "The Tailor Shop," is good. I particularly like the rape of the widow in black velvet, who, after falling, asks the young hero, "You'll always love me, won't you?"; while he is thinking, "Why did I wait so long? *Anyone* could have her. She's a push-over!" —This charts the difference between man's and woman's attitude to sexual intercourse very truthfully and clearly. I do think that's about what goes on in 99 cases out of, well, 102. . . .

* * *

Louise

1940-1949

TO MY BROTHER
KILLED: HAUMONT WOOD:
OCTOBER, 1918

O you so long dead,
You masked and obscure,
I can tell you, all things endure:
The wine and the bread;

The marble quarried for the arch;
The iron become steel;
The spoke broken from the wheel;
The sweat of the long march;

The hay-stacks cut through like loaves
And the hundred flowers from the seed;
All things indeed
Though struck by the hooves

Of disaster, of time due,
Of fell loss and gain,
All things remain,
I can tell you, this is true.

Though burned down to stone
Though lost from the eye,
I can tell you, and not lie,—
Save of peace alone.

February 15, 1940

Dear Morton:

So! —You still breathe. Gut!

* * * I refused, as I think I told you, to jump into the fire of mid-winter Truro, although Edmund kept the wires busy for about ten days trying to get me there. Had I gone, with what joys might I not have been able to regale you! * * * What wit and gaiety would have pounced and bounced around! What parlor games, what *bouts rimés*, what wassail, what widgeting! —I always have fun with Bunny, as you know, and I'm not trying to underestimate his hospitality. The pickled mussels are always forthcoming, and the gin, wine, beer and vodka. Also the liberty to partake of same: no Puritanical hidings of the bottle, or meachin' of the vittles. —I should have gone, perhaps, but the thought of that trip down the Cape was too much. Also, Maidie had a job [singing in church] and it would have been mean to leave her, when she was invited too. —So I have no wonderful details to recount. I read yours, with pleasure, instead.

* * *

That great editor, Harold Ross, really has a good deal of sense. I sent in a longish and rather pompous piece on Auden, and Ross, as I told you, asked, very politely, that I cut it to a column (it stood over two). Well, I did, and it came out ten times better than it began! Truly, I was amazed, when I saw the revised proof, this morning. All the points positively bristled, and the style had been stepped up no end. So you see how *wonderful* journalistic training can be.

* * * After spending several days re-reading the complete canon, I have made a great discovery: that [Katherine Mansfield] is almost major in her journal and letters, and pretty nearly minor in her stories, which she set so much store on. Her repressions were so strong that she could not get in any of her adult life, get it through, that is, to the stories. In the *Letters*, etc., however, there is a tragic picture of a growing personality: in spite of ill health, infantilism, egotism, show-offedness, meanness and plain foolishness. She knew something was wrong, and was on her way to fixing it. If she had lived, she would have out-grown the crudities of the Gurdjieff method (development of will through endurance of sadism), and really approached Chekhov, on his broad and human side. I really feel this, and will dish it all up nicely, tomorrow. Those letters are magnificent, in their way, and I

think Auden was right in putting her down among his ancestors. * * *
As for the stories, how much of them has faded. And she knew they
were fading. . . .
* * *

Ever, with love, your Pal,
Louise Andreas Salami [1]

1. Lou Andreas-Salomé made extraordinary friendships with extraordinary men,
Nietzsche and Freud among them.

February 19, 1940

Dear Morton:
* * *

And I think it would be a good thing if we both stopped whooping
up each other and ourselves, if you know what I mean. It's childish of
me to want your opinion, always. It's just that there isn't anyone else
whose opinion matters, with whom I share a word, for months on end.
And I know you are brave and fearless; only I wish you could be un-
hampered by any academic afterthoughts (in the sense of "Will this
be bad for my salary ten years from now, when I am put up for Old
Prof. Higgins' place, and a nice fat stipendium?"). —It was a shame
that you could not have published the MacLeish letter, for example.
And that you could not come right out and slam Blue Butter Balls [1] in
the eye. (Did you see the good word Auden put in for her, a few
weeks ago, in the *N. R.?*) And that you have to hedge *the least little
tiny weeny bit*, on palpable fudges like Delmore Schwartz. But that's
your business, and you are coming out into the open more and more,
all the time. * * *

The dinner and evening with the Man with the Off-Color Epergne
(and I am not being moral: people have to act as best they can, and
it's none of my business) turned out to be a bit sordid. We went to
that Ticino place, and were the sinecure of all eyes, because Wolfson [2]
had John Garfield and wife along. Garfield is really quite a darling:
exactly like something out of Clifford Odets (early). Don't be a ro-
mantic-eyedealist, he said, at one point, sternly, to his wife. And they
had been to Mexico, and she (very cute and unspoiled Bronx in, of
course, a mink coat and hat and mink shoes, no doubt) loves Jean
Gabin and was cross because Hubby, not being a Romantic Eyedealist,
refused to go into "all those old churches," with her. Were there lots
of artists around, I asked, and she said, Lots of painters, and poor

Garfield said, very pathetically, I thought: "Some people think actors are artists." Did you ever? —But very sweet and very serious and quite simple. * * *

> Ever with really fine and true love, dear Morton,
> Louise

1. This would seem to be a reference to Laura Riding, a poet whom LB did not admire; neither did Miss Riding admire LB's criticism.
2. Victor Wolfson was best known for his work in the theatre, as producer and playwright.

March 1, 1940

Dear Morton:

What an imagination! Positively Shakespearean! Othello without need of Iago! Desdemona strangled on the tissue of a dropped handkerchief, dyed with mummy, alone! One stale old quotation out of Maeterlinck, and he's off. One word of pity for a sad character, one of appreciation for a fellow lyric poet [Ivan Goll], made pitiable by his status of refugee, and really admirable in talent, and he sees something out of Sardou. *Sardou!* —I am really very much grieved. Even insulted as I am, by the innuendo that I can no longer wring bunches of roses from gentlemen, and that my state is a hard one, as far as masculine attention is concerned—I pass that by. But to put me in something by Sardou, that I can *never forgive.*

I don't know why I should try to describe the true situation to you. Perhaps I can't; it is rather a Chekhovian one, really. (And of course, I am *always* ready for the Chekhovian, *if not for the Sardouian!!!*) —How shall I begin? By the pictures of Madame [Goll],¹ as first given me by Jack, to whom she went with a novel on the subject of miscegenation (French woman versus Negro), on the recommendation of Mary Colum? —She took a great fancy to Jack, and kept going back, many times. So, the second time Ivan "dropped up" for his cup of tea here, I mentioned the fact that Jack had admired Madame's work, and why not bring Madame along? It was arranged that I go there, and I did, last week, arriving very late, because something else had come up. Ivan had gone out to meet me, but I missed him, so I went up to the top floor of the dilapidated house near Riverside [Drive], where they have two ex-servants' rooms and a little cuisine and took Madame *seule*, for about ten minutes. She is the small thin white-skinned red-haired type of Jewess, with good teeth and a small finely hooked nose. She must have been ravishing in the Munich-Rilke days (when she was about twenty, I should say, and Rilke in his forties, the old roué!). She is now still very attractive, although her hair has been dyed and overcurled. She wore a little get-up, rather Lesbian in character: white shirt and dark coat, with large O-so-Schiaparelli piece of junk jewelry in the lapel. She sat me down, said Ivan was "a good man, but a dreamer," and then gave me the works, which I recognized for what they were at once, having some knowledge by now of the refugee approach. Whom did I know, who was good to know, what were the best reviews in America, how much money did I make by writing, what was Edna Millay's address, was I married, was Jack my lover—no? O too bad!, then what did I live on? Etc., etc. Ivan had come back by then and was making tea, rather meekly, I thought, when she noticed him and started in on *him*. Everything he did was wrong, and I was horrified for a moment by the thought that I might have seemed to act toward Raymond like this, years ago: I think someone in Santa Fe said so, once. Never quite so bad, however, as Madame. It really made my blood run cold. All this was broken up by a messenger who came from Luise Rainer, in town for the night on her way to play St. Joan in Washington, D.C. —Madame was immediately galvanized into action, dropped the dissection of me, and the pecking of Ivan, flung on a FUR coat, asked Ivan what hat she should wear (this was rather touching, I thought, and really showed the relationship up, for one moment), and was off, like an arrow. —Well, after that, if Ivan attempted to stroke my hair and invite me to stay part of the night, can you blame him? Did I yield to this? NO. It took me about two hours to break away, and I must say I haven't fought so for my virtue for years, but fight I did and away I got.

And then you drag me into a sordid little play by a degenerate Comédie Française! Shame, shame!

Then, on Wednesday, Ivan came here. He is sweet, and he is pathetic; and underneath there is the refugee drive, I understand perfectly. They have everyone lined up, naturally, beginning with the Jewish intellectuals: Babette [Deutsch] and Jean Starr [Untermeyer], etc. Then come the "reviews," and they've done pretty well there, too: Claire with her reminiscences of Rilke in *Twice a Year*, and Ivan with Dwight Macdonald and Dupee.[2] (He met Dupee chez Wittenberg, in Brooklyn, after the night of the great attack, and Dupee was "very dronk" but impressed by the Goll family "niceness.") I have turned over that job of translation of Jouve, etc., to Ivan, thinking it might earn him a little money, and make him a little so important as Claire. —The Claire-Ivan relationship is, of course, one of master and slave (mistress and s.). I intimated that I thought Madame somewhat spoiled (we had to look this up in the dictionary, and it turned out to be *gâtée*). He waits on her hand and foot; she is completely dependent on him, and he is rewarded, as slaves always are, by pecking. He takes this in a philosophical way. —The passes are very sweet and gentle, and, I should say, harmless. I have managed to disabuse him of the fact that I am "so alone," and he now, I am sure, thinks I have at least eight lovers. He still thinks he might do something in the way of awaking my sleeping passions, so that I shall begin to turn out great lyrics by the score. Maybe this is true, but I haven't tried, yet. Maybe I will. . . . He is such a pathetic character—although with a real base of Jewish strength and acceptance of suffering, which takes him out of the dish-mop class, and makes him a man—that maybe I will. Why not?

Something out of *Sardou*!

Shall I ever forgive you? You'd better be nice, or all is ovaire.

Awaiting your reply, I remain,
Louise Mélisande Goulaud

1. Little known in America, Mme. Claire Goll is the subject of No. 167 of the Éditions Seghers series *Poètes d'aujourd'hui*.

2. Macdonald (a controversialist who wrote on subjects ranging from biblical translations and films to politics) and Frederick Dupee (critic, teacher and Henry James expert) were on the editorial board of *Partisan Review*.

March 19, 1940

Dear "Poet"!

* * *

—I can't remember where I left my little ídyll, as Edmund pronounces it. (E. showed up last week or so, by the way, and we had a terrible row over *Finnegans Wake*. E. is now in the throes of a big Affair with Thornton Wilder: thinks him ducky, etc., and swears by his interpretation of Joyce, which is taking all the salons like wildfire: the last I heard was that Thornton was holding forth on the subject at Mabel Dodge's—she's in town having her teeth filled, or out, or something.) *Well, anyway*, Time certainly flew past, during Feb. and the first part of March. I woke up one day and discovered that

I owed about a dollar's worth of fines on seven library books *I hadn't had time to take back!* The kingdom totters!

Actually, things tapered off a little last week, and I actually turned down a couple of telephone come-ons. The week before everything was simmering and glimmering: long walks, ending in bistros, up and around 181st Street, with a few huggings and tuggings before and after. —As a matter of fact, this apartment is not made for love-making: not with Maidie with a key, and irregular hours, and windows on all sides, and snoopy neighbors with whom I have a feud, down-stairs. *And there is no bed,* either, say what you will. Ivan had all this impressed upon him, by me, while I was leaning away at a slant, and he agreed. Instead of finding an odalisque, with patchouli and frangi-pani in her hair and a peignoir wrapped about her sturdy person, he would find Louise, all nicely gotten up in her latest little Black Num-ber with a Touch of White at the Neck, on her feet, and in her senses. This finally got him down to such an extent that he began taking me out for cocktails, after about an hour of fruitless struggle. He *does* talk wonderfully, and is the *same person* we are, with a tinge of The Seven Tribes and Alsace-Lorraine-Montmartre thrown in. (I can't see how this can be, because he seems to have been born in March. Something zodiacally screwy there.)

Well, last week he finally gave up, and began inviting me to the movies at the Museum of Modern Art. (!!!) I turned down the first invitation, because, as I told you, I had little Brown [1] on my hands. (Little Brown turned up laden with Homer and Pindar in the Original, under his arm. He has a very small face and smaller features, and has been through the regular mill: sitting at Ransom's feet at Kenyon, and hearing Allen at Benfolly, and knowing Auden and everything. He was born in Portland, Maine, and has a fine Harvard accent, and is worried because he doesn't know why he writes poetry: Did I think it was because he couldn't dance? I told him: What difference does it make? and that only men tried to explain things in abstract terms. It then turned out that he didn't care much for Sappho; had I ever read her in the original? The interview ended on a rather inconclusive note but it was pretty horrifying to see anything so young, and so talented and earnest, all at the same time. Heart-breaking, really. . . .)

Yesterday I gave in and *went* to the Mod Museum. Ivan floated in, armed with an international press card of some kind, which got him by the door without paying. The picture was René Clair's *The Italian Straw Hat,* and why haven't we known about this before? I always thought it was a sort of experimental short-subject. It is a full-length picture and the most wonderful satire on late-19th century French middle-classishness that I have ever seen. It is done in imitation of the earliest and most primitive movie technique; and from the moment it starts a terrible war is waged between inanimate objects and human beings. Boots are too small; furniture becomes a menace; neckties fall off; and a long sequence flays the French marriage ceremonies (right through the *mairie*, the church, on to the supper and speechmaking and the sad quadrille danced in the caterer's hired rooms—festooned with paper garlands). Then there's a killing sequence wherein a husband, middle-aged, is discovered taking a foot-bath behind a Moorish screen in his *salon*, and this really does sum up the whole period. *Both* Ivan and I laughed till we cried. I must have this put on for you when you come (but how can I, not being a friend of Iris Barry?).[2] You must see it! The furniture and the ornaments: correct down to the last ormolu clock and the final bowl of Carrara marble with doves perched on the edge—*remember those?* —And then the wedding guests, a little *beschwipst,* get into the wrong apartment and can't tell the difference: the same furniture and ornaments and looped-back hangings! —It's a work of the purest genius, and Miss Barry sums it all up admirably in the program enclosed (please send this back). . . .

Listen, darling, I am not taken in. I know that Ivan is after some translations of his immortal works, by me. Clark Mills has done several, but now Goll has decided that I am the female queen-bee in the poetry line, and could give him quite a push upward and onward. I have balked at the translations because they would be one hell of a job; but yesterday the whole thing came up again, and he suggested that I could use two rhymes only, to a stanza. The hell with eeet! —And Life is closing in, because in a fortnight or less, he oars away to Cuba, and then goes to the sea-side for the summer! (O leave it to the refugees!) —So Bogan will turn into Ariadne, I suppose, full of *sehnsucht,* on Manhattan's Naxos! In a pig's ear, if you'll excuse the irreverence. . . .

* * *

It was so beautiful today. I went up to the Park, for the first time since last October, and men were pruning trees ("That whole top part is as dead as temorrer, Mike, ya *dope,* ya!"), and some very twirly bird was singing its heart out. And the doves are getting as burnished as anything; and aren't there *any* cuddly female doves? —I think male doves get an awful cold break, with the female *always* trotting away, but maybe they like it that way. —I shall never forget the ducks I saw making love in the Borghese Gardens in Rome, with all the young seminarists looking on. . . .

Life, life! How beautiful! How mysterious, as you have pointed out, before this! Ah, *Vorfrühling!* Ah, poetry! Ah, Kindred Souls, Brought Together by Inscrutablenesses Not to Be Scrutinized. . . .

Write soon.

Ever with love (the old-fashioned kind),
Lou-Lou

1. Harry Brown, who then worked for *The New Yorker*, would in 1944 write *A Walk in the Sun*, one of the first novels about World War II.
2. The film curator at the Museum of Modern Art.

April 1! 1940

Dear Enobarbus:

This is to warn you that *Pinocchio* IS ONE MASS OF FREUDIAN AND GOLDEN BOUGH SYMBOLISM! Do not fail to mark this, when you see it again. I saw it on Saturday night, along with Edmund and Mary and others, and sat right down in front, and the whole redemption-through-rebirth-in-the-womb, the frightful-female (mad whale!) and search-for-the-father sequences almost overwhelmed me. And don't forget that little homosexual interlude, with Lampwick as its chief youthful expositor, and Honest John as Adult Initiator. . . .

I point all this out to you because, apart from the wonderful observation and the "art" involved (and how!), these are the reasons for the thing's tremendous pull. It's a sort of Dante's *Inferno* and story of Noah, in simpler fable form. It is a true fable, in other words, and a masterpiece of its kind because it runs so true to type. —Edmund thought it was full of faults; he didn't care for Jiminy Cricket or Cleo. THE CONSCIENCE does not make cricket noises in his mind, evidently. Has a firmer and more bellowing voice, perhaps.

I sold the "March" poem, and have written another called "The Sorcerer's Daughter." Have also started in to translate Supervielle. . . .

* * *

Riggishly and hoppingly yours,
Cléopatre

1940

/ to May Sarton /

April 24, 1940

Dear Miss Sarton:[1]

Thank you for your letter. —What can be done concerning the general distrust and even hatred shown toward lyric poetry, so prevalent now, I can't think. Nothing, I suppose. These turns of the wheel of taste always happen; the distrust of form and emotion is always present, in every generation. The particular form this distrust takes, in our day, may be symptomatic of a social neurosis that only the future can trace down and name. . . .

As far as Spender goes, I never thought he knew anything, beyond his special infantilism. Auden, I think, is a man of genius, but he, too, has been protected and swaddled against any reality but the fashionable kind.

I often remember that Hall Caine rejected at one time a sonnet of Hopkins'. . . .

The only thing to do is: do what one can, and not sell out.

Believe me to be,
Faithfully yours,
Louise Bogan

1. May Sarton, the novelist and poet, was at this point twenty-eight years old and had already published two books of verse. Her friendship with LB is documented in letters beginning in 1954.

/ to Morton D. Zabel /

June 17, 1940

Dear Morton:

Well, well! So you're discovering America at last! —I remember the places you speak of, from having received postcards from them when I was a little girl, and my mother was making the Western Tour, in 1907, the year after the Great Fire. —I remember cards of Pikes Peak and the Garden of the Gods, and of Goldfield, Nev., and Tonopah, and I don't know where else. —The means of getting about in those days was horse-carriages; or, if you were very grand, *teams* of horses, or tandems, or some such thing. Mother had an admirer who had cleaned up in Goldfield, and who showed her the West in a big way. She was forty-two at the time—just my age now—and in the full bloom of her beauty. —After she came back from California, in 1908, she declined rapidly, and never was really the same again. This, I trust, will not happen to you. . . .

Do tell me: is San Francisco all that has been said of it? I'm sure it is a very civilized and beautiful town; and has always had the Bohemian, as they say, gay, unstuffed kind of life, which it took the rest of the country so long to learn. —On the other hand, I have never seen a San Franciscan whom I could tolerate for ten minutes: man or woman. They were always perfectly hollow, pretentious, yearning and would-be, and they usually end up as promotion agents for Alfred A. Knopf, or something like that. —Or else they are like Rolfe; nice but slightly ambiguous and cracked. * * * —And Lucius Beebe likes the town so much that I am sure *something* must be wrong with it. —What can it be? —All its poets are bad, and all its minds punk. —Perhaps you can clear this up for me. —I have also known some honeys (in the line of punks) from that place across the bay; I can't remember the name. . . .

* * *

Here several things have happened. I was shanghaied by Jack Wheelock into a dinner-party, a week or so ago. He swore that there would be no one there but Van Wyck Brooks, and wife; and he also swore that Brooks wanted to meet me. But when I arrived I found * * * a Southern (Mobile) Novelist, as well as the Brooks'es. * * * Brooks [is] really quite a twirked-up, conceited little man. Later, in the living room with coffee, Brooks and I had a run-in on the subject of the Arts; and he turned to me with the remark (designed to put me forever in my place)—"Of course, Miss Bogan, you and I differ fundamentally on the subject of aesthetics. I think that the aesthetic content and value of a work of art is its smallest ingredient . . ." or words to that effect. —I took this, too, with a smile, and sat listening to him go on, in rather a footless way, about the South, and how snakes do not hibernate in the winter in South Carolina. As he left, he turned to me and said, "I'm sorry that I brought the aesthetic question up, Miss Bogan!" "Think nothing of it, Mr. Brooks!" said I to him, thinking in my heart, "Dearie, works of art will give wonder, refreshment and delight, long after you and your horrid little utilitarian Roosevelt Administration ideas are quietly mouldering in your graves." * * * Poor Jack! He is such an innocent, and thought he was being so smart to get me there at all! —And his is the one dinner table in New York which I cannot leave, with a kick that sends the solid silver to the ceiling, when dopes go on not to my liking, and against my principles.

And this is not because he is my publisher, but because he is a poor lost soul, who has really been wonderfully kind to me, in time of need.
＊ ＊ ＊

Love,
Louise

/ *to Rufina McCarthy Helmer* /

June 23, 1940

Dear Rufina:

I was so glad to hear from you, and to know that you and Bill are about to come to town. —And thank you for the clipping. In spite of the fall of France, I still am without wild feelings of rage, hatred, and revenge. —France is an example of a very high point of civilization, surely, but so are lots of other places I could name. And to wipe out all thought of the excellence of one civilization, and all mention of the faults of another, in order to concentrate hatred and detestation, etc., seems to me to be an uncivilized thing to do. —And, in spite of all that has happened, I am still wasting no tears upon Britain. She has done all, and more, than any other nation has ever done, to brutalize and bully, and now. . . . Well, as Yeats said, "The ghost of Roger Casement is knocking on the door!" . . . (Look up a book by Nevinson, Henry, sometime in the Library. It is called *Last Changes, Last Chances* and has a full account of the Casement case. Also, of some other horrors, such as the French occupation of the Ruhr in 1923, now, of course, never mentioned. . . .)

Well, we'll soon be a dictatorship like another. That's what hatred and fear does: it makes one exactly like the hated and feared. . . .
＊ ＊ ＊

Ever affectionately,
Louise

/ *to Morton D. Zabel* /

August 22, 1940

Dear Morton:

＊ ＊ ＊ The dance, as I see it, should be the open and unabashed exploitation of beautiful bodies, in something frankly sensuous, or something frankly gay; just as a lyric poem "should be either a song or an epigram." I don't think that the dance, in our day, should get epic on

/ 209

us. And it can't be a ritual, either, without being phony; since the religious feeling behind the early dance rituals is entirely dead, and was too sadistic and orgiastic, anyhow, to appeal to the denatured audiences of today. So all these story-telling arrangements, and all these probings into the soul of Emily Dickinson, are tripe. Emily Dickinson was what she was because of Father Dickinson, and Mother Dickinson; and the really interesting things about her are too silly or too tragic to be "danced." [1] (How could you "dance" her correspondence with Col. Higginson, for example; or her recurrent attacks of insanity?) So Martha Graham is nuts, on that score. Dancers and actors, I have found, always have a very marked phony philosophical side. They are always Prying into the Secrets of the Universe, in a dumb way. They feel that they must Understand Things; and, since they are all pure mindless narcissists, with nothing at all working in the brain-pan, they are enough to bore, as you say, the pants off anyone. If they don't go Hindu or Buddhist, they go *REWOLT!!*—and some of them have dabbled in both, in their short but vivid careers. —You should read the memoirs of Ruth St. Denis, if you want to get all this in pure form. * * *

Louise

1. What has LB exercised is Martha Graham's "Letter to the World." The "rewolt" echoes Fanny Brice's parody of modern dance, and dancers.

/ to Margaret Marshall /

September 26, 1940

Dear Miss Marshall:[1]

The Swift book is one of those biographies reduced to "popular" terms. In it Swift sounds like a perfect idiot; and nothing at all, of course, is made of his reasons. —This sort of thing gives me the creeps; and I'd pass it by, if I were you. —Do you want the book back?

I'd like to see the Blackmur [*The Expense of Greatness*]. Writing criticism about criticism can get to be pretty tenuous; but Blackmur is a special case. He has escaped the taint of the academic approach by never going to college (or going only a little); and he can be really intuitive. —For Heaven's sake, if you want the review fast, give me a deadline on it! —Although I have reformed somewhat, and hope to pound things out right away, this year.

Every good wish,
Louise Bogan

1. As literary editor of *The Nation,* Margaret Marshall would offer LB what she hoped were tempting books to review, but "I never can see what purpose 'popular' descriptions of artists serve. People who don't understand the figures won't understand them any better, and the lives are always so sweetened up and watered down." (To Marshall, January 13, 1939)

/ to Edmund Wilson /

October 7, 1940

Dear Edmund:

I have just finished reading *To the Finland Station,* which I finally managed to get from Womrath's. —I want to write you at once, to tell you what a moving experience this reading was. I think that here you have produced something absolutely new in the expository genre: something that has the emotional sweep of both music and drama; the sensitive insight and the tough fibre of the finest novels, together with analysis which would do credit to a great writer of briefs. —I say this from my heart, and I could give you chapter and verse, taken from the book, to back it up. I was particularly impressed by the whole drama of Marx, as you give it; the change of tempo when you get to Lenin is remarkable too: and it is a change of light as well as of tempo. The whole book, after it gets going, is full of these brilliant and moving effects. Just on structure alone, the whole thing stands as a sort of First Symphony, by Edmund Wilson, and makes even *Axel's Castle* seem like a youthful sonata. And what the book does to pastiches like *The Flowering etc., of New England,* is a caution. Everywhere where Brooks sheers off from his problem, you go right to it; and you waste no time in flinging in cadenzas; you keep right on with the variations. . . .

I hope you see what I mean, musical as hell as the above sounds. . . .

Another thing which will make the book a source of strength and inspiration to people, once they wake up to what it's all about, is the fact that it lays forever the guilt, promulgated and laid on with a trowel, of the Marxists who deny the artistic processes. For what you prove is: that "history" is itself a stream of energy, is "generous inconsistency"; and that those who work with it succeed best when they realize this, as the artist always realizes it. It can't be pawed out of shape; it must be listened to, before [being] acted upon.

All you need now to be a great man entirely is a Sense of Awe! I hope you will look into this Sense, and work it up, in your next work. (But you have it already, you know, in spite of your protestations to the contrary.)

Well, anyhow, I'm proud and humble to be your friend, you old woggo....

Ever,
Louise

[P.S.] How good you are on the diseases of "exiles' colonies"; on Bakunin; on Lenin's childhood home....

/ *to Allen Tate* /

December 15, 1940

Dear Allen:

No, I don't think I was too hard on Blackmur. Do you remember that wise remark of Hopkins': A palace should at least be a house. It seemed to me (and to other people whose opinion I respect) that Blackmur's writing has too much self-indulgence in it. We all have been forced to learn how to write prose clearly, forcefully, and without fanciful and baroque curves, because we have written for an audience; and have had to sell our stuff. Blackmur has been coddled in this respect, it seemed to me. Arrow Editions is, after all, a sort of coddling publishing set-up. Blackmur has not learned that one proceeds step by step toward complexity: both of thought and expression. H. James *earned* his later style through process of long growth. He (James) knew how to write simply too.

After all these years, you still do not think that I work under *animus*, I hope.

Ever cordially,
Louise

/ *to Morton D. Zabel* /

January 21, 1941

Dear Morton:

* * * The Auden meeting occurred a week ago Friday. Mrs. Connolly [1] has installed herself in one of those apartments which look like a stage set; and are slyly disguised in a walk-up tenement house building—this time on the corner of Lexington Avenue and 72nd Street. I hadn't seen an example of this sort of thing for years; it still goes on, unimpaired. Everything, in this case, was late Empire! The walls and draperies (such draperies: all thin and layered and valanced!) were

putty colored and lamps made out of old embossed coal scuttles stood about. Negro *putti*, entangled in gilt sconces, peered at one from the mantelpiece; there was a fine copperplate engraving of one of Napoleon's soldiers framed severely in gunmetal; and everything else in proportion. I sat on an uncomfortable little *bergère*, and chatted with one of those blank faced, humorless interior decorating types, until Fred [Dupee], etc. showed up. Gerald Heard's name came into it a good deal: the group seems to be going in for monkhood, now, under G. H.'s leadership. There is a farm in Pennsylvania: the Trappists all over again, it would seem. . . . —So we sat and sat (Mrs. C. was out doing "exercises" somewhere), "waiting for Lefty" as Fred charmingly put it.

Then Mrs. C., just out of her hockey suit, appeared, with Auden after her, and a whole cloud of mysterious little male presences all looking, as someone of us said afterwards, like pressed flowers. Auden had on a dinner jacket and a black tie, of all things. He sat down beside me, and immediately asked me what I had done about *The White Cliffs*.[2] I told him I had thrown it out, last September. This seemed to break the ice; and he said it was bad, but that "Edna was funnier." We then talked along perfectly naturally. He is very homely, with a large mole on one side of his face; and looks lined and concentrated: much older than I had expected. He said he liked my glass-flowers poem ["Animal, Vegetable and Mineral"]: that his best critic was Frederic Prokosch; and said he would like to come up here for a visit sometime. It was characteristic, I think, that he wanted to know just what number of 8th Avenue train to take.[3] —He said he lives very quietly in Brooklyn, not seeing anyone for weeks at a time (I think this unlikely; but maybe he doesn't think the little pressed flowers anybody). I soon rose (I was reeking of cold, and snuffling away like mad, the whole time), and said I would write to him. "Care of Bennett Cerf?" said I. His address was 7 Middagh Street, he revealed. So off I went; and I wrote him some days ago, telling him that I was ill; and would he let me know sometime next month. —So that's that. Somehow, when meeting these boys, I think of the distance which separated 709 W. 169th Street, some years ago, from Iceland and Spain. —It's amusing to see Destiny working out its little literary plans, is it not? —O, yes. He also said that I was the best critic of poetry in America. —I wish I felt more excited about this, but I *have* had such a cold. . . .

* * *

M. Marshall wanted me to do something about Joyce; but I couldn't bear to go into all that again. It was tragic; but I prophesied last year that all he could do now was die.

> Ever your Sybil, in or out of caves,
> Louise

1. The mother of Cyril Connolly, the British essayist and critic.
2. A long, sentimental and immensely popular poem by Alice Duer Miller, celebrating British grit in wartime.
3. Happily enough, one took the A train.

/ to Edmund Wilson /

January 27, 1941

Dear Edmund:

Thank you for your letter, with its interesting and valuable points about the rise and fall of conjuring. —I was about to set my hand to the pen, on this subject, when, last Thursday, Maidie came down with one of the worst throats I have seen in years. She was pretty bad for a few days—high temperature, and real agony of soreness—but today she is beginning to recover. —I will try to get you the poem, at the end of this month, but if I cannot, do not think I am being merely "fastidious." You know, as few others do, that I am a housewife, as well as a writer; I have no one to sweep floors or get meals, or get out the laundry, or, in the case of sickness, make egg-nogs and squeeze orange juice. All these tasks are very good for me, but they are tasks I never can allow to slip; and in the crisis of illness, I have no free time. Please bear all this in mind; and believe that the conjuring poem will be written sometime, if not now.[1] I know that the *N. R.* will not publish it, probably, after you leave, but that's their tough luck. . . . Someone will, and I shall owe the whole idea to you. . . .
　* * *

> With love to you all,
> Louise

1. No poem on the subject has been discovered.

/ to John Hall Wheelock /

Dear Jack:

Thank you for your kind letter. —I still don't know about the *Collected Poems*. —I know that you have been for the idea for some years; and Edmund, last Christmas, spoke quite seriously to me about the matter: saying that it was ridiculous for me not to have a collected volume, etc. And I have heard plaints from one or two young people (but only one or two!)—that they couldn't find *Body of This Death*, and couldn't afford to buy the two others.

I still don't know; and I'm not being coy. In the set-up of the literary world, I sometimes think that the best thing to do is to do nothing; and to let the wave pass over the head. The American cultural situation is now lower than it has ever been before, so far as conscious art is concerned. There is a great deal of vigorous folk-art, and I am all for this; and people are excited about painting (I had to *elbow* my way around at the Metropolitan, the other day, in order to get a look at the French pictures). —All this means that there will be a poetry "revival" in about fifty years: maybe twenty-five. But I am so out of the general line, now; and I really have been so battered about that I don't care any more. What good does it do?

* * *

All best, as ever,
Louise

/ to Malcolm Cowley /

Dear Malcolm:

I apologize for being so insulting to you, in my letter. I do get cross, but I cool off and I don't bear grudges. No. So I'm sorry if I imputed all sorts of things to you. As a matter of fact, I know very little about you, having met you about ten times! [1]

PLEASE GET ME RIGHT! I wasn't cold to [Conrad] Aiken, in my review of him, because he had (supposedly) done all these and those horrid things. The reason I mentioned these and those was: To show that Aiken wasn't above a little envy and malice, himself. I WRITE MY REVIEWS AFTER ALL MALICE IS SPENT! Believe me! In great calm, in a little blue closet, right out of William Morris, trimmed with ivory of the purest hue! [2]

I think all this Schools of Poetry stuff is old-fashioned. Aiken, himself, was terribly worried about "schools" in *Scepticism* (1919). But I don't think anyone is, any more. Except Nicolas Calas and (on the other hand) the *New Masses*.

Look, Malcolm, I wouldn't bother with you at all, if you hadn't, once, written some real poetry. But you have, and hence these lines.

Actually, what has Aiken got to kick about? He was off in Deakes House, Rye, Sussex, for *almost 20 years*, meanwhile getting all the American honors: Pulitzer, Guggenheim, etc. —I have been sitting right here in New York, and did anyone ever invite *me* to join the A. Academy of Arts and Letts? —I think I'll start a society called Friends of L. Bogan. Why Doesn't She Get the Pulitzer? Down with Audrey Wurdemann and Marya Zaturenska!

Well, as I say: I am sorry to have been insulting.

Take it easy.

Louise

1. This claim has more passion than veracity to it. LB had known Malcolm Cowley and his first wife as far back as 1920, when she first came to the Village; and Cowley reports that they had visited easily and fairly often in those years.

2. According to Cowley, Conrad Aiken's novel *Conversation* (1940) included a portrait of LB, "and Louise never forgave him for writing it. Maybe she thought all passion was spent before she wrote reviews of his works—but not quite, not quite."

The novel, which does use John Coffey (see p. 3) as a character, has one figure—presumably LB—who never appears on the scene. Instead, in the other room, she sits at the piano, playing interminably, badly and, more often than not, Gershwin's *Rhapsody in Blue*.

/ to Margaret Marshall /

April 3, 1941

Dear Peggy:

It *would* be interesting to do the Tate and Ransom together. But one of those things is involved: Allen T. has recently been pretty sharp about me and the *Nation* review of Blackmur, in the *Partisan Review*. He might think that I asked for the book; and that would be bad. He has recently written me a friendly letter, expressing his friendship and admiration, and I never mentioned the *Partisan Review* thing to him; ignoring it was best. But you can understand that it is perhaps best to have nothing to do with his new criticism—for me to have nothing to do with it.

Ransom knows so many more *words* than I do, that perhaps I might come a cropper there, as well. When man soars into the regions of the abstract concept, I have no way to describe these flights except by concrete images. But perhaps I could sprinkle in a few words like *dichotomy* and *empathy!*

> Ever sincerely,
> Louise

/ *to* ——— /

May 14, 1941

Dear Mr. ———: [1]

Thank you for your letter, inviting me to offer some criticism concerning the anthology edited by Richard Aldington, which [your press] is about to publish. —Because I write criticism for a living, I shall not be able to give you this criticism without pay. I have always made it a rule to keep my reviewing on a strictly professional basis. I never write blurbs for books I have not reviewed, for example, and remarks of mine quoted by a publisher are always from published reviews. And your kind offer of a free copy of the anthology means little to me, since I should get it gratis in the natural course of things.

My criticism of the modern English and American portion of Mr. Aldington's book, I find from a glance at the table of contents, would run to at least two typewritten pages. This is the section upon which I feel myself most fitted to speak. Writing two such pages would take time and effort. I am a poor and busy woman; and I am sure you can find others more fortunately situated, who can afford this time and effort, as I cannot.

> Believe me to be,
> Sincerely yours,
> [unsigned]

1. It is not clear whether this letter was sent; it certainly represents what LB said and wrote on many occasions. She broke the rule set forth here only once, when she joined with Auden and Lionel Trilling and a number of others in attesting to the greatness of Ford Madox Ford's *The Good Soldier* on its appearance in paperback.

/ to Morton D. Zabel /

June 2, 1941

Dear Morton:

* * *

My pleasantest experience has been the renewal of a beginning
friendship with Little [William] Maxwell. I have seen him several
times this winter. One afternoon he came up, and we played records,
and he is the most wonderful record-listener I have ever met. He really
breaks right up, and is shattered, and is frank, and is disapproving,
and is delighted, so that it seems another *you* is involved: another expression of one's own taste, only fresher. [Schubert's] *Gruppe aus
dem Tartarus*, for example, actually laid him out. "That was a terrible
experience," he said. And, of the final record of [Mahler's] *Lied v. d.
Erde*, he remarked: "That is a perfect expression of the romantic's
yearning for the Infinite. . . ." —Maxwell is really an exquisite human
being; and I wish there was something between love and friendship
that I could tender him; and some gesture, not quite a caress, I could
give him. A sort of smoothing. I may be able to work out something
along these lines later! Seriously, I simply love him like a brother. He
had me down to tea last week (Patchin Place), and such a lovely little
apartment you never saw: plants on the windowsills, and pale furniture, and faultless bibelots, and a fireplace and books. He is all for the
"light verse" you wish to exclude from the book. Something will have
to be worked out, in that connection. The whole MS must be in
Scribner's hands before July 1st. Have you any suggestions?

* * *

Ever with best love,
Louise

June 4, 1941

Dear Morton:

I feel like the Marschallin, if you must know; but that is absurd, because there never has been, and never will be, of course, anything
remotely resembling that Overture, in the M[axwell] business. No
foamings of lace out from the big baroque (rococo, rather) bed; no
scampering of slender young male legs around the boudoir; no large-
bosomed breathings and swellings and flutterings and burnings. I
haven't any of the appurtenances pertaining to such a situation, from
the rococo bed through the bosom; and my whole emotional set is

also away from all these things: the cold stern light of the-response-with-insight having burned under the ribs for seven years. Howbeit, I *should* feel like the Marschallin if I could! * * * We were speaking of how Rolfe's book was dedicated to me, and had been turned down by every publisher in New York. "You should have told him to put the dedication in after the book was accepted," said M. "O," said I, as quick as a flash, "so you admit I have enemies." Slight pause, and perfectly straight glance of the large brown eyes. "Of course you have enemies," he answered. Now WOULD YOU OR E. W. OR J. WHEELOCK OR ANYONE ever admit that, to my face. NO.

* * *

Sorry to have been so Abstract. I have been trying to get through *The New Criticism*, by John Crowe Ransom, for the past two weeks, and the coloring has seeped into my own style, no doubt. What a true old bore that Ransom is! His greatest feats are his diagrams: the round one wherein the affect slides down from ten minutes past, to half-past, on the dial, when hit from the outside by the stimulus (the *attitude*, not the *affect*: excuse me!), is enough to make a cat laugh. I have still to read his great Binomial Theorem Theory, farther along toward the back. Ontological Criticism, indeed! Of course, Stephen Potter had this all taped, some time ago. The Schools are all around poetry; the same old methods of mediaeval university teaching are beginning to creep back, and all over, the teaching of Mods. And what did I once tell you about the deleterious effect of Rhodes Scholarships upon Southerners, or upon Northerners, for that matter. I can never forget (although this is, of course, in Ransom, analogous to a Horrible Past) that his first book of poems was called *Poems about God*, was written in free verse, and had an introduction by that other famous Rhodes Scholar, C[hristopher] Morley.

* * *

> Best love, though not of the Marschallin kind, after all these years; of a more distilled and brandied (spiritual) potency!
> Louise

/ *to William Maxwell* /

June 23, 1941

Your letter was exactly the kind I always want, when my friends go back to their native towns; I want to see and hear the town, but I seldom do. Yes, it is the birds and children, along those streets with their lawns and trees, and I'm glad you remembered the clothesline. Clotheslines always stir my heart, and it is a pity that they have never really been touched by American art, except by the people who draw soap advertisements for the *Ladies' Home Journal*. . . .

And it's fine about my first name. I simply *can't* first-name people until I've known them quite a while: a provincialism, no doubt.[1] I have always shrunk up inside when casual acquaintances began Louising me, right away. —But if I start in calling you William, it will turn out that you never have been called William in your life. I started to call E. W. Edmund, way back in 1923; and I soon discovered that no one else called him that. But then I couldn't stop, and only this last year or so have I been able to call him Bunny. Edmund, by the way, is one of the few people who have ever got behind my masculine-protest side, far enough, to spring LULU on me, from time to time!

* * *

As ever, sincerely,

Louise

1. Explaining the same problem to Margaret Marshall, whom she Miss'ed for years, LB wrote: "I have always dealt with male editors up to now (Harriet Monroe was more a great-aunt to me than editor!) and, when they were not friends of my youth, I have always found it a good idea to be as formal with them as possible. When they come to be friends, I keep it up, even then. William Maxwell, on *The New Yorker*, a male angel if ever there was one * * * is always 'Mr. Maxwell,' just the same." (March 30, 1941)

/ *to Theodore Roethke* /

[July] 1941

Dear Ted:

We are having a heat wave, but I answer your moaning letter, in any case! —I *am* sorry about your mother, and hope that she is steadily improving. I know, in spite of all your protestations, that you are a v. tender nurse. A v. tender guy, under all that Purple Gang side. . . .

Auden respects and likes you thoroughly, I should say. He wrote that review, you must realize, against all his decisions not to review con-

temporaries. He thinks you a good poet, a good teacher, and a fine person generally; but we both agreed that you should GROW UP, and stop pretending that your childish side is melancholy, WHICH IT ISN'T. Now, worry over that one! * * * I think him a swell person, complicatedness and all. We drank a pint of Scotch together, and toward the end of the evening he made one of the most profound remarks, in re neurotic fears, that I have ever heard. I told him about the man who broke into tears in a taxi-cab, and confessed to E. W. that he had a vestigial tail. "I shouldn't have minded a vestigial tail," said I. "No," said he, "one can always stand what other people have."
* * *

> Love,
> Louise

/ to Morton D. Zabel /

July 10, 1941

Dear Morton:
* * *

I finally had another meeting with Auden. He came up here, under circumstances which I will relate to you, orally; and we had a grand evening, just *crammed* with Insights and Autopsies, and Great Simple Thoughts, and Deep Intimations. I should have written a good deal of this interview down, the day after it occurred; but I find that I remember most of it. He is reading H. J., and had some charming anecdotes. He gave me some Profound Advice (in a rather oblique way) just before he left; and I do think him a real and natural person. Complicated as all hell, of course; and I should hate to cross him; but fundamentally sound, tender and full of Recognitions, and AMOR. He was wonderful on Van Wyck Brooks's imitation journal; and said of Allen: "If you're going to set yourself up to be the greatest highbrow on earth, you must at least be a tremendously clever man." He couldn't get over my obscurity; and I told him that it was because I wasn't respectable. "But that wouldn't count among members of the academic world," SAID HE, INNOCENTLY. —He left me with the gift of a package of Lucky Strikes; and didn't drink up all his share of the Scotch.
* * *

> Ever, with love,
> Louise

July 28, 1941

Dear Jack:

I find it easy to send back this proof quickly; there is nothing controversial in the choices. —I don't think, however, that we can keep "A
Letter." There is something wrong with it; I can't say just what.
Something sentimental or unfinished or mawkish. Whatever it is, I
don't like it. So please let's take it out. —I don't like "Love me because
I am lost," either. Don't you think we might dispense with that, as
well?

It isn't that I'm turning on my early self. But the girl of 23 and 24,
who wrote most of these early poems, was so seldom mawkish, that
I want her not to be mawkish at all. —You understand, I am sure. . . .
So please do make excision marks in *both* instances; and let's get that
choice off our minds!

   * * *

                   Ever, dear Jack,
                   Louise

September 5, 1941

Dear Morton:

I know I am often hasty and perhaps passionately unfair; but I know
from long experience that you do not, very often, give me credit when
I am generous; and you tend to judge me by things which your own
often too cautious character pushes me to do. I miss you when I don't
hear from you; but I think we ought to come right down to cases, and
clear up a few matters, before either renewed friendship, or eternal
silence.

In the first place, no one could have been sweeter or more generous
than you were to me during my visit. I was deeply touched, and have
told everyone as much. On the other hand, I do not think that you
even begin to realize how your attitude about my letters has hurt me.
I thought: He will have them there as a surprise, and we shall have a
wonderful time going over them. It is the only whole record I have
of the past ten terrible years; and, in addition, my letters from Ireland
were written him, on the express condition that he let me have them
back. "Don't keep a diary," said he. "Write me every day; and then

I'll give the letters back to you." This, I truly think, is a broken promise; and I really can't forgive you it.

I have finally come to realize that you are not treating the letters as a gay correspondence between friends, but as *a collection*. In other words, everything I write you is being put into a kind of coffin, and kept there. I am being treated like a character out of some memoirs; I am being put in cold storage while still alive.[1] This realization must, of course, break my correspondence with you. I am a live, growing object; and I'll thank people to treat me as such. I'll write to people who think of me as a human being, and not as a museum piece.

This tendency of yours to chill people into literary figures has grown on you, I think. It came out during our last luncheon, when you started to run down *The New Yorker*, call Auden no good, and whoop it up for W. Stevens and M. Moore as the greatest living poets (Amer.). —I thought, as I came back on the train, that your professorial side wanted to throw life out. Of course, M. Moore is a remarkable writer; and so is Stevens. They will continue to write good poetry, I hope, for a long time to come. But the thing that attracts you to them, instead of to Auden, is THAT THEY ARE FIXED AND FINISHED. They will never *surprise* anyone again. They will never break down or up or take to drink or religion or run off with anyone's wife or husband. They are half-dead already; whereas Auden might surprise everyone by becoming either a circus clown, a caterer, a caitiff, or a killer or a clergyman, tomorrow. He might do anything. And the one place he enjoys being published above all others is in *The New Yorker*. That, too, is alive.

There's nothing I can do to change you, Morton. Not now. I think I have done you a great deal of good, if I do say so myself. And you have been of great help to me. But I can't become a corpse; not yet, God willing. I love and revere life; and intend to keep on being vulgarly alive, just as long as possible. I'll never fit into a seminar, while above ground. . . .

Well, goodbye. I'll miss you. But think of my side of things, once in a while. You can't laugh or shrug me off. I'm no Germaine de Staël; but I pack a heavy, living wallop.

Ever affectionately,
Louise

1. The charge LB makes here is supportable. Although Zabel did finally return the letters written to him from Ireland, every other letter or postcard LB was ever to

send him was preserved and, at his death, deposited in the Newberry Library in Chicago, along with all his other papers. (The bulk suggests that Zabel began collecting in the second grade.) In his defense, however, it should be noted that saving her letters seems to have been an automatic cultural pastime (Edmund Wilson even retained envelopes), and, indeed, she kept all the letters written to her.

/ *to Theodore Roethke* /

December 7, 1941

Dear Ted:

Thank you for your kind letter. —I am really surrounded by encircling glooms, at the moment; but perhaps I can fight out of them by spring. I just heard from Jack Wheelock that he fully expects a few "token" bombings, anytime now; but those don't seem to bother me so much as the problem of eating and getting my rent paid. . . . Everyone seems to have folded up at once. . . .

I am v. glad to hear that Kunitz thought the book [*Open House*] "impressive," and is to review it for *Poetry*. I think *Poetry* has long since gone into the most fatal of tail-spins, but a good review from someone you respect, anywhere, always warms the heart. —Mary Colum certainly did a job on me, in the *N. Y. Times*. Rolfe has written a letter in answer. Rolfe and I seem to be the only two people who aren't scared of the b. . . . She seems to have frightened many people out of their wits; why, I can't imagine.

Today I turned down an offer to read, and be "interviewed," God save the mark, over WQXR. I simply haven't got the sales instinct, it seems.

I saw *The Maltese Falcon* and thought it fine. —Did it ever occur to you that the only Academy, in America, which gives awards, is the Motion Picture Academy? This must mean something.

* * *

Ever,
Louise

/ *to William Shawn* /

December 9, 1941

Dear Mr. Shawn: [1]

I am writing you this letter against the grain, because I am not a person who likes to push or shove, or ask favors, etc.

But I find myself, this winter, in the most precarious financial position. Everyone knows those periods in which all the members of one's family need attention at once. My father is now 80, and needs special care. There are other claims upon me. I am trying to sub-let my apartment, in order to meet these obligations; and I have been forced to economize down to subsistence level.

My job writing the Verse department has now gone on for ten years. Until 1936, I did two omnibus reviews a year, and was paid space rates for them. Katharine White, in the spring of 1936, put me on a salary (she said the magazine has kept books on me, and that the salary of $15 a week comprised a raise of about $200 a year over what I was then earning, writing articles and blurbs).

Since 1936 I feel that I have made the Verse department, step by step, into a real influence. I have had many letters from people whose opinion I respect, telling me that they have respected my criticism, and have always read it with both interest and profit. I feel that I did something toward keeping the flag flying (not to speak of the torch burning!) during the darkest days of political pressures upon writing. And I was touched, last winter, to hear that W. H. Auden had spoken his mind freely, saying to many people that I was the best critic of poetry in America.

I don't know how to ask for "a raise." But if the magazine thinks it can add something to my weekly check, I should feel that I could see my way out of my encircling glooms; and, next summer, begin to pay back what I still owe to the magazine. —And let me add that I have always felt the deepest gratitude to the magazine for asking me to keep on with the job, which has been good for me in every creative sense.

> With every good wish,
> Sincerely yours,
> Louise Bogan

1. William Shawn, who became editor of *The New Yorker* on the death of Harold Ross, was at this time the managing editor.

/ *to John Hall Wheelock* /

April 27, 1942

Dear Jack:

Forgive the paper. I am fresh out of white.

Things seem to be going along well; and I was touched at your efforts to cheer me on the subject of the royalties. I wonder that they were as much as they were. Poetry is on its way out, for the duration, at least. A new consciousness is forming, I feel sure; and it is a consciousness which is quite different from what anyone supposes. I think that many attitudes will be swept away, before this far flung thing is over. I don't believe that we shall get anything which is remotely a repetition of post-War poetry, or of 19th century poetry. It will be quite different; and it is coming into being this very moment, among the soldiers in the field, as such poetry always does.

Auden wrote that he is "trying" to do a review of the book for *Partisan Review*. He said: "Comparisons are supposed to be odious, but I find the last half of your book a finer body of work than any similar body of English lyrics of this century, bar none." I think that a little excessive—but how nice to get some encouragement from one other person whom one respects!

* * *

Ever,
Louise

/ *to William Maxwell* /

July 8, 1942

TWO ORIENTAL POEMS
(offered instead of Job, by one who has always been rather frightened of the morals of the Old Testament)

> *Chinese*
> It is better to be a crystal and broken,
> Than to remain perfect like a tile upon the housetop.

> *Japanese*
> The morning-glory has taken hold of the well-bucket;
> I'll borrow some water elsewhere.

Louise

October 9, 1942

Dear Maxwell:
So nice to hear from you, and to get the MS pages.[1] —I truly think that the narrative goes, and interests. I can see the terribly tough job you have; but, after a month of absorbing the trials of Flaubert, year after year, book after book, as put down in his letters, I can see that

no profoundly conceived idea can come through, in narrative prose, without the most gruelling work. As I see these paragraphs, you are right about shifting from the first person. If the first person is to be the delicate observer, too much irony and sardonics have to be thrown in to keep "him" ("I") in his natural place. With the third person you can get more slight mockery in, as notice your use of "legged it out to the field." . . . What I mean, and am trying to say is: that the sensitive observer has so much more insight than the other people, that one has to play him down a little, merely for proportion's sake, and that is difficult, working with "I." Proust was *out* to make the s. observer well above the bunch; but Proust is a special case; and even he gets terribly tiresome.

The one thing I jibbed at a little was the description of Latham's physical set-up: "wide in the shoulders and narrow hips like a boxer." A little too easy? We've heard it before?

Did you see my S[*entimental*] *Education* piece in *The Nation*? If not, I'll save a copy for you, because I worked so hard on the damned thing, and it really came out quite well. I should think that, when you flag, you could pick up that translation and open it anywhere, and refresh yourself with those wonderful crisp passages of description which always move things along, at the same time that they have both density and brilliance. And [Flaubert] wrote them with such difficulty! One sentence at a time!

I'll be busy until after the 16th. Let me know about the walk thereafter.

Ever,
Louise

1. LB refers here to Maxwell's third novel, which, when completed, would be called *The Folded Leaf*.

/ *to Margaret Marshall* /

December 2, 1942

Dear Peggy:

I was right about _____ (infallible Louise!) He sent me quite a saucy note when I turned down his book. I think he might do something if he got enough extra–New York shocks; but that isn't likely. *I predict* that he is in the big money in a Fadiman way, within ten years. —The glitter and jingle at lunch could have been explained (I used to g.

and j. myself, ten years ago, when not sure of myself) but there's a bully underneath, and I can't be bothered with bullies. They're boring.

The reason I feel so warmly toward *The Nation* is that I started to review for it when I had finally matured, and had all my wits about me. The *N. R.* stands for my wobbly youth; and besides, it represents all the disgust I have felt [over that] crowd of sycophants all writing *tough*. The place hasn't a nice smell. At *The Nation* I've always been free and trusted, and I think that attitude of the Literary Section has shown in my work for the Literary Section. . . .

Let me gather myself together this month, and do a nice essay for you in January. I still have a piece for *The New Yorker* due, before December 14, and then there will be Christmas. On January 1st I'll bring all notes together, and see if I can't get at least an outline of that *roman policier* article to you. That or something on *The Bostonians*.

> Ever affectionately,
> Louise

/ *to William Maxwell* /

December 4, 1942

Dear Maxwell:

Still good and right. Oh, how sad everything was, in those apartments on those afternoons. Sad as the Naturalists never realized. And the boy asleep, as though shot. . . .

I am sending you the novel today.[1] Let me explain it a little, or you will be puzzled somewhat, as you go along. V. Meynell is the daughter of Alice, the really fine poet, and of Wilfrid, who, I judge, is / was rather a stuffed old Catholic shirt. She wrote the novels I hope you will read while she was young, and, I think, psychically as well as materially tied to her mother and father. Her brothers were brilliant and did rather wild things, like marrying Americans. One, [Francis], founded the Nonesuch Press and became a typographical expert. So you can see what the background was like; and I think that a knowledge of its specialness and airlessness (of a sort) makes these novels all the more remarkable. Now, I came upon this one in 1916, the year I was in college. It made me feel, for the first time, that there were other people in the world who had the same sort of sensibilities as myself. I had never read any French or Russian fiction (being taken up with poetic works at the time) and I did not know that there was anything outside the Naturalistic—Wells and Maugham and Frank

Swinnerton, say—in English literature up to then. I have written a long article on Viola, which I'll show you sometime, and we have corresponded, and it's a long story. But just keep in mind the circumstances which made for her stiffness; and then marvel at what she can do within her limits. —I'll have the others for you soon, if you like this. I want them for myself in any case, as they are not in the library any more and my copies were burned.

Yes, the McCarthy novel [*The Company She Keeps*] is certainly odd, as far as background is concerned; but those people exist, I assure you. Mary has a certain twisted and mixed kind of power, though: the way she *explores* things. She isn't on to herself at all, however, and may never be. —What wheels and circles! Do you realize I knew *The New Yorker* before there *was* any "21," and when [Wolcott] Gibbs lived in as unfashionable a place as Tudor City?

More, please!

Ever,
Louise

[P.S.] Virginia Woolf, by the way, once said that Viola was the finest modern English female novelist, but no one ever paid any attention to this remark.

1. Most probably *Columbine.*

/ to Margaret Marshall /

December 30, 1942

Dear Peggy:

Happy New Year! I couldn't share any cheer with you, although I'd like to have, because the wave of Christmas passed only to leave me in the clutches of those fiendish *New Yorker* copy-readers (who can think up *every* way to query proof). * * *

The enclosed letter is touching, I think (and may I have it back, because I must answer the man). It would be wonderful if *The Nation* could put out a special number, or at least scatter articles throughout the twelve months, designed to clear away some of the fog and hatred now attached to James' name and works. Morton could do some fine things, and Edmund. I'll have *The Bostonians* for you, in any case. And the point which the man makes about a decently arranged cheap edition is very important. And perhaps some civic-minded person could start an agitation to have Washington Place renamed James Place. (Henry was born on the corner of W. P. and Washington Square.) If we can enshrine Minetta Brook, I don't see why Henry James should go unlaureled, in his native city. Perhaps someone could even put up a statue to him, but that's too much to hope.[1]

But I hate to think that the surface-creepers, in the form of the *Kenyon Review* crowd, will have Henry all to themselves.

Ever,

Louise

1. The new year was to bring the centennial of Henry James' birth, but he was not to be honored by the city until 1967, when LB was present to see a plaque unveiled on a building at 29 Washington Place. (A second plaque on the same building commemorates the Triangle Shirtwaist fire of 1911.) Minetta Brook, after which a lane, a street and a tavern in Greenwich Village are named, was an underground stream.

/ *to Rufina McCarthy Helmer* /

May 14, 1943

Dear Rufina:

   * * *

The literary season is about over. I have just reviewed T. S. Eliot's new book [*Four Quartets*], with much groaning and many trips to the Library—for the poet gives no help in notes, any more, probably on the assumption that those who want to find out what the background is, will; and to hell with the others: a very sane idea, really. So I had to look up a lot of *Anglican* saints. These are usually poor imitations of Catholic saints, Catholic saints having folk-lore on their side, and therefore making more color and sense. Anglican saints tried hard— getting martyred and setting up religious communities, and one thing and another—but they always had a mother or a family of sisters and brothers tagging along behind. This especial A. saint had his "religious community" destroyed by the Puritans. That is amusing, the thought of Puritans burning and ravishing: the pictures we had of them in youth were so mealy-mouthed and colorless: Priscilla and John, etc. . . . Well, it seems that they could burn and ravish with the best. . . .

   * * *

Ever with love,

Louise

/ to Rolfe Humphries /

August 24, 1943

Dear Rolfe:

❋ ❋ ❋

The poisons DO accumulate. The first two days [in Swampscott] I spent emotional energy, as well as analytic powers, on the piano practice of some girl or other. I sat there *sneering*: when all that was required of me was to *listen* and understand just why she was playing as she was: all the notes, in tempo, but badly out of time, and with the twists and *rubatos* of the amateur *expressing* herself. Now, I am a little cured of that. Perfect love casteth out fear; that is true. One has to stop being nasty and hateful, both concerning oneself and others, if one is to stop suffering and stop getting panicky. It is not enough, to get rid of oneself; one must really feel at least *kindly* toward others. Not superior. All right; I knew that she was hurrying those triplets in the *Moonlight Sonata*. But I shouldn't have *hated* her and felt fine myself, in a horrid way, because she was. —So, in your katharsis poem, the same thing comes out. Supposing you ARE better than "all of them together"? That's only the first step. The next is to feel humble, whatever you are. This humility is the point where we touch the spirit: and it has to be a happy, *supple* humility, of course. —Stay open and relaxed. It comes. It also goes again. But do GIVE UP, my dear, in your worst moods. Give right up. —We *hate* too much: yes, WE who put on this great act of *loving*.

Louise

/ to William Maxwell /

October 18, 1943

Dear Maxwell:

This note is late. —Maidie and I managed to get my father into the Presbyterian Hospital on October 6th. We still do not know if he will be able to get out, and go on to some sort of nursing home, next Wednesday, when the two weeks which it is within our power to pay for are up. We don't know just what shape he is in, and the doctors are working on the problem. But I have put the burden on the Lord; I do all I can, and that is all anyone can do. ❋ ❋ ❋ Meanwhile, the old gentleman is having a nice rest; and seems not to mind; to enjoy everything, in fact—including the cigars we buy him and his daily paper and food. It all goes to prove that Spirit is neither wholly Kind nor wholly Good nor wholly Non-Time-Wasting. Infinitely Complicated, as those "leakages" over into our own consciousness of which W. James speaks, ever show it to be . . .

Well, anyhow, as Gertrude Stein often says.

Let me get these two or three notes on your MS off to you before more Complication sets in.

On page three of the initiation chapter, I have marked the paragraph beginning "It is just as well that the committee didn't attempt the rites of etc. . . . ."

When I first read this paragraph, I thought it a little too much, and as one goes on reading the chapter, I think that this feeling grows. The point you are making is the point of *torture*: I think that the words following "the only awe-inspiring part of the initiation" . . . up to the end of that sentence could be omitted or compressed or put in elsewhere; and that the torture motif could be leaned on in just the *faintest stronger way*. (Remember that nothing here is actually *wrong*. Only not the swiftest kind of rightness. . . .) When the anthropological motif comes in on page 6, it comes in with absolute rightness, I think, and makes the elaboration of the paragraph spoken of, unnecessary. —Now I've made my point; it's your prose; and you know best what to do with it.

Everything else is fine and moving. The last sentences of the last page are really the finest you, or almost anyone, has written on the theme of the knowledge of love.

Good luck; and shall I cook you supper sometime soon?

Ever,
Louise

[October] 1943

Dear M.:

The sight of the check (which fell out of the letter in the most graceful way, and slid along the floor) at first flabbergasted me to some degree; but I shall not pretend that using the money it represents won't solve the problem of my father's board and room at the Presbyterian Hospital, for another couple of weeks. —The hospital has "shaved" the bill, after Maidie gave them a general view of our situation, as they well might, as the first week, with all the special services and laboratory work, etc., had spiralled up into the sum of $90! * * * I'm taking the money. And now I can always give you presents (up to $100, and not a cent more!) without having all those thoughts about an older woman and a younger man, etc., which so quickly spring into my meticulous (as far as human relations are concerned, at least) mind. I can give you, when the tide turns (and after seven years of hard luck, it will, I know), and I have an occasional $25 around loose, four presents to that amount—a bunch of Swedish table glass, a rare pear tree or rose-bush, and some linen sheets are the first things that come into my thoughts. —Thank you for a couple of weeks of peace. * * *

Did you ever think of doing some needle-point, by way of letting the subconscious run around and through psychic blocks? * * * Men need this sort of thing as much as women do; the hands being extensions of the brain, and I see that great burly men are sewing with glee, after various experiences in war; and not merely for muscle therapy, either. Do you ever do anything with your hands, outside of sweeping the floor and peeling potatoes? It is such a comfort to use them in a perfectly monotonous way. The King of Sweden does v. nice sewing, and is the only intelligent K. in Europe.

Just a suggestion for the winter evenings. —Now get back to work!

Ever,

Louise

/ *to Margaret Marshall* /

January 4, 1944

Dear Peggy:
* * *

The book you mention (*Clowns and Angels* [by Wallace Fowlie]) might be interesting; do send it along if you'd like. It is one of those Sheed and Ward volumes, wherein the Catholic Church begins to take some notice of what has been going on in literature, during the last fifty years (or a hundred years, maybe); and tries to do something with it beside merely disapprove of it. I have seen one of these volumes: a life of Baudelaire; quite a good one, as a matter of fact. It would be interesting to see if the Church still thinks Gide a victim of demonic possession, as some of Its sons did, not so long ago.
* * *

Affectionately,

Louise

1940-1949

March 26, 1944

Dear Morton:

Your v. fine letter received. How happy I am that everything was sublime and magnificent: the trip and the situation when you arrived [in Rio de Janeiro]. * * * All that now remains is the quest of Violetta della Liana Frangipani; and perhaps even she has by now appeared, fragrant lacy bosom and all: blood sister to her who made Mallarmé's life so vivid, and gave even the firelight on his humble armoire such meaning and refulgence!

Here, it is much the same, except for the fact (and I say this in a hushed voice, not wishing to waken You Know Who) that a few small swishes of the tail of Fortune have swept some ripples my way: silver ripples, if not downright golden ones. In the first place, I got a raise. Quite a considerable one—ten dollars a week. This was due to the machinations of Katharine White, and to the fact that I am not on salary but on a sort of space basis. —After this * * * the most unheard of thing happened. I was summoned by Mr. Moe to give him some of the benefit of my wide experience in the world of letters. I went down [to the Guggenheim Foundation] one rainy morning, and went through a remarkable session. He presented at least twenty-five current literary characters for my appraisal and judgment: not their works, just their names; and I just sat there, and told the truth, so far as I knew and understood it. —This, after ten years of believing that Moe never listened to a word I said for or against anyone. We had a *real* nice chat; he escorted me right out to the elevator after it was over. Then I reported on the works of two people, the MS being sent up here by messenger; and, on the day I lugged the material back in my market-bag, I had another heart to heart talk with the gentleman, on some characters who might as well be nameless; but you would be rather surprised if I did name them. Suffice it to say, that they are established figures, my seniors, etc. . . . I felt that all this conversation might well bring forth a little honorarium, and it did: $50: and I wrote my heart-felt thanks, as why should I not? So I can never go around and curse prize-committees for never giving ear to the sensitive and enlightened, to those wise in life and loaded with learning, again, can I now? —Frankly, I think the whole thing was fine, for everyone concerned. It was about time that that committee got a salt-breeze of Boganian taste, now don't you think so?

* * *

Mr. Moe told me, by the way, that you are getting a G.! Let me be the first to congratulate you, dear Morton; although I must say, you were pretty mum about it all! Were you afraid I might want to commend you?

Write soon!

Ever with love,
Louise

April 19, 1944

Dear Morton:

I hasten to give you my vote in the matter of the Harriet Monroe poetry award.

Allen wrote me, giving as his first choices 1.) Eliot and 2.) Marianne. I answered him yesterday, saying that I thought Eliot was out: not an American poet; has not been one for almost half his life-time. I also said that I thought Marianne represented a decadence, instead of a freshness, in American literature. I do think this, but let's get on to some of your points before I go into what I think, when Marianne is put alongside the other people you mention, in her generation and out of it.

Let's turn to the poets under 40, that you mention. Of these, I should certainly vote for [Robert Penn] Warren as first choice. I have just reviewed his *Selected Poems* and admire his qualities. He is remarkably deft, I was surprised to see, at sensing the trend of the background in general. The running comment in "The Ballad of Billie Potts" is *far too much* later Eliot; and he is, for my taste, too darned smart at being a naturalist when naturalism is in, and a pure aesthete when that is the trend, etc. . . . His poems imitating Marvell and Hardy *might well be* Marvell and Hardy: and I don't think that *absolute* powers in this direction of approximation are all to the good. They are the sign of the second-rate; not the first-rate creator. Warren is head and shoulders above all the rest of the people in his generation, however, in his feeling for language, his sense of "life," his general breadth. And when he is working on his own material, in his own way, all the sedulous side disappears. Well then, Warren first, in that class. —[John Peale] Bishop, poor man, died a few weeks ago. *Gregory* I have never considered a poet at all (you know this, and know that the opinion doesn't stem from the personal dislike I hold for him. I have always thought him a fifth-rater; a man who never wrote an original line, or cut a "new-minted" phrase). *Delmore Schwartz,* as well, in my opinion has mistaken his calling. I agree with you that *Shapiro* has had enough for the time being, he just received a Guggenheim, and an award from the American Academy of Arts and Letters. He needs to assimilate his success and get out of the army, before we can see what he is really worth, in endurance and growth. . . . *Jarrell*, too, as you say, is still unformed. *Agee* is highly talented, but is a freak of some kind; and has his development ahead of him, if any.

So I can't give you any second or third choices in this group. Robert Penn Warren first, and second and third, if you will.

To turn back to poets over 40: I certainly think it should be Marianne, in spite of the remarks I have taken pains to make, above. She represents, decadence or no, the high formal line that needs to be stressed and helped. She should have received every prize in America, long ago, including the Pulitzer and anything the Am. Acad. of A. and Letters had to hand out. She has developed, and writes more beautifully now (in the last book) than she ever did. She has a spiritual side, in working order (to put it crassly!). She is really, as you say, a sort of saint of American poetry; and although I feel that saints should be outside their mothers' leading strings, and, like St. Theresa (of Avila!), be able to run a convent and dance every day before the Lord, and have visions and ecstasies, but also a fine, firm, human and tough point of standing (if I make myself clear!)—well, we can't have everything, and Marianne's decadence has been channelled off into her life and her prose, leaving the poetry pretty firm and pure and clear. Yes; that is true. So I give my first, second and third choices to Marianne Moore! (Of the others, Stevens, as you say, has stopped, and become an affected old fool. Léonie has stopped, actually. I do think Harriet would want someone who has gone on, fought through, endured. Don't you?) [1]

Love,
Louise

1. LB's final choices for voting purposes ran: (1) Marianne Moore; (2) and (3) R. P. Warren. The prize went to Miss Moore.

/ to John Hall Wheelock /

May 1, 1944

Dear Jack:

There isn't much to say about the lecture. It is called The Hopwood Lecture, and is an annual thing; and such stuffed characters as Christopher Morley and Edward Weeks and Carl Van Doren have given it in the past. —Mary Colum gave it last year.[1]

You will forgive my complete frankness: but I don't want to get involved with any book-selling, or autographing, during my visit to Ann Arbor. I feel that if Dr. [Roy] Cowden had wanted some of my books to be on hand, he would have ordered them himself. —I still am amazed at the ways of publishers! Scribner's did not take the trouble to give me even a small advertisement in *The New Yorker*, a magazine with which I had been associated over ten years, when *Poems and New Poems* came out. Numerous people were surprised and shocked at this, including, after I finally awakened to the fact (I awaken to these facts rather slowly), myself. But when there is a chance to make some money and sell some books without an outlay of cash, the publisher becomes interested. —I am sorry, but I am not interested.[2] And I should consider writing Dr. Cowden in this matter, when he has shown no interest in the selling side of the thing, rather a vulgar thing to do.

> With every good wish, as ever,
> Louise

1. "The lecture went off rather well. The set-up out there [at the University of Michigan] is quite magnificent. The whole commercial trend is, however, v. bad. Publishers' agents were right on the spot, to grab up the immature works of those kids." (To Maxwell, June 8, 1944)

2. LB had broken with Charles Scribner's Sons early in 1943.

/ to —— /

May 13, 1944

Dear ——: [1]

* * *

I am very much interested in the problem of the small magazine, devoted to literature, as that problem exists at the moment. —The problem is by no means the same as it was ten years ago; and totally different from the whole problem of "experimental" writing twenty years ago. I know that you have difficulty finding interesting work; and I feel that a magazine devoted to a purely aesthetic point of view must in some way widen its character, without in any way letting down any of its standards. I have never believed, as you perhaps realize, in the various materialist and political patterns that have been imposed upon creative literature; and I believe less in the academic textual analysis which has become fashionable in some quarters. I feel, however, that the period of "experiment" in poetry and prose is definitely over. What we need now is writing with a full measure of insight into life, society, culture, at large; writing with a firm background of that historical sense of which Eliot has spoken. Re-evaluation; interpenetration of one art with another; the relation of them all to the actual moment and the actual situation. —I find much more of this kind of wholeness in books concerned with painting and music, than I do in books devoted to literature as such. —It is time for the young writer to prove his sensitiveness by understanding what is really happening in the peculiar culture in which he finds himself. He can apply himself to the material he uncovers with the aid of satire, or with the aid of imagination. But he can no longer spin literature out of himself, in an unrelated way.

I say all this fragmentarily and badly. I should like to write you again later, at more length, when I have more time.

Sincerely yours,
[unsigned]

1. Because this letter, available only as one of the rare carbons in LB's papers, may not have been sent, the name of the addressee is omitted.

/ to Morton D. Zabel /

May 24, 1944

Dear Morton:

* * * I saw Allen and even Marianne—rare vision!—at the big party given by the *P. Review,* about ten days ago. This was the first party I had attended—of this kind—in ten years; and the experience was interesting, if rather mild. Marianne appeared, in a very nice hat and grey get-up, with a sort of shawl and reticule; and it was a great lesson in Time, for me to look at her; for the last occasion when I had seen her had been in the run of work in the St. Mark's Place Branch Library, in 1922! —This was the winter before I went to Vienna; and I was in a dazed state of mind, and Marianne, as well as everyone else, came through to me rather foggily. But I remember very well, working with her in the winter afternoons, upstairs in that library with its dark-brown woodwork, its noisy children, and its general atmosphere of staleness and city dinginess. —Her hair was then a beautiful shade of red; she wore it in a thick braid. She was continually comparing the small objects with which we worked—mucilage brushes, and ink and stamping rubbers—to oddly analogous objects; and she smiled often

and seemed happy. Mama kept running in and out as if she owned the place: I remember that, too. They lived across the street. She had no idea that I wrote poetry, and always treated me kindly, but rather like some assistant more or less invisible to her (as indeed I probably was, being, at that time, more or less invisible to myself, as well). . . .

In any case, she greeted me at Philip [Rahv]'s [1] (the party took place there) with great pleasantness, and kept remarking that I had done her a great service in writing that poem to my brother. (I never quite understood this.) Allen took her over, and we all had a pleasant talk on the virtue of Prudence: sitting on the edge of Natalie's [2] Bauhaus sofa. She looked v., v. ashen: the hair, once having been red, looked particularly burned out. * * * The rooms were crowded with such an assortment of talent, stupidity, ugliness, beauty, sects, septs, spies, *agents provocateurs*, and just plain hangers-on, as was seldom seen in the history of man! * * * Then, I was continually being led up to small groups of very small Young (usually female) writers of verse and "admirers." . . . One small female writer, Janet Terrace, has just produced a v. good Jamesian story, in the *P. R.*, and I was amazed to see that this gifted person was of about the general size and shape of a young drownded kitten. —Some of the young were Very Rude: not to me, but to Allen, who I must say, was being rather rude to them. "Tell 'em nothin'," he kept repeating to me; "Let 'em find everythin' out for themselves. . . ." Allen and I made our get-away together; it had begun to rain and we rode up here in a cab; and many were the anecdotes and memories—of those far away days when we all lived in tenement houses, were young and thin and beautiful, loved our husbands and wives, worked hard at everything, including shovelling coal and cooking large dinners for ten people. "You used to be *emaciated!*" said A. to me; and all this is a part of life which you knew nothing about, dear M., since you came upon the scene some four or five years later. A touching *rencontre*, don't you think?

Edmund I haven't seen; he telephoned that his mother was exceedingly ill; that he was going to Wellfleet, and would turn up later. Mary published a v. snippy set of remarks on the subject of Graham Greene, in the Variety columns of the *P. R.* She was even rather snippy about your article; she thinks everyone has been Taken In. So I told Philip that the last word had not been said; and that I was the girl to say it. So I shall expand my theory of How Certain Writers Live Their Psychic Life in Public: or, The Split-Man, His Criminal and Religious Tendencies, in a short rebuttal to Mary (and, partly, to you). For the Autumn Number. * * *

Actually, as that character in Isherwood was so fond of saying, I am not really as filled with cantankerousness as the above might sound. I have relaxed on life; as I darned well had better, what with the things I'll Have to Go Through, in the next week or so. —I think everything will be fine; there will be brushes with certain smarties, of course; but I will say of Providence: He forbears to give one really sassy enemies until He has also given one the power of fairly sassy rejoinders. Isn't that the truth?

—The new Osbert Sitwell—an autobiography, called *Left Hand! Right Hand!*—projected in several volumes, of which this is the first—is full of v. amusing things. The account of how Sargent painted the family is enchanting. Mrs. Sitwell was painted in a ballgown and a large hat, arranging flowers in a silver loving cup; and it was explained that she had put the hat on in order to go into the garden and cut the flowers. Sir Osbert explains that his mother was such a Manchu that she was incapable of tying her own shoes, let alone going out into the garden to cut, etc. . . . The emergence of Edith will be interesting; Papa's attitude toward her was rather Chinese: that it would have been just as well if she had been exposed on the river bank at birth. I am sure her later style reflects this Psychic Scar.
* * *

Allen has just wired me that he will get you his final decision—and mine—by Diplomatic Pouch! O, those happy days, when we were Young and Thin and Beautiful!

Write soon!

Best love,
L.

1. The critic Philip Rahv was editor of *Partisan Review*.
2. Natalie Swan, Rahv's wife, was an architect.

/ *to William Maxwell* /

September 18, 1944

Dear W. M.:

I sat down and read the novel all through, that very night; and, as I told you over the phone, I was much impressed by the new *largeness.* It has kept all its old poignancy, along with this extension of dimension

(I sound like someone in *Time: The News Magazine* . . .). The last chapter I liked; but I can see that you might want to give it more depth and sweep. And is it true that the boy actually gets rid of all his childhood, then? —Couldn't there be a loophole remark, in which it could be hinted that getting rid of one's childhood is almost a lifetime job; unless real steps are taken? Of course, Lymie has taken what would seem to be the ultimate step—attempted oblivion—but he has come back to life where everything is so partial that one has to renew the fight almost day by day. —I came upon a remark of Goethe's, famous to everyone but me, no doubt, from the last part of *Faust* II, in which he says that one must fight for one's spiritual freedom *every single day*. I had been wondering why I felt slack; and I hadn't really taken thought about these matters, consciously and conscientiously, for some years. I just thought that I was leading a good harmless life; and that grace would keep right on flowing in. This isn't the way it always works, it seems.

You should be *real* happy; and enormously relieved. You have gone beyond your former attainment; you have changed yourself "in an upward direction." Now all you have to do is, plan to do it all over again, as soon as possible. (I *know*: look who speaks; but wait until I get that TABLE!)

   * * *

Ever,
Louise

/ to Rufina McCarthy Helmer /

September 21, 1944

Dear Rufina:

* * * You have produced a book. Now you must stand outside it, tear it apart, and put it together again. I know how sacrosanct a first book is. One thinks: well, I've done it—all those words, all that time and effort and suffering—and I won't touch it; I won't change it; I will cling to it as it is, through hell and high water, and anyone who doesn't like it or understand it is wrong, terribly wrong. (Think nothing of this typographical ghost that seems to intrude here; I'm awfully low on paper.) Well, if you want to go through the difficult middle terrain, the Waste Land, the Valley of Doubt, that separates the *writer* from the amateur, you must take a firm grip on yourself, right AT THAT MOMENT OF DESPAIR AND CERTAINTY. You must put the book away, for

about a month or so; and start writing something else; or start studying something else. You might start reading some Great Novels, and
taking notes on them. You might read a few treatises on Dramatic
Form, and how to get effects in plays, and in the theatre. You might
start doing all of these things at once; and get so interested that you
stop thinking of the already completed novel. *Madame Bovary* and
Sentimental Education and *Crime and Punishment,* and one of the big
Victorian set-pieces (anything but Thackeray!) and Jane Austen and
more of E. M. Forster: those novels would keep you busy for quite a
while. And you might read some well-made "mystery stories," too, and
watch how they get their effects, build up their suspense and *get at the
reader,* in general. —Then, and only then (after you have a few notebooks all full of perfectly realistic notes on FORM), you can go back to
your book, and start re-writing it. Once you start working at it, in this
journeyman way, you will have taken the *first step* toward getting on
your own feet as a self-critic; and no matter what anyone says, you will
be working as a conscious artist works, and not as someone who merely
has written a FIRST NOVEL.

   * * *

Love,
Louise

/ *to William Maxwell* /

September 28, 1944

Dear M.:

* * * I'm sorry I didn't snap right back, in approval or disapproval of
your *Julius Caesar* title. I think it v. good. —But why don't you just sit
around for a month or two, reading all sorts of snippets of things, in
anthologies and elsewhere (in books opened by chance)—while your
publisher is going through the manuscript; pray to St. Anthony (of
Padua) and St. Theresa (of Avila)—and I'm sure the most beautiful
and appropriate title possible will just fall in your lap. —Not that I
have undergone a *conversion* in the last couple of weeks; but isn't it
true that just waiting and praying (to whatever illustrious or charming character, now in the shades, that you will) is just as productive
of Beautiful Accidents, as any other way you can think of? —Marianne
Moore has a lovely new book [*Nevertheless*] (v. small, as books of
poetry should be); and she has a lovely poem on patience in it; and

a lovely *aperçu*: namely, that skunks ("don't laugh," as she puts it) have sweet faces. . . .

The prettiest title for a novel I have heard for some time, is being held in suspension for the book to be written to it, by a frail young man in the Library called Herbert Cahoon. He is rather given to surrealism, but the title comes from "The Last Rose of Summer," by Thomas Moore: *All the Lovely Are Sleeping*. I'm sure that there are numbers of other titles hidden under our very noses, in the most familiar poetry and prose possible. . . .

Auden wrote me a nice letter, thanking me for the review, and asking me if I would come down and visit him in Swarthmore, where he is, he says, rather guiltily getting tired of the Quakers. —I think I'll go; it's such an unheard of thing to do: to spend the night in a poet's home on the "spare-bed," as he calls it, surrounded by Quakers, and drinking a few drinks, and listening to records (he mentioned having both of these last). Then I could skim out the next day, and have a nice ride on the train, an experience I have come to love, these last iron-bound years. —And I want to talk to him; he has such piercing insights into the bare spots in one's spirit. . . . I wish you could come along. And I hope that the "spare-bed" is surrounded by the walls of a spare-room. . . .

    * * *

                           Ever,
                           Louise

                                       [October] 1944

from CHORIC SONG from "The Lotos-Eaters"
stanza 3

Lo! in the middle of the wood,
The folded leaf is woo'd from out the bud
With winds upon the branch, and there
Grows green and broad, and takes no care,
Sun-steep'd at noon, and in the moon
Nightly dew-fed; and turning yellow
Falls, and floats adown the air.
Lo! sweeten'd with the summer light,
The full-juiced apple, waxing over-mellow,
Drops in a silent autumn night.

All its allotted length of days,
The flower ripens in its place,
Ripens and fades, and falls, and hath no toil,
Fast-rooted in the fruitful soil.

                           Alfred Tennyson 1833 (aet. 24)

Dear M.:

I first saw this in a book on Shakespeare by J. W. Mackail. He used it, speaking of *Romeo and Juliet,* and the sense of young beauty and doom in that play. —I think it has a real *adolescent* sorrow about it. It is particularly lovely if you stop with the 10th line.

It has the adolescent sorrow about *growth*; which always seems tragic to the young; and this is one of the moving themes of your novel.

                           Love,
                           Louise

                                   November 10, 1944

Dear M.:

This poor young man has been bombarding me with poems for a week or so. —It now appears that he is in *France*; so everything becomes more touching. I have written him; but in these situations it is better if you write him too. —There isn't time to send them back to him; so will you write a note?

                           Love,
                           Louise

[P.S.] They came *Air Mail.*

                                   [November] 1944

Dear M.:

I send you another of Sgt. Salinger's letters. Perhaps getting in touch with this here agent, Harold Ober, would help stem the tide.

I am full of the strangest kind of news. Did you hear about the National Eminence I lately attained; and how I went to Washington and sat on the right hand of Archibald MacLeish? —You don't believe it? Neither do I; but it happened.

   * * *

                           Love,
                           Louise

/ to Allen Tate /

January 16, 1945

Dear Allen:

❀ ❀ ❀

The New York Letter forms cloudily in my mind; and I have already put down a brief outline. The question arises: Do you want the article to deal with Literature alone? I find that some contingent questions keep coming in: the low state of the theatre, for example. But I haven't seen anything this year but Billy Rose's rather old *Carmen Jones*. This spectacle shows v. clearly the prevalent trend of decanting all tragedy and Meaning out of literature and drama, with the result that one finds oneself watching a cheap comic strip effect—in the case of Rose's *Carmen*, for example, we get an exquisitely costumed, staged, lighted dirty joke about a little tart who runs off to Chicago with a soldier. The fact that Negroes make up the cast of this production might complicate matters. So I hesitate to use the example. —Shall I just mention the thing in passing; and stick to Literature as Such? —I think I'd better, on the whole. But do advise me.

I have received a strange communication from some Bryn Mawr females who teach at Yale, about Marianne Moore's transcendent worth. They want to *meet me*, and, no doubt, judge if I am a person in my right mind, before they go to Bryn Mawr and demand that something be done to decorate Marianne. —I wrote the spokeswoman of the group that I could not see her this month (I cannot see why I should!)—and then I gave some facts concerning the H. Monroe judges; and mentioned your name. Perhaps this character will write you a letter. If so, I am sure you will write good and true things about Marianne's worth. —Aren't people funny? —Katharine White of *The New Yorker*, herself a Bryn Mawr graduate, is all for getting Marianne money and publication and one thing and another. So perhaps we have started Fortune's wheel in the right direction—Marianne-ward. I do hope so.

How many words for the Letter? I can't remember that you said.

Every good wish,
Louise

/ to William Maxwell /

April 5, 1945

Dear William:

I was so touched! [1] —But I did v. little, as I look back on it: just nagged now and then at the beginning. I remember how long it took for Spud to *wake up,* on that porch. After that things began to work for you. Surely that wasn't much *patience* on my part!

The last touches you gave everything are really wonderful. They always happen, don't they, if one has been a good writer and torn oneself to pieces on the foundation drudgery. *Then* the lovely little additional ideas just come floating in, like feathers from angels' wings! —The book is completely right throughout: not a false note. With an added firmness of fibre, and more spiritual scope than the others.

Now get started right away on another one!

Last night my *persona* (only it's masculine in the case of women, but I don't know the masculine form) kept telling me that now I knew the way to write a long piece of prose fiction: start in; work; see what happens. "For how do I know what I think until I see what I say?" as E. M. Forster remarks. —So I will! —Who is this man living in the room with the bobbles? I never have had the faintest idea. But now I know how to find out. I thought I could think him through first. But I see that he'll have to be *created.* . . . I have the first sentence, and I'll send you a sheaf of MS really soon.

I've just done three *New Yorker* reviews in *three weeks.* This would have put me out of commission, a year or so ago.

How is the marrying coming along? I hope you have the ring, at least. Give my best affectionate wishes to Emmy.

Love,
Louise

[P.S.] I'm so glad you printed the *whole* quotation, and Alfred's age.[2]

1. The dedication page of *The Folded Leaf* read "For Louise Bogan."
2. See pp. 243–244.

/ *to Morton D. Zabel* /

July 6, 1945

Dear Morton:

I'se so wicked!

Not that I wish to begin this long overdue letter in a purely coy and Topsy-like way! —Maidie has been bringing all the weight of her moral disapprobation to bear upon me, ever since Christmas, in the matter of my writing you. "You haven't written *Morton*!" she would say. "I think it is terribly mean of you! Why don't you write Morton? He's been down there for two years now (she got this a little wrong) and yet you never write him! I think it is terrible of you not to etc., etc. . . ." "I *will,* I *will,*" I kept saying. And I have written you many letters, while riding around in subways and doing the dishes and sweeping the floors, and while giving the whole house that lick and a promise of the duster, which really annoys me more than it does the house, but *how* I hate to dust! —I *don't* hate writing you letters. But this has been one of those years. A year unprecedented since I went into my "obscure period" in the spring of 1937—remember? When I renounced the world, and settled down to doing a lot of journalism to prove something, I can't remember just what. Well, anyway, I as suddenly decided to come off it, or come out of it, and accept all invitations to speak, read, teach or turn handsprings, in public.

Not that I was overwhelmed by such offers. But they began to mount up, at that. One thing led to another and before I knew it, I was actually sharing a platform at the Young Men's Hebrew Association with none other than Dorothy Parker! —Wasn't that a surprise for the gods and the men? She took it all quite nicely, too, and I rapidly worked out of my dismay at facing a totally Parker audience (Maidie sat there sweating with sheer terror, after seeing what I had been gotten into. * * * —I had been wooed into the job by the promise of speaking alone, and then, who turns up but Dottie, all gotten up in a magenta turban and a coat lined with summer mink) and gave them the works. —O yes, I have learned a great deal since I saw you last. I am now an expert at judging the saturation point of any given audience to my works. I can now rise, as cool as a cucumber, and look them over, and shape the thing up. I can even cut and edit my own prose, *on my feet,* when I feel things are running overtime. The Michigan lecture taught me something. * * *

The great and overwhelming surprise occurred last November; and I can't think why you have not heard about it. I think that the whole business really startled me so, that I thought it might startle you even more. Perhaps I have a psychic block about it. Perhaps I think that *you* will think that I have sold out! O dear! Yes; I have perhaps been keeping this from you. Well, let's get it over with. Let's face up to it.

Last November I received a letter from A. MacL. telling me that I had been elected, or appointed, a Fellow in American Letters of the Library of Congress! —And would I come down to a meeting of the Fellows which was to take place the following week. —So I went. And there was Allen and T. Spencer and Willard Thorp (the Princeton one) and Mrs. Biddle and others.[1] *And* A. MacL! And we had meetings and listened to experts, and had a drink or so, and a dinner or so, and I returned. I can't tell you all the details; wait until you get home. It was v. good for me, because I had for so long indulged in tail-lashings about the good seed being passed by, etc., etc. I was becoming a little peculiar on the subject, and it did me good to face reality that was somewhat rosier in hue than usual. —So there you have it; and there has been a sequel to all this which you will perhaps hear about before this letter reaches you. —Remember, whatever reaction you have: that the sequel requires a good deal of courage on my part. I have gone into it (I just heard about its confirmation today) because I think I can help keeping the gill standard; because I am now a chastened person who does not go all stiff and bug-eyed at a little success; and because it really is the damndest development. . . .[2]

* * *

So goodbye for the moment, dear Morton. Write me *at once*; and I shall send back all the details of the Mysterious Development (which by then will be in full swing, I hope) by return. Have a wonderful time. I do miss you; and hope you won't prolong your stay after this coming autumn. —Auden has gone to Europe on some kind of government job.

Ever with best love,
your old friend and comrade-in-arms,
Louise

1. Theodore Spencer was a poet and a professor at Harvard; Thorp of Princeton, a critic. Katherine Garrison Chapin Biddle, wife of Francis Biddle, who served with distinction as attorney general under Roosevelt, is a practicing poet.

2. LB was to become the Consultant in Poetry to the Library of Congress.

/ *to Allen Tate* /

July 9, 1945

Dear Allen:

It was nice to get your letter. —Perhaps by now you have heard that I have decided to take the Consultant job. I take it, you can be sure, with both eyes wide open to the difficulties involved. * * *

The New Yorker has been wonderful, in agreeing to keep me on as reviewer. At first I thought holding two jobs would be simony, or whatever you call it, but evidently a writer has to write. . . . Then, I have been given three full weeks during which *the books will be held.* This is the first freedom of that sort I have had since 1936. Always, wherever I went, the books would follow, and there hasn't been three full weeks during which the nagging responsibility was not continually present. * * *

I enclose my map of Ireland. *Guard it with your life,* as it is a particularly good one. I have marked the town of Clanabogan, outside Omagh. I think you might write to Omagh, asking for records. That town name shows that an actual Bogan clan existed: and that is where you should start; in the cradle of the clan. Ireland is full of antiquarians, and you may get hold of one in Omagh (a sizeable place) who could tell you everything pertinent.

Ever,
Louise

/ to Rolfe Humphries /

September 11, 1945

Dear Rolfe:

It would take the application of a major Victorian novelist—Dostoevski or Trollope—and the innermost "apple" of Rilke's eye for *dinge* to describe to you the events and accouterments of the last week. —Briefly, I have been landed by the Rodman generosity under one of the strangest roofs in the universe (including Saturn, Uranus, Mars, Neptune, Pluto and Jupiter).[1] And I have done more concentrated "deskwork" than, I am sure, 18 *other* bureaucrats in the same time. —I have had a few side flashes at Washington, the Nation's Capital—of the *Capitol*—I see it out of my front window (I have a *suite* of offices, in case you care!) any time I please. Head on. Flights of steps and dome (which is really impressive, even though a work of cast-iron of the early 19th century)—complete.

A strange angel hovered over my birth. During those eight long years in Washington Heights, I thought the magic influence which wafted me in 1917 into a concrete Government flat in the wilds of Panama had tapered off. But O no! Once the Subject of Queer Events and Places, always such a subject. I shouldn't surprise myself if I spent my old age in 1.) The Kremlin or 2.) a grass hut in Malaya. * * *

Louise

1. Selden Rodman, a poet and anthologist, had lent his Washington apartment to LB, who described it in a letter to Maxwell: "A combination of something out of Joseph Conrad's earlier period (*Almayer's Folly* or *An Outcast of the Islands*) and those Josef von Sternberg chicken coops in which Marlene Dietrich used to find herself, ten or twelve years ago." (October 8, 1945)

/ to William Maxwell /

The Library of Congress
Reference Department
September 23, 1945

Dear William:

I was so happy to hear of your enchantment; and I hasten to write to you on my handsome new stationery (which doesn't go to everyone, you may be sure, seeing as how it is bought with tax-payers' money) to show you how truly your personal happiness has sealed you off from events, these last months!

For it was in June that at least one person on the magazine knew of my appointment to the *Chair* of Poetry, at the above printed institution. * * * —Amazing, isn't it? Particularly after all my cracks about official positions for poets, and one thing and another? —Well, you see! Is it hauling down the banner at last?

In most ways: No. I was elected by a jury of my peers, and owe nothing to "influence" or politics. (Certainly I am the most unlikely person in the world to get anything that requires any degree of boot-licking.) Then, I found that all my thought-up *refusals* were actuated by pure fear. So then I had to embrace a non-fearing *acceptance*. . . .

In any case, here I am; and the work at the Library is delightful: I have an intelligent young assistant who treats me like a Mandarin; and between us we are compiling a *valuable* "check-list" of British books since 1939.[1] I get v. homesick, and get back to town every other week-end. —So perhaps sometime next month you and Emmy and I can have that dinner, in any case. —Do write meantime, and wish me luck. —I shall have to live here for about a year; and I can't say that Washington has endeared itself to me, so that I look forward to such a period without some heart sinkings. . . . But Dr. Wall said I could be as eccentric as I pleased, so long as I didn't take to drink. And I am so busy reading wonderful books that I don't seem to find the time to tip up many bottles.
     * * *

(Incidentally, I'm being rather well paid!)

Ever with every best wish, to you both,
Louise

P.S.—I *still* can't understand how the *New Yorker* grapevine broke down. . . .

1. *Works in the Humanities Published in Great Britain, 1939–1946* (Library of Congress, 1950).

1946

/ to Theodore Roethke /

> 1207 35th Street, N.W.
> Washington 7, D.C.
> November 22, 1945

Dear Ted:

I take my pen in hand on Thanksgiving Day (which I am spending alone and hemmed in—as the street-cars are on strike) to answer your letter. Perhaps if you saw the bee-line kind of life I at present lead (home-to-office; office-to-home) you would forgive my lateness in answering. —But no! I'm sure you'll NEVER forgive me; never, NEVER. . . .

Be that as it may, the fact remains that I liked your long poem "The Lost Son" very much. —It is a poem written to be read aloud; I suppose you realize that. —You have rather got into the way of thinking of your writing as something for *you* to read aloud—or am I wrong? In any case, "The Lost Son" loses certain effects—these effects do not completely come through—when the poem is grasped by the eye alone, and not by the ear alone. —The impact of the whole *is* effective, however, even in print! "What a small song. What slow clouds. What dark water." (*adagio con moto*, as it were)—that whole *slow* movement is beautiful. Also, the *last slower* movement, "It was beginning winter, etc. . . ." And the exhortation at the last is really lovely. —But don't you think that giving the whole some sort of musical sub-title (like *Rondo* or *Suite*—*not* Sonata, for it isn't a sonata—much more Impressionist and Debussy-an) would be a good idea?

How are you? —How *I* am is too complicated to sum up here. —Write again soon; do. —Sorry I didn't see you that week-end in town. —Can the L. C. lend you any new English books? It has practically everything. . . .

Do write!

> Love,
> Louise

/ to Allen Tate /

> The Library of Congress
> Office of the Consultant in Poetry
> January 7, 1946

Dear Allen:

Your letter of December 13th, in which you outlined to me, as a Fellow in American Letters of the Library of Congress, the problem of assigning the Grants-in-Aid of the Rockefeller Foundation to suitable projects, received.

I have for some years felt the lack, in books concerned with American culture, of an all-over picture of the culture existing in America at any given period. —The works concerned with literature in America, for example, rarely "mesh in" with works concerned with music, painting, and the graphic arts, architecture or theatre. And I have thought that "popular art"—so-called—should be brought into some relation with the more formal arts. An anthology of poetry, which included "popular songs," ballads, etc., along with "serious" and formal poetry (the two kinds of expression being printed without any lines of demarcation between) would, it seems to me, be extremely interesting and valuable. What "popular" verse was appearing in America when "Thanatopsis" was published? What was the popular background to Longfellow (himself a semi-popular figure)? —An anthology of this kind should be illustrated with vignettes of the period or periods.

It is my opinion that some collection of this kind would do much to correct certain misapprehensions concerning the intellectual and moral climate existing in America at one time or another. Such a collection— of prose or verse, or of prose *and* verse—would serve to correct the notion that Poe was an isolated tragic figure—and that his works were peculiarly colored; whereas, as a matter of fact, Poe in many ways merely rejected the "popular" Gothic romanticism of America in the 40's. . . .

Sincerely yours—
Louise Bogan [1]

P.S. I know, from experience, that a project of this kind has little or no appeal for the ordinary commercial publisher. Both Houghton Mifflin and Henry Holt and Company were much interested, but both thought that such a project should be projected in some other way than the ordinary commercial one.

1. The formality of this letter results from its official nature. Tate is being addressed here in his role as editor of *The Sewanee Review*, by LB as a government officeholder.

1946

/ *to Edmund Wilson* /

The Library of Congress
Office of the Consultant
in Poetry *in* English
Washington 25, D.C.
March 20, 1946

Dear Edmund:

Thank you very much indeed for the copy of *Memoirs of Hecate County*, with its memory-laden inscription. I read the book over two week-ends, and think it by far, and in innumerable ways, the most impressive piece of writing you have ever done. It is dense (in the best sense), complex and interwoven in a way that makes other contemporary reading seem thin in the extreme. The diabolic fumes that rise from it (especially in the Canby, etc. fantasy) are also well-managed (if one can *manage* a *fume!*). And I was impressed by the moral courage displayed throughout; you have not left an opportunity unused—an opportunity of the kind opened up and bequeathed and made possible by the great *martyrs* of writing—from Baudelaire through Joyce.

I hope it made the Canby–Benét–Fadiman axis tremble a little over its excessive ὑβρίς. —I hope I live to see the day when Fadiman will be selling shoe-strings for a living in Union Square.[1]

> A habitation giddy and unsure
> Hath he that buildeth on the vulgar heart.

> Write me sometime,
> Love,
> Louise

---

1. Clifton Fadiman had preceded Wilson as book editor of *The New Yorker*; he was also master of ceremonies of the radio program "Information Please" and a judge of the Book-of-the-Month Club. Many years later, after a stay in a sanitarium, LB was happily to quote a friend as saying that the only way she had proved her "derangement" was by making favorable mention of Fadiman's abridgment of *War and Peace*.

/ to William Maxwell /

Library of Congress
Washington 25, D.C.
June 26, 1946

Dear William!

   * * *

Now that the time draws near that I shall leave (a bad translation from the Sanskrit, that last!) I am feeling rather warmly toward Washington, Georgetown, the L. of C. and even toward the incredible little people who inhabit this place of exile. I have nasturtiums in my flower-boxes and it is pleasant to have a door onto a balcony in one's bedroom, even though the bedroom itself has a navy-blue ceiling. I have given up trying to reform my mad young assistant. He *writes* and *writes*; so I plan never to have a *literary* helper again; just a young woman who can barely *read* (let alone *write*) who loves files and filing. * * * The Library machinery still baffles me; but I have leaned over backwards to be cool and detached and cheerful and obliging. As a matter of fact, it has all been v., v. pleasant, and I have learned a lot; and the Library has learned a few things, too. Such as the fact that R. M. Rilke is a man, not a woman, and writes in German, not Italian. . . .

   * * *

Isn't my handwriting queer? I lost my old one, typing for years; and *this* one showed up last winter. Odd!

I'll write you again. Good luck to the new novel. . . .

Love,
Louise

/ to Rolfe Humphries /

October 7, 1946

Dear Rolfe:

I am beginning to feel some of the backwash of my activities in September. All seems rather stale, in spite of the fact that my bank-account (God save the mark!) is better than I ever can remember it having been; and in spite of ruddy health, good expectations, etc., I don't seem to be able to *self-start*, as I once did; and I am frequently stymied by writing jobs: I just don't write things on time! This sultry, sullen Indian summer weather isn't helping any, either. It condenses and reflects too many sultry (and sullen) feelings in my own breast! O dangerous age of 49! O thoughts like dahlias and all late, coarse summer flowers, that linger on till frost! "Emotionally mature," indeed! If I could only write poetry, all would be well, and all manner of things would be well. Or fall in love with gusto, in a coarse, dahlia-like way! (Why don't *you* do something with the thought above expressed!)

Well, the discipline of the writing table will probably save me in spite of myself. —I have to do a piece on the surrealists, this week. And I think I'll begin my memoir-in-the-form-of-a-horror-story—behind my consciousness' back, as it were: by writing a journal, and hiding it away from myself—under the linen in the middle-drawer of the chest. —No creative work in five years! "No wonder you are calm," as you said to me once, ". . . the daemon has been silenced, and whatever silenced it is sitting pretty."

Well, it looks as though the calm were healing up. I don't really take much pleasure in reading, any more. I get restless and guilty. So little time left, before decay sets in! * * *

Your dahliaesque friend,
L.

October 9, 1946

Dear Rolfe:

The weather has changed, thank God; and I no longer wish to be an Old Languorous Tiger-Lily, yearning by the Pond; or an Old Blowsy Dahlia by the Fence ("peering through the railing, In a manner unavailing . . ."); or even a Left-over Ragged Rose, banging against a Trellis. —Far better to be a Nice Old Cool Cucumber, tendrilling circuitously in a cucurbitous way; or a Fine Old Melon, coyly resting on a nest of Straw; or, best of all, a Monstrous Old Huge Pumpkin, swelling with sun and memories, and not afraid even of frost; and with a certain secret kinship to the Witch and the Warlock, who, in November, keep the last of their Summer Covens, under the Hill. —Now why don't you rhyme *that* up, as you once did the Druids?

Love, and write soon.
Louise

1940-1949

October 13, 1946

Dear Morton:

* * *

All sorts of delicious news, since the great Wilson arrived late last night, shouting for the *finest* brandy. "I can only drink the v. *finest* brandy," he said, "now that I am so rich and have the gout." He said that E. Millay had written him an extraordinary letter, admitting the fearful sins she has committed against art and the Creative Spirit, during the war years. She pleaded a nervous breakdown; and now she is better, and has memorized quantities of *good* poetry: all of *Endymion,* I believe, among other things. She now feels that *no dreadful Evil* can ever enter into her mind again, with all that treasure under her mental hatch. She sent him three poems (lyrics), two of them good, E. said. Well, well. . . . —E. is worried about his book [*Memoirs of Hecate County*] being on trial during the next two weeks or so. He thinks that some of the old fuddy-duddies in Doubleday will try to keep the publicity down, thus hampering his v. good lawyer. If the book loses,[1] it will, of course, be banned from the U.S. mail, and that will be the end of E.'s income. He apologized for his bad *NYer* reviews, and he is leaving the mag. soon; fed up after two years. So he may not be so v., v. rich for long. He is going to stay in Wellfleet all winter. * * * Mary's story in the *NYer* v. well written, I thought: classic syntax. But how shut up she is in *Mary!* I have had some light thrown on *pure* narcissistic types, by Dr. W., recently. Wall says that they are hopeless, and that their trouble is so fixed and deep that it seems to be *somatic.* One sign of the pure narcissistic character is that they never can say "I love you!" So that lets me out! How often have I framed those words with my careless lips; and perhaps, even at or beyond *fifty* (dreadful milestone) I may yet frame them at *least once* more. Who can say? Life! life! etc., etc. Well, the brandy arrived (Martell) and we proceeded to down it; and Edmund got a little *bearish* toward the end, but not alarmingly so. He accused *me* of being self-righteous—can you *imagine!* And he is about to marry again: some gal whose first name is Ileana,[2] and who comes from the Middle West. Sounds like a Communist *agent,* to me. (I liked *Hecate Co.* by the way. Really excellent social satire, and all true.)

So we get older. . . . I really cannot believe that I am 49. But I look forward to my 50's with a certain amount of eagerness. White hair, a calm philosophy, some extensive dental work, which will give me back my *radiant* smile; soft shawls of gray-blue, and a pliant mask (with a "living face" behind it)—what fun! So many books still to read and music to hear, and so much work to do. My poor old father was as good as new at 80. Of course he is a little closer to those Derry peasants than I am; and I have that streak of *bad* O'Neil and Murphy blood: *bad* in the best sense, if you know what I mean. However, with luck I hope to be running smoothly at 75. You too; why not? I hope that we'll live within visiting distance, in our 60's. So we can play 4-handed piano music and grab books away from each other, and be able to TALK gossip, not forced to write it.

The great impending *horror* is the expected arrival, in a day or two, of the great Gregory–Zaturenska opus [*A History of American Poetry, 1900–1940*]! E. has seen it; and it is dedicated to *Louis Untermeyer!* And, he says, it is all toned down, so that the really waspish side is not evident; and the result is that it is just nothing. They have knifed E. W., however, and have tried to shuffle ME out of sight by placing me between H. Flanner and G. Taggard and hurrying on as fast as possible. Many mistakes of actual fact, such as the statement that J. Peale Bishop derived from a rich influential family. —I can hardly wait. I'll try to be fair; you know that. But Louis Untermeyer! [3] * * *

Love,

L.

1. It did, attitudes toward descriptions of sexual encounters being what they then were.

2. The fourth Mrs. Wilson's name is Elena Thornton, and considerably happier comments will be made about her later.

3. "On the subject of the *Terrible Book:* —when it arrived * * * I spent a weekend going *mad*, I tell you, *mad*; taking long sheets of notes, and querying and exclamation-pointing—all this labor directed toward a terrific job of *demolition*. For three nights I went to bed with my eyes bugging out; and, as I remember, I took to drink the third night, guzzling tall glasses full of white wine and seltzer in order to make the agony more bearable. —'This will require some advice,' I decided, on the fourth day, still reeling from those strangely serpentine sentences with the subject not related to the predicate; still soggy with *the authors'* leaps into the empyrean and descents into the inferno; still clogged with the residues of *the authors'* paranoid hatred, fears, malice, misinformation, fake erudition, quotations from Sam Johnson, etc., etc.

"So I telephoned Mr. Shawn at the magazine. 'What shall I do,' said I, 'with this awful book? Shall I go all out; or shall I by-pass it?' Shawn, who has had some experience with an enraged H. Gregory * * * immediately decided that by-passing was best. So I *blurbed* the *thing*; about eight typewritten lines." (To Zabel, November 12, 1946)

January 4, 1948

Dear Morton:

* * *

What glittering meetings can I present you with, besides? —There was a luncheon with Katharine White and E. B. —What a place they live in: a dream-duplex in Turtle Bay. Raymond and Scudder Middleton and I used to frequent those rich "liberal" purlieus in the 20's; I haven't seen them since. But surely the loveliest apartment in N.Y. —A circle of lemon-colored couches; one fine painting over the fireplace, a broad black cocktail table; and, best of all, four windows (one of them behind a concert grand) onto the communal garden. And, upstairs, a bedroom, duplicating the four garden windows once more. * * * —I have promised K. some new "fiction"! I remember your dislike of my last (1932–34) productions in this line, but in February (after a six-month trying out the subconscious, from August 1947 on) I shall try again. At 50 one has stories to tell. Whether or not I am the girl to tell them remains to be seen.

As for E. W.: SILENCE. PASSING-OVER. Not even a Christmas card! O dear! What shall poor Robin-Bogin do? —Certainly not make bitter comments about friendship remembered not. —But I hear from *les jeunes* that the [*Europe without*] *Baedeker* was v., v. bad. Cold, bitter, unsympathetic, etc. So where is E. W., who laments for his generation? An admirer of Anaïs Nin . . . , a . . . well, let kindness reign! His latest remarks in the *NYer* are nothing to brag about, surely; and Katharine had stories (she is all for him, as I am, fundamentally, of course) of *really shocking* shifts of responsibility, etc.[1]

* * *

Love,
Louise

1. Explaining to Zabel what he apparently did not understand about her relationship with Wilson, LB had written: "As for his friendship and mine, and my opinion of his middle-classness—some of this was thrashed out, and more will be. We have been having knock-down and drag-out fights for twenty years now. And more to come, I have no doubt." (November 5, 1943)

/ *to Katie Louchheim* /

February 25, 1948

Dear Katie: [1]

Your *nice* letter arrived just before I pushed off into N. England, on one of my trips to oversee my father's health. I meant to write you from Portland or Boston, but matters moved too fast. The hideousness of the winter had penetrated to all the cities I saw; although the country-side, from the train-window, occasionally looked *pure and good!* My father is much better than I had hoped; and, after eating several large hearty meals of lobster, clams, etc., I came back to town rather refreshed than otherwise. —A whole set of mad people (many of whom I haven't seen in 20 years) suddenly appeared out of the blue, however. So that it is just today that I have been able to gather myself together and sit down at my desk for an hour or so.

I have been doing my best for you with the *liberal* papers. *The Nation* seems to have fallen into some obscure kind of decline, so far as reviewing of books is concerned; but I haven't lost hope. The *N. R.* has had another shake-up, and B[ruce] Bliven is back in command * * *. What this forebodes, God knows! Meanwhile, why don't you write a few sample reviews (on any book that interests you in any field) and send them on to me? Good practice, in any case; and valuable samples perhaps later. Make them crisp! Start with a short sentence, and keep your EAR on your nouns and verbs!

This "writing with the ear" (as it were) is really the best technical practice you can give yourself. Remember that the reader's attention span is usually v. short. I *cut* and *cut* my sentences, right up to the last version; always keeping the adjectives down to a minimum and the adverbs practically down to zero. The *verb* can do so much! I don't mean to make you write *completely* without color or sound; but try writing as barely as possible, at first. *Then* put in your connectives, etc. (Although I think that writing "at full spurt," and then paring down, is the best all-round way. Don't censor yourself in the beginning! Keep the feeling fresh, and be sure some *tension* is working at all times. But be severe, severe—at the end.)

Be sure and come to see me when you're in town. It's not so hard to get up here, really.

Love to all,
Louise

1. Katie Louchheim, a deputy assistant secretary of state under the Kennedy and Johnson administrations, published her first book of verse, *With or Without Roses,* in 1966.

/ *to Morton D. Zabel* /

March 20, 1948

Dear Morton:

* * * I went to Washington in January, and saw the usual meeting of
the Fellows through. R. Lowell looks very handsome in The Chair;
and I stayed again in Katie Louchheim's guest house in O Street in
Georgetown, and saw my other old friends. Mrs. Biddle gave an exceedingly dull evening party. Auden and I sat at a table and just ate
and talked; and various other people looked in at this feed, from time
to time. * * * Then, in February, I went up to that awful conclave at
Sarah Lawrence. Really, Morton, the academic world is degenerating
rapidly. We sat around in a smoky room for an entire day, and listened to one *madman* after another expound their views on poetry—
their fantasies, their hatreds, their delusions concerning it, rather.
—*Everyone* was there: except Auden, who sensibly had a sick eye. I at
last *saw* peculiar little oddments like R. P. Blackmur (who is on the
way out at Princeton, I hear); Norman Pearson (who gave an insane
talk, advising people to take poems away from poets, as one would take
a babe from the arms of a nursing mother); Joseph Campbell (who is
rather nice, but so very *mythic*); and I don't know who all. Poor
Robert Fitzgerald, in a Christ-like beard, arrived late, and proceeded
to pour forth a speech on Christian perfection, the dark night of the
soul, etc. . . . * * * Marianne Moore, looking like the saint she is, was
there; also M. McCarthy, looking very demure in a black dress and
some beads. —And over in a corner, coiled up in snake-like dignity
were no other than our two serpent friends: Marya and Horace. *We
did not notice each other* * * *. And in the midst of all this sat
handsome E. Spender, pleading for an *aura* for poets! * * * "What you
have said is very small," said Spender to Pearson. [Lionel] Trilling
was mediating like mad (I like him less when he is so very concilia-
tory). The Walgreen heiress who runs *The Tiger's Eye* was also in
evidence, looking very *golden*: she is a sweet, simple, yearning type,
who means well, I am sure. Marianne, Mary and I shared a train back
to 125th Street where I got off. I must see Marianne in the spring. She
keeps making rather awe-struck remarks about my nature, the sources
of which I can't make out. She thinks I live in some sort of danger. . . .
I don't understand where she got that idea. . . .
   * * *

I have just finished a piece on D. H. Lawrence's poetry. How good it was, to return to! I had never really read *Pansies*; and I was amazed to find so many of these jottings so filled with power. (I have liked the Anna and Vronsky poem for many years, as it appears in the *Oxford Light Verse* and in *The Poet's Tongue*.) Auden certainly learned a great deal from Lawrence—from these later poems which H. G[regory], I discovered, called clots of venom, or blots of filth, or something of that kind, in his *strange* Lawrence study. That was the Soviet influence working, in those days, I suppose. But how good those "pansies" are, when they are good! —I think that Yeats tends to bore us, now that we are ripe and mature, because Yeats, unlike all the other poets of his stature, refused *to give in, to flow*. Yeats and [Stefan] George remained transfixed in power and will. Lawrence and Rilke and Mallarmé *flowed*. . . .

   * * *

Ever with love,
Louise

May 31, 1948

Dear Morton:
   * * *

The dinner of the *maudits* passed off v. well indeed. Bill [Troy] was almost painfully sober and was not rude to us—or to Léonie, until the tag end of the evening, when he began to complain that "my wife interrupts me." Maidie played many *lieder* records; and it turns out that Bill was once a boy soprano; so he liked all this v. much. (Léonie, although she conceals it cleverly, is tone deaf.) * * * Then, on the following Tuesday, the great "poetry festival" went off well at the New School. I read first (like the acrobats or trained dogs in vaudeville!); and then came R. Lowell (who is now quite pert); and then darling Marianne (who was in a cunning little Quakeress get-up). Then Allen closed the proceedings in his usual smooth way. A good largish audience. Sherry upstairs afterward. Marianne attended by the Gotham Book Mart woman [Frances Steloff]. Djuna Barnes casting baleful looks around, from under a Paris hat. Many old friends: Dave Mandel, E. L. Walton, the –?–, Betty. Also E. Bishop, Caroline [Gordon] (looking smart and *satisfied*, if not exactly *holy*), Maidie, Peggy McKee, etc. —I enjoyed it all. —Léonie and Bill, again v. sober and straight. —O yes, Margaret Mead and Ruth Benedict in the front row: I hadn't seen them in years. Ruth looking old and beautiful; Margaret as "earth-bound" as ever. Such celebrities, yet!

* * *

Love,

L.

/ *to Katharine S. White* /

October 14, 1948

Dear Katharine:

Thank you for the check, and for your thought and hopes directed toward *stories*! Just after my return to NYC in September,[1] I plunged into a piece of translation, with Elizabeth Mayer,[2] which fascinated but exhausted me. We were commissioned by a set of learned German professors to do a new translation of Goethe's *Werther*; and we managed to push the thing through in less than a month. W. H. Auden has just approved of the MS; and I hope the professors will do likewise. —I wrote the whole thing out long hand (in order to keep the tone flowing and natural) and I must say that a pile of MS, written in this way, is a v. satisfying object to contemplate. . . . * * *

So now I go to bed at night, and lie awake in the morning, turning over the "stories" in my refreshed mind. They will be memories, and, since I am not the "confessing" type, it is hard to start them off. I tend to surround the facts with a certain amount of "philosophy," as well; and that is not good. I intend to throw the material onto paper v. soon, however; and then shape it afterward. Criticism, when practised over years, makes the creative side rather timid. It is a pity that one cannot use the disguises usual in the 19th cent., when one could tell a story through posthumous letters (as in *Werther*!) or through eight or nine made-up observer-narrators: Colonels B. and C., or Mr. H. and J., for example. . . .

Well, I'll try!

I do hope you are well. You sound very well indeed.

Affectionately,

Louise

1. LB spent part of the summer in Seattle, where, at Roethke's invitation, she taught at the University of Washington.

2. "She has lived about five or six lives, and is as full of intelligent curiosity and intellectual fire as she ever was, I am sure. She it was who took Benjamin Britten under her wing, when he was young and unknown here in New York, about ten or

fifteen years ago. He lived at her house on Long Island for three years; and a year or so ago he invited her to his English summer festival; flew her over; and entertained her with all the grandeur possible. Elizabeth loved it. Wystan she has also befriended; he dedicated his *New Year Letter* to her. She lives at 1 Gramercy Park now, with her husband and a large black Bechstein that has come through all her difficulties in splendid shape. . . ." (To Sarton, February 12, 1954)

/ *to Morton D. Zabel* /

October 24, 1948

Dear Morton:

* * * The usual blurb-writing goes on in all its usual autumn fullness. —I had the task of reducing *Allen* to a paragraph; and it took me a careful week to scan *On the Limits of Poetry*, from beginning to end. What a really good mind he has—erratic, but really depth-revealing. I can't make out just *how* he fails; he is astonishingly right often, at the same time that he is *cagey* and suave and circling. *Circling* seems to grow on him as he grows older; although the five essays that the Cummington [Press] boys are about to bring out under the title of *The Hovering Fly* are v. good indeed.

Well, things are narrowing down somewhat. Only a MS to be read (at a $15 fee) for Macmillan, a talk to be written ("On the Pleasures of Formal Verse"), to be given at Bard, in *opposition* to W. C. Williams, on the week-end of November 5–6; and plans to be made for clothes, etc. for the Fellows' Meeting at the L. of C.—a meeting moved into this November from January next, because of T. S. Eliot's presence at the earlier date. So I shall at last behold Him in the flesh: yellow eyes and all! —Léonie has written that things go rather well for her. . . .

—You may well imagine how pleased I was for my name to stick in your mind, in relation to the job of Visiting Lecturer at the University of Chicago. —I have turned the idea over and over in MY mind. In terms of Challenge and Response: I have, for the last four or five years, Faced Up to all Given Challenges of this sort, as you know. The Washington D.C. business was the hardest. It was a true exile, in many ways, in spite of the frequent week-ends. I could not move about freely at night, for example, because of my situation on the edge of a Depressed Area (no one will ever know how brave I was, alone in that shack for a period, lying in bed listening to the drunks of all shades cursing up and down the street and breaking bottles on the front piazza). I was also—then—pretty recessive, still. Now, not so much so. Indifference comes with humility; I no longer think v. much in terms of my own importance; and the importance of human beings as such has shrunk a good deal, too. . . . All this makes me more free to Go Away Alone. And Chicago, with you in the city, would be less an Exile.

So far as the actual teaching is concerned, I feel I can do exactly what you say: "give your *all* to the students, cordially, openly and generously." Nothing else, in such a situation, is really important, I discovered last summer. Everything goes down, in a classroom, before the real and intense interest of the instructor in his (or her) subject.
* * *

The money side of things is important, since I am now 51, and circumstances have prevented me, up to this time, from being able to set much aside for old age—or even for emergencies—as you know. The *taxes* have been with me during my high-earning years, as well as my father's hospital bills, etc. Thank God, I have been able to manage without going into debt (except to you!); and I have a tiny surplus now. * * * But I *must* earn more money before I am 60! I had planned to go out job-hunting this fall, if nothing was put in my way by *Fate*. At present, I am willing to consider this offer—which comes through your generosity—as Fateful. Let us keep things open, and wait and see. —As for living arrangements, I *must* have a quiet, light room—preferably *not* with a lot of academic women! A room where I can at least make tea, coffee, and an occasional bowl of *soup*. . . . I really was beside myself in Seattle, having to run out for every meal. . . .
* * *

Love,
Louise

/ to Rolfe Humphries /

November 1, 1948

. . . Yes, I got a bid to the *Life* party-photograph, and turned it down at once. —Things ended up with Marya Z. and H. Gregory (great friends of the B. aristocracy, in their latest phase), one holding onto SIR Osbert and the other clinging to DR. Edith. —The Sitwells are prime publicity hounds, and deserve what they get.

L.

1948

November 28, 1948

Dear Morton:

   * * *

!As for Washington!

    My Love is of a birth as rare
    As 'tis for object strange and high:
    It was begotten by Despair
    Upon Impossibility. . . .[1]

I sat beside the Great Man [T. S. Eliot] at lunch; and I looked into his Golden Eye! How beautiful is the combination of physical beauty (even in slight decay), high qualities of mind and heart, and *perfect humility.* ("Humility is endless . . .") We talked, during the end of the entrée and *through* the coffee and ice-cream! Of form, and Youth's fear of form; of rhythm (we got it back to the heart-beat and the breath); of the true novelist talent; of Henry Miller and little magazines; of Brancusi and modern architecture ("who wants to live in a machine?") and, finally, of the *cat* poems! I asked if he had enjoyed writing them; and he said that he had tried them out on "various young listeners." My favorite, I remarked, was the cat who taught the mice how to crochet. O yes, said he; that, among others, had "scandalized my adult readers." —One adult reader, namely, Allen Tate, was being visibly scandalized, just across the luncheon board. —Then, that evening, the lecture on E. A. Poe scandalized quite a few Southern die-hards. * * *

Eliot had sat in on all our Fellows' Meetings:[2] v. quiet, shy, reserved. He smokes incessantly, and at one point took time off to *sharpen a pencil* (with a pen-knife, in his lap). He looks quite frail, really; but what beauty! Well, it is all too late and too sad—but I must love him, in a mild distant, sisterly way:

    Therefore the Love which us doth bind,
    But Fate so enviously debarrs,
    Is the Conjunction of the Mind,
    And Opposition of the Stars.

* * *

Léonie, by the way, conducted the meeting with great charm and acumen and poise. She is being visibly benefited by Washington. What a good idea to send her!

* * *

Poor Harry Harvey died last week, I see in today's *Times.* * * * He telephoned me a week or so ago: as conventional in a Geneva, Ill., way, as ever. . . . And Genevieve T. died. And Ruth Benedict died. —Harry was 73, and Ruth was 63, however.

Now I must polish off E. Sitwell—rather late. I *do* hope that they feed T. S. up well, in Sweden! Don't you!

Ever, with remaining love,

L.

1. The first and, below, the last stanza of Andrew Marvell's "The Definition of Love."

2. The Fellows met to award the first Bollingen Prize. They gave it—as everyone knows—to Ezra Pound. Following this occasion, Eliot went to Stockholm to receive his Nobel Prize.

/ to William Maxwell /

The University of Chicago
Chicago 37, Illinois
Department of English
February 8, 1949

Dear William:

Thank you for your post-card, with its kind remarks concerning [?] the poem! [1] —I have been so very rushed that I haven't answered *anyone*, this last month. The writing class keeps me hopping; for, of course, there are at least two *real* intelligences in it, who *query* everything. The lecture class is better; but there again, I must be meticulous—more so than last summer in Seattle.

One student has just finished a novel that is, I think, sensitive and powerful. I thought of you as a reader for this MS. I have given the young man—Richard Cheney—your name and address. Would you do me the great favor to write to him, expressing your willingness to see the MS, and he can then send it to you? —I hope that this isn't an imposition. Do not think it one. The boy's work is so much *akin* to your own that I thought of you immediately in connection with it. Cheney has just read *Time Will Darken It* (did I ever *thank* you for the copy and tell you how good I thought it was?); and is excited about your various story-telling skills, as well as about your *locale*: he thinks he recognizes "down-state" Illinois.

I enclose the first letter I had from Cheney. He is, as you see, serious; and he has found a method by which to project his seriousness as well as his sensitiveness.

Love to Emmy.

Ever,
Louise

1. Humphries was instrumental in bringing the poem—"Song for the Last Act"—to its final shape. Originally written in four stanzas, it was turned by Humphries' "three stanzas mathematics" into a triptych. "I want to thank you for your *great help*," LB wrote him in January. "Katharine took the poem with great glee; so at least one more poetic work will be published, proving that *women* can carry on to some slight degree, *in* their 50's!"

/ to Rolfe Humphries /

June 27, 1949

Dear Rolfe:

Thank you for the inscribed copy of *The Wind of Time*. I think the book is very impressive; I like it better than *Forbid Thy Ravens*; you seem to have ridden another wave of your development with "success." You have explored another, and I think, deeper level, of your innerness; and your wit and satire function v. well, too. Good luck to the book!

I am still occupied with Goethe's *Elective Affinities*, although the end is near. This translation took too long; my collaboratrix [1] sort of folded up in the midst of it; and I had to take time out (2 weeks) to get some sun and sea-air at Swampscott (the dirt and darkness of Chicago penetrated pretty far . . .). —Now I am faced with a couple of *NYer* pieces: including a long one on Goethe, for Aug. 1st.

Did you note the dirty attack made by that unspeakable fellow, Robert Hillyer, on the Fellows, etc.? A statement from us all should be printed soon.[2] We all should sue the *S. R. L.*, and its horrid editorial crew; but what good would that do? The middle-class mind is dominant, certainly in that sheet. Harrison Smith sent letters to me and Allen (and to others, probably) before this thing broke, asking us to elucidate a long passage of *The Pisan Cantos* for *nothing*. —We sensed the hatchet-man in the background, ready to hack at us, what*ever* we said; so we ignored the request. You can see how carefully the campaign was planned!

* * *

Love,

Louise

1. Elizabeth Mayer.

2. *The Saturday Review of Literature* led the attack against the Fellows' awarding the Bollingen Prize to Pound, who, at the time, was under indictment for treason. Hillyer's S. R. L. article and the resultant rather one-sided correspondence in the magazine were soon followed by a pamphlet, *The Case against the S. R. L.*, in which the Fellows and their defenders grimly explained the procedures followed in making the award, and the principle upon which it was made: the value of the poetry, *not* the value of Pound's patriotism.

/ *to William Shawn* /

September 27, 1949

Dear Mr. Shawn:

The number of books I have found myself kept from reviewing, over the years, have been few, as you know. —I cannot bring myself to deal with Robert Hillyer's book, *The Death of Captain Nemo*, because of the attack by Mr. Hillyer upon a group of which I am a member. After the workout he gave to our characters and aims, I feel that I should be fighting *prejudice* in *myself*—and that would never do! —I am returning the volume to you, therefore, under separate cover, and you can deal with it as you see fit.

Regards!

Louise Bogan

/ *to Hayden Carruth* /

November 19, 1949

Dear Hayden: [1]

* * *

About the pamphlet—I should advise you to send it direct to:

Mr. William Shawn
% *The New Yorker*, etc.

—Shawn is the man who "handles" me; and he is also the working book editor—in that the books come into his office, are listed by his secretaries, etc., before they are sent out to the various people who blurb them. —You might (*do*, in fact) send him an accompanying note, telling him what the pamphlet is, and how important it is to get the other, anti-*S. R. L.* point of view over. —*Do this right away!* It will be better for it to come from you than from me; but tell him I suggested your sending it, if you like.

❋ ❋ ❋

How about that money we all were supposed to put up for the pamphlet? Is that now precluded by the fact of possible sales?

Ever sincerely,
Louise Bogan

1. The editor of *Poetry*, which published *The Case against the S. R. L.* (see p. 268).

HENCEFORTH, FROM THE MIND

Henceforth, from the mind,
For your whole joy, must spring
Such joy as you may find
In any earthly thing,
And every time and place
Will take your thought for grace.

Henceforth, from the tongue,
From shallow speech alone,
Comes joy you thought, when young,
Would wring you to the bone,
Would pierce you to the heart
And spoil its stop and start.

Henceforward, from the shell,
Wherein you heard, and wondered
At oceans like a bell
So far from ocean sundered—
A smothered sound that sleeps
Long lost within lost deeps,

Will chime you change and hours,
The shadow of increase,
Will sound you flowers
Born under troubled peace—
Henceforth, henceforth
Will echo sea and earth.

March 26, 1950

Dear Karl: [1]

* * *

Now, about reviewing for *Poetry*. —I am trying to get away from any reviewing which is not directly bread and butter; or, rarely, whipped cream and macaroons. That is, I do the *New Yorker* stuff; and an occasional piece when the pay is extra good. Otherwise, not. —Straight articles are a little different. I find that stray wisps of *theory* are beginning to form in my mind, now that I am over fifty; and if / when any of these shapes up I'll send you a sample. I am fascinated, as you perhaps know, by some aspects of the 19th century; and perhaps I can do some pieces on these aspects, [between] now and the time I'm sixty . . . or even fifty-five!

* * *

I am not an intimate of Auden's, but I know him well enough to have him to dinner, etc. —I advise you to write him direct concerning his abstention from *Poetry* contributions. He is about to go to Italy for six months; but his mail is either held or forwarded. He perhaps shared the feeling of a good many poets, while G[eorge] D[illon] was editor, that it wasn't any fun being published along with a lot of trash.

Well, good luck to you and your family; and remember to telephone me when you are in town. I expect to be here until the first week in June; in Utah, the West Coast and Indiana thereafter, until about the last week in July.

Every good wish,
Louise

1. The poet Karl Shapiro was then editor of *Poetry*.

January 6, 1951

Dear Maxwells!

It was such a pleasure to hear from you at Christmas time. —I had seen Katharine White during the fall, and she had told me that Bill was back at the magazine, but not that you both were in town. —I am so glad that Emmy is enjoying her Manhattan neighborhood. I once lived on Lexington Avenue, near the corner of 38th Street, and remember 3rd Avenue in that district as a place of great shopping charm: there was then a Swedish delicatessen that sold wonderful dark bread, along with *whisks* made out of birch-twigs. . . . Does this place still exist, I wonder?

* * * —I know that my restrictive and restricting work-habits are boring to hear about; but I think you will both be thrilled (and astounded!) to hear that I actually managed to write the first draft of a little history of poetry since 1900, since August.[1] The printed volume will come to about 100 pages. I am now writing the whole thing over in longhand (so that the subconscious can have a chance to flow from the end of the arm); and I hope to be out of the woods on March 1st. But I no longer have to shut myself up, when working, as I once did. So perhaps we can have a meal and some wine soon. You say when . . . or nearly when. . . .

Best love as ever,
Louise

1. *Achievement in American Poetry, 1900–1950*, published by Henry Regnery Company as part of its 20th Century Literature in America series.

/ *to Morton D. Zabel* /

June 8, 1951

Dear Morton:

* * * We had a v. nice visit with the Tates, late in May. We drove down, and found Caroline extremely hospitable and warm; Allen too. We had lunch with Allen in Princeton, and stayed on for a party that night. The house is now quite *large* and charming. About eleven people showed up, and the [John] Berrymans came over later with— of all people—Edmund! Edmund had been squiring Mrs. [Arthur] Koestler around town (he knew her in London); and came over when he heard that Maidie and I were present. He was in a wonderful *alcoholic* glow, and even partly apologized to Caroline for his cruelty. He then swept M. and me off in his mother's big black limousine (chauffeur-driven)—*me*, that is; and Maidie followed us all the way to Red Bank in the Chevrolet. He put us up for the night, and we had a wonderful long talk the next day, leaving after a shad lunch, cooked by the held-over cook. E. is selling this Red Bank house; but he will have 2 others: one in Talcottville, N.Y., and the Cape one. I never saw him in better form. He is now in Wellfleet. He was v. funny about the Institute award, and sent me several scurrilous post-cards on the subject.

The Institute thing went off v. well: I wore black—with a v. effective new big black hat! The place was jammed with all kinds of people. Léonie was on the platform, together with K. Burke, and L. Trilling.[1] Bill Williams and J. C. Ransom gave me nice words from their places of honor; and old sour-faced Mark Van D[oren] said "Hello" later—and there was *Archie* (later) shaking my hand with such *vigor!* —The citation was quite nice and rather amusing and got a laugh. —Then everyone trooped up to the terrace for refreshments; and all my invited friends were there, including M., who didn't know *who* had invited him but came anyhow. Peggy [Marshall], Elizabeth M[ayer], Katherine [Anne] Porter, R. Jarrell, N. Arvin, B. Gill were in evidence; and many faces I hadn't seen for years reappeared. Bill Troy flashed through the assemblage looking like a wounded bull; and Léonie looked v. proper and happy. * * *

Ever—

Louise

1. These three were inducted into the National Institute of Arts and Letters. LB received a $1,000 grant, as did Newton Arvin, Brendan Gill and Randall Jarrell (plus Elizabeth Bishop and Vladimir Nabokov, who, if present, were not remarked upon by LB).

December 30, 1951

Dear Morton:

It was fine to get your card, and a letter (at long last!) plus an acknowledgment of the little book; to tell the truth, I had thought that you were being rather *rude*, in the last connection. But I should have sent you a Christmas greeting in any case (though quite late, and at the end of the list, you realize . . .) if it had not been for the fact that my poor old father died of a heart attack early last Monday. I received the news around 9:30 A.M., and was on the train to Boston at 2:00. —I arrived in Portland the next noon, after spending a night in Boston, and took up whatever had to be done in the practical way of things. Fortunately the funeral director is one of the Bogan cousins (twice removed), so that everything was very quickly in hand. The poor old gentleman looked v. noble, and very much at peace. Many unexpected friends and acquaintances turned up for the "wake" ceremony, and the funeral took place on Thursday morning, after a High Mass at St. Dominick's: the church where Dad was christened, served as altar boy, and was married. The chapel where the Mass took place has the original altar of the old church, built in 1830; and I never saw a purer piece of early Gothic

Revival: exquisitely simple in white and gold wood. The sun shone brilliantly at the cemetery; and I was moved by the whole churchly ritual anew: the meeting of the coffin at the door of the church by the priest and acolyte is particularly impressive, is it not? —I am still *lapsed,* however. * * *

You have been having your share of notables in Chicago, have you not? Miss [Elizabeth] Bowen, I hear, * * * expressed the wish to meet me, but I have not had time to do anything about this, although I have her N.Y. address. (E. Starkie was quite amusing about Bowen's family and *Irish* pretensions: "Cromwellian!" she remarked, rather coldly. Starkie sent me a copy of her autobiography, *A Lady's Child—*very moving and full of Edwardian detail.) * * * —The Yale librarian, Mr. Babb, informs me that the meeting of the Bollingen judges will be informal, and that the men will not dress for dinner. . . . It looks as though I am to be the only woman involved: a fact which pleased Léonie no end, when she served a year or two ago. —My resignation from the Fellows in American Lit. of the Lib. of Congress was sent in last week, by the way. Your name is on the list, and you will no doubt be tapped before long. —I really couldn't feel happy going back without Allen and W[illard] Thorp and some of the original group, present. So that phase of things is over. . . .
* * *

Love,
Louise

January 19, 1952

Dear Morton:

* * * I want to tell you that all went quite smoothly in the matter of Marianne's choice for the B[ollingen] Prize. The only snags were Auden's belief that a younger poet might perhaps be chosen, at this point, plus L[eonard] Bacon's choices of Frost and *Jeffers!* —Bacon was v. amenable, however; and Wystan was not v. firm in his insistence on youth (R. Jarrell, of all people . . .). So the vote was unanimous at the end. —I must say that the little room in which the committee sat was filled with more *bad* modern art than I have seen for some time, including a large paleolithic portrait of Gertrude S., by Picabia, a *frightful* early Picasso and some v. gummy looking Matisses. The Stein collection is formidable—all housed in super-slick steel filing cabinets; and they have that statuette by Davidson which makes her look like

Erda—or the miller's wife, all done in and tired out with heaving the sacks she so much resembles. . . . Wallace Stevens came over from Hartford for the party the night before—quite a feat, because the roads were exceedingly icy. Still a *strange* man, but truly formidable; and nice, after he thawed a bit—in all senses.

The really *crashing* news is that I have been *elected* to the Institute of Arts and Letters! This was a surprise; but evidently my old friends got together, after P. Colum had made a speech in my behalf. L. Bacon told me that the yearly banquet is quite fun. I get my *diploma* next May.

Part of my time-consuming duties has been the cleaning up of files; and I came upon a mass of letters by you written from 1938–41 which certainly are of your *best period*. Such glitterings of epithet, fierceness of opinion, enthusiasm in discovery, and range of interest and of taste! —This is the line we should re-discover, and fruitfully explore, in our 50's and 60's. No moaning over the dark mysteries, but a continued thorough exploration of what mysterious Life and equally mysterious Self have to offer. * * *

Ever,
Louise

/ *to Rufina McCarthy Helmer* /

616½ Ida Street
Fayetteville, Arkansas
February 27, 1952

Dear Rufina:

Your telegram came yesterday, and I was grieved to hear of your mother's death, for old time's and old friendship's sake—for I was v. fond of her, as you know. —The factor of release for her poorly lighted later years we both know and understand. Believing in God, we must think of that side of things as a mercy.

You will have sad days, and a flood of memories will come back to you, and you will feel that a part of your life is over. —We must *mourn*, in these situations, while our grief is still fresh; for if we do not, and suppress our sorrow, we shall have to go through it later, in a more bitter form. But what we *must* not do is feel *guilt*, of any kind. Dr. Wall told me, after my mother died, that I must think of her as a complete person: with all her faults as well as all her virtues. Thinking of the dead in this way relieves us of our own guilty sense of mortality; and leaves us free to live our own lives—which is our *main task.*

Do write soon!

Love,
Louise

/ to Katharine S. White /

English Department
University of Arkansas
Fayetteville, Arkansas
March 9, 1952

Dear Katharine:

I was delighted to get your letter, and to hear that Mr. Shawn is going to be more receptive to "difficult" (so-called) poetry, than Mr. Ross (in spite of his generous attitude toward sound writing) could ever allow himself to be. —I have been turning over in my mind your request for a list of names of poets that you now might try to print in *The New Yorker;* and I must admit that I have not come up with much. You yourself have been so open to new talent that you printed Richard Wilbur,[1] for example, in the first flush of his youth; and Wilbur remains the finest talent among the American young, I should say. I *did* think of Theodore Roethke and Richard Eberhart; but they aren't so very *new*—and their productions tend to be spotty, so far as quality is concerned. But they are both basically authentic—and you might try them for samples. Auden in his present phase—writing occasional verse with great delicacy and lucidity—would be perfect, as you say: and I am sure that he would be amenable to the new largeness of taste, and not hold old grudges; for he is not a grudge-holding person. —Auden goes off to Ischia in Italy every spring; you might write him there. Marianne Moore will also be happy to send things in, I am sure, if you write to her and explain matters.

I shall continue to read *Poetry* and the *New Statesman and Nation* with an eye out for new talent, and send you whatever I find. * * *

Ever aff'ly,
Louise

---

1. LB had long admired Wilbur's talents. As early as November 1947 she had written to Roethke: "A certain Richard Wilbur is *very* good indeed: Harvard Fellow: have you heard of him? Variety, and real feeling for *objects.*"

1952

616½ Ida Street
Fayetteville, Arkansas
March 23, 1952

Dear Babette:

I spent a good part of a very *chilly* week-end (for Arkansas in spring wavers back and forth between balminess and semi-frigidity in the most *un-Southern* manner!) reading the galleys of *Poetry in Our Time;* and I want to write you at once to tell you what a solid yet delicately detailed job I think you have done. —Your grouping of poets under general ideas and tendencies has given you the opportunity to juxtapose poetic figures rather widely separated in time; and I think that this juxtaposition often dramatizes poets in different generations in a most effective way. —Your learning, of course, is immense; and your interpretive powers are impressive, as well. I enjoyed not only the chapters you mentioned in your letter, but was particularly struck by the job you did with Hopkins. You were beautifully detached in your treatment of Pound—detached and, again, in full command of the various critical tools it is necessary to have to hand, in dealing with a poet so full of human and artistic contradictions.

How about the following "remark":

Miss Deutsch has brought to her task not only an historical sense which places her material in focus, but also that wisdom of the heart which alone can truly illuminate poetic texts and the human scene which surrounds them.

I hope to have a copy of the book, when it comes out.

The two courses here are going along quite well. I have the kids' attention in both, I think; and the history one isn't v. hard to keep going. The writing course presents more difficulty, since one soon runs out of "rules"! But they *are* writing, and without inflated language, purple patches or *longueurs*. They all have such pleasant manners; and many of them resemble faces that one remembers having seen in old daguerreotypes: the original *settler* kind of face. . . . Let's hope that they produce something more valuable, sometime, than merely *regional* stuff. . . .

I'll see you in the early summer, I trust. Every good wish.

Louise

1950-1959

616½ Ida Street
Fayetteville, Arkansas
May 3, 1952

Dear Morton:

My visit draws to a close, and again, how strange everything becomes, when we have made it familiar, and know that we will never, never again see it, or possess it for a moment, again! —My little hutch here—with its paper walls, inferior plumbing, and slight air of the cracker-box—has just begun to fit me like a glove, in the material sense—and I shall never come back to it! —No more great bunches of flowers in all kinds of pitchers and vases, on the floor and tables; no more bourbon and Hennessy and Cointreau, lined up beside the bowl of lemons, the last two for friendly Side-cars * * *. No more mornings at the type-writer in the minuscule dining-room, or nights in the quite comfortable wide bed, or meals spread out of the refrigerator; or baths in the bath-room, where the water is so hard that the soap won't lather, but is quite convenient in every other respect! No more cars parked in front of the doorway; no more quiet reads on the couch! Well, I just sink into an-other rut, I suppose—a natural thing, at my age. I guess I'll go back to Manhattan Island and start my memoirs. After all, Edmund has started his. —What did you think of the Millay fragment, in *The Nation*? Do you suppose that he will serve us all up brown, in *The Shores of Light*? He wrote me that it is immensely long, this latest refurbishing of his pieces—this time the ones dating from 1920!!

   * * * I went down to Little Rock at Easter, and stayed with Charlie May Fletcher (Mrs. John Gould) and got another glimpse into the odd things that this place throws up: I think that it is, on the whole, a bad place for human beings. . . . Charlie May opened J. G. F.'s files to me—especially the files of letters written *to* him; and I must say that she has some remarkable material. Norman Pearson has begun to put the stuff in order; but it needs a lot of work; and Charlie May has some of that *lassitude* which is so prevalent below the Mason and Dixon line. —I told her to hop to it; that the world was waiting for this material, to fill in gaps in re the Imagists, etc. She really has some amazing stuff since J. G. F. never threw anything away. . . . I sat in J.'s study (the house they built is charming and colorful in all respects, and the old guy's library is really remarkable—filling the shelves in a large long liv-ing room, and overflowing elsewhere)—on the mornings I was there, turning over in my hands the *entire* Amy Lowell—J. G. F. correspond-

ence; and what an odd feeling that gave me: to see Amy's carefully typewritten letters, dated 1916 and earlier, filled with Amy's egotism and plans for a Poetic Empire run by Amy! —What a strange thing for the little Irish girl from Roxbury, to come upon after all these years! The copy of *Des Imagistes,* signed by everyone on the occasion of a dinner given on the day of its publication, was also extraordinary to see.... Etc., etc.... * * *

Love,
Louise

August 9, 1953

Dear Morton:

I was delighted to get your nice long letter, and to hear that you not only arrived safely, but in style. I am sure you will continue to enjoy every moment of your stay in Rio, its environs, and in South America at large. I still have visions of you flying over the Andes with the condors flapping their wings and dragging their long feet, beside you (my vision of a condor seems to be mixed up with the picture of flamingoes . . .). In any case, you will have been vouchsafed the beginnings of the healing process, by the time you get back. The wind in your case has certainly been tempered, by means of this trip; and you should say your prayers every night and be thankful.

I have certainly passed a lazy summer, compared to others I have known in recent years. The one effortful series of actions performed (over about three days) was the final rearrangement of my library: according to *subject* (roughly)! A period of cool weather helped to make me finally decide to get on my feet and get into action. The books are now arranged, quite definitely, according to poetry and prose; less definitely according to lesser categories. The Americans are divided from the English, in the poetry class; so that I have a whole three-shelved book-case filled with thin little volumes by Americans. The British have two book-cases (prose and poetry mixed, so far) to themselves; and then I have the French nicely divided off, also rather mixed, at present. Then come the Germans, the Greeks and Romans, and the Russians. Large and important modern *oeuvres,* such as Yeats, Rilke, James, Eliot and Hopkins, are set off by themselves; Pound, also. This arrangement by nationalities seemed the best over-all one; and I think it will serve, as time goes on. I am determined *not* to enlarge my library to any great extent, in the future, but to keep it pretty well pruned.

Large quantities of old dead French books went out, this time, along with several dead enthusiasms, bound in cloth. I do like to eliminate; and I now have several empty shelves, scattered here and there, as a result of my drastic (but not too drastic) clearing out. * * *1

Love,
Louise

1. In later years LB grew concerned about the disposition of her library. Believing that it would be "lost" in the one library that meant most to her—the New York Public Library—she willed it to The Western College for Women (see p. 303).

/ to John Hall Wheelock /

September 5, 1953

Dear Jack:
Thank you for sending the current *Georgia Review* with your poem, "The Cruel Song." —I cannot believe that the inscrutable universe turns on an axis of suffering; surely the strange beauty of the world must somewhere rest on pure joy! But *you* are the trained metaphysician! So I must read your lovely words with respect, as well as pleasure.

Greetings, as ever,
Louise

/ to May Sarton /

January 28, 1954

Dear May:
It was delightful to hear your voice, and to feel that you are working. Your letter this morning said many true things (and the poems, too). But what has never been explained thoroughly, by me to you, is the really dreadful emotional state I was trapped in for many years—a state which Raymond struggled manfully against, I will say, for a long time. In those days, my devotion came out all counter-clockwise, as it were. I was a *demon* of jealousy, for example; and a sort of *demon* of fidelity, too: "morbid fidelity," Dr. Wall came to call it. A slave-maker, really, while remaining a sort of slave. Dreadful! Thank God v. little of it got into the poems; but the general warp showed up in every detail of my life. Except for a certain saving *humor,* I should have indeed been a full *monster.* —During my illness, all this had to be relinquished, step by step. A new personality (that had been kept from coming into light and growth) slowly emerged; and it is this person that you now know.

The successful love-affair which began when I was 39 and lasted for 8 years was utterly different from anything that had gone before: perfect freedom, perfect detachment, *no jealousy* at all—an emphasis on *joy,* that is. This is the only kind of relationship that is possible for me now: something *given by me* and received in an almost childish way. * * *

What you say about my own development is perfectly true. I am trying to break through certain blocks in the "long prose thing": that will be "memory," if not "desire." So far as desire is concerned, I must wait. If it comes again, with a strength which I cannot withstand, and a *benevolence* (that is not the word, but then) I can recognize: good! But if not, not. —As I said to you the other night, quoting (I think!) St. Paul: With a great price bought I this freedom. —You understand.

Bless you. Keep feeling and working. For the work is really, for us, the important thing. The channels must be kept open so that it may live and grow.

> Love, dear May,
> Louise

February 4, 1954

Dear May:
* * *

The matter of a more regular appearance of my "blurbs," in the magazine, has been troubling me. * * * I spend an entire morning on *one* of those horrid little notices; and there are about twenty of them, at present, piled up in corrected proof. The women poet piece may be out today; I haven't seen this week's copy yet, having spent the morning writing two more short notices: one on Padraic [Colum] and one on Sir Osbert Sitwell's *Wrack at Tidesend.* —It is silly to worry about this sort of thing, but I do take the *New Yorker* job seriously. If anything should go wrong with it I should have to go job-hunting, in truth, and that is a baffling prospect, at the moment. . . . I am sure that nothing will go wrong; but you see I have my worrying and fussing moments.

* * * As for my eight-sided heart,[1] which you question, dear May, I can only say that the octagonal here is somehow symbolic of freedom. Love of things, I suppose, understood, more than love of human beings. . . . The delight in objects, both natural and artifacts, which has grown in me ever since the *obsessive* person was left behind (or buried, if you like, in the lowest layer of the dream). The delight of the col-

lector, which you sensed in my room; the delight of the naturalist (which I never had, when young, except in flashes, but which makes me scrutinize everything, from flowers to rocks on the shore, in these later years); the delight of the amateur in the arts (the piano and embroidery); the delight of the cook and the housewife. . . . All these are substitutes, I know; but they keep me alive and not only happy but occasionally full of joy. I do not speak of the delight of the maker, for writing has never been anything (except v. rarely) but tough and artisan to me.

* * *

Love, dear May,
Louise

1. The reference is to a parenthetical line in "After the Persian," part II.

February 16, 1954

Dear May:

* * * —I can't stand being in a *fog* about things. There is a rather sad joke between Maidie and myself concerning my mother, who had a rather terrifying way of picking out *one detail* which she presented as permanently baffling: the fact that she couldn't make soft custard, for example, because she didn't have the *right kind* of double-boiler. This fact kept coming up; and, although I am sure that the *right kind* of d.-b., in those days, probably cost fifty cents in the open market, *she* never bought one, and no one else ever did. —This is the sort of thing that I always try to put right immediately: if an *object,* or the lack of an *object,* seems to threaten my peace of mind, I either get rid of it or get it. In the realm of THINGS we can move fairly easily; and I refuse to make *things symbols* of bafflement. As for spiritual bafflements, or bafflements of situation, I want to get those out of the way quickly, too. To act *on* life; to be a *subject,* not an object. . . .

* * * —I am a v. poor stayer-in-other-people's houses, dear May; and I thought this a rare eccentricity until I began to come upon it in others, both in life and literature. My ideal visit goes something like this (and even in the full country!): arrival around tea-time; a fine series of cocktails and/or tea; a good dinner; a good sleep; a nice breakfast and perhaps a walk; lunch—and then away again! Purely selfish, you will note. The Chinese put the limit at three days—you probably know the adage; [1] but decomposition starts in, with me, no matter how much I love the persons and the place, around sunset of the second day....

* * *

"The Shocks" I liked, although can we use the word *beloved*? Why not, really; but that Romantic vocabulary comes v. hard, to me, having spent years getting away from it—since William Morris and Dante Gabriel R. were the people I imitated, during my apprenticeship. . . .

* * *

Be happy, dear May, and remember that I proffer you all that I can proffer any human being. Which isn't, I suppose, v. much; but all of it is fresh and real and non-*patterned*.

Love,
Louise

1. Guests are like fish—after three days they stink.

February 18, 1954

Dear May:

* * * I hope that your father isn't suffering,[1] and that he will *allow* himself to be an invalid, for a little. We understand how difficult that is; I can't *stand* being laid up for any length of time, and I am sure you can't. Tonight is the night of your reading; and I am sure that it has gone off well, and that you had a pleasant dinner with the MacLeishes. Archie has always been most kind to me, after an initial distrust which I can't blame him for, after the dreadful reviews I gave him during his "public speech" period. It is rare to find a person being magnanimous, after receiving what no doubt seemed to him a series of "slights." Anyone who can wake up Harvard to poetry should be cherished . . . and Archie has other virtues, as well. . . . He did a wonderful job of renovating the Library of Congress, everyone agrees. The moss and other detritus accumulated over the years was hauled out by the barrowload.

* * *

Love,
Louise

1. George Sarton, the distinguished historian of science, died in 1956.

1950-1959

March 13, 1954

Dear May:

* * *

Cecil Hemley [of Noonday Press, himself an author] seems genuinely interested in the book of prose criticism [1]—next year, perhaps. —This will mean searching and copying and fiddling around with files of magazines; but *The New Yorker* has all my stuff either pasted into a book, or listed; and quick tricks can now be worked, on material—photographing instead of copying out. This book I truly thought would appear only after my translation into eternity. I shan't let it appear if it turns out to be spotty, as it is. . . .

I think of you in your study, with the light rapidly gaining, day by day. How lovely the fact of the *equinox* is! What a Master of Effects keeps the universe in order and repair!

More later!

Love,
Louise

1. This interest would result in *Selected Criticism: Poetry and Prose,* published by Noonday in 1955. And the task of assembling her material required far more work than going through *New Yorker* files; she had written for such magazines as *American Quarterly, The Atlantic Monthly, Mademoiselle, The Nation* and *The New Republic, Partisan Review, Poetry* and *Quarterly Review of Literature.* "I wish I knew how to file things," LB wrote to Zabel in 1935. "I have never kept a scrap-book, and only one man who cared deeply for me, cared deeply enough for my work to start one, and he didn't last long, poor dear, and neither did the scrap-book. So I shall never know how much I have written, or where it is."

April 21, 1954

Dear May:

* * *

No, I'm not ahead of you, in the *Karmic* sense, I'm sure. I'm just *older!* At least twice in my present existence I have been forced to lose my life in order to find it. . . . This means losing people, for a time— and losing oneself—getting to the point where one gives up *completely* and merely keeps breathing, hoping that the power and the will to live will come back. The power of *persons* is lessened, after such experiences. It is a sort of amputation, I am sure; but one can manage, if one's heart and brain haven't been cut off. And one's hands—spiritual *and* corporal. . . .

You should have the book by now.[1] It is a *neat* book, I think, although it will never get a prize for the 50 Best.

* * *

Love,
Louise

1. LB's *Collected Poems 1923–1953* had been published by Noonday Press.

May 4, 1954

Dear May:

* * * On Thursday I must go to a cocktail party given by P.E.N., since both Léonie and I have beeen named guests of honor. I've never gone to one of these things, at the Sherry-Netherland, because I so dislike getting tight in the presence of a lot of intellectuals; and what can one do but *get* tight, under those circumstances? The Noonday boys will escort me, this time, and I'll stick to highballs, if possible. On Friday I *must* finish the blurbs which are in a fragmentary state at present, but which I'll scribble at off and on, from now until then.

Léonie's book [*Poems: A Selection*] is really very fine, at the center, although I can't care for the new poems as much as I like the old. And this morning I had the pleasure of hearing that Ted Roethke had won the Pulitzer Prize. I am v. pleased indeed, and of course, he will be delighted. It is true that Ted has made a point of knowing all the right people *everywhere,* since the start of his career, but he is certainly worthy of the prize, on the side of the angels, and an idiosyncratic person—it is good to see it given to such a one, and not to a stereotype... * * *

Love,
Louise

May 23, 1954

Dear May:

* * *

Marianne sent me a copy of the limited La Fontaine with the most *touching* inscription: "with diffidence—deference—love"! I've looked into the volume and find the combination of M. M. and the "incomparable" seventeenth century fabulist perfectly delightful. I have always held that Marianne had a good deal of the 17th cent. in her; she has that *curiosity* and connoisseurship which one finds in Evelyn for example. I really look forward to doing the review. * * *

This morning I got down five or six notebooks, that have been gathering dust in the back closet, and discovered how V. studious I was, in 1936. Pages and pages, in French and English, on Baudelaire, Mallarmé, and Rimbaud; with a few comments on the weather and other matters, thrown in, from time to time. —Directly I get back from S[wampscott] I plan to start gathering the prose together; and these annotations will help. —No poems, I'm afraid! Those will have to be brand-new!

I wish you could be here for the Academy-Institute Ceremonial; it promises to be fun, this year. For members (and their husbands or wives!) there will be cocktails at 12:30 and luncheon at 1:00. —Then, all mellowed with wine and food, we shall have the pleasure of hearing Léonie present David Jones (*in absentia*) with an award for poetry, M. Van Doren give Senator Fulbright an award for "distinguished services to the arts," and Archie present E. Hemingway with the Award of Merit Medal for fiction. Also, see John Mason Brown giving Maxwell Anderson the Gold Medal for Drama (I was against this . . .). The new Institute members include E. Bishop and R. Lowell. And R. Wilbur gets the Rome Fellowship, of course. Such goings on! I hope your father is better!

Sois sage.

> Love,
> Louise

June 14, 1954

Dear May:
* * *

You would have loved the Wilson *ménage*. Elena has really effected a tremendous change in Edmund's way of living. She really *loves* him, moreover! The little girl, Helen, is delightful; I must send her an *Orlando* book. The house couldn't be more attractive; and Elena has evidently put real elbow grease into decorating it: scraping floors and walls and making curtains. There is a "parlor" with a good deal of Federal mahogany (E.'s mother's) upholstered in yellow; a dining room with more mahogany against blue walls, plus lovely blue Staffordshire and silver; a "middle room" with more blue walls and blue chintz and linen; and Ed.'s magnificent study, with a bathroom attached, and a stairway to an attic, filled with overflow books. For the first time poor E. has attention, space and effectively arranged paraphernalia of all kinds. —Mary never really helped in the more practical ways; and E. has had a v. scrappy kind of life, down the years. Now all moves smoothly: tea on a tray for his "elevenses"; absolute silence in his working hours, and good meals at appropriate intervals. —Elena was v. hospitable, and fed me enormous luncheons (one of lobster), with highballs at tea-time. I slept in the little guest-house that has been fixed up for the children. —They aren't v. near the sea, but they have a man with a car (Mr. Peck?) who ferries them around. They have a tiny sun-trap of a garden by the side-door, and Elena has a little vegetable garden, v. European, with lettuces and beans mixed with herbs and the zinnias. * * *

> Love,
> Louise

June 18, 1954

Dear May:
* * *

The great and unexpected news is that yesterday morning I received a letter from Alan Pryce-Jones, the gentleman who is evidently now editor of *The Times Literary Supplement*, asking me to do an article (2000–3000 words) for a special American literature number he plans, on the contemporary situation in American poetry! [1] —Isn't that fantastic? Of course I am *no end set up*; and have answered yes. Not bad for the little Irish girl from Roxbury, I say to myself. . . . I know you will be surprised and pleased, for although the thing will be anonymous, I may be able to utter a few basic truths, and I do think I am better than Conrad Aiken, say—who would have been the person written to, twenty years ago. * * *

> Love and peace, my dear,
> Louise

1. "The check finally came through: for $75, really a large amount, considering." (To Sarton, October 15, 1954)

June 29, 1954

Dear May:
* * *

Your vignettes of people met have interested and amused me—although the picture of the old Communist lady was rather frightening, too. Marxist passions seem to bring to the surface all sorts of buried aggressions, do they not?—turning heretofore mild people into harpies and spiritual bruisers—at least in part. Thank goodness all of my friends who were former card-carriers have been converted back, and are now as mild as lambs. * * *

Tonight I go to dinner with Claire Goll, one of the most infuriating women in the world; but she has a pathetic side, in spite of her constant shrewdness and play-acting of misery and sorrow. . . . It is incredible to look at her—past sixty, with long loose red hair, still good teeth and a spare little figure—and realize that she once was loved by Rilke (she appears in the memoirs written about him as Liliane). She is a food fanatic, but she serves up v. pleasant little dishes in any case: the vegetables served as separate courses, in the French manner, with a wonderful *torte* of some kind to end with. No liquor!

* * * The only exciting outside reading I have managed is a little book on the nature of the universe, by Fred Hoyle, which really gives one a turn. The names that astronomers give the various kinds of stars are charming: red-giants, white dwarfs, blue dwarfs, black dwarfs, subgiants, sub-dwarfs and collapsed super-giants! Hoyle holds for millions of other populated worlds, in other galaxies, and this is so much more warming an idea than Bertie Russell's, who once wrote that despairing piece about the complete uniqueness and isolation of human beings in the universe. *Galactic* is another nice word. * * *

Love,
Louise

/ *to Edmund Wilson* /

August 31, 1954

Very Well!
(Never be it said that L. B. was
ever downed in a formal way . . .)

Said Edmund Wilson to Wilson Follett:
"I strive, while you're content to loll it."

"I've lolled since the time/days of 'The Prince of Pilsen,'"
Said Wilson Follett to Edmund Wilson.

Going back to the bastard form:

Said Edmund Wilson to Morton Zabel
"Please tell me your idea of a table."
"A table is what you put your pills on"
Said Morton Zabel to Edmund Wilson.

Love to y'all,
Louise

/ to May Sarton /

October 15, 1954

Dear May:
* * *

The separation between *life* and *things*—O dear, I can't command the vocabulary to bring out what I meant! —Briefly (and awkwardly)—are not trees and skies and water and earth, nature; to which man is added: *Homo additus naturae?* To which human life is added, and from which it is not wholly (certainly) derived. And with human life we get all the significant blood and the tears. And the gift of the intellect. And the common law. And art. The same current runs through the whole set-up —natural and human: true. But in man the power is transformed; and it is this transformation with which we must deal. The trees and the stones and the sea serve us as symbols, and stand around us like brothers and sisters—but they are inhuman siblings. . . . It is from life we must draw art; and philosophy must get mixed up in the horrors, as well as in the joys, of existence. . . . Now I stop!
* * *

The third class [at New York University] went off well. I gave them *texture* in a large dose: the silver cord, golden bowl passage from Ecclesiastes, really analysed down to the last vowel and consonant (I get this out of a book by a learned Oxonian); and a fragment from Keats' "Ode to Autumn" (beginning with the hazel kernels, and ending with the bees' clammy cells) brings out the *m* and *z* sounds complete, with the undertones of *l* and *s*. They seemed to enjoy all this. * * *

Next week: speed and tempo! I do think that modern poets write far too much at one speed. So I shall read a part of "Reynard the Fox," and perhaps the slowest poem in English: Collins' "Ode to Evening." —I find that the stuff they hand in is rather ingrown. I want to get them to look around and use material outside themselves. —Have you seen, by the way, the new James Kirkup volume—*A Spring Journey*? I think he is shaping into something really interesting. He is now 32.

＊ ＊ ＊

I hope that you're keeping a note-book. Dear May, I wish you all richness and deepness; and you are on the margin, I should think, of a new page.

> Love,
> Louise

November 16, 1954

Dear May:

It has been a difficult week, but now everything is "under control," and I can look forward to some fun—editing my prose works! —Your letter from the English countryside gave a colorful, if not a comfortable, picture. —Let us hope that we turn out to be hearty, eccentric old ladies. . . . The progress of the Cummings-Stevens piece was interrupted by an evening at the P.E.N.—where I was a member of a *panel* —consisting of me and two additional people: Kimball Flaccus and John Ciardi—with the task of discussing the *predicament* of poetry. Flaccus (what a name!) is v. dull indeed, and was tiresome. Ciardi certainly can speak off the cuff; *and* quote poetry by the yard (I envy him both talents). He has a fine voice, too. He and I were quite good: standing up for the modern *ethos* at some length. I spoke from notes; and I improve in this direction. ＊ ＊ ＊ *Last* night was the first Institute dinner: *wonderful* food, and the old familiar faces. L. Untermeyer got quite tight, sat beside me, and punned throughout the evening. But I *must* tell you about the waiter! He was passing the roast, when he heard Louis and me discussing *cats*. His face lit up; he stopped in his tracks, and gave us a happy description of *his* cat—who eats spaghetti with tomato sauce and evidently *drinks* red wine. "And his name is *Pasquale!*" he joyfully added. —*Cat people* certainly are a class in themselves, are they not?

＊ ＊ ＊ The gossip is that Stevens will undoubtedly win the Pulitzer, as he should.[1] —Perhaps, after all the returns are in, I may come up with some sort of booby prize! I really don't care. I told Louis that being a successful poet was like being a successful mushroom, and he seemed to agree. . . .

* * *

Love,
Louise

1. He did, for his *Collected Poems.*

The Winter Solstice: December 22, 1954

Dear May:

Everything happens at once, these days, and all of it time-consuming. —Morton arrives at the Biltmore, with a rather serious virus infection, and is in bed for days. Edmund comes to town with Elena; but Elena is called back to Wellfleet because of the defection of the little girl's nurse; and is then marooned in a blizzard! —Edmund and I had a *scrumptious* dinner last evening, in his miniature suite at the Algonquin: what fun that wheeled cart, with the white table-cloth and the metal dish-covers, always is! Much Scotch flowed, and the Master became rather inarticulate toward the end; but we *did* have a wonderfully amusing talk; and he gave me some good advice concerning the arrangement of the book, as well. His son, Reuel (by Mary McCarthy), was off with young friends, so we were uninterrupted and cozy. —The gathering at the Yarmolinskys (B. Deutsch) was rather mild. Isabel Bolton was there—a strange and rather pathetic figure, who is resigning herself to gradual blindness. . . .[1] O heavens, what a mixed world! * * *

Love, and every fortunate wish—
Louise

1. Mary Britton Miller, under the pen name of Isabel Bolton, wrote *Do I Wake or Sleep,* a novel "discovered" by Edmund Wilson and reviewed by him in *The New Yorker* in 1946.

January 4, 1955

Dear May:

* * * At 6:00 I rushed over to the Hotel Chelsea, where Léonie and Bill were giving a party. It was rather sad, seeing several people after a 20 years' lapse, now become so *v.* old and gray: Gorham B. Munson, for example! Margaret Mead was there, looking exactly the same as she did *30* years ago; and we had a really pleasant reunion, although there is a sort of *chemical* kind of *non*-attraction between Margaret and myself. She is *so* sure of everything, and has that *daring* career among the New Guinea natives to prove her mettle (but I still think she is a popularizer, and not a really dedicated scientist).

* * *

The new Whitman life is full of detail, but quite colorless. A set of essays issued by the Stanford Univ. Press—Richard Chase, Leslie A. Fiedler, W. C. Williams, K. Burke, *et al.*—gives more light, on what was certainly a strangely ambiguous personality and career. The insistence of Whitman in sticking to a plebeian background is a fact I hadn't thought of before; Camden was *exactly* like the Brooklyn of his youth. And all his *English* visitors were struck by the old gentleman's exceeding bodily cleanliness—"like a scrubbed deal table," one of them said. —A natural force, like Blake . . . but more earth-bound than Blake. People used to *warm* themselves before W. W.'s kind of interior radiance. . . . V. strange and touching.

Now *I* must bathe! Write well and be happy!

Love,
Louise

/to Edmund Wilson and John Hall Wheelock /

February 14, 1955

To E. W. and J. H. W., After Receiving
from Them a Congratulatory Sonnet, Written by Both [1]

> O had I a lute
> Or else a marimba
> Or a lyre made of shell
> Or a harp made of timber
>
> How sweetly I'd play
> Running over the strings
> A year and a day
> Of the happiest things:
>
> Such as sturdy young hearts
> And faithful old friends;

Of Valentine darts;
Of beginnings and ends!

Though art may be long
Though time tends to mottle,
There's nothing like song
Backed up by a bottle.

So let's lighten our lives
(Joy's more than we think it . . .)
Come up with your wives *
And help me to drink it!

Louise

* Sometime soon!

1. LB had won the Bollingen Prize, shared—$500 apiece—with Léonie Adams. The
sonnet, "written in alternate lines by E. Wilson and J. H. Wheelock, [was] delivered by messenger along with a fantastic bottle of Pin-Bottle Bourbon, done up in
a red-flannel bag! Edmund had found an old Valentine (roses, blue ribbon, clasped
hands) and they both had written the sonnet out. Wasn't that a sweet 'gesture'?"
(To Sarton, February 16, 1955)
    About the prize itself, she wrote to Katharine S. White in January: "I do think
that both Léonie and I deserved it, if only for *hanging on,* over the years!"

/ to May Sarton /

March 17, 1955

Dear May:
* * * —I want to write you rather fully about the problem of argument
in poetry, but cannot do it properly today. Of course, everything is
material for poems—even the "passive suffering" (sometimes) that
Yeats deplored; but argument should be dramatized, as Yeats learned
to dramatize, rather than projected straight—the dramatic monologue
helps. It is impossible really to argue, in lyric poetry, because too many
abstractions tend to creep in—and abstract ideas must get a coating of
sensuous feeling before they become true poetic material; unless one
is a born satirist. Auden argues, it is true, but with much satire involved; his use of the rhymed couplet in N[ew] Y[ear] Letter derives
from Butler's *Hudibras* (a sturdy satirist) more than from the more
waspish Pope. The element of wit has to be present; there is nothing
duller or more unmalleable than serious conviction, seriously expressed.
Even Eliot, in *Four Quartets,* keeps everything flexible, simple and

conversational, in the more argumentative sections. —Certainly "un-adulterated life" *must* be transposed, although it need not be "de-personalized." Otherwise you get "self-expression" only; and that is only half of art. The other half is technical, as well as emotional, and the most poignant poems are those in which the technique takes up the burden of the feeling *instantly*; and that presupposes a practised technique. . . . I have a pamphlet, the record of a Rede Lecture, given by C. M. Bowra, on "Poetry and Inspiration," which I'll tuck into an envelope and send you, some day soon. It has charming and fruitful examples of poets working at top speed—that speed when true fusion of thought and feeling occurs.

* * *

Love on the day of all the Patricks!
Louise

April 15, 1955

Dear May:

* * *

Your account of the chit-chat going on in Harvard sounds quite the usual thing; you mustn't mind "what people say." They are always "saying" something, and naturally they feel rather more like gossip than usual when a novelist has taken their *milieu* as a background.[1] If people's dark looks, or their mean tongues, could kill, we would all be dead long ago (all of us who have dared utter *anything* . . .). As for being a pariah, why not? once in a way. Some of our greatest souls have been pariahs. One should not actively *seek* that state, of course: not after the age of 19–22, say.

And how much of our inner substance is it good for us to give to public griefs? The whole modern tendency to agonize over the suffer-ing of the entire *globe* is surely something new. The great philoso-phers tell us the same things, over and over: that our greatest, if not our single, concern must be our own "soul"; and that we must love our neighbor as ourself. That means knowing and loving oneself first, does it not? And if we manage to love the people in our own *banlieu*, per-haps we do enough. So stop having nightmares! As a member of a formerly persecuted race, let me tell you that such an enclave contains intra-mural (racial) persecutions, too, as you say. Look at what the Irish did to Synge and Yeats! —I think that "intellectuals" cause a great deal of trouble trying to do it all with the mind. It is the heart that counts. . . .

I'm reading Elizabeth Hardwick's short novel, *The Simple Truth* (she is married to R. Lowell). It is excellent, I think: and the U. of Iowa should certainly be set on its ear!

Love and happy journeying,

L.

1. Miss Sarton's novel, *Faithful Are the Wounds,* was a faintly disguised dramatization of the story of F. O. Matthiessen, Harvard professor and author of *The American Renaissance,* who died a suicide.

/ to Morton D. Zabel /

July 7, 1955

Dear Morton:

* * *

I wish I could write you the fullest sort of account of the week-end I spent at the home of Glenway Wescott,[1] in New Jersey. The whole situation deserves the pen of a Chekhov or a Gogol. Monroe Wheeler [2] was off in Europe, arranging some exhibition or other, so there was only Glenway and his aged, but far from pixilated mother. The small white house gives no notion, from its outer aspect, of some of the v. odd treasures inside: quantities of drawings of handsome men and boys; scandalous needle-point (I must describe this to you at length, sometime later); a free-form dining-room table; records, books and art objects of every conceivable kind; great masses of flowers, etc., etc. —In addition to all this, there is the brother and sister-in-law set-up, which I didn't understand until the second day. G. would talk about his sister-in-law and of the farm just down the road and I immediately had a picture of a dirt-farm set-up, with the brother rescued from Wisconsin and meekly dependent on G.'s aid; and of a sister-in-law in a nice little cotton housedress, feeding the hens and cows. As it turned out, the brother, Lloyd (rather a Lincolnian type, in a soft sort of way), had married Barbara Harrison, a Californian millionairess who had some hand in a publishing venture with M. Wheeler, in Paris, during the 20's; the farm is an enormous gentlemen's venture, with 18 families living on the estate, raising a prize herd of Guernseys by the most scientific methods; the house, behind a façade of an old grist mill, overflows with art—they had just bought a perfectly *radiant* Renoir for something like $30,000! —All this came as a shock; moreover, I loved every minute

/ 297

of G.'s revelations concerning the great (Lady Cunard, "Emerald" for example); and marveled at what can come out of a Wisconsin hay-loft, as it were. I'll give you more details later. . . .
* * *

Much love,
Louise

1. Glenway Wescott is the author of such novels as *The Pilgrim Hawk, The Grand-mothers* and *Apartment in Athens*.

2. Wheeler was on the staff of the Museum of Modern Art.

July 7, 1955

My dear Dr. Modesto: 1

I was delighted to receive *yet another* copy of your manifesto, nicely underlined and annotated, this time. Perhaps you overlooked the fact that you had *already* sent me one, at which I was goggle-eyed, and which I would have sent off to my old friend Dr. Morton Zabel, except for the hot wave, which has been bothering us here in N.Y.C. for the last week. I am sure that Dr. Zabel has received a copy, however, since I feel that you have consulted *Who's Who in America* for your (excuse the expression!) "sucker list." *How I agree* with most of your state-ments! I myself have been living centrally, up here in Washington Heights, just behind the Psychiatric Institute, for so many years that I couldn't agree more with many of your tenets. With my string-bag de-pending from my right arm, I have mingled freely in the most central sort of way with the housewives in the A & P; I have called for my wash at the Elberon Friendly Laundry; I have frequented Frank's Fish Market, and even have darted into Savarese Bros. (Wines and Liquors) on occasion. A hush has certainly fallen on the crowd, as I made these peregrinations; and I myself have fastened my X-ray eyes on man-hole covers and pieces of drain pipe (exposed by Con Edison as it digs up the sewers to give them a look, from time to time); I have chucked babies under the chin and sneered at medical students. Nowadays I feel so central that I often seem to be flying around in mid-air, tethered to reality only by my *filet* (which is usually full of onions, carrots, small new potatoes, shrimp, ketchup, Angostura Bitters, bottles of gin and books I am taking back to the Inwood Branch of the NYPL). So you are asking me to do what comes quite naturally, dear, dear Dr. Modesto.

> Yours, right at the center!
> Weezie Bogan

1. Games-playing around Alan Harrington's novel *The Revelations of Dr. Modesto*.

/ *to May Sarton* /

July 19, 1955

Dear May:
* * *

Everyone in Bloomington put themselves out to be pleasant and helpful; and we were compatible, on the whole. * * * The two-hour tour which [Dr. Kinsey] conducted through his sound-proofed quarters was fascinating; only toward the end did he show any sort of extra-scientific interest in his files and other possessions. His library of pornography, he smilingly remarked (to Caroline [Gordon]'s well-concealed horror), is second only to the Vatican Library; and it *was* impressive: air-cooled, clean as wax, with all the leather backs shining. A slight compulsion to exhibitionism came through, I thought, as he held up that Musset thing, and turned the leaves so we all could get a good look at some v. larval looking maidens (in the ballooning figures of the time) engaged in some extremely odd pursuits. One didn't know where to look. . . . But he is a remarkable man, and is, no doubt, getting the most valuable sort of social, if not other, information together.
* * *

> Love, dear May, and appreciation of your
> non-provincial virtues!
> Louise

August 22, 1955

Dear May:
* * *

The news about Noonday continues to be depressing; I guess the press will disappear entirely, unless some real money is poured into it; Arthur Cohen and his father are withdrawing from a losing proposition, and putting all their funds into Meridian books. I don't even know about the party, at present! Poor Cecil is at his wit's end; and today is the day of lawyers' contracts, etc.; I'll hear from him later this afternoon. He will be there, finishing things up, for four months, and that period should see my book [*Selected Criticism: Poetry and Prose*] over the hurdles; although I *must* find out if there is to be *any* advertising. Cecil has promised to put me into the hands of some good other firm; I think it would be sad to go out of print again, almost immediately, so I am for this.[1] If he gets any money —and he may approach the Rockefeller Foundation, which seems to be open to experiment in the arts—he'll buy the inventory and start going on his own. —I refuse to tear my hair over all this; I feel that the book will get to the people who might care for it—the review copies have gone out, thank God—and that it will make its way in any case. The advance orders were quite heavy. But I'd hate to be remaindered right away! —It is fine to have a layer of Stoicism, in all this. The fact that my real bread and butter is not disappearing helps. I should be v. worried indeed if I found myself out of a job, or unable to work. A slight margin of economic safety is absolutely necessary to me—I had so much of the Micawber kind of thing in my childhood. . . .

   * * *

Love,
Louise

P.S. I am now 58!

1. Noonday was finally bought by Farrar, Straus, but it maintained its imprint. Not long after, both of LB's Noonday titles, *Collected Poems* and *Selected Criticism*, were remaindered.

October 22, 1955

Dear May:
* * * —I had a sad and rather eerie meeting, early this week, with poor old Evelyn Scott.[1] I say *old* advisedly, since she really has fallen into the dark and dank time—the time that I used to fear so much when I was in my thirties. She is old because she has failed to grow —up, in, on. . . . So that at 62 she is not only frayed and dingy (she must have been a beauty in youth) but silly and more than a little mad. She met me only casually, years ago, with Charlotte Wilder, but now, of course, she thinks I can *do* something for her—so transparent, poor thing. She is not only in the physical state I once feared, but she

is living in the blighted area of the West 70's, near Broadway: that area which absorbs the queer, the old, the failures, into furnished or hotel rooms, and adds gloom to their decay. It was all there! She took me out to a grubby little tea-room around the corner, insisted on paying for the tea, and brought out, from time to time, from folds in her apparel, manuscripts that will never see print. I never *was* able to read her, even in her hey-day, and her poetry now is perfectly terrible. Added to all this, she is in an active state of paranoia—things and people are her enemies; she has been plotted against in Canada, Hampstead, New York and California; her manuscripts have been stolen, time and time again, etc., etc. —We should thank God, that we remain in our senses! As you know, I really fear mad people; I have some attraction for them, perhaps because talent is a kind of obverse of the medal. I must, therefore, detach myself from E. S. I told her to send the MS to Grove Press, and that is all I can do. "But I must know the editor's name!" she cried. "I can't chance having my poems fall into the hands of some secretary. . . ." O dear, O dear. . . .

* * *

Love from your hasty
Louise

1. The novelist, and sometime poet, Evelyn Scott had lived in England with her husband, John Metcalfe, during World War II and had returned to America only in 1954. Metcalfe will turn up on p. 357.

1520 Willard Street
San Francisco, California
% Witt-Diamant
November 4, 1955

Dear May:
Your letter was waiting for me yesterday when I got over to the State College buildings, in the afternoon, and I was delighted to hear from the far-away *East*! —The trip was exceedingly pleasant: through the very depths of the Rockies, then across those amazing buttes and mesas in Colorado (quite frightening!) and then along the Feather River through the Sierras. Kenneth Rexroth [1] (looking v. *bristly*) met me when the Oakland Ferry docked in S.F., and whisked me up the hills to this pleasant little house. * * * My first reading (to a student group at S.F. College) went off well; and last night there was a party for the *young* (mostly), here. They are simply *bouncing* with life, have

read everything; and have a pet genius, whose name I can't spell, but who is a French-Canadian who spent his childhood in *Nahant!* [2] (He charms cats, which is a good sign * * *.) This "pet genius" thing is not a good sign; but Hart Crane was one, in the East, years ago, was he not? The young write *old-fashioned* free-verse, and were rather shocked when I told them that "the modern" was now the official style, and should be *revolted* against. . . .

    * * *

Love, as ever,

Louise

1. The poet Kenneth Rexroth, also a much admired translator of poetry from the Chinese and Japanese, was the father of the San Francisco poetry renaissance.

2. "Jack Kerouac, 'the world's greatest unpublished novelist' and a member of the S.F. Bay area writing enclave, sent me this, asking me to send it to the magazine's 'fiction editor.' So I send it to you!" (To Maxwell, June 11, 1957)

December 1, 1955

Dear May:

* * * My inclination is to do absolutely nothing useful—just sit and read all sorts of literature. I am beginning [*The Groves of Academe* by] Mary McCarthy: it's a pity she had to disguise Edmund into such a *caricature*—with a *Jesuit* education: he who is the most early American Protestant character I have ever known. * * * Well, she is a strange one—from the *Partisan Review* to Cecil Beaton in less than 20 years takes some doing. If someone could break through her veneer, she might write a fine novel. But surely that cannot happen, now that she is in her middle-forties (she is a perennial 32 in the book, you will notice).

Just as I was becoming rather interested in obtaining a little mescal (one chews peyote buds, they told me in S.F.), the terrors of narcosis in general (although mescal is not habit-forming) were presented to my frightened vision in the new play *A Hatful of Rain*—written by a gifted Italian boy [Michael Gazzo], and wonderfully played by several others. The younger set in S.F. seemed more or less permanently hopped up. The climate isn't extreme enough, but that's no argument really (what about the Mediterranean, that birthplace of mankind's art?). But I'll stick to whiskey and sodas, I guess. . . .

    * * *

Love,

Louise

1956

February 2, 1956

Dear May:

A belated letter, but I wanted to wait until I had seen Mr. [John] Barrett, before writing. —What a lovely little snuggery the Bollingen Foundation has fixed up for itself! Something right out of Bloomsbury, with modern conveniences added, and by interior decoration aided! And Mr. Barrett—what a lovely office, and what a charming man! The $1000 still stands, and he is really v. excited, and exceedingly hopeful about our collaboration. He evidently considers the fact that you can get the *feel* and *music* of Valéry over into English, as a sort of Heaven-sent find; he had been waiting for such an occurrence, he said. My part in the matter he seemed to feel had a place, as well. The year evidently starts right away, and can be renewed, if all goes well. —I am terribly pleased that the thing really worked out; the first evidence of interest I frankly didn't believe in; but now we are on wheels! Will you tell me what poems you have chosen to begin with, and I shall try to get them into flat English, and then await your more inner versions. Then we will have a conference, over a table, in March, when I hope to spend a few days at [Swampscott].[1]

* * *

Gossip there is none. On Saturday Peg Marshall is giving a largish party; which reminds me that I must give one soon. I have bought some charming recordings, including Kathleen Ferrier's rendition of Mahler's *Kindertotenlieder*: the first songs I heard in Vienna, in 1922, and always frighteningly lovely. I also invested in a disc of English music: Bax and Butterworth, etc. One tone poem, by Bax, called *Tintagel*, is full of those delightful English noises—and is a high piece of late Romantic orchestration, as well—the winds cum trumpets cum desolate pre-historic Cornish landscape. It's great fun turned up *real loud*. * * * And did you ever hear Vaughan Williams' setting of some poems from *A Shropshire Lad*? Morton has them; they're not yet on LPs.

Did I tell you that I'm to be made a Dottoressa, in June? The Western College for Women have told me that they will thus invest me; and Morton has written that it's a v. nice place, and I should be proud. I *am* proud; and I hereby promise not to go around calling myself *Dr.* Bogan!

Do write. And send me some steering notes on any Valéry you start.

Love,
Louise

1. The results of this collaboration were published in *The Hudson Review* and in *Poetry* in the spring of 1959. The poems they chose were "Birth of Venus," "Bather," "Canticle of the Columns," "Caesar," "In Sleeping Beauty's Woods," "Spinner" and "To the Plane Tree."

February 8, 1956

Dear May:

Well, the last—or rather, the latest—of the speaking hurdles is over, and I can settle down to a rather relaxed, if not unoccupied, period. It is true that the public thing takes it out of one, no matter how "unattached" one manages to be; and I think I manage to be pretty unattached. I want to put on a "pro" performance, it is true, but I don't let the speaking tear pieces out of my soul. * * * The New Haven thing went off beautifully. Mr. Haight [1] met me at the station in New Haven—it had begun to snow, hail and sleet, as soon as I set foot on the train—and off we went to a quite charming *Victorian* Yale building, where I signed the register and received my check, and we sat and chatted on a lovely Empire sofa. Then we battled through wind and rain, over to some chapel, where the lecture was given; and I must say I rather feared that there might not be an audience! Haight had said that all sorts of strange things happened, in the case of these Bergen lectures, which are open to the general public: sometimes only a few dowagers turn up, and sometimes a few students sprinkled in with what he called "ladies of the town." —Fortunately, the dowagers stayed away, almost completely, but there were rows and rows of students; as nice and as appreciative an audience as I have ever had. There was that charming reluctance to go, which so warms a reader's heart; they just kept on sitting there, even after an encore, and finally one of them asked me to read something of my own: "Cassandra." Then someone else asked for "Song for the Last Act." So that was that. I do think that I put together a v. interesting bunch of poems: all American, cheating a little by considering both Eliot and Auden Americans. . . . I did Dick Eberhart's "The Fury of Aerial Bombardment," which is wonderfully moving; and you could hear a pin drop. I also insisted on a group of what I consider pure and crystalline lyrics: two of Janet Lewis's and R. Torrence's wonderful "The Son." A boy who looked a little like a sturdy Shelley came up afterward and was introduced (evidently a star pupil of some sort) and thanked me for "The Son," and then said, "I like poem-y poems." Wasn't that exciting? —I realized the morning before

I was to read, that I hadn't included one gosh-darned poem by a Yale poet. O dear, I thought; but I couldn't bring myself to do any of Archie's (they are all *men's songs,* wouldn't you say?) and Steve Benét has always seemed v. third rate. I could have worked in E. Wylie, who had Yale affiliations, but I wanted to do Edna's "Little Elegy" (as an example of trochaic meter, among other things) and Abbie Huston Evans' "To a Forgotten Dutch Painter" (have I ever shown this to you?) so that there couldn't be too many women. Cleanth Brooks said, Never mind, so I didn't. —By the way, there was a good deal of talk at supper (which was reached through another snowstorm, out in the country, but was rewarding: delicious food and drink and masses of freesias and carnations over a bright burning fire) of Matthiessen, and of your book. I hadn't realized that M. was a Yale product; some of the men had known him; and everyone thought you had done a difficult job well.

* * * Peg's party on Saturday, by the way, turned out delightfully. Walker Evans (the photographer) was there; he used to live in the same house as my dear mad Do-Do Harvey, and we talked ourselves into fits of laughter (mixed with many tender nostalgic feelings) over her genius for parties, houses, food, drink and people. Walker has a show on at the Modern Museum, which I must see. He is really tops in his field, I have always thought.

* * *

Love,
Louise

1. Gordon Haight of the Yale English faculty has written extensively on George Eliot and other Victorians.

/ *to Robert Phelps* /

September 21, 1956

Dear Mr. Phelps: [1]
* * *

I was moved, after reading your letter, to write you a long analysis of the factor (often hidden) of responsibility, in any writer's life. All human beings, of course, must face up to this factor, but with the artist it is often a baffling element, which seriously affects his work. I myself came into responsibility at the birth of my daughter, when I was twenty; and I have not been able to get away from it entirely, although the death of my father, five years ago, at the great age of ninety, eased it somewhat. Responsibility forms and teaches, of course; but it also keeps one from the complete grasshopper's way, for if one should slip into complete destitution, one takes others along. I hope I am not sounding smug, but please realize that I have taken many jobs (including filing cards at fifty cents an hour) in order to keep myself, and others, from full need. And I have several drops of maverick blood, I can assure you!

Let us hope that something comes through. If Mr. Moe should write me, I'll let you know at once.

Sincerely yours,
Louise Bogan

1. Robert Phelps, novelist and journalist, whose devotion to LB and her work is recorded in letters that follow, had written to her in the hope that she might stir up some emergency financial aid for a hard-pressed poet. LB consulted the Institute of Arts and Letters and wrote, in addition, to Henry Allen Moe of the Guggenheim Foundation.

September 26, 1956

Dear Mr. Phelps:

I was happy to get your letter, which showed exact insight into the heart of the matter. I did not, for a moment, think you presumptuous at any time. But I wanted to intimate to you, in some way, my real *dread* of becoming in any way involved with anyone who might *claim* responsibility from me. I simply cannot, in these later years, give anything but some kind of direct help, and direct sympathy, to people; I cannot bear the thought of becoming wrapped, as it were, in all sorts of skeins and threads and webs, of other people's lives. I do not fear people "getting their hooks into me," as Cézanne did, in his later phase; it is the misty claim and the intangible semi-demand that matters. You will understand; you *have* understood.

* * *

Every fortunate wish,
Louise Bogan

October 9, 1956

Dear Mr. Phelps:

I hasten to add the name of Simenon to your French list. The early and middle books, especially. —The one *famous* novelist I have known

was Ford Madox Ford, in his rather loosened later years, around 1933. In those days he read Simenon continually, and called him the *finest* French novelist. Certainly there is something terribly close to the truth in this Belgian's passion for searching out "the tragic flaw" in the ordinary man and woman. One step divides ordinary life from the abyss; and Simenon's abysses are so terrifyingly squalid and everyday: the kitchen where the lodgers eat out of their tin boxes, in *Le Locataire*, for example. And how good he is with those secret interior shifts of mood and emotion; with smells; with times of day, particularly daybreak, and "the hour between the dog and the wolf." And how satisfying it is to meet that crisp prose, which can accommodate violence and tenderness equally well. *Do* read him—the *romans policiers* along with the regular novels. His power of improvisation is extraordinary, too—and it is all *right* and at the center. His autobiographical *Pedigree* is extremely moving.
❋ ❋ ❋

> Sincerely,
> Louise Bogan

/ to William Maxwell /

October 9, 1956

Dear William:
I was delighted to hear about your daughter's expected *sibling* (horrible word!). —It is so v. strange, the nature of one's children. We must never expect our offspring to resemble us. They shoot forward into the future, or have the character of some forebear we never heard of, who flourished in the late 18th century, or earlier. . . .

The "French Scarecrow" made me warm to the marrow. This is part of a *book*, I trust.

I'm taking piano lessons, and perhaps some lyricism will come out of a close association with Bach's 2 and 3 Part Inventions, etc. My teacher is v. good indeed. He quotes Schnabel and Debussy to me.

> Love to you and Emmy,
> Louise

/ to May Sarton /

October 22, 1956

Dear May:

Forgive the messy MS. I have tried to indicate my preferences—sometimes on your side, and sometimes on my own. It seems to me that we must keep this very literal indeed, if we want it to sparkle (or gleam, rather) with Valéry's own effects of diction; and since we are not rhyming, we can get right at the heart of the language, and bring it over almost intact. This intactness will be the only virtue of the poem, since so much has been lost by denying—or eluding, or subtracting!—the rhymes.

* * * Marianne M.—did I tell you?—is taking my YMHA class: how thrilling! She showed up last time—she had been in California—with a new marble-paper-covered note-book, in which she took a great many notes. . . . She studied with Auden last year, and someone takes her to the subway in their car. I don't know what I shall do when I come to syllabic verse, which I always illustrate by reading and analyzing "The Steeple-Jack"! I wish you could be there. . . .

* * *

Best love,
Louise

/ to John Hall Wheelock /

February 16, 1957

Dear Jack:

Your letter concerning "The Meeting" made me v. happy. The *materials* of that poem have haunted me for a long time; and I thought I must do it in prose. But one morning last spring the first lines hit me, and I sat on the corner of the chair and put them down. The rest came quite easily. I am glad you felt it to be "authentic." It certainly is the record of a recurring subconscious experience, concerning which I used to suffer a good deal; but now I am only curious and puzzled.[1]

This year I recovered two older first drafts—one from the summer of 1955, and one going back at least 15 years—and *carpentered* them up, and sold them. Their titles are rather old-fashioned: one is called "July Dawn" and the other "March Twilight." You and I both (and Léonie, too) have a thing about equinoctial light!

* * *

Don't ever call yourself *aged* again (without adding eagle, at least).

Ever affectionately,

Louise

1. "It came out practically whole, although a few shifts had to be made. The change in the dream-creature's personality had taken place; the creature started out by being Raymond at his most guileful, of course. And I always thought of the locale at the *bottom* of the dream." (To Wescott, March 15, 1957)

"Now [April 1958] the encounter has faded out, a little. —I wait and wait to meet my *personus,* and the Wise Old Man, and other Jungian archetypes; but to little purpose. For one thing, I can't *stand* Wise Old Men. . . ."

/ to Glenway Wescott /

March 15, 1957

Dear Glenway:

This answer to your letter has been delayed by various ordinary *cum* semi-fiendish tasks: a deadline last Monday, for one. Then I had to sign 150 poems in sheets—or however you describe a single finely-printed page. A San Francisco outfit has thought up this single-page-poem effect: *Poems in Folio,* they are called. The poem ["July Dawn"] looked v. nice (I'll give you one), but what a bore: signing and numbering and getting the darned things back into a package and off (this involved a taxi to the *Bronx*) by United Parcel—Air. How fortunate the rich and / or the married, who have servants and *wives* to expedite such matters.

Love,

Louise

/ to Robert Phelps /

April 24, 1957

Dear Robert Phelps:
    * * *

This is my most fatigued time of year, and a proper letter to you must wait. We were talking (*writing*) about the nature of the aesthetic experience. I agree that it approaches the experience of love. Sometimes it seems, however, that the aesthetically experienced object is less like a lover than like a long-lost child. Do you remember what Hopkins said: that when we look *hard* at an object, it looks back *hard* at us!

More later.

Sincerely,

Louise Bogan

/ *to Morton D. Zabel* /

Upper Lower Middle Croft
Puncton-on-Wye
Berks., England
August 3, 1957

Dear Dr. Zabel:

Your name has been given me by a *friend,* and I write you to ask if, by chance, you may be able to help me out of a dilemma! —I have recently published a novel, *The Thing Desired,* which received *mixed* reviews, here in the British Isles. I quote some of them, in rather condensed form:

> Witty!—*Observer*   Potty!—Dublin *Daily News*
> Pity!—*Listener*   Pretty!—*N. Statesman*
> Spotty!—*Times Lit. Supp.*   Hot!—*Encounter* etc., etc. . . .

Now, I have in MS, a *new* novel, which I should like you to run your eye over. (Your *friend* has assured me that you have one of (two of, really—ha-ha!) the best critical eyes in America.) The MS is 10,000 pages long (A TRILOGY, really) single-spaced; and it deals with LIFE—a sort of minnow's or earth-worm's view, if you follow me. (I have been devoted to *both* little creatures from childhood.) The cast of characters alone takes up several dozen pages; and then we get to CHAPTER ONE, and go on to CHAPTER TWO. (I have EPIGRAPHS chosen for all my chapters, taken principally from the ancient Greek lyricists.) The TITLE of the new book (or books) is THE MAN WITH THE GREEN MOUSTACHE. (He is a SYMBOL, and just darts in and out; he never really APPEARS.) O, I can hardly wait to get this MS into your hands! Do deal kindly with it, and give me some encouragement. I think I may go FAR. I hope you will agree.

    Hoping for the favor of a quick answer (double AIR-MAIL)

Faithfully yours,
Lalage Pulvertaft

Dictated but not read. . . .

/ *to Robert Phelps* /

October 19, 1957

Dear Robert Phelps:

I have read *Lolita* with a great deal of pleasure, and I am returning it to [you] by mail. —An account of a real *addiction* is v. rare, in any language, at any time—of a sexual addiction, all the more so. Part of the force here comes from the contrast between the *raffiné* protagonist and the crudity of the situation in which he finds himself; the concealed wildness and violence of the American "scene"; together with the *absolute* commitment. Nabokov has finally mastered the American idiom; it took him years, but now he has it. And such richness of perception! An end-product. I kept thinking of Chekhov's interiors and Turgenev's weather.

> Thank you!
> Write well. Lots of *pages*.
> Louise B.

/ to Morton D. Zabel /

December 29, 1957

Dear Morton:

I'm delighted to hear that you thought my choice to be *esoteric*—how I yearn for *esotericism*, every moment of every day! I gave the volume to myself, as well, in a mad rush of sentiment and nostalgia. The book [*The Liveliest Art: A Panoramic History of the Movies*] received a rather *cool* notice, in the *N. Y. Times B. R.*, a Sunday or so ago. Where is So-and-So and such-and-such? the writer demanded; and I *must* say that some people and pictures and directors were either left out or underplayed: Murnau, for example, and that whole German school, with their camera angles and shadows and trapezes and fireworks. That *Joan of Arc,* too, with its great close-ups. And the early René Clair, etc. And Marlene, in that feather get-up; and later, always sitting on station platforms, or in *pigeon coops!* I don't think we wasted our time! What would my youth have been without the *Bijou Dream,* on Washington St., Boston—on Saturdays (10¢)? Or the *Pastime* (5¢)? Or later, the *Modern* and the *Uptown* (all Boston)? I couldn't spend *all* my time in the B[oston] P[ublic] L[ibrary]! And then later, in the 20's, when we all used to go and make up conversation, and laugh ourselves sick! (So *rude!*) —I actually *saw* Nazimova do *Salome* all *in white!* And *Maedschen in Uniform!* And *The Blue Angel!* No, the time was not entirely wasted, for people like ourselves, to whom the visual is so *relaxing!*

   ❊ ❊ ❊

> Love,
> Louise

/ to William Maxwell /

April 8, 1958

Dear Bill:

Happy post-Easter! All goes well with you and yours, I trust. I have just finished the lecturing stint, under ΦBK aegis, which began last fall, and am pleased it is over, although all went well. Middlebury, Vt., and Wells College, in Aurora, N.Y., were particularly pleasant; that Lake Cayuga is lovely: deep enough to have marine colors.

Have you come upon Bianca Van Orden? Harcourt has recently brought out two stories of hers, in a volume called *309 East & A Night of Levitation*. I think she is v. good indeed; and she had good English reviews last year. She is an American, but rather a figure of *mystery*. Margaret Marshall at Harcourt's says that she (Margaret) will forward any mail promptly, however. Katharine told me that you are hungry for stories. Do read the book, in any case.

A great pleasure this morning, when I came upon a review in the March 22nd *New Statesman*, of my *Selected Criticism*. —One Richard Mayne liked it exceedingly! I'm delighted.

    * * *

> Love,
> Louise

/ to May Sarton /

Schloss Leopoldskron
Salzburg [Austria]
August 12, 1958

Dear May:

Such a *charming* birthday! Your card came early, and was cherished. Then, Maidie had the happy idea of cabling flowers. One of the maids knocked at my door. *"Grüss Gott"* said she, handing me an *enormous* bouquet of *dark* red roses, all ballooned with glassine paper! This was indeed heart-warming. Yesterday I had a delicious lunch downtown, and shopped for a party given at 5:00. Never sneer at Cheese Ritz: they are 19 schillings a box, here ($.76), and are made in *Italy*. I managed to find some thinly sliced Genoa salami, also Swiss cheese and *Austrian* Camembert, which turned out to be v. good. So all this was displayed, along with a bottle of Austrian brandy and two soda syphons, at 5:00, for the benefit of the faculty. The assistant director's wife, having heard me *yearn* for a doughnut, sent up a platter of sugared ones (fresh from the kitchen); and the management at large presented me with a little *round* bouquet you would love: *round*, dark red and pink roses; pink, lavender and purple sweet-peas, and bachelor buttons: v. Biedermeier indeed. . . . I went out to dinner at the pension-hotel where Maidie and I stayed in 1933, but was *lured* into the dining room on the way, to receive the traditional "Happy Birthday to You" and the *Austrian* addition of applause. —So it was *grand*, as the Irish say. All is compensated, says Emerson. Well, perhaps he was right. I certainly didn't *deserve* the tears shed here, so long ago. . . .

Every time the sun shines, the attendance at lecture falls off; enough come to make a slight noise, however. There will be a gala dinner on Friday, with toasts and general merriment; and on Saturday, at 1:20, I leave for Zurich (and private life!). —It has been delightful, on the whole, but a *little* too long. But I thank goodness for the lack of any real sour apples in the barrel. And such amusing surprises! Did I tell you about the Poetry Evening, when about six nationalities read poems from their literature, *plus* original poems? One large, shock-haired man, who is a Dutch journalist by profession, but a Frisian nationalist by avocation, arose and *sang* a long, loud hymn—*in* Frisian! And a Finnish girl (v. pretty and blond) joined forces with a handsomely dark Hungarian—since their languages are linked. And an Italian gave a translation of "Medusa," into the finest Florentine.

The trees are magnificent: larches, copper beeches; pines and aspens. Yes, old, *old* Europe. —I trust Switzerland will not chill me, as it (the *big* mountain section) did Rilke.

Love,
Louise

/ to Morton D. Zabel /

Brown's Hotel
London, W. 1
August 27, 1958

Dear Morton:
I can't leave London without sending you a greeting, from *Brown's Hotel!* Peace and quiet reign serene; and there is a large scattering of *ladies* and *gentlemen*, both American and British. Tea time in the lounge (chintz, brass and *brown* woodwork) is something to see. Also, any given meal, in the dining room.

My stay in Paris (after two days in lovely Berne) was rather un-
eventful, except for a trip, by bus, with Claire G., to *Ivan's grave* in
Père-Lachaise cemetery. Right opposite Chopin, under a large black
marble slab, with the Chagall portrait drawing now done in bronze
bas-relief, lies poor Ivan; and Claire is bursting with pride over this
final outcome—for she, too, will one day be included in this famous
precinct. Rather macabre, but a strangely fascinating trip. . . . * * *

Love,
Louise

/ *to Robert Phelps* /

October 22, 1958

Dear Robert:
    * * *

Your Tarot "fate" sounds rather improbable. *No one* has *no love*,
ever; even my poor father, who had a v. bad deal all round, was finally
adored by my daughter. *Years* of *hard work* are as it should be: how
boring otherwise. And money is nicest when you have a little of it,
late. So far as the malefic male is concerned, look out! Forewarned is
forearmed!

I hope you have stopped feeling the "guilt of success" by now. I
had it v. strongly, when I won my Guggenheim. Start another book.

Have you read [J. P. Donleavy's] *The Ginger Man*? It gets better as
it goes along. And by the way, did you ever come across the novels of
Jean Rhys? *After Leaving Mr. Mackenzie* and two others? They're in
the N.Y.P.L. *Total* self-defeat, but wonderfully written.

Yrs—
Louise

/ *to Paul Scott Mowrer* /

December 13, 1958

Dear Mr. Mowrer: [1]

I was interested in your letter, which, I am sure, was kindly meant.
—I am not the poetry editor of *The New Yorker*, but merely the magazine's poetry reviewer, so that the choice of poems which appear in
its pages is made by others. And, since I am a formalist myself, I could
not very well attribute formalism to others as a fault! I was writing,
in the piece you mention,[2] about empty, academic formalism, which
is a fault, in any language or period.

Modernism as such, in poetry in English, does go back more than forty years (modernism in French poetry, of course, goes back to Baudelaire—another formalist—or at least to the 1870's and 1880's). Poetic modernism is closely allied to modernism in the other arts. Whether or not the large audience has "liked" modern poetry or not, it is now a fact in the history of culture, and it has effected a change, which sets off poetry written in our century v. definitely from poetry written in Victorian England, for example. The reasons and the need for this change are also facts concerning which literary historians, critics and poets have written at length. Yeats states the problem with much truth, in his autobiography and essays, and Eliot's early criticism describes the shift in sensibility, which underlay the change, in detail. —As for the villanelle becoming a current cliché, among young formalists, I can only assure you that this form turns up with tiresome regularity, nowadays. It has become fashionable, and therefore, rather artificial and certainly dull.

Sincerely yours,
Louise Bogan

1. LB did not often answer letters quarreling with her reviews. "I get these, occasionally, when I hit old ladies and gentlemen in their Edith Wharton enthusiasms, etc. —If I answer them the old lady and gentleman answer right back, and become even more uppish. So what's the use?" (To Marshall, January 10, 1939) She did answer Paul Scott Mowrer, perhaps because he was himself a poet and a distinguished foreign correspondent.
2. LB's review of John Hollander's *A Crackling of Thorns.*

/ *to Ruth Limmer* /

February 1, 1959

Dear Ruth: 1
* * *

One bit of news which may not have reached you. The Academy of American Poets gave me that nice big prize [$5,000]; I was surprised and delighted. They are giving it to me in four quarterly sections! But no income tax. . . . So I can go to Greece when I'm seventy. Meanwhile, I'd like to build a hut or "willow cabin" by the sounding main, or in someone's *woods.* This is impossible, of course (or is it? I must read *Woman's Day . . .*).
* * * The Baroness Blixen [Isak Dinesen] showed up at the Institute dinner, last week: extremely feeble, but in fighting form.2 Great hoops

of black and diamond earrings. . . . She refused to put on her glasses, except now and then. The talk was entitled, "Mottoes of My Life." I forget the early one, but the middle one was *"Je reponderai"* and the last one *"Pourquoi pas?"* —Since this last has been mine, for years, I was warmed. Then, after she finished, she took out a large *fluffy* powder-puff and powdered her nose! Let's act likewise, when age really *gets* us.

Love,
Louise

1. The friendship between LB and Ruth Limmer began when, in Ohio to receive her Litt.D. at The Western College for Women, LB discovered that the then instructor of English had grown up, and during vacations still lived, within walking distance of her apartment on "our dear Washington Heights."

2. Earlier, in January, LB had been to a small dinner for the Baroness: "* * * she could eat *only* oysters and grapes, and drink *only* champagne. So there she was, incredibly big-eyed and emaciated, in black, doing just that: the oysters on a plate before her; the grapes to hand; the champagne in a highball glass! She has a slight accent, and talks *continually*. Even more than you and me. And such eyes! Like saucers, really. . . ." (To Sarton, January 14, 1959)

/ to Morton D. Zabel /

March 7, 1959

Dear Doctor!
   * * *

Things are fairly normal here, after a week or two of running about, staying up too late, and gabbling with too many people. I have been bothered, this fall and winter, by the difficulty of certain bristly books; I finally got blurbs written on Dame Sitwell's anthology and St. J. Perse's *Seamarks* (O, what monstrous lot of *tosh!*) and, finally, that dreadful imitation Odyssey thing [by Kazantzakis]. This last I tried to bypass, but, on hearing rumors that a band of rich Greeks was behind it and that Clifton Fadiman was walking TV screens saying that it was the greatest thing *since* Homer, I pulled myself together and wrote a short and bitter notice. I have been expecting masked Hellenes, all muttering in broken *demotic*, to waylay me; but nothing of this sort has yet occurred. What tripe! And the line drawings, like dirty Picassos. . . . * * *

Love,
Louise

1959

/ to Robert Phelps /

November 3, 1959

Dear Robert:
 * * *

Did I tell you that the *Times Lit. Suppl.* asked me for some poems for their *American Imagination* number (Nov. 6)? First off, I could find nothing to send; but I looked and looked and finally came up with a twenty-year-old poem called "The Sorcerer's Daughter," to which I added a set of lyric notes, entitled "The Young Mage." They took both! Look for them.

"You are at a nadir of popularity and influence," say my booklets.[1] "But in December the fruits of your labors will begin to show." —I saw the new moon last night, over the Hudson (through the glass of a taxi window).
 * * *

Affectionately,
Louise

1. LB and Phelps shared an interest in astrology, and she had already shared with him the appropriate data for the making of a horoscope: "My birth hour was (is) 8:30 P.M., at Livermore Falls, Maine (near Lewiston). * * * *Would* you ask your canny friend to cast her eye over my 'wheel'?" (April 10, 1958) The results predicted that LB would live to a great age. "Has there ever *been* an old lady poet? I look forward to the rôle with mixed feelings. . . ." (June 19, 1958)

/ to May Sarton /

November 13, 1959

Dear May:
 * * *

It is wonderful to know that my poems *spoke* to you: "The Daemon" especially, which was written (*given!*) one afternoon almost between one curb of a street and another. *Why not?* is always a great help. God presses us so hard, often, that we rebel—and we should. Auden once told me that we should *talk back* to God; that this is a kind of prayer. * * *

Love,
Louise

1960-1970

THE DAEMON

Must I tell again
In the words I know
For the ears of men
The flesh, the blow?

Must I show outright
The bruise in the side,
The halt in the night,
And how death cried?

Must I speak to the lot
Who little bore?
It said Why not?
It said Once more.

/ to May Sarton /

4423 Thackeray Place
Seattle 5, Washington
[April] 1960

Dear May:

It was delightful to get your letter about good days at Nelson, and the
news of your moving toward communion. Dr. Wall always told me
that it was the *work* that counted: Get it all into the work. That is what
we must do, ultimately. And you will do it! —Here, I live in close proximity to a cherry tree in *full* flower. I never had this experience before.
I look out my window, and there it is: some of the blossoms already
hanging in clusters, like cherries, and others like little white *muffs*, on
the upright racemes. So lovely; so *chic*! Nature's elegance. . . . The sun
has come out, and all is in bloom. [My landlady] brings me tiny bou-
quets—I have had garnet roses, freesias, and now a mixture of grape
hyacinths, with yellow and lavender-purple primulas. English daisies
grow well, along with dandelions. *Camellias* grow on bushes. . . .

* * *

I have written a *haiku!*

> *Rainier*
>
> The mountain comes and goes
> Like a watermark
> On celestial paper.

. . . It *is* a lovely mountain. And, in spite of bouts of mild homesickness,
I think things will work out well. * * *

Love,
Louise

Seattle
May 8, 1960

Dear May:

Your *good* letter, with the new poem, received with much pleasure.
You seem in good, creative "shape"; may the spring keep on enriching
you! Here, the red hawthorn (a tree!) is in full bloom. Also, dogwood
and *auricula*. Do you know *auricula?* They turn up in flower prints,
but I've never seen them in Eastern gardens.

My classes go well. One girl, who at first decided she "hated" me, has
now come around somewhat (she had been petted for throwing lan-

guage around in a semi-surrealist way). No one seems to *know* v. much, but they're all nice people. Pockets of Frost and Williams worship came to light. Also, quite a bit of Eliot-hating. —From now on, I don't teach on *Fridays* (Ted never did, but I tried to, for several weeks—conscience!).

* * *

The news about Ted was welcome, if a trifle disconcerting. He *always* clowns, I hear (I've never heard him read). The sleeping around talk is not well-based; he *paws* women at parties, but is true to Beatrice, I feel sure. B's brother, Irvan O'Connell, teaches classics here, and I have seen him several times. He *loves* Ted; and respects him. This would not be possible if Ted was deceiving Beatrice. . . . And, here, everyone knows what everyone else is doing, believe me. . . .

* * *

The weather continues to be spectacular: rare sunlight, with many showers, and tremendous cloud-effects. —A basket-hunting expedition yielded two small baskets only. These are from the Lapush reservation. (These N. Western Indians had a genius for language: Puyallup, Snoqualmie, Tatoosh. . . . And among their totem animals were the badger, the raven, and the killer-whale. They called Mt. Rainier the *Mountain That is God!*)

* * *

Love,
Louise

/ *to Ruth Limmer* /

Seattle
May 8, 1960

Dear Ruth:

The mountain is out today! A cloud it has just made floats above it. It is v. good at making clouds. . . .

* * *

Last Tuesday I was taken, by Beatrice's brother, Irvan O'Connell, to a little suburban Judo club. There it was, way off in one of those funny "districts": a small white building with an open wooden stair outside. Inside, boys from 6 to 12 and young men and adolescents sat on the floor along two walls, dressed in cream-colored pajamas, bare-footed. Some Italian and Irish faces among the Oriental ones—also a Negro or two. Well, they grasped each other (two by two) by the upper sleeves (thus immobilizing the arms) and sought for advantage with their feet. Watched by a *black-belt* Jap (highest Judo order). Tumbles, falls, prancing [?] around for position. The larger boys really lifted and twirled each other. This was the mild, non-killer Judo. Heaven help anyone exposed even to it!

   * * *

Love,
Louise

/ to Robert Phelps /

4423 Thackeray Place
Seattle 5
May 15, 1960

Dear Robert:

* * * I begin to get restless for home. Two more weeks, and I'll be on my way (to Boston via Albany). Did I tell you that a little Maine college (Colby) is giving me a doctorate (secret!)? On June 6. This touches me deeply. So I shall be there on time.

Almost certain cure for MS fatigue (and a *certain* one for MS fussing): Write several (1–2–3) pages a day, *and turn them over, without reading them,* as soon as they come out of the typewriter! This trick has worked for several people who were stuck fast! It worked for me with *Achievement.* Try it! Go back to the pages after some weeks—or after a week. Not sooner!

   * * *

(*God be with us all.*)
(Irish *prayer*)
Louise

/ to Elizabeth Roget /

August 17, 1960

Dear Elizabeth: [1]

   * * *

I quite understand your feeling about the Jünger book,[2] and your decision that the task of translation would be too difficult and too (momentarily) unrewarding. —I am always fascinated (as a good many people are not) by "off beat" speculations concerning reality and the nature of "the universe"; and I have always found Jünger's investigations into the matters original and freshly stated. Astrology is certainly an imperfect tool, but the fact that mankind has tried to introduce some "clocklike" order into time, and has tried to tie its individual destiny to the movement of the planets has always impressed me. Such elaborate reasoning, from imperfect data! Yeats, as you know, ran a good deal of his life according to astrological notions; it was through my study of his life and work that the notions of astrology first became familiar to me. —I didn't realize that this new Jünger book was an *apologia* for astrology: I thought it a new investigation into the historic facts, with some general conclusions drawn. —Well, I'll get into it somehow, sooner or later. Perhaps it will be translated into French.

* * *

Affectionately,
Louise

1. The pseudonym of a Swiss-born writer and translator whom LB had first met at the MacDowell Colony in 1958. Because they lived just across the Hudson River from each other, hardly any correspondence exists to document their growing friendship, which lasted to the end of LB's life.

2. With Elizabeth Mayer, LB had previously translated Ernst Jünger's *The Glass Bees*, which Noonday was to publish in the fall. Although a politically controversial figure—he had been an officer in the German army during World War II—Jünger held a strong attraction for LB, and in April, while teaching at the University of Washington, she had begun to puzzle through *Die Zeitmauer* (*At the Time Wall*), the book under discussion here.

/ *to Ann Rogers* /

August 17, 1960

Dear Ann: [1]

* * *

The ten days on the Cape did me a world of good. Everything seems more valuable and interesting * * *. I sort things out in the apartment, and look toward autumn with pleasure. Unwound!

I also look forward to the first installment of the cookbook! I'll show it, as I said, to Cecil Hemley, and try to get some sort of commitment from him, as to publishing. You must finish it, in any case. There are lots of publishers, and cookbooks continue to appeal, on all sides. . . .

There was a good deal of Portuguese cookery, on the Cape. One soup looked delicious: a brown, thick bean soup with *kale* in it. This I did not try, since I was concentrating on fish, lobsters, sweet corn, etc. But it was served in a place where working painters congregated. I'll try to get the recipe.

My mother's "Dutch supper" began with *bacon,* although sausage would do. Fry out several thickish slices; put aside. Fry onions in fat. Then thinly sliced raw potatoes, and finally, thickly sliced apples. Put bacon back and mix. Salt and *quite a lot* of black pepper.

It's hard to have to "swat down" love! In my declining years, I feel this should be done *only* when love becomes a menace to life and limb! A direct hazard, like a hole in the ceiling or the floor!

Do keep on.

Louise

1. Ann Rogers, a teacher of sociology and an author, was working up a book that would be published by Scribner, in 1966, under the title *A Cookbook for Poor Poets and Others.* LB provided an introduction, some advice ("a dollar or two must be spent at the beginning for staples") and some literary references ("I must dig up that story of the saintly little Jewish man [Bontsche Schweik] who wanted, in heaven, just one little fresh roll, with sweet butter, a day").

/ *to Ruth Limmer* /

September 28, 1960

Dear Ruth:

* * * I understand and sympathize with all *removal blues.* How many have I experienced! Especially in childhood, when often the barrels and packing cases stood around the house for *weeks.* . . .

* * * I saw *Hiroshima, Mon Amour* yesterday; it is exceedingly sensitive and moving. Did you see it? —It brings back all the impossible emotions of youth, and the girl in it does a supreme job; she is extraordinary in the mad scenes. And there are touches of business and *nuances* of facial expression seldom, if ever, seen before, done cinematically. The man looks a little bit as though he had drunk too much sake and stayed up all night, over too long a period of time. But such *hands!* and such tenderness. The horrifying side of the blasted city is also not neglected. Well, perhaps it will still be here when you come for Christmas.

I'll write May Sarton. She is in fine shape, surrounded by her lovely *objets* and her truly spectacular flowers. If she would only stop writing sentimental poems! I had her take out two mentions of "kittens," from one poem. "Cats," yes, "kittens," no. . . .

* * *

Love,

Louise

Dear Ruth:

* * *

The party at Peg Marshall's was a good one: all sorts of people I never see, hardly. Diana Trilling, for example—who gave me a run-down of women's characteristics. And was v. *blaming*, on the subject of Dorothy Parker (who, according to her, had sold her birthright, etc.). She also said that Clifton Fadiman *suffers* (she went to school with him). This last I cannot believe. Lionel T. was also there, looking far less baggy-eyed than 10 years ago. Also Alice Morris, who chooses poetry and short fiction for *Harper's Bazaar*. * * * Dear old Abbie Evans was there, too, looking charming in a ladylike way. * * *

The event of the week was my reading of John Updike's new novel, *Rabbit, Run* (Knopf). The boy is a genius. Every sentence counts. The story is rather contrived, but one believes every word of it. And the flashes of weather, and of the "American scene": drug-stores, highways, main streets, factories, used car lots! And the passion and the *grief!* The sex gets out of hand, once in a while; but for the most part he uses the sexual aberrations to striking purpose. And he believes in God ("something there")! [1] *Do* get it at once; it's worth buying—($4.00).

* * *

> Love,
> Louise

1. "Dr. Wall says we are in God's hands. (He doesn't know what that means, he adds, but he believes it.) I believe it too." (To Maxwell, December 28, 1960)

Dear Ruth:

I hasten to send you a few words of comfort. Not that I'm in any too good shape myself, having spent the *entire* morning reading Lawrence Durrell's *Collected Poems*. There's something v. irritating about that guy. A wonderful sense of words—and of place—but no *base*. Everything is everything—and a good many things are blue. "By our blue Aegean which forever / Washes and pardons and brings us home." Too much washing and pardoning, for my taste; and when he really goes overboard (as in a poem, dedicated to H. Miller, on the closing of the Paris brothels—O how he misses those girls!) he is *horrid*. He is also horrid when he sees a *yellow* woman ("a half-caste"), in Rio, drinking coconut milk. It reminds him of the "patrimony of the ape"! He's Irish! The Irish should stay away from the Aegean. . . .

* * *

Love,
Louise

March 10, 1961

Dear Ruth:

I promised myself a session at the typewriter this A.M. (such a relief to my correspondents!) but it's too darned hard to get it onto the desk —the desk's cluttered condition being what it is. So you must decipher!

First: about the enclosed clippings. —I have always felt that clipping-senders were rather a nuisance: slightly soft-headed old ladies, etc. But I seem to be joining their number! Those old *Nat. Geographics*, which were gone over recently, certainly offer temptations. I couldn't get away from the off-beat hummingbird: so chic! And the contrast between the "surface temperature" of the hummingbird and man was too good not to share. We humans have a tough time, but we don't have to get all tanked up on honey, in order to migrate. . . . * * *

I have been having a spell of depression. * * * I *have* had a rough winter, I keep telling myself. And the weather turned horrible, on Wednesday, so that I had to sludge my way home, after class, in a sleet-storm. Well, I haven't come to the weeping and wailing aloud stage, at least. And tasks impend, which will keep me busy, busy, from now till June. (The Guggenheim material descended, on schedule. *Terribly* bulky, this year. —I remember last year—how I had to do it against time, since I was wafted away, westward, on March 16. It seems a century ago.) [1]

* * *

Green grass blades in the Park (Central!).

Love,
Louise

1. LB had been judging applications for Guggenheim Fellowships in poetry since 1944. While she felt the job was very much worth doing, she found the judging increasingly burdensome. By 1963 she was saying: "I struggle with the Guggenheim stuff. Academics and beats; beats and academics. Pretty poor stuff. And the spiels of the Sponsors ["nothing but ass. profs"] are really something! On and on,

in jargon, in jargon. . . . Severity is the thing." The following year, faced with a new batch of applicants and twenty-three *re*-applications, she quoted herself as writing to the Foundation: "It is a depressing spectacle—this great file of writers who range at worst from the pretentiously incompetent to the naïve minor. In any case, the Foundation, by this time, must realize that my intentions are serious, however frivolous or sharp-tongued they may seem, when written down in type-script."

April 12, 1961

Dear Ruth:

Well, I heard R. F[rost] speak (and read) last night at the Institute dinner—and he really is remarkable! Of course, the vanity was quite evident (he's about to reform the entire Washington scene, and pull it toward *The Arts*) as well as the well-calculated "baggy" attitude. But he still makes sense, and has his rote memory intact (for his own poems, at least). I shook hands with him *without any sparks flying*. "Nice to see you again," said he! (Glenway was standing by, *grinning*.) —As for the piece, I came upon some v. good fresh stuff in Eleanor Farjeon's *Memoirs:* R. F. and E[dward] T[homas] in England; how the Frosts lived, etc. Writing starts next week.[1]

* * *

Then, a sad-pleasant surprise: E. Wilson dropped in on Sunday evening. He looked ghastly: and has *angina*. A little J. Walker helped, but when we went out for the taxi, he could hardly *walk*. We re-pledged fast friendship, however. *Time!*

Love,
Louise

1. LB had been engaged to write the section on Robert Frost for the two-volume *Major Writers of America;* this task also involved putting together a selection of Frost's own writings: poetry and prose. Although she was not given to admitting it in later years, LB had once known Frost well, through his friendship with Raymond Holden.

April 24, 1961

Dear Ruth:

The most beautiful day of this unbeautiful spring—and I was trapped in a theatre seat, watching Martha Graham unfold her idea of what went on in the House of Atreus. A v. strange experience. I last saw

Graham in the early thirties, as I remember: much lithe-er and leaping-er. I must confess that, yesterday, I thought her rather earthbound. Clytemnestra, to me, has always been a great tall woman of tremendous power and—efficiency, shall we say? A ruthless wielder of *will*. A semi-tribal goddess. A non-Mother. . . . Graham made her into a sort of skulking middle-aged frump, in a bun-on-top hair-do and a damned black tea-gown (damned in the sense that it might have been kicking around the closets of Hell, for about 40 or 50 years, or millennia). One favorite posture: a sort of mobile *scooch*, by which she advanced to and from on *bent knees*. Also, a great deal of staggering, walking in circles, etc. Terrific emotion always accompanied by a great big kick, forward—involving the tea-gown in a great big swirl.

The company, let me say at once, was v. good indeed. Everyone had evidently taken a serious course in Greek vase figures: those drooping attitudes, contrasted with a great deal of angular arm jerks, and flat-footed jumps. Frieze effects. Shield and sword gestures. Several lovely young men. —Agamemnon was made rather a comic. Also Cassandra. And Iphigenia was hard to distinguish: a mere white headband distinguished her from the other girls (they all wore black, with a trouser-shirt combination—v. odd). *Surely* she could have been *all* in white: the sacrificial lamb. —But no old-fashioned symbols for Martha! And no straight-forward story line! Clytemnestra is in *hell*, to begin with, and *reviews* what happens (prowling around a neo-phallic throne the while; or just sitting on the floor, looking gloomy). The music turned out to be by a Coptic* from Cairo: dissonances in various tempos—one rather effective *jig-time*. Two singers—male and female—howled, from time to time. Also, some exceedingly bad poetic-prose issued from their vocal chords: "a mother's *curse*" (repeated on six or seven occasions); "flesh-mesh"; . . . "I am *Clytemnestra*!" . . . etc. . . .) —Why must dancers attempt to be poets, as well? (Did you ever see Martha, in the E. Dickinson thing, lying on what seemed to be a park-bench with one toe pointed to heaven?)

Well, everyone got everything possible out of their physical equipment, I will say. *Everything*! Crawling on the floor was usual; also the slant and the upside down. I could go on. . . . And I hope you're not a great M. G. fan! —The place was packed—with v. ordinary (for the most part) looking people. I wouldn't have missed it, in spite of all that

* V. fashionable, Coptics. . . .

crouching and lurking, on M.'s part. Maybe C. *was* a *damned* house-wife, at heart.

* * *

Love,
Louise

May 25, 1961

Dear Ruth:

* * *

A large crowd showed up for lunch, which was laid out in the library of the Institute: v. nice. The bar was set up by the front windows that face on the graveyard; this locale looked particularly charming: full of new green and sunlight. Dear Ben Shahn was there, in a brightly striped shirt: arsenic green and magenta. It made him look like an elderly Mack the Knife. Robert Graves, who gave the Blashfield this year, also in full-blown, gray-haired character (the address was delightful, on the word BARAKA, which means hand-made and lovingly produced, I gather). I had quickly absorbed several Gibsons, my first drink in ten days or so, and things became rather hazy after wine at lunch; upstairs on the terrace I found myself gabbing—not too tipsily, I trust; no one gave me hard looks, or walked away! * * * Malcolm and Glenway (of course with a pink carnation) [were there] and Carl Van Vechten (a new member, looking 100000 years old). Time is moving on, for us all; this was my tenth appearance at this do. I didn't see young George Starbuck, who got the Rome thing, to speak to. Well, *some* talent keeps coming on. . . .

* * *

Love,
Louise

October 6, 1961

Dear Ruth:

[Edward Gorey's] *Unstrung Harp* received, and remarkable contents noted. I feel that I must *live* with this *chef d'oeuvre* for some time. It is reposing in a decorative niche: beside the *papier-mâché* ink etc. stand, on the front-room desk. What an imagination! I hope that the fur-coats and the sneakers and the rest of his *decor* don't prematurely either stifle or strangle him. . . .

I, on the other hand, have discovered the *depth* and *strength* of Ionesco! Far from being merely a Romanian surrealist, he is a true poet and humanitarian, I have come to think. His face, moreover (re-produced on the cover of a little book about him, in that Evergreen Pilot Book series), is sensitive and intelligent to a degree (I had thought him to be rather bright-eyed and bushy-tailed, again in a cliché Romanian manner). Not at all! There are practically no details given of his life (the Leeds prof, who writes the commentary, leaves all that out—but Ionesco *was,* evidently, a teacher, under the Nazi regime). And here is a passage from *Jacques, ou La Soumission*—well-translated; Donald Allen made hash of it:

Roberte II: Below stairs in my country house, everything is puss. . . .

Jacques: Everything is puss.

Roberte II: One name for every single thing: puss. The cats are called puss; food, puss; insects, puss; chairs, puss; you, puss; me, puss; thirty, puss; all the adverbs, puss; all the prepositions, puss. It makes talking so easy. . . .

Jacques: To say: let's go to sleep, darling. . . .

Roberte II: Puss, puss.

Jacques: To say: I'm very sleepy, let's go to sleep. . . .

Roberte II: Puss, puss, puss, puss.

Jacques: To say: bring me some cold spaghetti, some warm lemon-ade, and no coffee. . . .

Roberte II: Puss, puss.

Jacques: And Jacques, and Roberte?

Roberte II: Puss, puss.

Well, there goes logic, that dangerous weapon! Do you remember the logician in *Rhinoceros* who proves that Socrates was a cat? —Ionesco states (his statements are scattered, as yet, in essays and interviews, mostly in French, but his opinions and *aperçus* will be devastating when gathered together) that he did not want or plan to become a playwright; he only wanted to learn English. So he bought himself a *Method Assimil,* and the terrors of everyday reality burst upon him. Do you want to see the little book?

All of this is, of course, terribly ANTI-BRECHT. But I am convinced that Brecht was confessing his sins, in those last plays.[1] * * * —Ionesco has wit, warmth and form, under all his fooling. And he seems to be getting better all the time. What fun! (Puss, puss!)

* * * Yesterday there was a really delightful lunch meeting of the Grant Committee. Not many grantees were found, but I sat next to John Hersey, who has become much more human since this second marriage. Delightful, in fact. I very nearly made a terrible *gaffe,* being

about to say: "Have you ever been in Japan?"—but I changed the wording in time. —We decided that I should go to Thos. Cook and Son(s) and ask for their best set of literary pilgrimages. "No, Madame, we can't oblige with George Herbert, but we have a nice bus tour to Henry Vaughan." ... * * *

Puss! (Love)

Louise

1. "I have finally capitulated to Brecht. *The Caucasian Chalk Circle* is v. fine indeed; also *Mother Courage*. And he is confessing his duality throughout. His tender, loving *persona* is v. moving. And such *fiber!* A strange split man—full of guile, craft—but also *love.*" (September 16, 1961)

October 22, 1961

Dear Ruth:

I'm glad you like "The Dragonfly." As I said, it is all based on FACT. And I am rather proud of the last line—which is a piece of pure "inspiration." Get those repeated *u* sounds—one of them disguised.[1]
* * *

Many books from the Institute, to read for the Grant Committee, including the Mark Schorer life of Sinclair Lewis: really an extraordinary tale, well told, and with *masses* of data. The poor guy ended up so tragically: the pawn of a conniving courier-valet. And I must say that Dorothy Thompson's letters, after their separation, are v. womanly indeed. —Do get this. —The Virgilia Peterson [*A Matter of Life and Death*], on the other hand, is a sort of Electra-complex nightmare. The old girl has absolutely no insight into her situation, and she writes like a simple-minded Proust—all curly sentences, which sometimes do not come out right. This you should see, as well, if only for the wry laughter it engenders. * * *

[Harold Pinter's] *The Caretaker* was extraordinary. This you must take in. The dreamer brother, the extrovert brother—both wonderfully and tenderly done; while the old rogue—a Welshman, it is indicated—puts through a set of tricks and tergiversations that we have seen and despised—and that we all have some human share in. And as for the old gent's underwear! British, long and separate, and frayed into a kind of chiffon raggedness. In itself worth the price of admission.
* * *

Love,

Louise

1. "With the other husks of summer."

/ to May Sarton /

October 31, 1961

Dear May:

* * *

Now for the book [*Cloud, Stone, Sun, Vine*] (*briefly*).

My objection to the sonnet-sequence is in part a general objection: I don't think that such sequences can be written, nowadays, with any hope of effectiveness. They have received the kiss of death; not only in the 19th century, but in our own time—Millay's and Wylie's are, on the whole, pretty bad. —*Women* should not write them, any more! The linked formality makes chance of discursiveness too great; and the sonnet, *as such*, is *never* discursive. It is dramatic; *the* dramatic lyric framework. Shakespeare, even, gets rather woolly, at times; although he continually keeps tightening up and slashing out: "the expense of spirit in a waste of shame," etc. The early sonnet sequences (Sidney's, for example) are based on a terrific concept of courtly (*demanding*) passion, and *morality*. They are pointed. They are channeled. —With D. G. Rossetti, etc., the whole thing begins to *dissolve*. One thing leads to another. Etc., etc.

I think, too, that it should be clear that your sonnets are written to a woman. This is not clear. (In 14 you mention a *father* and a *son*, where, I think, it should be a *mother* and a *daughter*.) These are the two main objections. One other small one: I feel that the sequence should end in a kind of unresolved positive *anger*, not in a questioning acceptance. "To hell with you." —But that's my Irish *vulgarity*, no doubt!

Otherwise, I think that the book *marches*; proceeds; opens out. You know how much I have always admired "Humpty Dumpty." From here on you begin to come down to facts—and state terms. And the *actual* begins to break in. "Somersault" is excellent: a true image for a spiritual complication. ("The Phoenix" and "The Furies" are also v. good indeed.) The poems on the deaths of your mother and father are also v. moving—and true—and difficult to do. —I must admit to almost total dislike of the poems in "To the Living" section. *With* the exception of "What the Old Man Said," which is *lovely*. "These Pure Arches," *also*. You have transcended the awkwardness which *must* reside in the "humanitarian" poem, here. —You know how much I like the European evocations. And the Nelson poems.

On the whole, you have a *metaphysical* bent; you desire the universal behind the apparent; you have a passion for the *transcendent*. That is why I am perturbed when you seem in the sonnets to put so much spiritual capital in the *temporal*: in a *person*. —I feel that you will not need to do this again; that this is a transitional phase; that your *big, unrelenting, drastic* poems (*life or death*) are to come.

Now, take all this as the advice of one so *much older,* whose every second thought must be of death!
* * *

> Love as always,
> Louise

/ *to Ruth Limmer* /

November 4, 1961

Dear Ruth:
* * *

The November gloom descends, although some early mornings and late afternoons have exquisitely delicate skies with masses of flocculent clouds. And, of course, the end is not yet. It is when one lights the lamps at 4 o'clock that the dark is hard to bear. But, as we have agreed, an *hexagonal* universe would be even more depressing. At least we have an *oval* one.

I have been reading the 1 vol. edition of Ernest Jones's life of Freud. What an *eloquent* career! Ideas kept descending on F. at fairly regular intervals, throughout his lifetime. Sometimes these were all wrong, and he had to go back and correct them. My poor friend Dr. Frink shows up as F.'s favorite American, and the scandal is outlined. Frink, according to Jones, went crazy in 1924 or so, and "never recovered." Raymond and I saw him v. close at hand, from 1926 through 1927, and he was taking care of his children (in the country), and had a girl, and was only fitfully peculiar. His trouble was manic-depressive schizophrenia —Lincoln's trouble, they say. Being a split manic-depressive is pretty hard. . . .
* * *

Next time I'll send you a short run-down on Jules Renard, together with some of his *aperçus.* —A short study of the delicate insight, the happy linkage (down the ages?) is certainly in order. I'll start taking notes. —The notion of writing a lecture (for Bennington) on E. Millay and Elinor Wylie has also crossed my mind. With some sidelights on the female sonnet addiction. With some *aperçus* on the sonnet sequence, from Sidney on. How about that? The whole thing could be kept v. detached and factual, and analytic—but warm. M. Sarton's sonnet-sequence turns up again in the book. I wrote her what I thought about it; she will never forgive me, maybe.

The Renaissance Conference sounded exciting. O well, nature meant men to be radiantly intellectual (when they *are* gifted). Women tap the life-force more successfully at other levels. But it's sure fun to have a few brains, of whatever sex. Mulling over personalities, all one's life, must be pretty tiresome. ("And *I* said; and *she* said . . .") —But imagine being Sinclair Lewis, or *Citizen* Hearst!
   * * *

                Love,
                Louise

/ to May Sarton /

                            November 21, 1961
Dear May:
   * * *

Your preparations for the trip [to Japan]—shots, etc.—must bring the whole plan close to you. —I do feel unenterprising, not to go; but there is some reason in my decision. —What I am looking for—or would be looking for—is the old imperial, romantic, feudal, beautiful and horrible chrysanthemum and sword set up, which has vanished forever, from all accounts. The thought of little privacy, continual flitting-about service, crowds and *noise* (*one* transistor radio can drive me wild and the gossip is that there is one such in every other hand) defeats me. The only way out would be to have everything partially European and semi-deluxe; and that would never do. —So you will have the fun of exploring, and of *going on* (as opposed to *going back*) if things get difficult. —Perhaps I'll take a *literary* tour of England and Scotland, instead! I must say that the literature put out by the British Travel Bureau is stunning; not a machine, not an electric light bulb in view! * * *

The new piece on the prize books, et al., goes on slowly; this has been a swamping season, with practically everyone in print, including John Ciardi, Dick Wilbur, and Jack Wheelock. The Yale Series winner, Alan Dugan, is pretty mad; Dudley Fitts loves odd-balls! But he can write. So many of the serried bunch *can't.* What I shall do about the egregious Peter Viereck play [*The Tree Witch*], I am at a loss to say. The academic world has coddled him; both Harvard and J. Hopkins gave this crazy piece of balderdash a hearing, and *Poetry* printed the *poem* version. Well, I mustn't talk about it while I'm writing it! —The *Marianne Moore Reader* is great fun. Eccentric again, but so humble and shy. She has the soul of a little boy who has not had much fun, and is trying to make up for it with later fun (books! objects! pets!) and games (baseball!). She has a new poem in which she speaks pidgin Italian to a *crow*! Enchanting!

* * *

> Love ever,
> Louise

/ *to Ruth Limmer* /

> Thanksgiving morning
> November 23, 1961

Dear Ruth:

Well, I'm thankful for a great many things—heaven knows: health, and the temporary, at least, holding off of the bigger and better bomb; and enough money to get by on, and quiet neighbors; and for the small chicken which Maidie is about to cook, in *her* kitchen. * * *

The books still straggle in; and the *NYer* piece is in fairly full notes. I see that Winthrop Sargeant, this week, writes a little general essay on the difference between music and painting, so perhaps *I* can ramble a little, at the beginning. —Meanwhile, I pulled myself together and wrote a blurb for * * * R. Lowell's "translations" (*Imitations*). This last better than I first supposed. The Rimbaud and Baudelaire (and the Villon) really sizzle the way they should; and he's v. good with Rilke: makes him bitter and a little nuts. O the madness of poets! How carefully we must tread! For that [Michael] McClure guy, who writes out of a "peyote depression," may yet connect with the sacred fire in no uncertain way: look at Clare, look at Hölderlin, et al. And Chris Smart. . . . It's so easy to be stuffy. But it's the pompous paranoids that are the worst. Charles Olson, for example, who calls himself Maximus, and states that HE IS THE ONLY MAN WHO UNDERSTANDS MELVILLE. . . .

* * *

> Love,
> Louise

Dear Ruth:
* * *

The two days [spent judging the Bollingen Prize] at New Haven were v. pleasant indeed. I went up with Cal [Robert] Lowell, who loves trains, and who kept up a continual chatter, mostly of a personal nature, on poets and poetry. He described the life he led, in Bridgeport, as a parolee C.O. (after having done time in Leavenworth): mopping floors in a Catholic hospital, and reading all of Toynbee on his off days. —We took a taxi at the station in N. H., and I went to my v. nice room at the Taft—with a lovely view over the Green. Dinner at the Lawn Club was augmented by various visitors—R. Wilbur and wife among them. The black lace and pearls was just right! Norman Holmes Pearson then had us all over to his house—filled as it is with wonderful Elizabethan editions, bad modern paintings, and all sorts of small, ancient, rather junky little carvings. Also, paintings by poets! H. D. was one of his great friends! * * * A good deal of standing-chattering went on, and I got home to the Taft before 11. —On Saturday morning, bright and early, we all foregathered in Mr. [Donald] Gallup's office (filled with G. Stein *memorabilia,* most of it in the form of terrible little paintings). Malcolm C. was the chairman. Allen T. (who looks wonderful, by the way, and whose new wife is quite nice * * *) was in good form; then there were Lowell and Donald Hall, to boot. We all gave little speeches concerning our favorites. I plumped for Wheelock and Abbie [Huston Evans]. No agreement was reached, at first; and then Allen had the bright idea of letting Eberhart (who had a *Collected* last year) into the game. Finally it came down to Jack W. *and* Eberhart—a good choice, I think. We then trooped down to the Librarian's office and called Jack up, long distance, and congratulated him. He was in tears, poor old gentleman. I'm delighted that he got it, although shared; the sum is now $2500, so a share isn't so bad. —I didn't stay for lunch, but went back (again with Lowell) on the 1:07. No snow, thank God.
* * *

Love,
Louise

1960-1970

Dear Ruth:

   * * *

The Helen Burlin Award (YMHA) judging has also become a nightmare. A pretty little secretary (who is also studying ballet) comes up for the batches of MSS—v. blond in an Austrian loden coat and a stocking cap. She goes to Lowell for a batch; then to Kunitz for a batch; then to me. I've one more batch to come. Terrible stuff, mostly. Several raving madmen who celebrate their stays in Bellevue in scatological terms. . . . Well, I'll get paid for this. . . .

   * * *

It's sad about your pretty, sweet dumb freshman, but what can you do? If all girls were born smart, the human race would die out—men would be rejected [?], and babies would stop being born. So you must play along with the life force. . . .

                    Love,
                    Louise

February 6, 1962

Dear Ruth:

Two enclosures about the M. Moore evening [under the auspices of the P.E.N. club]. —The reporter female certainly made a hash of the proceedings (even though I lent her the notes). Marianne was wonderful, as always. (She had seen the questions ahead of time.) She has really worked out her public persona—half pedant and half child—and she *jumps* to her feet and *projects*. Have you seen the *M. M. Reader*, by the way? —I'm not entirely happy about "The Steeple-Jack" being *revised back;* that Student Ambrose, and those salpiglossis, etc. However, it's her poem. —She looks v. old, but is still bright-eyed.

C. should arrive, pretty soon, and we'll put up the china. The little *objets* will come out of hiding. I miss them. They soften the edges of life, as well as the edges of the furniture. They *speak* of life. I can understand perfectly why primitive man (and others) took their dishes into their tombs. Not mortal!

The YMHA thing *should* terminate this afternoon, with a meeting between Lowell, Kunitz, and myself, in some quiet nook in the Lexington–92nd St. building. The proportion of really crazy contributors was high; and Lowell, of course, is all on the side of one of them: a big, wild, hallucinatory manic, with no publications and several *terrible* obsessions—all of them excremental. Good heavens! Then there are a few *possibles*—including a little nun from Spokane, whom I have met—Sister Mary Gilbert. She sees things rather panoramically, and is not at all pietistic—hardly any Jesus, and *no* Holy Mother. Unusual.

Madness, for some reason, seems to dog me (the confluence of the planets, no doubt). In an unguarded moment, in the 179th Street Library, I picked up the latest work of that *great Australian,* Patrick White—*Riders in the Chariot.* I *knew* better! But I thought I could skim through. Not at all. I am compelled to read it fairly carefully, for one never knows what great blob of horror will happen next (if a blob can happen—and with P. White, it CAN). —And what a terrific portrait of P. White adorns the back wrapper flap! Such a solemn, yearning-eyed, *shovel-chinned* visage! A 4th generation Australian! A dweller on the outskirts of Sydney. —All I can say is: Something happens to men, women and the English language (not to speak of the human soul) in the Antipodes.
   * * *

                      Love,
                      Louise

                              February 7, 1962

Dear Ruth:

The YMHA jury for the H. Burlin award went through some strange gyrations yesterday afternoon. The result is as you see.[1] —This Seidel guy is, according to Cal Lowell, about 23; Harvard; v. sophisticated; married to the granddaughter of Learned Hand. The MS, as I told you, is v. shocking indeed; an orgy that outdoes Suetonius is described in *one* longish poem. Also, a great deal of Sade (so S. Kunitz said). Slime, excreta, pederasty, etc. —It is, however, a *fiercely* projected set of inner experiences; and certainly not just dirt for dirt's sake, as in the case of the Beats. * * * There will be a scandal, I should imagine. This is really a publisher's prize, by the way: Atheneum. —The Sward book is pretty far out, but delightfully original, on the whole. —What Sister Gilbert will think of it all, knows God!

I'm exhausted! Last night I had a series of dreams, wherein the nightmare side of existence kept reappearing. The result of the conjunction of Patrick White and Seidel! * * * Down, rising flood of darkness!
   * * *

                      Love,
                      Louise

1. Frederick Seidel's award-winning book of poems was called *Final Solutions*. Robert Sward won second prize with *Uncle Dog, and Other Poems*. Honorable mentions went to Robert Bly, Donald Finkel, Barbara Gibbs and Sister Mary Gilbert.

In December 1963, LB lunched with Seidel and said it turned out very well. "He is medium-sized, with rather gooseberry eyes, and rather too-slick (palish) clothes: tie matching gray of suit, etc. And he liked to address waiters in French. Other than that, he is a v. well-mannered, intelligent, Harvard type, with *no* devilish overtones. And a sense of humor. So perhaps he *may* go on writing. (He is quite conscious of everything and everybody—in the poetic field * * * but that sort of awareness is natural in the young; they have to keep up.)"

/ to Rufina McCarthy Helmer /

February 28, 1962

Dear Rufina:

Yes, Brandeis is giving me one of their *senior* awards—which is for an entire career and carries *both* a medal and an honorarium of $1500 (not bad!). —I am v. much touched, of course, since it is the first recognition ever to come to me from the good old Bay State. —There will be a presentation reception on March 18. Maybe you can fly down! Let me know, if you can.
* * *

Love,
Louise

/ to Ruth Limmer /

March 4, 1962

Dear Ruth:
* * *

I saw *The Innocents*—did I tell you? With Deborah Kerr wandering around making a British face, and holding a candelabra and jumping at noises. Quint was properly fearsome, and Miss Jessell looked exactly like a Chas. Addams witch (the young kind). * * * The death of Miles really shocked the Coliseum audience. The two old ladies in front of me jerked about and showed distinct negative agitation.

Good old Henry J.! I came straight home and read the original story straight through. How wonderfully managed it is! and that "frame" bit—at the beginning! What the old boy knew—and was determined to express—was the hypocrisy of children, as well as the delusions of suppressed old maids. We get this duality in Maisie—although *she* is sort of a moral moron, rather than a little fiend. —*Maisie* I have always found hard to read. —I then went right through *The Aspern Papers*, and found new joys in it. That "lame" dressing table, and that "peevish" lock on the desk, or whatever it was! Such epithets! And such *ease* of language! * * * Come; why don't *you* take a dip in these wonderful waters! Read the preface to *A Portrait*: see H. J. holed up in Venice, trying to get the book finished, but continually running to the window to watch the life and the color, outside. *Most* moving. * * *

New Intelligence: I HAVE BEEN INVITED TO THE ROBERT FROST DINNER, by the Secretary of the Interior (WHY HE?), on March 26. Pan-Union Club, Washington. Black *tie*. M[aidie] says I should go. Do you think I should? It's a pre-publication do, and Holt, Rinehart and Winston appear as co-hosts. Should I be lured into such a framework? Certainly not in a *Ball-Gown*! (although M. thinks that I should immediately get a swank get-up, toe-length). O dear! Seduction of reviewers, really. Although they've never tried to seduce me, before this.
* * *

Love,
Louise

March 28, 1962

Dear Ruth:

Well, it was all as grand as you please. The high table included R. P. Warren (looking v. red in the face); Sec. and Mrs. Udall (he is a dark visaged gent, with a rather *low* forehead; she is pretty); Adlai Stevenson, looking like his photographs; and M. Van Doren, looking striking, as usual. *Also*, the Poet, the Poet's publisher and a sprinkling of anons. The Poet disappeared, for most of the feast. Then he came back, and the eulogies began: Udall, Publisher, Warren (far too long and rather rambling), Felix Frankfurter (looking v. brisk and noble), Stevenson (good!) and Van Doren (really excellent!). *Then*, the Poet arose, and, I regret to say, rather maundered on. He let out one or two vulgar truths (such as that he had made himself and his publisher *rich*) and struggled with a few immensities ("matter is transformed into spirit"). Then he began to *recite* his own poems, which was fine. That mother of his certainly trained her boy well, in those gloomy evenings beside the oil-lamp and the nice warm kitchen stove, in S. F. and Methuen, Mass. —But I thought it went on too long, even this *good* period of platform appearance. A touch of senile vanity and a touch of vulgar exploitation. . . .

There I sat, between Reuben A. Brower (Harvard), who wrote on Yeats in the Harcourt *Major British Writers* (he is *nice* and we enjoyed our chat), and Someone-or-Other, the Ambassador from Mexico! Also, farther on, Lesley Frost, done up like Mrs. Astor's pet etc.: low green dress (showing pushed up rather *freckled* bosoms) and all sorts of Indian silver and turquoise jewelry. Our eyes met once: a chill! * * * My little black dress did v. well, by the way—but such sweeps of black lace and satin panels and embroidered gussets! —The big dining room is lovely: all white and crystal—and the *food*! At one point the waiters brought in platters with full-feathered pheasants sitting on the edges!!! And the wines kept coming on: champagne with the dessert! —The AAA treatment. A cultural breakthrough!

The Attorney General went up the stairs one step in front of me. He looks about *eighteen*. . . . No Pres or Vice Pres. J. F. K. had had Frost to lunch.

I had lunch with my old, dear friend Emma Chase, at the cafeteria in the Methodist Building. * * *

So there! Home seems lovely.

Love,
Louise

April 18, 1962

LAST WORDS (MAYBE)

(For don't forget that I am about to advance into *Peter Viereck* country! Perhaps he and the Tree Witch will hex me *good*. —His poor father [George Sylvester Viereck] passed into eternity recently— did you hear? And what a handsome guy he was, according to *20th Century Authors* (new ed.)!)

But I am going toward it all, *v*. bravely indeed.[1] * * * I'll be put up at the Brookstone Inn, in S. Hadley; drinks that evening; then the kids reciting, after dinner; and then *me* reciting, at 11:00 on Saturday. —From thence to Vermont, and all-night sessions at the Smiths[2] (no doubt). Home on Mon. or Tuesday.
* * *

Love,
L.

P.S. Don't pay any attention to Charles Williams as a poet! —He's just what *The Kenyon Review* would care for, at this point: holy, sententious, and not a little batty. . . .

1. The occasion was the judging of the Glascock Prize, at Mount Holyoke College. (In 1938, a very young Robert Lowell won this prize, when LB was also a judge.) Hexing, LB thought, would be an appropriate response to the very severe review she had given Viereck in 1953, and again for the *Tree Witch* the month before, but: "Perfect poise on his part! He even detained me a moment on the back porch, to tell me how fascinating he had found *Russia*. Criticism doesn't really touch him, the general opinion finds. Who are these people? says V. to himself—and this *is* true, I now believe. Those globular eyes; that beard! And I had forgotten that his father was an *authenticated* natural son of Wilhelm II—the 1914 Kaiser—and therefore, partly Hohenzollern! *Naturally,* therefore, *above* the rest of us. . . ."

2. The Smiths—William Jay and Barbara Howes—are both poets. His memoir, *Louise Bogan: A Woman's Words,* was published by the Library of Congress (to which he was consultant in poetry) in 1971.

May 15, 1962

Dear Ruth:

Well, I have survived Mother's Day and am set for a spell of hardish work, in order to get rid of the one or two books which continue to plague me by sitting on top of the chest of drawers in a semi-annotated state. * * *

I went to a highly praised French movie, entitled *Jules and Jim*—and this turned out to be a strange production indeed: a sort of disguised homosexual fantasy, wherein a wife (that depraved looking Moreau woman) shuttles back and forth between her husband and a couple of lovers. The style is all 1912, to begin with, and this is charming, although strongly derivative from the early René Clair—*The Italian Straw Hat,* for example. The clothes, the furniture and the street-scenes all have that now-so-appealing awkwardness—an awkwardness which was far from appealing *as I remember it*! Then the Great War turns up, in old movie shots, and then the triangle-quadrangle of lovers go to the country, into a darling little *châlet* filled with cunning *objets,* including a bent-wood rocking chair. (A rather depraved looking fat little girl turns up, at this point: the daughter.) Moreau really looks frightfully crazy and concupiscent; she finally drives off a bridge into a lake, along with Lover No. 1—in an antediluvian closed coupé. A rather grisly funeral scene follows, and the husband is last seen walking downhill out of Père-Lachaise. —Several reviewers found all this *simply delightful.* You must see it, if it ever turns up again, merely for its undertone of fancy spiritual horror.... * * *

I am also in the midst of *Ship of Fools.* It is a strange and rather frightening book. Katherine Anne [Porter]'s powers of realistic description are wonderfully available, at all times, and she has pulled out the realist stops to the full in certain passages concerning the baser instincts of man, woman and child. Her whole mixed inheritance and experience is finally all in the open: the Southern (Texas?) lady and the young Bohemian rebel, and the slightly older Mexican expatriate, and the Villager in her forties, and the aging Southern lady again (a writer, this time). She has split herself in two in the book, in the persons of a youngish female painter, with mixed generosities, and a middle-aged divorced *élégante,* who yearns for Paris and its classier environs. The book is dedicated, by the way, to Barbara Wescott, who is, of course, Glenway's millionaire sister-in-law; I've told you about her. Katherine Anne was part of Barbara Harrison's *entourage,* in the beautiful French days: *O saisons, O châteaux!* Rambouillet was one of the châteaux. —The book is a remarkable piece of narrative, in spite of its episodic pattern; and moves along steadily, in sets of almost cinematic "frames." What is it that is lacking? Pity and tenderness, I guess. It is not so much *fools* that human beings are, but creatures incompletely wise. Or so I prefer to think. —I will say that K. A. leaves out few of the horrors and sordities [*sic*] of human motive and action; she is as brave as any woman writer has ever been, in that respect.

Now I must do some work on the Neruda-MacDiarmid piece. Would I had an attendant angel, with a pen of gold, to touch in a few glittering phrases, here and there. * * *

Love,
Louise

Swampscott
Memorial Day
May 30, 1962

Dear Ruth:

A most moving little parade—and set of ceremonies—was presented this morning, under rather cloudy skies. Led off by fairly ancient members of the Am. Legion, a colorful bunch of *young* people advanced down the street *toward* the Civil War Monument, and toward the ocean: the S. High School Band (dark blue, and *boys*) tooting and drumming away; a firing squad and some color-bearers (regular army, in khaki); a squad of regular soldiers, in battle dress, helmets and *red* scarves; a squad of sailors of assorted sizes (also with flags) and *then* (horror of horrors!) a bunch of girls, all gotten up in shakoes and high boots, some with little *guns* on their shoulders, and some with little swords, with *their* band (but with no high-stepping majorettes, thank God). Who were these last? Well, I will tell you. They were the band, etc., of the Sacred Heart School of Roslindale! Sacred hearts in red, complete with little *crosses* on top, showed up over *their* respective hearts!

But everything else was delightful. All the flags were at half mast, but there was absolutely *no* other sign of mourning. The firing squad, after a prayer (Congregationalist? Presbyterian?), faced out, over the rail of the esplanade, and fired a salute at the ocean, in memory of the Swampscott sailors, lost at sea. Then two Legionnaires went down the steps to the beach and put flowers at the edge of the waves. (Also, they stuck a little Am. flag in the sand, I saw later.) Then the rifles went off (*v.* impressive, always) and they played *Taps*—also v. moving, *always*. The G.A.R. "ceremony" followed, at the foot of the Civil War Monument (which had a pretty, round, fresh green wreath suspended on it). And what a colorful crowd of spectators: with *balloons*, and little Am. flags, and bright print dresses, and plaid shirts, and baby-pushers. Dogs, bicycles, little boys running and wrastling and yelling (prayers or no prayers); little girls all gotten up, in a *dégagée* kind of way; flags; balloons. V. *Prendergast*! V. small town. V. Memorial Day. . . .

After the Civil War dead were taken care of (*and* the sailors) the whole bunch (including the Sacred Hearters) went up by the grass-plot and the flower-beds (full of tulips) and memorialized the *other* S. veterans of all the *other* wars, by the second monument. I didn't stay for this. —But I was *v.* moved—really choked up. America seems so *innocent*, in these gatherings in N. E. —And one red-haired baby, just able to stand, in his pram, with checked pants outlining his cute little bottom, will, undoubtedly, end up on the MOON. . . .

     ❀ ❀ ❀

Love,
Louise

/ to May Sarton /

August 9, 1962

Dear May:

* * * Bryher's book [*The Heart to Artemis*] set me off on Dorothy Richardson, the full run of whom I can get at the Mercantile Library. D. R. was *certainly* a forerunner; *Pointed Roofs* came out in 1915; and both V. Woolf and J. Joyce learned from her. She *is* quite tiresome when she gets off on *cosmic* themes, but she does that *v.* seldom. Wonderful on sight, sound, smell, the tactile sense (washing her hands with good soap becomes a shining moment!). And wonderful on men *versus* women. Men she dismisses as hopeless (spiritual) bunglers: creatures shut out from *the center*. She's not feminist *or* Bohemian at all. And O, those 1890 London streets and parks and interiors!

You want me to be frank, my dear:

I think you are still writing *around* your travel experience. I want to *hear* you and *see* you *right in* the gardens; right *beside* the river; right *next to* the stone god! I feel that you have *distilled* the moments too much—enveloped them with too much *calm*. "O God, how tired and miserable I was in this place or that"; or "How hot it was"; or "How restless and mortal I feel," or "How perfectly wonderful". . . , etc., etc. "The great god sleeping" stanza is *v.* good indeed. But again, I feel that you are doing too much in *one poem*. Make three poems! And don't keep the question and answer form (which slows and dilutes). Just let's have *you*—right in the midst of one experience after another.
* * *

Breathe in! Breathe out!

Love,
Louise

September 6, 1962

Dear May:

I am, of course, very sorry indeed that my professional critic side has come to bulk so large in your view. —This will not always be the case, I feel, and we shall be poet-friends (or just human friends) once again.

Get all the *bear* into your work! Get all the bitterness, too. That's the place for it. —And twenty years doesn't seem such a tragic length of time, to me, dear May. I have been writing since 1912, the year of your birth!

* * *

Warm greetings, as ever, dear May,
Louise

/ *to Ruth Limmer* /

October 26, 1962

Dear Ruth:

What a coming and going! What an array of poets: bearded (R. Jarrell), plain (no names!), dark, light; snowy polled (Shapiro, surprisingly, and Nemerov, prematurely); fat (Rukeyser), thin (J. V. Cunningham, Kunitz, and *me*); learned, foolish, hung over and sober as judges. —The librarians, I must say, in all echelons, fell over themselves to be courteous, and there was a large public, particularly for the afternoon (reading) sessions. * * * [1]

The chief event of the morning was my reconciliation with M. Zabel: right on the platform, in full view of the audience, a "cocktail kiss." I'm glad this happened; he insisted he had done nothing, but was "sorry" in any case. I will hand it to the old prof.: he introduced the first panel session with an exceedingly well-organized, and crisply written, description of American poetry prior to 1912; followed immediately by a eulogy of Harriet M. which couldn't have been bettered. I then got to my feet, and read my "notes"; [2] people said, afterward, that they were "most effectively written." Then Kunitz spoke, well, too. (Henry Rago introduced us all.) Then the silly questions began, and we all did quite well there. . . . The afternoon reading went on, all of a lump—too much of a good thing, but fascinating, none the less. —I passed up a reception, that evening, and just ate and went to bed. (R. Jarrell spoke for 2 hours *that* night!) * * *

The Tuesday afternoon reading was cut by an intermission; much better. John Berryman read first, in a high state of manic excitement. Then me—not bad—and a v. good response, even from the adolescents. Then the dark Miss [Gwendolyn] Brooks, with poems about cockroaches, dead white men, etc. J. V. Cunningham * * * read well, and included a v. dirty Martial-like epigram, which must have shocked the nuns speechless. —A "tea" at Mrs. Biddle's followed, whereat I saw Katie Louchheim, looking v. beautiful in red furs (to match her hair)

—just back from Germany—an assistant Secretary of State!! . . . Lovely food here, and Morton and I and Marie Bullock and Eliz. Kray [3] were whisked off to the Frost reading in Marie's chauffeur-driven car (the chauffeur's name was Washington!). Frost was pretty maudlin: painful! —A party was given, later, by the Udalls, to which I was not invited, and this festivity, I have just heard (by telephone from A[nthony] Ostroff, who stayed on), was followed by 1.) Delmore Schwartz tearing up his hotel room, and being nabbed by the police and 2.) John Berryman going to Delmore's rescue, and also being nabbed! —So, you see, there was a touch of the Dionysian, after all. No more, perhaps, than in a convention of brassiere makers, but still a touch. . . .

I enjoyed the whole thing, taken by and large. —To see Rexroth get up and roll his eyes around, while telling stories about his exploits, made Morton sick. ("And you like him? What do you see in him to like? He rolls his eyes *up!*") Little old Miss Steloff was there, and we all gave her a hand.[4] * * * The Capitol, lit up at night, was exquisitely lovely; and we walked back and forth to the Library, through its park, with those great old trees. Washington is really becoming a lovely place. Fountains play. And the weather was as balmy as spring. . . .

* * * William Meredith came through with a grand long poem, and several v. perceptive remarks. He is such a dull fellow, seemingly. But I want to see more of him. The pictures in the exhibition were frightful, mostly. In mine—as you will soon see—I look like *Pearl Buck*. . . .

Your p. c. just arrived. Snow here, too. And won't the Nobel Prize infuriate Frost??? [5]

Love,
Louise

---

1. The occasion described was the National Poetry Festival, held by the Library of Congress through a grant of funds by the Bollingen Foundation, on October 22 to 24.

2. "The Role of the Poetry Journal" (uncollected).

3. Mrs. Bullock is the founder of the Academy of American Poets; Elizabeth Kray is its executive director.

4. Frances Steloff was the owner of the Gotham Book Mart in New York City. In that role she was a very real benefactor of poets and poetry, because, among other things, she always stocked books of poetry. Her shop also gave room to the meetings of the James Joyce Society.

5. The Nobel Prize in literature went to John Steinbeck.

1962

November 10, 1962

Dear Morton:

(I trust you do not mind this rather workaday paper. I have begun to use it, these last years, when *we* were in the *non scribere* state, with my more voluminous correspondents; it is pleasant to write on, giving one the impression of *creative effort.*)

Your lovely, voluminous letter received, and warmly appreciated. —What goings on, as the Festival progressed (we had prophesied some such outbreak, if you remember). * * *

I'm glad that Sir Herbert [Read] wowed them. He is a strangely pliant and flexible thinker—his ideas so carefully *managed,* down the years; but he is informed, certainly, and serious and a force. —Old Ransom should be retired from the scene, I should think. Enough is enough. And it's a pity no one came through with some really pertinent remarks about *form.* There's a lot to be said—and it can be said simply and effectively, so that any audience can be *really* enlightened. . . . You and I could have given them / it some *real* information.

Well, I went to the do for Frost, given by the MacDowell Colony: an invited audience, *black tie.* Aaron Copland and Mrs. Bullock (she radiant in a white ball gown) introduced the old Fox, and presented him with yet another *medal,* and we all got up and sat down and got up and sat down. (No *kneeling,* but that may come when the old F. hits 90. . . .) HE was in full control, this time, and put on an excellent act. He insisted that "Stopping by Woods" was NOT concerned with Death, and gave a little scratch to John Ciardi: as a *new critic!* It's the *tune* that counts, he kept saying. He really is remarkable, when he recites a long poem (such as "Birches") by heart. Everyone (and the large auditorium at Hunter was *packed*) loved him. —Maidie, who had never seen or heard him before, was *charmed.* —Many friends and acquaintances in the audience, including Ogden Nash and Bill Meredith. No reception afterward, thank goodness. . . .
* * *

Louise

November 11, 1962

Dear Ted:

Your letter came just after my return from Peterborough, and just before my two rather taxing "jobs" in October: 1) a paper read at

Bennington (called "What the Woman Said") and 2) an appearance (and a set of notes *and* a reading) at the great Library of Congress Poetry Festival. Both of these do's went off v. well. The audience at Bennington (* * * including the pleasant, and gifted, Ben Belitt, and lots of kids) laughed in the right places—and it *was* a *well-written* lecture. The original assignment (from Fowlie) had been women poets; but I must say this topic came to bore me excessively, as I sat in my studio at MacDowell, drinking coffee and feeding the open fire with massive logs. —So I just wrote about women, in and out of literature—poets *and* novelists, from the Bronze Age (Homer) on! —An exposé of Simone de Beauvoir as an analyst of women artists was included. —I'll send it to you sometime. They wanted the original MS, and a promised typescript has not yet arrived.[1] * * *

Love to Beatrice and to you (*semi*-wretch that you are!).

Louise

1. At the present writing, this lecture remains unpublished.

/ to Ruth Limmer /

March 7, 1963

Dear Ruth:

* * * Last week—and on two days of this—I arose every morning saying: Now, Louise, just a few paragraphs more!—and then a look at the thing as it stood brought on such acute nausea that the A.M. was spent in re-write. O, the stale and sluggish mind of Miss B.! Sentence by sentence, however, it began to brighten up a little; and it went off on Tuesday. I did a rather nice job on Anne Sexton, and really clobbered that Sandra Hochman dame, she who was chosen for the Yale Younger Series, this year, by D. Fitts. And some praise for May Swenson. (I heard that that talented Sylvia Plath had died!)

Now the Guggenheim stuff awaits. But this is *easy*, compared to dragging bright clauses out of the tired brain. * * *

The Auden party, did I tell you, went off well. *So* many faces—including that (dug-up looking) woman (name?) who wrote *G. Prefer Blondes*. —Then I introduced W. H. A. at the NYU Loeb Student Center, the next Sunday. *Large* audience, and Wystan in v. good, serious form. Then I went to a MacDowell Admissions meeting, where Kay Boyle appeared in a *large fur* hat (antique?), with her usual load of eye-shadow and feminine charm. I *do* like her, but I wish she'd wash her face (meow, meow!). —She brought along her daughter, Clover, who is perfectly lovely. * * *

Love,
Louise

March 21, 1963

Dear Ruth:
   * * *

E. Wilson came up, the other night, with Léonie, * * * and he was v. sour indeed on Frost. He took my [Frost] piece away with him, and wrote me that it was "solid," but that he still couldn't see the poetry. He was particularly cross because I called "The Pasture" a "love poem"! Good God, said he, how could you! So I wrote back and said of course it was a love poem—either to a woman or a child, and perhaps to both (the cow and the calf point to that, do they not?). *He* thought that it was addressed *to the reader.* Well, the Tainian method falls down, sometimes. . . .
   * * *

A terrific anthology, by Brinnin–Read, illustrated by that Rollie Mc-Kenna, who was around about ten years ago, just came this morning: *The Modern Poets* (McGraw-Hill). I appear, in my former, pre-1953, fat-faced version; [1] others look v. idiosyncratic indeed, usually against walls, or looking out from behind bars (or sitting on the floor). . . . But it's quite a book, really. * * * Now, all I want is the salt, salt sea; and a few banks of wild thyme, at the other end. . . .

More soon. Love.
Louise

1. The picture shows LB beaming out through an opened front window of her apartment; to take it Miss McKenna had crouched on the fire escape.

R.M.S. *Queen Mary*
At sea
May 24, 1963

Dear Ruth:
Why can't I turn out to be a female Anthony Carson,[1] and spit out several pages of gay-bitter stuff about the dear *Queen M.* and her present bunch of passengers—surely the *ugliest* bunch of assorted human beings that I've seen in some time? * * * Really, London was so *full* of hand-

some people, comparatively (at least Bayswater–Queensway–Padding-
ton was: of all colors, too). Two v. blonde mothers with café-au-lait
babies rather threw me; the mothers *did* look miserable, and the babes
unloved. —But those blonde male and female giantesses! And those
noble faces, seen for a short span, on the underground—so full of intelligence and—insouciance (??). —And the scraps of well-balanced periodic sentences one heard, behind one, from time to time, full of long
words and abstract concepts, and close reasoning! Really, what a
people! Somehow they seem to be blooming nowadays. I never saw
them so strong, fresh and varied. Carrying (men and women) their
market baskets, full of bread and fruit principally (it seemed); with a
bunch of flowers in the other hand. Was it thus in Chelsea?

Of course, on the other hand, they *do* tend to *blither* somewhat, as
you say; and a provincial upper class hotel (such as I struck in Bath),
in the midst of a wedding, certainly resounds with the loud, certain,
rather shrieking voices of the ex-Empire builders of both sexes. * * *
How *flat* our native American sounds, in comparison! How low-pitched,
how without accent or rise or fall: plain American, that the cats and
dogs can speak, as Marianne M. remarks. * * *

Love,
Louise

1. An essayist for the *New Statesman.*

/ to Glenway Wescott /

June 12, 1963

Dear Dr. Wescott!
(Robert Phelps told me about your Rutgers honor. Good, good.)

The list you sent to me, in April, contains a good many interesting
names, along with some (to me, at least) duds. Norman Mailer I cannot ever be for; and is the remarkable Hannah Arendt a *creative*
writer? The shining lights [for possible election to the Institute], in my
opinion, are:

John Updike	Loren Eiseley
William Inge	Truman Capote
Leon Edel	James Baldwin
Caroline Gordon	May Swenson

followed by the lesser brilliance of Dwight Macdonald, Erich Maria
Remarque and Morton Zabel.

The younger poets are all so very *flat*, somehow, at least the lot in Donald Hall's new Penguin anthology. A bad patch, as Wystan would say. (There's a great deal of flatness in England, at the moment, too.)

It's grand to be back, even though living in a little hotel on the verge of Bayswater (transitional territory!) was fun, too.

> Ever, dear Glenway,
> Louise

/ to Ruth Limmer /

> MacDowell Colony
> Peterborough, N.H.
> September 8, 1963

Dear Ruth:

* * * E. A. Robinson was v. wise to stick to this one studio, from 1915 to 1934. Built on a slope, of large cobblestones, with a pitched roof inside, and windows high up, in the gables, it *stayed cool*. Also, a view of Monadnock exists, through pine branches—v. Cézanne and Mont-Sainte-Victoire. —The woodpile is *in* the room, but one gets used to this.

I've done little but read Freya Stark (*Beyond Euphrates*, which I've missed up to now), since I finished the K. Koch–F. Seidel review. *So* restful, not having to make up one's mind about what to leave out, or put in. —And Freya S. certainly awakens one's admiration: a neurotic girl with *masses* of demented relatives, who figured out *just* what she wanted to do, and how much it would cost—and *did* it. Did you ever look into the first vol. of her autobiography—*Traveller's Prelude*? Get hold of it, if you can.

Mary McCarthy's *The Group* showed up in the little paper and book store, downtown, so I *bought* it. I'll send it on to you, as soon as you get settled. Women's secrets again, told in clinical detail: a seduction, told as though by slides in a microscope, is the best; also, various involvements of high-minded girls with low-minded men are wittily put forth. M.'s style has become v. sharp and economical, too. But the semi-Mary protagonist gets killed again (suicide?); while her *other* half (rich, soignée, onto everything) turns out to have been a corrupt and corrupting *Lesbian*, all along. V. strange! Meanwhile, there's the usual picture of Mary, looking just the same as always—neat, clear featured and pulled together—gazing out over a Parisian suburb, this time.

Did I tell you that my little Swiss friend [Elizabeth Roget] finally broke down and decided to join me in the J. Renard translation? She is rather *over* meticulous (never having been to school!) but she is certainly good on subtle idioms, etc. —And she works fast and accurately, so I'm starting right in, marking passages, and comparing versions. She'll get some of the advance, of course; a third seems fair.

O, what a *laughless* bunch of characters September has cast upon the MacDowell fields and meadows! —One young painter, with loose wrists and v. unpleasantly flat red eyelids was *shattered* by one rainy day. "O, it's wise to rise above the weather," said I to him. "But I'm so *emotional!*" said he. (He staged "a happening" in his studio—did I tell you?) Appalling! And such affected little daubs, on his walls. Who let *him* in? Virgil Thomson was amusing enough—but so hard, and such a snob. * * * Then there's Robert Sward, whose little Greek wife is about to give birth to a second child, while Bob writes far-out poetry which will never help support him, her, or their young. *Plus* Hortense Powder-maker, who is intelligent but *also* heavy (anthropology; Queens College); and a large lanky male character from Tucson, who has lately switched from poetry to composing and doesn't believe in "the nuance." Heavy, heavy! * * * But Bill Smith will come over next Friday, to work on that children's anthology. We may get a poetry evening out of it.

How were the Wallkill flowers? Write soon.

Love,
L.

/ *to William Maxwell* /

MacDowell Colony
Peterborough, N.H.
September 20, 1963

Dear William!

Thank you for the Roethke proof, and your note. —The poem is lovely; one of his most tender lyrics. It is sad to think that all that incredible energy is now "undone." [1] The nearer one comes to *vanishing*, the stranger it seems.

Yes, I still love pavilions: particularly an octagonal one, that I have made up for myself. Also, those wooden towers that appear, attached to Victorian (American) houses. Quite a few of these appear in this countryside.

Mushrooms and Shirley poppies were contemplated here, this time. —I'm afraid the woman who lived under the roller coaster is gone for good.[2]

Love,
Louise

1. Roethke had died at the beginning of August; in October *The New Yorker* published six of his poems, including the one she refers to here, "Wish for a Young Wife."

2. In 1941 LB had told Maxwell "about a woman called, actually, Mrs. Breed, who lived, in 1912, under a roller coaster, and had a husband who ran a bowling alley. She was a wonderful woman; and I don't think I am worthy to put her down."

/ to Ruth Limmer /

October 9, 1963

Dear Ruth:

Your postcard received, and contents noted. How flat that [Kenneth] Patchen-wit falls. And imagine taking on the subject of representing *tigers!* —A genius who needs a little talent, as Renard said of Mme. de Noailles. * * * The weather has been perfectly lovely, and I sat on a bench in Ft. Tryon yesterday morning, and read *You Are Not the Target*, by the present Mrs. Aldous Huxley, all the way through—but not every *word*. She advises tense people to 1.) Go into a room and take off all their clothes, and turn on the radio, and DANCE, and 2.) Go into a room and take off all their clothes, and PRETEND THAT THEY ARE SOME KIND OF AN ANIMAL. Goodness! I think that the dancing part might be rather fun, though. I don't suppose you can go in for this form of therapy (not that you need to) with your landlady listening and learning. You can try it on West 174th Street, sometime, maybe. (Silent animal?)

* * * There's a rather good article on *Fanny Hill*, by that dull but scholarly John Hollander at Yale, in the current *Encounter*. He thinks that pornography in the novel goes over into poetry. This I do not believe. Poetry excites, too, he says. An odd thought. . . . They're selling *Fanny Hill* in that new bookstore, right beside [the supermarket], by the way. Women telling about naughty doings, in the first person, is part of the tradition, and of the fun, Hollander says; and I guess this is true. Mary McC. departs a little, by putting it in the third. But

women always sound more depraved than men—*when* they *are* depraved; vide *Moll Flanders* (but not Molly Bloom, who isn't depraved in the least . . .).

* * *

Love, and write soon,
Louise

/ *to May Sarton* /

December 2, 1963

Dear May:

What nightmare days we all went through! —The beautiful funeral observances, seen everywhere on TV, helped to ease the shock (I did not see them, as I had had enough, by Monday), from all the accounts I have heard; the fine young soldier who *led* the horse became a sort of symbol to at least two of my more sensitive friends. —The young people at Williams, Bill Smith says, are desolate. —And Dr. Wall (whom I saw on Saturday) said that this sort of *violence* is the price we pay for being the Republic we are. *One person* the target for all the mixed hate and love. . . . One *removable* person; one *chosen* person. . . .

* * *

Love,
Louise

/ *to Ruth Limmer* /

December 8, 1963

Dear Ruth:

* * *

BIG NEWS!
I have been *approached* (over the telephone) by one
Victor Harris
of
Brandeis University

in respect to my teaching there for the entire academic year of 1964–65!
Salary: $12,000. Two courses. About 4 hours a week!
(Short pause!)
Shall I do it? I should give him some sort of answer by Friday, 13

December. J. V. Cunningham and P. Rahv are there; also (as visitor) L. Kronenberger. —Where would I live? Could I stand Boston? Could I really receive enough of that dough, after taxes? Please advise! I can put them off until after Christmas, I think.

Love,
L.

January 30, 1964

Dear Ruth:
* * *

Meanwhile, much time has been taken up by *humane* actions. 1st of such: my visit last Friday to old Mr. Metcalfe (E. Scott's husband); did I write you about him? In *extreme* want; in a little room in one of those awful *communal* (kitchens) upper B'way hotels. *Shaken* by his wife's death, and, I suspect, nursing the whiskey bottle somewhat. WELL, I've got hold of his doctor, and I've written the Carnegie Fund for Authors, and something will be done. Not just *money*. A plan.[1]

Then, yesterday, I sat from 9:30 through 3:30, at (in) the court of violation claims (or whatever it's called); trying to get the landlord punished. For reasons too fantastic to go into, our (the tenants') pleas and accusations came to naught. —It was a nightmare experience; think of it going on, day after day! Outside, and the ham sandwich eaten at the noon recess, seemed paradise. *Never* complain!
* * *

Love,
Louise

1. Continuing to help John Metcalfe, LB wrote in April: "My *crown* gets starrier every day, no doubt; but I do wish these demands on my charity would let up, for a while. Or that *grace* would flow, so that I might stop being so *irritated* at being so good. . . ."

MacDowell Colony
February 19, 1964

Dear Ruth:
Well, it is snowing and it is going to snow, in the words of that great weather-watcher, Wallace Stevens. —We have already had a 19th century poetic snow-storm (in the *Whittier* manner), with great flakes as large as oyster-crackers, floating down for a day and a night. —*This*

is the light, fine variety, and it will produce a foot and a half in no time, so they say. —I am sorry to say that my townee side is coming out big. On Sunday (the *Whittier* day), I had planned to spend a good deal of time in the library, which had been specially heated. All was well: pianoforte, heaps of music, comfortable chairs, books, ashtrays—everything but trays of fruit and bottles of Scotch. Through the high window, however, I could see *everything* being obliterated, including my own footsteps. And the water was turned off. So I panicked, and beat my way back to Colony Hall and the Eaves—an *ignominious* retreat. —It is strange how one's neuroses—long quiet—waken to ancient pressures.

    * * * But I wouldn't have missed this winter wonderland effect. When the sun comes out, all that intense blue overhead and unmarked *crisp* white, underfoot, is v. thrilling indeed. In addition, we have had a new moon and two bright attendant planets, since the 13th. *Orion* is also always there: a lesson in drawing a straight line. . . .
    * * *

> Love,
> Louise

/ to Miss —— /

April 6, 1964

Dear Miss ——: [1]

I was interested to read your poems, and perhaps I can give a few words of advice. —You are at the age when talent usually shows itself, and I think that you have a talent for language. You express yourself in a naturally pleasant rhythm, and you evidently take pleasure in this expression. You vary your sentence structure, instinctively, in an interesting way, and you see things and hear them, in (usually) an interesting way.

For a writer, a feeling for words—for language—must be the principal thing—the central endowment. Without such a feeling it is useless to apply oneself to the hard, hard tasks which face the writer, throughout his or her career. You have this feeling for language, but you have not developed it very far. For you do not write, as we say, "in form." You write free verse. At seventeen, if you are to go on writing poetry, you must not only begin to acquaint yourself with the effects of formal verse, but you must begin to use these effects. You can begin by imitating this poet or that as long as you admit that you *are* imitating. You must begin to practise—as a pianist practises (only you are practising *creatively*, of course—not merely performing). You show a slight tendency toward form, in these poems of your manuscript, but not consistently. I should say, from present evidence, that you might very well turn out to be a writer of prose—a novelist, say, if you have any storytelling ability.

So try writing all sorts of things! And look into some textbooks on prosody. *Poetry Handbook*, by Babette Deutsch (Funk and Wagnall) is a valuable, recent such book, that has received high praise from many people, including myself. Any book store will order it for you.

Write and read! Read and write! —Those are the two rules.

Every good wish.

[unsigned]

1. Because the recipient of this letter (available only as a carbon in LB's papers) cannot be traced, her name is omitted.

/ to Ruth Limmer /

April 10, 1964

Dear Ruth:

* * * The party for Eliz. Mayer's 80th birthday, at her eldest daughter's house in Bayside, was v. pleasant. Both Wystan *and* Hannah Arendt (sp?) were there—the latter in a determinedly feminine get up (large print bow on bosom, etc.)—the former looking more creased and battered than one would think possible. How *does* he get that *crumpled* look? Drinking? Working? Thinking? Being a genius? He had an Irish sweater on, under his coat; and this was removed, and put on again, with *lumpy* results. He's translating Hammarskjöld's diary. —H. had quite a messianic delusion, it appears, from what I've heard. Wystan seems unperturbed by this fact; all that troubles him is that he can't track down some of the English quotes.

* * *

Love,
L.

April 30, 1964

Dear Ruth:

* * *

The sad news of Morton Zabel's death has just reached me. O how truly sad! I had sent him a card at Easter; our tiff was healed. —It must have been cancer. * * * I tried to get the Wheelocks, but they are out of town.

He and I laughed in the same places, too. I shall miss him. Write soon.

Love,
L.

May 9, 1964

Dear Ruth:

Delighted to receive the *Encyclopedia of Sexual Behavior* promotion. —Years ago, when I was a *girl* in Brentano's, I discovered that the Rare Book Department would forward all sorts of *rare* pornography (high-toned) to *anyone* who had an established business or profession, *and* a bank-account. So you are in good society, with your name on that list. A good deal of this stuff ended up in the Indiana Sex Museum Library; the relatives, on the death of some old lecher out in Kansas or wherever, immediately packed up the racy books and sent them to Kinsey—*as gifts!* (So Dr. Kinsey said . . .)

No Western (westward) trip, this year. —Morton's death really shook me up (it was a coronary, following surgery for gastric ulcer); all I want to do is to get beside the sea, as soon as possible. * * *

Love,
L.

16 Chauncy Street
Cambridge, Mass.
October 11, 1964

Dear Ruth:

* * * O, this is a strange area! With Washington taking command of his troops, only yesterday, down by the Cambridge Common; and with a statue of a poor, miserable little Quaker woman, in front of the State House, and right *opposite* the Boston Athenaeum (they *spell* it right): sitting down, with clasped hands, and her dates, and her facts (fighter for religious freedom)—with the added legend *Hanged on Boston Common*, sometime in the 1600's. Goodness! —And the Athenaeum itself—so granitic, so gray, with all *its* dates incised on marble slabs inside the front door (this building dates from the 1840's). And then one sees the librarians, in a room overlooking the Old Granary

Burying Ground—v. brisk and up-to-date, with a few potted plants disposed behind them. To the *left* is the Periodical Room, with every known periodical in English laid out neatly on *tables*; and there are *many* potted plants here, in the window (to take the curse off the view, I suppose)—some on wooden planks and with a largish watering can, attendant. (The Newspaper Room is at the front, adjoining, with *The Observer* and the *London Sunday Times* right on the first table; and with all the U.S. papers hung up on those wooden things that they have in European cafés.) —I haven't been up to the *belles-lettres* stacks yet. The array of new books—to the librarian's *left*—is too staggering. British, American, French—and all arranged under *subject* (from history through thrillers). What a plan!

But you are dying to hear about my meeting with H. Calisher.[1] —She is extraordinary to look at: hair all black and bushy, and brushed up into a kind of smart hay-stack; v. pretty teeth, and big black eyes; and gotten up in a black dress with white *broderie Anglaise* sleeves. —She is not at all mean or hateful—or edged in any way, temperamentally. None of the *talk* you might expect from such a flamboyant mask: a rather quiet *persona*; no crackles or darts. *She* thought the blankness I had encountered a Brandeis *thing*. (I am *convinced* it is just *ignorance*, with a little stupidity mixed in. There hasn't been time for the force and originality of the set-up to take hold.) —At the English Dept. get-together cocktail gathering, on the *Thursday* before the Saturday, one intelligent young man told me frankly that I would have a *big* class if I were teaching the 20th Cent. *novel*—with Hemingway shocks to hand out, etc. —*He* had had a class of *three*, one of whom could only communicate in *Swedish*. Cheer up, he said.
❊ ❊ ❊

Love,
Louise

1. The novelist Hortense Calisher first came to LB's attention with, I believe, a *New Yorker* story, "The Middle Drawer."

November 22, 1964

Dear Ruth:
One has one's paranoiac days, Dr. Wall once told me. I think that the enclosed review (by some bitter little Briton, trapped in a London French department) should be counted on as (perhaps) providing

a paranoid *week.* —Well, the dislike of the *N. Y. Review* for L. B. has, at least, been flushed out into the open. * * * ANYHOW, it's the first time my motives have been called *meretricious*; and I didn't put in the Sartre quote anyhow—and can't think who did. "If the book was so minor, why go on so at length?" said J. V. C[unningham]. *Persecution!* A *banding-together!* —I guess I'll forget it.[1] Healthier, all round. . . .
            * * *

Love,

L.

1. The review of *The Journal of Jules Renard* was written by John Weightman. But LB did not forget that the *New York Review of Books* attacked this translation (which recollection was sharpened when it ignored her collected poems in 1968). Her response was to refuse to purchase copies when they appeared on the newsstands, although in fairness it should be noted that her quarrel with the publication was more broadly than personally based.

The Neurological Institute
710 W. 168th Street
N.Y.C.
June 12, 1965

Dear Ruth:

Yes! I have moved over to this far-from-forbidding spot, after a severe seizure of pure depression, early in the week. —Dr. Wall put me in touch with a Dr. H. (who is the big anti-depressant-drug man) who is attached to the Psychiatric *and* the Neurological. And as it happened (and fortunately, I think, on the whole) a room was vacant on this, the 12th floor—the "emotionally disturbed" sector. —There is no doubt that my *depression* has become the main problem. Dr. H.'s pills are called "psychic renovators"—or some such term. Dr. Tyson called yesterday, and explained that these drugs went straight to the hidden sources in a most extraordinary way; they are by no means *tranquilizers.* —Yesterday, after my first doses, I became exceedingly dopey. This first effect wears off, I am told. —In any case, I have *taken action!* —And am being taken care of, down to the last detail. And am *eating!* and sleeping (fairly well). And with doctors on every side. . . .

This depressed state began last fall, I think—with the return to the scenes of my childhood—or adolescence. Boston is really filled with sorrowful memories of my family, and my early self. —I thought, because I had "insight" into it all, that I could rise above it. But H. has told me that a depression can *seep through*, as it were, in any case.

This is a most attractive set-up, with lovely *views* on all sides, and no grisly, sloppy hospital atmosphere. The patients are, of course, pretty mixed—with some exceedingly vocal ones. And the "treatments" include electric shock (which has been much "improved," I hear—but Lord preserve us). —Some young people receive these, as well as older types. —I feel that they are not for me—since my mental *confusion* is nil. (An exceedingly pretty little Italian woman doctor puts one through a short stretch of baby-psychoanalysis, right away; and I was surprised to find myself subtracting *sevens*, counting backward, etc.)

* * *

Just let us hope that the "drugs" connect with the *psyche*.

Love,
Louise

Neurological Institute
710 West 168th Street
New York, New York
June 26, 1965

Dear Ruth:

* * *

Well, I guess I'm over the worst of the fringe effects of the strange "medication" ("wonder drug") treatment. Believe me, it was rough, for about five nights: heart palpitation—the feeling of the center of the citadel being invaded. And blood pressure taken in all positions: sitting, standing, etc. And the semi-knowledge that the doctor was just as much at sea as you were. (This was nonsense, of course, as H. is tops in his field.) THEN—finally, the pill is changed, and the heart quiets down, and you say, "I'll never worry about *anything* again." One evening, with a gibbous moon hanging over the city (such *visions* we have!) like a piece of red cantaloupe, and automobiles showing red danger signals, as they receded down Ft. Wash. Ave.—I thought I had reached the edge of eternity, and *wept* and *wept*. * * * —I'm now on a little white pill which makes me rather woozy, but is mild otherwise. . . . (I'm writing *through* it, at the moment.)

The shock treatment patients are a group to themselves. No interest in anything, even when they're coming out of it. "You *read!*" they say. —But their condition changes right before your eyes: more quickly than mine, for example. Right up out of speechless melancholia to *smiles*. But that is not for me. My trouble is not cyclic; and the physical side is mixed in with it. * * *

A dull letter, for someone as peripatetic as yourself to receive. But you might be interested. —The Salinger ["Hapworth 16, 1924"] is a disaster. B. Maxwell came to call, and rather deplored its total cessation of talent. More!

Love,
Louise

July 10, 1965

"Sprung" the day before yesterday; and just in time, as "the disturbed patients" were gaining on the undisturbed. —The depression is lifted, but I *have* fallen a couple of (harmless) times. O those medications. We will laugh when you get back.[1]

Love,
L.

1. There *was* laughter, but life grew increasingly difficult as the summer wore on, and LB returned to the hospital in September. These months may best be approached through the opening stanzas of a rondel written the following February, when poetry again became possible.

Cleanse and refresh the castle of my heart
Where I have lived for long with little joy,
For Falsest Danger, with its counterpart,
Sorrow, has made this siege its long employ.

Now lift the siege, for in your bravest part
Full power exists, most eager for employ;
Cleanse and refresh the castle of my heart
Where I have lived for long with little joy.

New York Hospital
White Plains, N.Y.
September 26, 1965

Dear Ruth:

I have been neglecting you—and many other far-flung friends—in the course of the development of my "mind shock" experiences. —First off, I was *demoted* from the "class" I entered this hospital in; secondly, the days pass in a strangely disjointed manner. —I should like to hear from you, however. My letters are posted in our living room here, unsealed

—and are sent on later, through the patients' respective doctors. Which makes for formality.

I have learned to *tolerate* TV programs—v. interesting, from space flight to "giving away" programs. —All v. much [?] a *psychological* set of actions and reactions.

My *depression* is much improved. It is an *eerie* process, however, with rather frightening lapses of memory in between. I wish I could see you and demonstrate—if not explain.

Keep well. The weather, at least, is lovely.

Love,
Louise

/ *to May Sarton* /

N.Y. Hospital
Westchester Division
White Plains, N.Y.
November 3, 1965

Dearest May:
  * * *

One ray of happiness: the appearance of Bill Smith's, and my, children's anthology: *The Golden Journey.* It has awakened v. warm praise from all and sundry. I'll get a copy to you, sometime soon. We did it, you will remember, practically by reciting the stuff to each other *out loud!* This liveliness of approach comes through.

Dear May, how wonderful it is to be unburdened by depression once more! To be at the mercy of that *oppression* is one of the most frightful experiences possible. —Evidently, I'm not going into a *high* phase.

I trust that all goes well with you, and your teaching. Write again!

Love,
L.

/ *to Ruth Limmer* /

January 26, 1966

Dear Ruth:
* * * I am trying to pack in some NYC diversions [but] the truth is, that a good many of the possible companions-in-recreative action rather bore me! Isn't that a poor kind of confession to make? Either that, or they are actively climbing out of their own particular difficul-

ties—impending age among them * * *. Well, it is all much, much better than being shut up with those egregious suburban neurotics * * *.

Reading matter is not terribly exciting. * * * I have managed to read all the back numbers of *Atlas* and *Encounter*, and the *N. Statesman*, and thrown them out. I also read the new Graham Greene [*The Comedians*]: a pale replica of former thrills and evil. The entire world of the mystery novel has collapsed, it would seem. And I'm not yet ready for *War and Peace*! —I should *take up* something, I suppose. Perhaps Hortense Powdermaker (who is nice, near by and v. friendly) could give me a course of anthropology—with the accent on the tribal practices of upper Manhattan Island. But alas, I find Hortense rather boring, too. . . .
* * *

I have been told of the Stanley Kauffmann outburst against homosexual playwrights, in last Sunday's *Times* drama section. I didn't see it, because it was snowing so hard I feared to venture out. No names named, of course, but a direct attack on Inge, Williams and Albee, and their woman-hating. This seems to be getting things out into the open, and starting a controversy. All to the good, although *Time*'s animadversions, a week or so ago, had a prissy, Establishment fussiness about it.
* * *

The gulls are flying up the Hudson. More, and better, soon.

Louise

March 10, 1966

Dear Ruth:

This is an add on the subject of Susan Sontag's remarkable book, *Against Interpretation*. I actually bought this volume, and I shall be glad to send it on to you, if you'd like. —The publishers say nothing whatever about her, and her work stands quite detached, from any stated education, origin, etc. She is extremely pretty, and smiles enigmatically on the back of the jacket, clothed in a semi-beat get-up. (She has just led a protest of artists, in Los Angeles, of all places, against Vietnam, I see in the paper.) —The work shows that she has read *everything*, ancient and modern—in several languages; that she has formidable powers both of abstract thought and of *argument*; and that her knowledge of all sides of the modern situation—aesthetic, political and philosophic—is extraordinarily full. —She is v. informed—and usually quite good—on the movies as well; in fact, the cinema comes through as slightly more important to her than any other "art-form." She even has hopes for the future of TV. . . .

One strange characteristic struck me—and I don't think I'm being square to separate it out as a fault—a drawback—among Sontag's multiple gifts. She seems hung up on an eroticism so far out that it verges on what we must call—for lack of any decent word—pornography. She is particularly wild on the subject of blue movies—the artistic kind, of course. But sexual shock in general attracts her. She is on to herself in many ways—and she stands up for both *mystery* and *form,* in a kind of backhanded fashion; but give her a movie in which women are having an orgy, and she goes all out. —Is this Sontag, or is it post-Beat? Or what? —Shall I send the book on?

Love,
Louise

May 11, 1966

Dear Ruth:

* * *

The Librium effect gave out a little over, and just after, the weekend; with some reason. You know how fond I am of Rufina, and how long I have known her; and the sight of her, bravely gotten up in her pretty hat and her little mink short wrap, after her some-years-ago tangle with surgery; and the memory of the fun we have had together —and other such thoughts, really threw me, after I had walked her down to the Boston train, through that ugly tunnel at G. Central. (The sight of her room in the Hotel Roosevelt, all Louis Quinze in pale colors, with about eight lamps, also threw me, for some reason. Plus the dames going into some party or other in the Grand Ballroom . . . with their gents . . . O, is this the reward of American virtues, I said to myself.) Well, anyway, we had a nice walk up Fifth Avenue and saw the flowers, and had lunch at a new "pub" called Charley O's; and finally ended up by seeing that happy little Soviet youth movie, called *Meet Me in Moscow*: perfectly beautiful young people putting lots of butter on their bread and telling each other how *happy* they are; and making a little fun of officials. V. peculiar . . . but certainly a different sort of propaganda.

* * *

Love,
Louise

/ to Rufina McCarthy Helmer /

July 25, 1966

Dear Rufina:

* * * You should see the Village, these days! I went down recently to see an anti-Vietnam free-form play (written by an Irish girl from Seattle) [Megan Terry's *Viet Rock*] and it's really hard to make one's way around the streets. But all this is *ferment*—which should lead to something, someday.

My strange little (for it *must* be a child-ghost, embedded in the subconscious) morning visitant is, I believe, yielding to work-exorcism, more than to medication. *It* vanished at 10:30 A.M. today, and hasn't been back. Work at the typewriter seems to bore it. For all it wants to do is *weep.*[1] O heavens, am I seeing the end of the tunnel, *at last?*

Love, and write,
Louise

1. LB is here describing an understanding that will be expressed in "Little Lobelia's Song."

/ to Sister M. Angela, I.B.V.M. /

August 20, 1966

Dear [Sister] Angela: [1]

Thank you for your letter. —It is difficult to analyze lyric poetry, because, if it is at all authentic, it is based on emotion—on some actual occasion, some real confrontation. "Exhortation" and "Henceforth, from the Mind" were written in my early thirties, in the midst of a state which bordered on despair. "The Mark" is earlier, and is much more contemplative. "Juan's Song" is earlier still. In the last named, I think one can detect the bitterness which comes with a breakdown of early idealism. The bitterness has become deeper later on, and is deepest in "Exhortation," which was written on the verge of a psychic and physical breakdown (which had roots in reality, and partook v. little of fantasy).

"The Dream" is a later poem, written in my late thirties, after a complete change in my way of living, and in my general point of view about life (and the universe at large!). It is the actual transcript of "a nightmare," but there is reconciliation involved with the fright and horror. It is through the possibility of such reconciliations that we, I believe, manage to live.[2]

About form, I can say nothing. It comes, if one is lucky, and in a state of creative grace.

I hope these few remarks help. Thank you again.

Sincerely yours,

Louise Bogan

1. Sister Angela O'Reilly, I.B.V.M., who teaches at the SS. Simon and Jude School in Arizona, was at this time working on her thesis.

2. " 'The Dream,' by the way, is a poem of victory and of release. The terrible power, which may v. well be the psychic demon, is tamed and placated, but NOT destroyed; the halter and the bit were already there, and something was done about *control* and *understanding*." (To Sarton, August 14, 1954)

/ *to Ruth Limmer* /

September 19, 1966

Dear Ruth:

* * * —It *is* difficult to see the world run by anything *but* a demon (the universe, too). The only hope is: that there must be an edge (a sort of *selvage*) of good, that holds and defines. And, of course, the very spectacle of crowding, hungry life, crowding into every crack and cranny of the material situation (cracking the *Manhattan schist* with an oak tree, as well as the spectacle of a piece of lichen accumulating in a crack of same) should continually excite, if not reassure us. —That new laboratory building of Columbia-Presbyterian just echoes with the barking of dogs; and I shudder every time I go by it, in the early morning. But there, mind is actively working over matter; and Maidie once told me that they are the best-tended dogs in the world. . . .
  * * *

A bunch of books went to the Phoenix [Book Shop], but I have been unable to find anything truly readable anywhere, although I actually bought, for $1, one of those maundering, tenuous late S. Sitwells, because the index was so fascinating—ranging from (to begin in the middle) *God* on to *Uganda*, Walruses, Waldteufel, Witches, Yoshowara (beauties of the), to Zumbo (Gaetano) and Zurbarán (Francisco). —Another purchase has been B. Britten's *Curlew River* (at Goody's, from the same decayed but smart old gentleman). One mono record. I sat down to listen to it, having plied myself with a mild Scotch and soda, and really enjoyed it. It's full of extraordinary detached noises, in the background, including a truly eerie gong; and P[eter] Pears, as the Madwoman, is suitably watery and wavering (I do get tired of that Britten waver-waver noise). The voice of the little ghost is also v. touching: just a little *needle* of sound, coming in as an echo to some monkish chanting, in both Latin and English. I wish you had been here to share this experience. I simply don't know one other person (with the exception of Maidie) in the company of whom I can listen to music. That is bad—and strange.

* * * And I have started brooding over an approach to J. Mac-Donald.[1] Two longish blurbs will appear in this week's magazine. When the long piece will shine forth, no one knows. —I'm typing out those last scattered poems, too. —A new book by Anne Sexton has just arrived—with the compliments of the author, no less. O why can't I write psychotic verse! Neurotic verse pales into insignificance beside what those girls—Sexton and Plath—can (could) turn out.

Love, and write when you can.

Louise

1. LB had for some time been an admirer of the non-series novels of John D. Mac-Donald, whom she often compared to Georges Simenon. For fun, and change, she thought she might do a piece on him for *The New Yorker*. Also at this time she was preparing the MS for *The Blue Estuaries*, her last collection of poetry.

November 9, 1966

. . . Well, the YMHA reading went off v. well indeed. Bill Smith introduced me most fulsomely ("the greatest living woman *lyric* poet") —forgetting that Léonie was in the audience. (This brought on some cane-waving, from L., later; only *half* in jest. . . .) A fine audience, and I hear my *relaxed* reading was v. effective.[1] * * *

Love,

L.

1. Always somewhat platform-shy, and convinced—no matter who was reciting her poetry—that dramatic projection was inappropriate to its interpretation, LB gave readings that often sounded like lessons in perfect enunciation. Edmund Wilson, writing in *I Thought of Daisy*, described LB's reading "—when she read at all—as if her poems had been compositions which she had never seen before, poems written by some other person and by someone of whom she disapproved." Still, her austerity had its effect. As Ruth Benedict wrote (in *An Anthropologist at Work*): "Louise was a lovely figure—read with an accent of disdain, very becoming."

Although these descriptions both come from the 1920s, LB's performances did not differ much in the decades to follow, as can be demonstrated in her recordings for the Library of Congress, Spoken Arts, the Yale Series of Recorded Poets and Poets for Peace. They are "dry," slowly paced—as opposed to the very swift tempo of her conversation—and each vowel sound and consonant is given full measure in a pure contralto that never lost its New England shading.

November 15, 1966

Dear Ruth:

* * * From now on I may disappear into—not a cloud—but the *fat*
W. Stevens *Letters*. He was v. touching, in youth, taking long walks
and looking at plants and animals, and going to the N.Y.P.L. (just
after it was built) and the Met. Museum—in a most studious and lonely
way. (He boned up on *French* poetry, as I always knew he had; and he
got himself a piano-playing wife—hence those Debussy-like titles. . . .)
Good God, what an experience lies before me: W. S., becoming
more and more abstract and garrulous and Republican. —His vignettes
of *Miami* and of Florida in general, circa 1912, are delightful. Coconut trees full of coconuts; *little* houses; hardly any hotels. *Miami!*

I have just this minute finished my report on that 400 pp. plus MS
(on Stevens' "poetic") sent to me by Rutgers. For a time, I thought
I was lost in the labyrinth; for the guy's "doctoral dissertation" is
embedded in the middle of this heap of slippery typewritten paper.
You should have seen me, paper-clipping the chapters together, on
my bed; everything sliding around, and the paper-clips *bending* under
their burden. Thank God, I didn't have to read every word. But then
the W. S. commentaries began to come down off the shelves! —I had
to chide myself: *Stop it, Miss B.* —The *Letters* will be much easier,
really.[1] *What* a strange man! *Dutch*, he keeps saying. . . .

Love,
Louise

1. "The W. Stevens letters are indeed *formidable*, and one gets to like the old guy,
in spite of his lousy politics, exceeding carefulness, and general circuitousness. He
was scared to death, half the time, I think: of poverty, other poets, and *himself*."
(November 18, 1966)

/ *to Howard Moss* /

January 25, 1967

Dear Howard: [1]
These three "songs" seem to go together, in this order—although the
third one is older than the other two. But it seems to belong to the
same world (of dream and aberration). The first and second songs
are new: this winter.[2]

How I wish I had heard you read. —But getting about at night continues to be a chore.

Best!

Louise

1. Howard Moss, poet and critic, is the poetry editor of *The New Yorker*.

2. Published first in *The New Yorker*, the poems—"Little Lobelia's Song," "Psychiatrist's Song" and "Masked Woman's Song" (which LB would later describe as "a fairly old erotic song") were to conclude *The Blue Estuaries*.

/ to Ruth Limmer /

May 4, 1967

Dear Ruth:

* * * I agree about Lenny Bruce. —A true obsession there, along with great talent. Everything became fuzzy and paranoid, toward the last. —Novels keep on disappointing; but I have *40 Years with B. Berenson,* which ought to yield some nuggets (although I thoroughly dislike the old boy: such a hypocrite *cum* snob).

   * * * But one experience must be seized, and passed on to you. —Yesterday I saw, in the 8th Ave. local, a teeny bopper, complete with knit miniskirt, white raincoat, and hair down to her *waist*—reading WHAT?

JANE EYRE!

Love,

L.

August 27, 1967

S.S. *Bremen*

Dear Ruth:

All is proceeding calmly and rather endearingly (for the flood of German which swirls around me, at table, and everywhere else, seems to be having a soporific effect). ANGST—possibly recognizing *its own* language—seems completely to have disappeared. —The sea is a millpond. The food is good. A brass band plays every morning, and "gaiety" goes on until 2:00 A.M. —A gaiety more hips than hippy . . . literally *dozens* of large people drift around; but do not think that the younger set is unrepresented. Plenty of miniskirts. And not a few outfits verging on the *whorish.* —I have a feeling you'd hate everything. But when one old lady after another—who have ended up either in Hamburg or Heidelberg or Oakland, Cal.—tell you the story of their lives, somehow it is soothing to listen. For those stories come from the v. center of the middle . . . and are often filled with unexpected moments of pathos. . . .

* * *

NOTE: Cheerfulness still prevails. I really feel extraordinarily *free*. Of what, I am not sure.

Wednesday

Freedom is still the feeling, but I am beginning to bog down with the *food*. A large fruit salad is what I crave. Meanwhile, I sit and watch a large, pretty lady (who runs a "bridal consultant" shop in Detroit, has four daughters, and wears *v*. loud prints and *much* jewelry)—dig in. "What is that?" I ask, as she attacks a slab of something, all over some sauce. "A smoked porkchop," she answers. (She has already surrounded the fish course, which course I have eaten *solo*, without surroundings. . . .)

NOTE: The library has v. odd books, bought about 5 years ago in a rummage sale. The unreadable, half-popular kind. So this is where they end up: riding the Atlantic.

* * *

Love—

L.

/ *to Josephine O'Brien Schaefer* /

December 11, 1967

Dear Jo Schaefer: [1]

Thank you for being so prompt with the V[irginia] W[oolf] notes. —I typed out the first set, and I plan to send *you* some comments later in the week. * * *

Everything you say is pertinent, I think—and fits into the pattern of my own insights. Her alternation of mood was, of course, a result of her illness; manic-depressives are swept from one extreme to the other. Her euphorias seem to have been fairly equally divided, as to timing, with her depressions. (This does not always occur. Ted Roethke, for example, was more manic than depressed in *his* cycle.) It is amazing that she was able to level off for considerable periods. She struggled v. hard indeed, constantly. —One point I made, in my article on V. W., done as a book review of a posthumous collection (title?), and re-printed in *Selected Criticism* (I don't have a copy to hand), was: that she was incapable of judging her contemporaries. Joyce was a low-bred fellow; Lawrence was a shocker. But she was v. good indeed at reconstructing an atmosphere of the past, and the color and motion of the genius of the admired dead—Jane Austen, for example. —Her feminism was bound up with her fears. Men were out to *get* women, etc.—and always had been.

We can keep these peripheral ideas floating around the *Diary* as a center, I think.

Don't worry about time or space! We can always cut and revise.

Best,

Louise

1. Having been asked to write an afterword for the New American Library edition of Virginia Woolf's *A Writer's Diary,* and deciding that to do a collaborative piece would be easier and more pleasurable than to work alone, LB enlisted Josephine O'Brien Schaefer, professor of English at The Western College and author of *The Three-fold Nature of Reality in the Novels of Virginia Woolf.*

LB had last written on Virginia Woolf in a review of *The Captain's Death Bed.* Comparing her to Isak Dinesen, Colette, early Elizabeth Bowen and others, LB criticized her "skirting of evil" and pointed out that "Mrs. Woolf is frequently intellectually pretentious and always emotionally immature."

When May Sarton objected, LB wrote: "I agree that my treatment of V. Woolf was rather partial; but I am so tired of people *mooning* over her. She had a v. inhuman side." (September 21, 1955)

/ *to Rolfe Humphries* /

May 18, 1968

Dear Rolfe:

I was v. sorry indeed to hear of your illness; but I feel sure that you must be on the mend, since you have just written such a fine poem, which I am happy to see. —I myself have had a rather mixed winter. By a series of events which no one could control, my circle of friends in N.Y.C. has rapidly dwindled. Betty Huling [1] has been in a recurrent, and severe, depression, for a long time; the two old gals who live across the street from me have both become pretty senile; Peg Marshall is in California, and so are you; and my closest woman friend—Ruth Limmer, who teaches at The Western College for Women—you have heard me speak of her—took herself off on a grand tour of Europe, including Russia and Prague. (She seems to have survived both locales.) I see Dave Mandel [2] for lunch, every once in a while, and there are other people I can talk to. Léonie is rather difficult, since she never *stops* talking . . . and is a fanatical Catholic Rightist, to boot. —Maidie I see about once a week; and I visit a literate youngish psychiatrist twice a month. But I get pretty lonely. This is a new feeling, for I have always been pretty vigorous and self-sufficient. A slight failure of nerve, no doubt. . . . But I hate it, and wish it would go away.

Meanwhile, there are stories about this apartment. Columbia has bought the building; and that means ultimate razing. I plan to hold on. For Manhattan Island is evidently part of my destiny; I can't imagine living anywhere else. If I could live in the country, things would be simpler. But I can't envisage not being a townee. . . .

* * * The books of verse that pour in are usually horrible, with titles like *The Lice* and *Body Rags*. But this kind of downgrading will have to change sooner or later. —Have you read the new Norman Mailer [*Armies of the Night*]? He seems to be the king of the mountain, with the v. young, just at present.

The U. of Washington Press sent me Ted's *Selected Letters*. You and I figure in them, of course; but on the whole they are horribly dull—and exhibit Ted's worser, ambitious side far too clearly. And hasn't the *New Yorker* poetry been grim, recently? One poem, by Anne Sexton, made me positively ill. These ingrown and degenerate Yanks!

Write soon, and stay out in the sun. I go to Ft. Tryon, often; it is lovely at this time of year, with azaleas.[3]

Love,

Louise

1. Betty Huling had been for many years on the staff of *The New Republic*.

2. David Mandel, author of *Changing Art, Changing Man,* is a labor lawyer whose energies for many years have been directed toward stopping the war in Indochina. It was he, primarily, who convinced LB to end her resistance to all forms of political action and join in the Poets for Peace reading at Town Hall in November 1967. On that occasion she read "To an Artist, to Take Heart" and, for the first time in public, "To My Brother."

3. Rolfe Humphries died, at the age of seventy-four, in April of 1969.

/ to William Maxwell /

January 11, 1969

Dear Bill:

* * * One or two troubling thoughts—to pass on to you before I leave [for Virginia]. . . .

In the first place, I have been having *scruples* about my reviewing any poet who seems to be *in competition* with myself—my having published a book of verse in 1968, and the prizes being what they are. (I was able to help judge the Bollingen, recently, since I have already received it.) My critical honor is, of course, impeccable—but even so. ... What do you think?

Then again, I find myself rather unwilling to write *short notices*, concerning this one or that. Omnibus reviews, every so often, seem to be more effective, somehow, at present. For the talent is so scattered— and so *scarce*. —Would you ask Shawn what he thinks of this? And I have been fighting the good fight against the academic *thesis* sort of thing.

* * * I do brood about the material; but I'll need some adjustment, away from the old pattern, I feel.

Best as always,
Louise

/ *to Robert Phelps* /

Hollins College
Virginia
January 22, 1969

Dear Robert:

I write you from my current habitat, to which I *flew* a week and a half ago. (This appointment runs for a *month* only; and is proving warm and varied. An "inter-short-term.") Bill Smith is here, part of the time; and the English department in general is varied to the point of the semi-bizarre * * *.

My own *first flight* went from N.Y.C. (La Guardia) to Washington airport—first class, Maidie insisted. *One* martini—and I was there. A much smaller jet (of the Piedmont Line) then took me over the beginnings of the Blue Ridge Mountains (and "the shade of the lonesome pine"). No panic whatever! So either my ID has burrowed down into one of its more inaccessible *dens*, or my nervous system has become blunted. . . . Over the ocean, at night, still scares me.

Your account, however brief, of the *Alphabet*, whets my appetite for more.[1] *Do* send the MS to Ruth. —As for the *prizes*, I don't know.[2] My *Karma* has always allowed prizes; while other ordinary human successes have been denied me. Odd! But let us put our faith in that sun ("and the other stars").

As I write, some perfectly lovely [?] piano Brahms is seeping down through the ceiling, from a practice room, above. A fresh young voice breaks into song, too. —I think I can "go back" to music, when I get home. Of course, my apartment will need attention, at ONCE. Plans for a general paint job are in hand. Once cleaned, perhaps I can "have people in." Or hire a summer cottage on one of the estuaries.

I read, last night, in a *beautiful* auditorium, to a fine audience. Virginia, Virginia! A veritable little pocket culture. And there's Scotch as well as Bourbon.

Keep me posted. Here until Feb. 8.

Love to you both,

Louise

1. Phelps was working to collect LB's criticism for a volume that, given its alphabetical arrangement, he thought should be called *A Poet's Alphabet*. In her classically severe way, LB felt the title "too fancy," but came to approve it after a time.

2. The *Alphabet*, which saw publication nine months after her death, won neither a National Book Award nor the Pulitzer. Caught between her dismissal of the latter prize as an award for literary merit and her desire to win it, LB wrote to Phelps in May, when *The Blue Estuaries* was passed over: "Let's not give it another thought. ° ° ° The Pulitzer comes from a school of *journalism*, we must remember."

/ to Ruth Limmer /

February 23, 1969

Dear Ruth:
      ° ° °

Did I tell you that everyone sat around and recited poetry, after dinner, that night at the Louchheims'? —Sen. [Eugene] McCarthy is certainly handsome, but there's something *small* about his mouth; and his mother is a German—a fact not usually brought out. He and his wife are splitting, rumor says. —And I liked Mr. [Jacob] Beam. I told him of your trip, and he said for you to come right over to the Embassy, when you're next in the USSR. "We like to have visitors," said he. Knowing your opinion of Embassies, I said nothing.

I *must* get out into the AIR. More soon. And keep me informed.

Love,

Louise

P.S. The Philip Roth book [*Portnoy's Complaint*] is raising a great noise. The Id breaking through—(I have a new theory about outbreaks of the Id. The Id has no sex—did you know?).

March 10, 1969

Dear Ruth:

* * * I went into a small but severe [slough of despond] last week, when the news of Betty Huling's death reached me. We had been friends ever since 1930; and we had many a "good time," together: matinees and parties and this and that. —It was impossible for me to see her, in her last days, because of the general impact—and she wouldn't have known me, in any case. Her death was a mercy, of course; but I miss her.
* * *

The last pressure is concerned with the *NYer* books. They have appeared (again) in quantity. —I want to start off a piece with a mention of the *Id* rampant. But it's so hard to be definite about the *Id*. Impossible, in fact. —But I have a picture of it snorting like a dragon, and lashing its tail, like demons. . . . Say a prayer!
* * *

Love,
Louise

March 26, 1969

Dear Ruth:
* * *

My poems seem to have fallen down that deep, dark well. Not a review! This doesn't bother me much.

But I *was* bothered by a letter from one Paris Leary (an American, evidently, teaching at the University of Leicester), taking me to task for my last review in the *NYer*. Shockingly superficial, he thinks. Why don't I write like Miss [Pauline] Kael: voluminously. Why don't I resign? —He states that he considers me a "1st rate" poet, which, evidently, makes matters all the worse. —This is someone whose name I have heard; and Robert will know all about him. —I feel that I shall have to answer him. Robert will advise me about that, too. Good old multi-functioning Robert!

The movies are terrible; and so was *Hair*, which I saw (and *heard*) last week. Violence, noise, rocking on the floor and a naked flash of two badly proportioned girls, pubic hair and all. A *revue* without laughs. * * *

Love,
Louise

1969

April 13, 1969

Dear Ruth:

* * * I waken at v. odd hours, having gone to sleep so early. —Remedy I: Put on light and try to read. II: Get up, and *do not* light a cigarette, but pour yourself a nice slug of Gordon's Gin. This usually works. . . .

* * *

[Ruth, I think I'm becoming an alcoholic! *Schnapps* in the A.M.—never more, all day, than ½ pint. But I simply cannot settle down to *work*, in the A.M. —My notes on the Id lie unruffled. The books have piled up. Perhaps I should get out, while the getting's good? Well, I'll give it a little more time.]

I'm re-reading *Death on the I[nstallment] Plan*, after having managed the v. last one, *Castle to Castle*. This was hard, because he had begun to go in for those three *dots*. But there's one hilarious incident, on a train, in a freezing storm, with all the dignitaries tearing up the "drapes," in order to keep warm. —Don't you think that crazy Céline should have a place in your autobiographical list? Those vignettes of Paris in summer, before 1914, are really something.

* * *

Added to everything else, I have forgotten large chunks of the *multiplication tables*, and have to count even more on my fingers. Senility?

* * *

Oh, to placate that Id!

Love,
Louise

April 27, 1969

Dear Ruth:

* * *

I have read a lot of tripe, and can't seem to get going on the *NYer* piece. I have decided, however, to mention the fact (at least) that Anne Sexton is the first woman in history to have written a hymn to her uterus. . . .

Love,
Louise

May 10, 1969

Dear Ruth:

* * *

S. Hadley, followed by Washington, was tiring, too. The undergraduate contestants at Mt. Holyoke were quite interesting this year: more idealism and positive statement than one would expect. I liked a hippy boy's offerings best; he had a Czechish name and a great fall of hair, and tight pants. But he was right in there with *reality*: gutsy stuff. A Bennington girl was also good. She wrote a poem to her *stomach* (as distinguished from her uterus . . .). Everyone was pleasant, and the Scotch flowed like water, at the evening party. Goodness! Those N. E. academics have fun!

Washington was quite formal: a black tie dinner at the Sulgrave Club, followed by a *packed* house at the L. of C. E. Bishop was there, and A. Tate (with ex-nun wife); R. Lowell, R. Fitzgerald, and dear Jack Wheelock (still in voice). Also, Marie Bullock in a petunia-colored dress. *And* E[ugene] McCarthy, at the cocktail party (calling me *Louise!*). K. Louchheim was in Paris. Bill Smith was about to leave on a State Dept. whirl through the Far East: Japan, Malaysia, etc. He has done a fine job of giving life to that consultant job. After J[ames] Dickey, things had fallen rather low. . . .

And did I tell you that a lovely old gal, draped in amber, *rushed* up to me and *pressed* my hand? This was the redoubtable Mrs. [Alice Roosevelt] Longworth, who is as lively as a cricket, with shining blue eyes—at 80 plus. . . .

The Pulitzer Prize committee certainly scraped the bottom of the barrel, in choosing Mr. [George] Oppen. Well, I'll never receive that accolade; not enough time left. But I do not weep. —I wish you could be here for my Academy investiture (on May 21st). I am the one elected person, and I *may* weep, then.[1]

Many strange books. *Ada,* by V. Nabokov. A super-Lolita, with language flowing from three or four fonts—and some non-words thrown in. A sticky life of E. St. V. Millay. New poems by J. Updike, with all the dirty words on display; to say nothing of descriptions of perverse copulation.

When will you be back? I'll be here off and on.

Love,
Louise

1. "Well, the *investiture* went off splendidly! I sat in the front platform row, alongside V. Thomson, and *he* sat beside L. Stokowski . . . and *he* sat beside T[ennessee] Williams (who was quite stoned with something, as it later appeared). The place was packed, and I got a nice hand when [George] Kennan shook hands with me (no *money*, this time)."

The American Academy of Arts and Letters is made up of not more than fifty members elected from the National Institute of Arts and Letters. Of the seven women who held chairs at this time, only two were poets: LB and Marianne Moore.

/ *to William Maxwell* /

June 30, 1969

Dear Bill:

The struggle with *silence* still goes on. —But I plan some secretarial help, after the holiday. If this doesn't help, I'll have another conference with you; and plan some strategy. Surely I can outwit this thing! I don't want to give up just yet.

As ever,
Louise

/ *to Ruth Limmer* /

October 1, 1969

Dear Ruth:

What a lovely letter! —And I am answering it, in my scrawl, to give you some *news*. Helped on by Dr. B. (who said, recently, that I had worked myself into a *circular* situation, which would have to yield, at some point, by means of a *break* of some kind), I have *decided* to leave the magazine. After 38 years; and 7 years beyond normal retirement age. —I know that you are against such a move; but really, Ruth, I've *had* it. No more pronouncements on lousy verse. No more *hidden* competition. No more struggling *not* to be a square. Etc. —No more weekly checks, as were; but Mr. Novak (broker) assures me that a *monthly* check, of feasible proportions, can be forthcoming. And I can stop *saving*: turning everything back. —And no income tax on the monthly S. Security check (which amounts to $156.50). Etc. Plus the extra jobs, as usual—with no limit to the amount that can be *earned*.

Plus no *guilt*, and v. little *fear*. . . .

I am writing this at 10:00 A.M. at which time I am still a little *shaky*.

So forgive. —Maxwell and I had lunch yesterday. He did not *press,* and I've given myself 10 days—in which the damned books can be *sent back.* —Let's pray that J. Dickey doesn't get the job. The [*Poet's Alphabet*] MS has reached McGraw-Hill. *This* I can work at. Also, at a new anthology with Bill Smith.

    ❋ ❋ ❋

Robert is *for* my retiring, by the way. And those 38 years have not entirely gone down the drain.

    ❋ ❋ ❋

Remember: this takes *courage.* But I'll come through!

> Love, and happy journey!
> Louise

October 9, 1969

Dear Ruth:

I've exorcised the demon! I'm free! No more A.M. weeping. No more *fear.* —*The books* go back to the magazine tomorrow—by messenger. —And I've had a lovely session with Robert, in the matter of the *Alphabet.* What a job he and you did! I shall acknowledge it. How about dedicating it to you?

    Really more, soon.

> Love,
> Louise

November 21, 1969

Dear Ruth:

(Edgar Cayce said: *Ohio* will not be destroyed, when all the eastern seaboard is. How about that?)

    The trip to Washington turned out to be v. pleasant. —I *flew* down on Sunday—*1st class.* A lovely hotel room, near the Library, and a pleasant evening with the Smiths. Then, on Monday afternoon, Bill and [William] Cole and I did a reading-chat [on poetry for children] to rather a small audience. —On Monday evening, however, we had a *packed* audience, with P. Colum pulling long poems out of his 89 year memory. Fantastic! I'll repeat some of his cracks to you, when I see you.

    ❋ ❋ ❋

The only *real* news is the fact Robert P. will bring up his "portrait" of Miss B., on Sunday. I feel that this will have to be re-done. However, we'll see.[1] * * * Well, the book may make the Christmas list in 1970. I *do* want to see it! If all that work had gone down the (journalist) drain, it would have been sad. As it is, I can *crow* a little!

The [Vietnam] moratorium was over, when I reached D.C. —But it will have its impact. —I came back in the plane with a real "short haired executive." He was delighted that "the Republicans" were going to *stop* the war; after the Democrats starting it.

Nothing (still) to read. (Except Lillian Hellman's memoir [*An Unfinished Woman*]: kooky but nice.)

I must go out and buy some food for my little inarticulate cleaning girl. She polishes, but does not speak. I'll really write more. At least my handwriting does need fixing (!?).

Love,
Louise

1. Prepared to reject any introduction that was too personal in nature, LB turned the "portrait" down; the *Alphabet* was published with *The New Yorker*'s obituary, written by William Maxwell, in place of an introduction.

Thanksgiving
November 27, 1969

Dear Ruth:
 * * *

What book do you think the most *neglected* of the last ¼ century? The *American Scholar* wants to know. Abbie Huston Evans's poems, I should say.

I am mildly hooked on Doris Lessing, at the moment (the latest book [*The Four-gated City*]). She is so inclusive when she gets going (manic-depressive, the Doctor tells her). How I envy such ease. Well, I *must* get my typewriter fixed. Handwriting, with my one bum eye, becomes increasingly difficult.
 * * *

Love,
Louise

Dear Ruth:

I'm still not good at writing letters; but here are 2 clippings that seem to be *yours!* Better next time! [1]

Love—L.

1. The clippings, from *The Times Literary Supplement,* were of an advertisement for a book of verse for children and a long review of Betty Askwith's biography of Lady Dilke, George Eliot's source for the character of Dorothea in *Middlemarch.* Early the next morning, alone in her apartment, Louise Bogan died of a coronary occlusion.

From *AFTER THE PERSIAN*

III
All has been translated into treasure:
Weightless as amber,
Translucent as the currant on the branch,
Dark as the rose's thorn.

Where is the shimmer of evil?
This is the shell's iridescence
And the wild bird's wing.

IV
Ignorant, I took up my burden in the wilderness.
Wise with great wisdom, I shall lay it down upon flowers.

V
Goodbye, goodbye!
There was so much to love, I could not love it all;
I could not love it enough.

Some things I overlooked, and some I could not find.
Let the crystal clasp them
When you drink your wine, in autumn.

Index of Recipients

The numerals in parentheses indicate the number of letters.

Sister M. Angela, 368
Anonymous, 187, 217, 237, 358
Ruth Benedict, 17, 21–22 (2), 27–29 (3), 35–38 (2), 43–44 (2), 45, 51
Hayden Carruth, 268
Malcolm Cowley, 215
Babette Deutsch, 279
Wolcott Gibbs, 74
Robert Hague, 134
Rufina McCarthy Helmer, 158, 183, 209, 230, 241, 277, 340, 368
Rolfe Humphries, 5–16 (10), 24 (2), 40, 88–95 (2), 100, 105, 124, 127–29 (3),
    131, 133, 143, 146, 148–50 (2), 170–73 (4), 175–81 (5), 184, 231, 249,
    254–55 (2), 264, 267, 374
Ruth Limmer, 315, 322, 325–32 (9), 334, 336–40 (5), 340–45 (5), 347, 350, 353,
    355, 356–58 (3), 359–65 (9), 365, 369–71 (3), 372–73 (2), 377–80 (6),
    381–84 (5)
Katie Louchheim, 258
Margaret Marshall, 210, 216, 227, 229, 233
William Maxwell, 220, 226–27 (2), 228, 231–32 (2), 240, 242–44 (4), 245, 250,
    254, 266, 273, 307, 312, 354, 375, 381
Harriet Monroe, 3, 4, 49, 55–56 (3), 59, 73, 74
Howard Moss, 371
Paul Scott Mowrer, 314
Robert Phelps, 305–07 (3), 309, 310, 314, 317, 323, 376
Theodore Roethke, 96–100 (2), 101–04 (2), 107, 110–13 (3), 116, 119, 122–24
    (2), 126, 137, 139, 151 (2), 157, 163, 167, 169, 220, 224, 251, 349
Ann Rogers, 324
Elizabeth Roget, 323
May Sarton, 207, 282–90 (11), 291–94 (4), 295–96 (2), 299–305 (7), 308, 312,
    317, 321–22 (2), 333, 335, 346–47 (2), 356, 365
Josephine O'Brien Schaefer, 373
Karl Shapiro, 273
William Shawn, 225, 268
Allen Tate, 33, 60, 63, 212, 245, 248, 251
Glenway Wescott, 309, 352
John Hall Wheelock, 40, 44, 46–48 (4), 50, 57, 77, 85, 114, 118, 132, 138, 158,
    165, 173, 181, 182, 215, 222, 225, 236, 282, 294, 308
Katharine S. White, 71, 76, 126, 262, 278
William Carlos Williams, 3
Edmund Wilson, 5, 18, 23, 30–33 (2), 38, 58, 79–82 (3), 84, 137, 142, 150, 152,
    154–56 (2), 168, 174, 185, 193, 211, 214, 253, 290, 294
Morton Dauwen Zabel, 61, 64–71 (5), 71, 75–76 (2), 78, 83–84 (2), 95, 108,
    114, 119–21 (2), 129, 134, 141, 144–46 (2), 147 (2), 152, 153, 160–63 (2),
    164, 166, 170, 181, 183, 186, 191–93 (2), 194–96 (2), 199–206 (5), 207,
    209, 212, 218, 221, 222, 234–36 (2), 238, 246, 256–58 (2), 260–62 (2),
    263, 265, 274–76 (3), 280–82 (2), 297–99 (2), 310, 311, 313, 316, 349

General Index

The letter i *refers to the page on which this person is identified.*

Index

Index

Index

Index

Index

Index

Motion Picture Academy, 224
Mount Holyoke College, 343n, 380
Mowrer, Paul Scott, 315i
Mozart, Wolfgang Amadeus, 70, 93, 125
Mr. Pope and Other Poems (Tate), 34n, 63
Munson, Gorham B., 293
Murnau, F. W., 311
Murry, John Middleton, 70
Museum of Modern Art, 204, 305
Musset, Alfred de, 123, 299
Mussolini, Benito, 133

Nabokov, Vladimir, 275n, 311, 380
Napoleon, 190, 213
Narrative of A. Gordon Pym (Poe), 12
Nash, Ogden, 113, 193, 349
Nation, The, 16n, 22, 160n, 211n, 216, 227, 228, 229, 259, 280, 286n
National Book Award, 377
National Geographic, 327
National Institute of Arts and Letters, 61n, 274–75, 275n, 277, 288, 292, 306n, 315, 328, 330, 332, 381n
National Poetry Festival, 347–48, 348n, 349, 350
Nazimova, Alla, 311
Nemerov, Howard, 347
Neruda, Pablo, 344
Neue Gedichte (Rilke), 87
Nevertheless (Moore), 242
Nevinson, Henry, 209
New American Library, 374n
New Criticism, The (Ransom), 219
New Directions, 196
New Gossoon, The (Shiels), 69
New Masses, 84, 106, 113, 133, 167, 216
New Republic, The, 15n, 48, 49, 60, 61n, 65, 72, 86, 87n, 105, 110, 112–13, 124n, 193, 200, 214, 228, 259, 286n, 375n
New School for Social Research, 261
New Statesman and Nation, 278, 312, 352n, 366
Newton, Isaac, 106
New Writing, 150
New Year Letter (Auden), 263n, 295
New Yorker, The, 10n, 11n, 28n, 65n, 67n, 71–72, 74, 78, 79n, 81, 91, 108, 113, 115, 124, 126n, 134n, 136, 138, 153n, 178n, 206n, 220n, 223, 225n, 228, 229, 237, 245, 246, 248, 250, 253, 256, 258, 267, 268, 273, 278, 283, 286, 293, 315, 336, 355n, 361, 370n, 372n, 375, 378, 379, 381, 383
New Yorker Book of Verse, The, 113

New York Review of Books, 362, 362n
New York Sun, 113
New York Times, 224, 266, 366
New York Times Book Review, 311
New York University, 291–92, 327, 350
New York World, 27, 133n
Nicholl, Louise Townsend, 5n, 6n, 14
Nietzsche, Friedrich, 106, 180, 188, 200n
Nin, Anaïs, 168, 169n, 196, 258
Noailles, Mme. de, 355
Nobel Prize, 266, 348, 348n
Nonesuch Press, 228
Noonday Press, 286, 286n, 287n, 299–300, 300n, 324
Notes on Novelists (James), 123
Not Mine to Finish (Taggard), 81
Novak, Nicholas, 381
"Novaks, The" (Isherwood), 150

Ober, Harold, 244
Obey, André, 131
Observer, The, 361
O'Connell, Irvan, 322
Odets, Clifford, 200
Odyssey (T. E. Lawrence), 70
Ogburn, William Fielding, 5n
Olson, Charles, 336
"Omelet of A. MacLeish, The" (Wilson), 175n
On the Frontier (Auden-Isherwood), 186
On the Limits of Poetry (Tate), 263
Open House (Roethke), 97n, 104n, 224
Oppen, George, 380
Orlando (Hale), 288
Orphée (Cocteau), 115
Ossian, 16
Ostroff, Anthony, 348
Other House, The (James), 20
Our Town (Wilder), 176
Outcast of the Islands, An (Conrad), 249
Out of Africa (Dinesen), 196
Ovid, 6n
Owen, Wilfred, 109, 142
Oxford Book of Light Verse (Auden), 261
Oxford Book of Modern Verse (Yeats), 141–42

Pansies (Lawrence), 261
Pareto, Vilfredo, 163
Parham, Percival, 116n
Parker, Dorothy, 30, 247, 326
Partisan Review, 194, 194n, 203n, 216, 226, 238–39, 286n, 302
Patchen, Kenneth, 145, 355

Index

Index

Index

Index

Index